Penguin Books
Russian Writing Today

RUSSIAN WRITING TODAY

EDITED BY
ROBIN MILNER-GULLAND
AND MARTIN DEWHIRST

PENGUIN BOOKS

Penguin Books Ltd, Harmondsworth,
Middlesex, England
Penguin Books, 625 Madison Avenue,
New York, New York 10022, U.S.A.
Penguin Books Australia Ltd, Ringwood,
Victoria, Australia
Penguin Books Canada Ltd,
41 Steelcase Road West, Markham, Ontario,
Canada
Penguin Books (N.Z.) Ltd,
182–190 Wairau Road, Auckland 10,
New Zealand

First published 1977

Made and printed in Great Britain by
Richard Clay (The Chaucer Press) Ltd
Bungay, Suffolk
Set in Monotype Bembo

Contents

PART TWO: WRITERS IN THEIR GENERATIONS

1 *Veterans*

2 *The 'New Generation' in Poetry*

Introduction

It is difficult and no doubt pointless to try and characterize the individual features that set the literature of one nation apart from that of others, strongly as one may sense that such features exist. Part of the virtue of such anthologies as this one, if they are to be in any measure successful, is that they put the reader in a position to make up his own mind on such matters – or not to, as he prefers.

Yet how problematical (indeed impracticable) the anthologist's task remains! A fully 'representational', and hence impersonal, approach never works well, for a variety of obvious reasons – one of which is that works of art or literature cannot really be 'representative' of other individual works anyhow. At the other extreme, total subjectivism puts the reader irrevocably at the mercy of the compiler's fancy, which he thus – egotistically and irresponsibly – elevates to a position of greater interest than the very subject with which his volume deals. Somewhere between these extremes the cautious anthologist will try to strike his balance. He may discern overall patterns in the matter he is presenting; he will try to clarify these to the reader without foisting them upon him or indulging in artificial schematizations. He will use his best judgement to select for his book – out of an enormous mass of possible material – what seems most likely to interest, enlighten and entertain the reader with a different cultural background; but ultimately he will rely on personal choices, conditioned by his personal enthusiasms and taste. Whether we have managed to strike proper balances in *Russian Writing Today* will be for the reader to judge.

*

Even if we avoid an attempt to delineate it exactly, we may well agree that the 'profile' of Soviet Russian literature is more distinctive than that of most, perhaps any, of the other modern European literatures – a cause for pride among its proponents, for regret or disdain among its detractors. This distinctiveness has been conditioned by various factors, which include: pre-Soviet and early Soviet Russian literary traditions; numerous social and political pressures in accordance with, or indeed against, which the writer may react (e.g. 'social commands', the requirements of publishing-houses, the varying rigours of censorship); the public's expectations from the writer; the writer's view of his own role. To trace the operation of such factors throughout the Soviet period, and through them to come to recognize the distinctive physiognomy of Soviet literature as a whole, the reader will need to turn to full-scale specialist works: the complexity of the Soviet literary achievement is greater than is often imagined in the West. Fortunately our task in this volume is much more limited and (one hopes) more capable of fulfilment: to set before the reader a picture of Soviet Russian writing today. Its chief impediment is the fact that, of course, in literature there *is* no 'today'. With any definition of such a word one snaps the basic cultural threads linking the isolated works that together make up a literary heritage. Arbitrarily, but not, we hope, illogically, we have looked back from the beginning of the 1970s (a moment that will probably be seen to have brought a new orientation to Soviet literature, with the retirement of the great editor Tvardovsky from *Novy Mir* and the widespread emergence of *samizdat*) about the length of a generation – to the end of the Second World War – for the unit of time that for our purposes most adequately represents the 'today' of Russian literature:

the writing, in other words, that is felt to be 'of our time'. Historically this period may not be an obvious unity – broken as it is, above all, by the 'de-Stalinizing' Twentieth Congress of the CPSU in 1956 and the subsequent great qualitative changes in Soviet cultural life – but it has unifying factors. It has been a period of an often uneasy search for stability, following as it does on an age of titanic upheavals: Revolution and Civil War, NEP and Party schisms, the terror of the late thirties and finally the forging of a sense of Soviet nationhood in the War. The fundamental principles of Soviet life, including (for example) the promulgation of the 'Socialist Realist method' (cf. p. 356) in all branches of the arts, had been firmly established. Soviet literature had suffered, and somehow learnt to live with, enormous losses – through emigration, through the purges, through early deaths from privations or on the battlefield – but it already had achievements to its credit that in many cases were waiting to be recognized or followed through in subsequent decades. For better or worse, the familiar image of Soviet literature (which was to be modified, but not fundamentally altered, in the so-called 'Thaw') was formed from the War onwards. From the Western point of view this literature may seem weak in formal innovation, in sheer variety or scope of achievement and (thematically) in the exploration of complex inner states, but strong (at its best) in traditional technical competence, in its pervasive humanist-ethical concern, and in its penchant for the evocation of place and incident. Such a generalized picture remains valid, we feel, whether one is referring to the work of the newer, post-Revolutionary writers or to that of older survivors from the experimentally minded generation of the early twentieth century.

★

This anthology – for obvious reasons of space – concentrates on the shorter genres: lyric poetry and the short story. While this somewhat distorts the picture of Soviet literature as a whole, our loss is not as great as might be feared: longer forms such as the novel and the drama have contributed proportionately less to recent Russian literature than to that of Western countries. Modern Soviet writers have tended to cultivate in particular the 'long-short-story' (*povest'*), partly in reaction against the sprawling and over-ambitious novels which were one aspect of the nineteenth-century legacy to pre-war Soviet literature. But we have tried to cast our net wide – taking cognizance of memoirs, letters and criticism as well as more narrowly literary genres. It is worth noting at this point that the great majority of (though not all) the items in this volume have been published in the USSR – often some time after having been written. For several reasons we have given little or no space to the 'desk drawer', designedly anti-Soviet literature whose full extent and nature we can at the present stage only imperfectly know and to which great, possibly too great, attention has been paid in recent years in the West. The boundaries between 'acceptable' and 'unacceptable' writing from an official Soviet viewpoint (if such a thing exists) are continually shifting, in any case, and to record them is more in the province of the political commentator than the literary critic; we deliberately pay little attention to them in our selection and commentaries. If it is not too much to hope, we feel that this volume represents a sample of the common ground between what the typical educated Soviet reader and his Western counterpart would find enjoyable within Russian literature of the past generation. But it should be noted that among the most important literary 'events' since the Thaw are the frequent first publications of works, by both famous and unknown writers, that originated long before the period covered by our volume began.

*

Instead of a lengthy introductory essay outlining the history of post-war Soviet literature and placing the writers represented in their context, we have decided to introduce them in a different way: through brief comments that link the various items together. Our commentary can be skipped by those who do not like an editor to interpose himself between the author and themselves; we hope that others will find it useful, if only to give them an indication that there are wider perspectives in Soviet literature than a brief anthology can present. Our material has been loosely arranged by dominant themes or characteristics, so that one item follows another without total arbitrariness; it must be stressed that there is nothing rigid about our categorization, and that many, if not most, pieces could have been differently placed – we recognize this by making many cross-references between items.

Though we have preferred to present material previously little known or unavailable in English, we have not dogmatically stuck to this principle where it would have weakened the anthology to any great extent. Our translations aim to be readable English versions – particularly with respect to the poems – rather than stilted cribs. It is notorious that approaches to poetic translation differ widely, and we refuse to be drawn into the unending controversies surrounding it here: the reader will soon see that our translators, while all attempting to produce acceptable English poetry, have adopted a variety of solutions to the problem of finding an equivalent to original forms. As far as editorial tasks were concerned, M.D. was largely responsible for the initial selection of material, and commissioning and checking of translations, R.M.-G. for certain subsequent additions, the ordering of content, and drafting of this introduction and the commentary; but both of us are equally answerable for the ultimate shape of the volume.

Acknowledgements

Thanks are due to the following for permission to include works or extracts from works in copyright:

To Keith Bosley for Antokolsky 'All we who in his name ...', Brodsky 'Étude' and Kovshin 'Trinity Sunday' from *Russia's Other Poets*; to Carcanet Press for Gorbanevskaya 'Turn the Sky Over ...' from *Poems/The Trial/Prison*; to Aleksandr Solzhenitsyn and *Encounter* for the three Solzhenitsyn miniatures, called 'Études'; to Victor Gollancz Limited for Sosnora 'Kitezh' from *The Living Mirror*; to Harvill Press for an extract from Tertz *The Icicle*, Kazakov 'Arcturus' and Pasternak 'The Wind'; to the *Honest Ulsterman* for Platonov 'The Seventh Man'; to Ivor Montagu for an extract from Ehrenburg *Men, Years, Life*; to Oxford University Press for Voznesensky 'Homeless', 'Autumn in Sigulda' and 'Sketch for a Poem' from *Antiworlds and the Fifth Ace*; and to Weidenfeld & Nicolson Limited for an extract from Okudzhava *Good Luck Schoolboy!*, Akhmadulina 'Volcanoes', Voznesensky 'Antiworlds' and Solzhenitsyn 'Matryona's Home'; to Stephen Spender and *Encounter* for Pasternak 'Letter to Stephen Spender'; and to Robert Daglish, Progress Publishers and VAP, Moscow for Shukshin 'Depth of Character'.

Part One
Writers and Their Times

I Aftermath of War

Clearly any writer may be looked at within the context of the major events of his time, with results that can be to a greater or lesser extent worthwhile. Such an approach is especially likely to be appropriate in the case of modern Russian literature: behind it stands a tradition of the artist's civic responsibility and responsiveness, while writers, commenting on, and indeed initiating discussion of, public matters, have often taken on roles that would elsewhere seem more the province of the journalist or the historian. In any case twentieth-century Russia has had more than its share of mighty events that its literature and the arts could scarcely avoid reflecting.

Central to the Russian experience in the last generation stands the Second World War. Much of the lyric poetry of the war years themselves was, predictably, of ephemeral quality. Since then war themes have inspired some of the more important Soviet novels (e.g. by Konstantin Simonov and Viktor Nekrasov) – often the occasion of sharp controversy – as well as poems, stories, 'documentary novels' (Anatoly Kuznetsov's horrifying *Babiy Yar*), straightforward memoirs. Early catastrophes, civilian and military endurance, the forging of a sense of national common purpose, the human toll, heroism and cowardice, have deepened simple wartime patriotism as motifs lending Soviet war literature an importance that is more than merely historical.

★

Andrei Platonov (1899–1951) was a writer dogged by ill-fortune; his remarkable short stories of the 1920s and 1930s were severely criticized (on one occasion by Stalin himself) and he was undervalued in his lifetime. Curiously enough, Hemingway came across his tale *The Third Son* and praised him highly. Only since 1958 has his work, much of it previously unpublished, gradually become available to Soviet readers and subsequently in the West. Though the historians of literature have largely passed him by, his originality of style and idiosyncratic vision of the world mark him out as one of the masters of modern Russian prose. Himself of working-class origin, he writes about 'simple' people with a calculated naïvety of manner; but for Platonov 'simple' people and phenomena are almost unbearably complex, and 'simple' language is charged with an inexhaustible potential for ambiguity, macrocosmic implication, irony and mystery.

The Seventh Man, written at the end of the War, was published in 1966. Though commentators sometimes dismiss Platonov's late work as insignificant, this tale with its hero at the extremes of endurance and its strange metaphysical reverberations seems fully characteristic of his talent.

*

Andrei Platonov

THE SEVENTH MAN

I

A man crossed the front to our lines. At first he wept a bit, then he looked round, ate some food and calmed down.

The man was poorly dressed in black rags, tied on to his body with cords, and his feet were wrapped in straw. There was little flesh left on him, no more than on the corpse of a man long dead – only the bones had been preserved, and around them life still lingered. A patch of dark blue had begun to cover his face, as if death's hoar-frost had appeared on it. It did not have a normal expression, and only if you looked into his face could you understand that on it was imprinted the sorrow of being alienated from all other men – a sorrow which this man, who had suffered so much, was evidently no longer aware of, or felt to be his normal condition.

He must have been alive only from the sheer habit of living, and not from any desire to live, because everything he breathed, ate, believed in had been removed and taken from him. But he went on living and growing weaker patiently, as if he wanted to carry out fully the will of the mother who had borne him to a life of happiness, hoping that he had not been deceived by her, that his mother had not borne him to a life of torment.

Already his soul – the last desire for life, which spurns destruction until the dying breath – already his soul had emerged from the dried up recesses of his body, and his face and vacant eyes were therefore so little animated by any earthly need that they signified nothing, and it was impossible to define the character of this man, the good in him, and the evil – but he went on living.

His papers gave him as Osip Yevseyevich Gershanovich, a native and resident of the town of Minsk, date of birth 1894, formerly employed as a senior planning official in the Regional Manufacturing Combine; but in real life he was already another being, perhaps a traitor to mankind in the impenetrable protective mask of the martyr. In our time, in time of war, when the enemy has decided to kill off restless, inconsistent humanity, leaving only an emaciated, servile remnant of it – in our time wrongdoing can appear inspired and righteous, because violence has instilled wickedness in man and squeezed out of him his ancient sacred essence, and man gives himself over to evil deeds, at first in desperation, and then with faith and satisfaction, so as not to die of horror. Evil and good can now appear in the same inspired, touching and tempting form; in this lies the special condition of our time, which formerly was neither known nor feasible. Formerly a man could be capable of wrongdoing but felt it to be his misfortune and, when he had got over it, again embraced the habitual warmth and goodness of life; nowadays, however, man has been forcibly brought to the position of being able to live and keep warm by a burnt offering, destroying both himself and others.

2

Gershanovich had reached us with the help of the partisans, whose astonishment and interest had been aroused by so unusual a man – unusual even for them, who had had their full share of misfortune – a man capable of harbouring death within him and enduring it. They had led him through, protecting him with their lives, and had carried him in their arms past fortified enemy positions, so that his heart would be free of suffering, even from the memory of it, and he would begin to live normally.

Gershanovich's speech was like the speech of a man in a dream, as if the mainstream of his consciousness was in a world we could not see, as if only a faint glimmer of his distant thoughts came through to us. He kept calling himself the seventh man and saying that he had not pulled out the pin of his hand-grenade because the pin was stiff and he had had no time to pull it, and the pin had been stiff because the work of the Quality Control Department was not of the requisite high standard, not like in his Minsk Regional Manufacturing Combine.

Later Gershanovich spoke to us more clearly, saying that he used to take home extra work in the evenings: he needed the money because he had fathered five children and all of them had grown up strong and healthy; they ate a lot and were eating up the fruits of his work without leaving any and he had trained himself to go without much sleep, so that there would be enough time for extra work. But now he could sleep as long as he wished, and even die – he no longer had anyone to feed: his children, his wife, grandmother, all were lying in a grave of clay near the Borisov concentration camp, and there with them lay another five hundred people who had also been killed; they were all naked, but they were covered with earth; in summer there would be grass there, and in winter snow would lie and they would not be cold.

'They'll keep warm,' said Gershanovich. 'Soon I'll come to them too, I'm tired of being without my family, I've nowhere else to go any more, I want to call on their grave ...'

'Live with us,' invited one of the Red Army soldiers.

'I'll be living here but they won't be living there!' exclaimed Gershanovich. 'Things are so bad for them, they're in such a poor way, where is the truth then? ... No, I'll go to them through death a second time. I didn't make it the first time, now I'll go again.'

And suddenly a dark memory made him shudder.

'And again I won't die. I'll kill, but I won't die myself.'

'Why not? It depends on the way things go,' said the soldier who was listening to him.

'That's the way they'll go,' said Gershanovich. 'The Germans are sparing with death, they're mean. They used to give us one death per seven men – it was me who invented that rationalization for them – and now they'll give even less on the deal: the Germans have grown poor.'

At the time we didn't understand what Gershanovich was trying to say. We thought: let him ramble on.

Soon four partisans arrived at our positions. It turned out that they had known Gershanovich for a long time as a member of partisan brigade N; they told us that Gershanovich was a very wise man and the most skilled partisan in his brigade. His family had indeed been killed near Borisov when five hundred people were shot at one go to avoid having extra mouths to feed and Jews.

'But death didn't once get him, although he wouldn't have complained,' said one of the newly arrived partisans. 'You can understand why it's like that: Osip Yevseyevich is a clever man and he needs a death to match his cleverness, but the Germans make a lot of noise when they fight and shoot like fools and so far it's been no great trouble for us ... In Minsk Osip Yevseyevich had his head right in the way of a bullet – at close range too – but it didn't enter his head, he forestalled it by the power of his mind.'

We said that that was impossible.

'It's not,' said the partisan. 'It depends how you fight. If you fight skilfully, then it is possible.' To prove it, he felt the back of Gershanovich's head with his fingers; then we felt the same place – there, under the hair, was a dent in the skull, the result of a deep wound.

3

When he had lived with us a little longer and eaten some good food, Gershanovich became more rational and normal in appearance, and then, together with the four partisans, he went off again into the far rear of the enemy. He wanted to go a second time over the same course where death had failed to overcome him, where he had not completed his victory, and then to return to us soon.

Dressed in a Belorussian coat, wearing bast shoes and armed, Gershanovich went off at night into the thick of the enemy, to destroy it and to call on his dead children.

Having reached Minsk along paths used by the partisans, Gershanovich left his companions and again, as on his first journey, came out at dusk on the outskirts of the town. Calmly aware, a solitary figure, he walked, comprehending the world around him as a sad fairy tale or a dream which might pass him by for ever. He was already used to the absence of people, to the deathly ruins of the German rear and to the constant chill of the human body, still alive and toiling down here.

Gershanovich went past a camp for Russian prisoners of war. Behind the wire there was no one to be seen for the moment. Then, in the distance, a Russian soldier got up and went towards the wire. He was dressed in a charred greatcoat and was bareheaded. One of his feet was bare, the other wrapped in a rag, and he was walking across the snow. As he moved his emaciated, painful legs he was muttering deliriously – the words of his eternal separation from life. Then he fell on to his hands and lay face downward.

The entrance to the camp was crowded with people. 'It was crowded then as well,' Gershanovich recalled. 'There's always people here.'

On a bench beside the guards' hut two Germans were sitting – senior Gestapo security men. They were smoking their pipes in silence and smiling at what they saw before them.

Two Russian prisoners in good military clothing and with well-fed faces were chasing two other people out of the camp, also Russian prisoners, but so gaunt, broken and indifferent that they seemed to be already dead, dragged forward by an outside force.

The Germans said something to the Russians, and the two who looked all right pushed their two fellows, who fell down submissively, because they were helplessly weak. Then the two well-fed Russians forcibly lifted the weak ones up and threw them to the ground. After this the well-fed Russians halted expectantly, wanting a rest. The Germans began to shout at them to go on working until every breath of life had left the weak and useless men. The well-fed traitors obediently lifted the exhausted soldiers and again threw them head-first on to the frozen hummocks of earth.

The Germans laughed and ordered them to work faster. Gershanovich stood at a distance and watched. He understood that this murder was taking place to save cartridges, with which the Germans in the rear were extremely sparing, and, besides, they had to turn murder into educational edification for those prisoners who were still alive.

From inside the camp five prisoners came up to the gate and silently watched the death agonies of their comrades. The Germans did not chase them off; they watched the Russians with a smile of customary, almost indifferent hatred, ordering the traitors to work more slowly. But by now there was no sense in their working: it was mere corpses with battered heads covered in cold, clotted blood that they were lifting from the ground and throwing down again on to the hummocks. The men must have already died from inner exhaustion when they were thrown to the ground the first time; there was already nothing in them for their breath to cling to. Nevertheless the Germans continued this execution of corpses, since they wanted its educational significance to appear to full advantage for the living.

Gershanovich quietly made his way towards the Germans sitting on the bench. At the same time the weary traitors also came up to them and, standing to attention, requested the extra food ration to which they were entitled for their services.

The Germans grinned and said nothing; then one of them answered that there would be no more extra food rations: some partisans had attacked the supply convoy, and now they had to get the bread back from the partisans.

'Join our punitive corps,' said the Germans, 'and take the bread from the partisans, then you'll have enough food; we haven't got any bread for you ...'

Gershanovich pulled the pin of the grenade under his coat and from short range hurled it right into the middle of his four enemies.

The grenade burst violently into flame, as if a man had uttered his last cry, and the enemies of the people stood for a moment in frozen immobility, then fell to the ground.

The previous time, at the other entrance to this same camp, Gershanovich's grenade had not gone off; he had merely cut open a German's head with it, as if with a dead lump of metal, but now he was delighted and ran off with satisfaction in his soul.

However, the guard in the hut had not been killed; he began to fire at Gershanovich and into the air.

Five armed volunteer militiamen appeared from a pavilion where refreshments had once been sold and, shouting at one another in order not to be frightened themselves, fell noisily on Gershanovich and disarmed him.

4

They delivered Osip Gershanovich to the Regional Commandant's Headquarters, where he had been once before. Here in the cellar they shot men in groups of six with one bullet – they had to do it like that to economize on ammunition. To do this, they stood the six close together one behind the other and made them all the same height by putting thick volumes of somebody's works under their feet.

At the Commandant's Headquarters they asked Gershanovich whether he would say anything to stay alive. Gershanovich replied that, on the contrary, he would say nothing, since he wanted to die, and that there was no need to beat him up – not because they mustn't, but so as to conserve the strength of the field gendarmery, so that the noodles and mutton, eaten at the state's expense, would be left intact inside the soldiers.

The officer possibly thought that Gershanovich's words were rational, and ordered him to be taken away. However, Gershanovich was not yet dead; he was living and struggling and hoping to win.

This officer was not the one who had interrogated Gershanovich the first time, and so Gershanovich again made an offer of his invention: you can kill not six, but seven men with one bullet, the seventh not dying straight away, but later; all the same he too dies and there is a saving to the state of fourteen per cent on ammunition.

'The seventh won't die,' said the officer. 'The penetrative force of the bullet is considerably weaker in the sixth head. I have had reports that on an earlier occasion here they tried to add a seventh man; he survived and escaped from an unfilled grave, wounded in the back of the neck.'

'He knew how to survive,' explained Gershanovich. 'He knew what was what, and even then his head hurt, they had injured it for him. I know!'

'Who was it?' asked the officer.

'How should I know who it was? It could have been anybody. A man lived, he did not live long, they tried to kill him, he lived on and then died because he pined for his family ...'

The officer thought for a moment:

'We're trying a new type of modernized gun – you'll be the seventh, but for an experiment I'll put an eighth there as well.'

'Fair enough!' Gershanovich readily agreed.

'It'll be interesting to see', said the officer, 'if the bullet stays in your brain or goes through your forehead as well and into number eight. These guns have a strong firepower but we don't know what their penetrative force is ...'

'It will be interesting. We'll find out together,' said Gershanovich, deciding that the officer was a fool. Then a soldier took the prisoner away under escort.

5

In a common cell, inhabited by men who would soon be dead, normal life was going on; people were mending their clothes, chatting, sleeping or thinking about what their life was like and what it should have been like according to universal justice. The cell did not have windows; all day long a small paraffin lamp burned in it and only the newly arrived prisoners could say what time of day it was, but soon they forgot the time again, argued about it and no one knew for certain whether it was day or night outside, and everybody was interested in this.

Gershanovich found himself a place on the floor and lay down to rest. A thought now troubled him – who would be the eighth man when they were shot? This eighth man was guaranteed a sure salvation if he did not turn out to be a coward or a fool. 'That would be a pity,' thought Gershanovich. 'The bullet won't hit him hard if it kills me – well, it might damage a bone, that's all – but he'll think he's been killed and die of fear and anticipation.'

Some time passed; Gershanovich had not yet managed to get any sleep, but the whole cell was ordered to go outside. Gershanovich was expecting this; he knew from the first time that the Germans did not keep those designated for death very long, so as not to give them food or drink or think about them at all and expend mental effort in vain.

For the second time in his life Gershanovich was going

down the dark, stone steps to a death in the cellar. Among his comrades who were walking with him to their doom he did not recognize a single familiar face, and from their speech he guessed that these people had recently been brought from Poland.

A lance-corporal counted off eight men, among them Gershanovich, who was second in line, and let them into the cellar; the rest were left on the staircase.

In the basement the timid light of a solitary candle was shining and by the light stood the officer who had interrogated Gershanovich. The officer, a gun enthusiast, was inspecting some sort of short rifle. 'They're all trying to economize and reap the benefits,' Gershanovich reasoned. 'But we mustn't economize; even if we need two bullets for every German it'll still be worth it.'

The lance-corporal began to place the prisoners one behind the other.

'I'm the seventh,' Gershanovich reminded him beforehand.

'You don't want to be the first to die?' asked the lance-corporal. 'You want to outsmart us? Well, die seventh, as a privilege, and put a brick under your feet, you're a bit on the short side.'

Gershanovich put a brick under his feet and stepped up onto his place of death. He looked at the eighth and last man – in front of him was an old man's bald pate, covered with the down of infancy.

'I shall die,' Osip Gershanovich realized. 'But what of it? I haven't lived badly down here; I'll arrive in the next world and there too I'll try to exist, and it'll be good there and I'll see my children. And if there's nothing there, that means I'll be like my dead children, I'll be the same as them – and that'll be good too and just. Why should I be alive, if my murdered heart is lying in the earth?'

'Ready?' asked the officer. 'Breathe deeper!' he ordered the prisoners and then promised them: 'Now you'll sleep a sweet, child-like sleep!'

Gershanovich did just the opposite. He stopped breathing and listened to the silence which had fallen, wanting for his own curiosity to hear the shot; but he did not hear it and fell asleep straight away: his kindly senses blacked out of their own accord, protecting him from despair.

When he woke up Gershanovich tried his forehead – it was smooth and clean. 'The bullet's in my brain,' he decided. Then he tried the back of his head and felt there only the old dent of his earlier injury. 'I'm still alive, I'm in this world, it's like I thought,' the prisoner reflected. 'Their new gun – it's no good at all, they don't put enough powder in their cartridges – I knew it. Well, how many have they killed with one bullet? Well, three, four maybe, but the bullet reached me, number six, last time. They're getting weaker – I can sense it!'

As he lay, Gershanovich grew accustomed to the darkness, which was barely illuminated by a mysterious light, scarcely breathing and flickering in the distance. Beside him lay the man who had stood next to him in front – the bald-headed man with the child-like down on the clean skin of his head. Gershanovich put his hand on the old man's head; his head had grown cold and the whole man had died, although he had not been harmed in any way. 'There, just as I thought – you mustn't be afraid,' Gershanovich concluded. 'Life can end through fear, and then what would happen? You mustn't be afraid!'

He realized where he was; it was in the cellar where they had shot them, the eight men, and the candle in the distance had still not burned down. 'It's a pity that we're here,' Gershanovich reasoned. 'I shall die. Well, what of it! Before death there's also a little life. Last time they carried me off to a grave, and I managed to go on living from there ...'

The officer bent down to him. Gershanovich sensed him from the alien breath, from the stinking foulness of his innards, carried into the open on his breath.

'Well, how do you Bolsheviks put it?' said the officer. '"It didn't come off"? He stood seventh in the queue, how he tried to stay alive, the Jew!'

'I think it was your plan that didn't come off,' replied Gershanovich. 'I'm alive!'

'You're already dead!' corrected the officer and aimed the barrel of his small pistol at Gershanovich's forehead.

Gershanovich looked into the officer's pale eyes, which were deadened by secret despair, and said to him:

'Fire at me ... Here I have life, but my children are there – I find good everywhere, everywhere life is good to me, everywhere life is pleasant ... Here we were men, humanity, but there we'll be even higher, we will be eternal nature, giving birth to human beings ...'

The bullet entered Gershanovich's eye and he died; but for a long time his body remained warm as it slowly took leave of life, giving its warmth back to the earth.

6

A long time afterwards an elderly partisan came across the front to our lines and told us this story of Gershanovich's end. He had been the eighth and last in the queue of condemned men, and Gershanovich had stood behind him. So well had he been able to feign death and stop breathing that his body had even grown cold and thus, in his fight for life, he had deceived the German officer and even fooled Gershanovich when he felt the back of the old man's head.

The candle in the cellar had gone out and they did not bother to light another, and this old man, without any real check to see whether he was dead, had been carried off and thrown into a gully together with those who were genuinely dead, and he had later slipped quietly away from there. To save manpower the Germans don't always dig graves, especially in winter, in the frozen ground.

1945–6, published 1966
Translated by Alexander Pavlov and Michael Pursglove

Soon after the War short-story writers began to move away from the more obvious heroics to explore the small human incidents of life as war affected it – tragi-comic human situations, hurried meetings and partings, fear and tedium as well as bravery. Our next two stories come into such a category.

Konstantin Paustovsky (1892–1968), a much-loved and respected upholder of high standards in Russian literature, has become famous in the West for his vivid multi-volume memoirs of his early life. But he made his reputation as the author of 'well-made', sometimes rather sentimental, short stories; his unobtrusive craftsmanship makes him an important link in the tradition of the Russian short story between the time of Chekhov and the 'young prose' of writers such as Kazakov (see p. 269).

Vladimir Dudintsev (b. 1918) is a somewhat younger, but not dissimilar, writer. He has published little, and is known chiefly for his controversial novel *Not by Bread Alone* – a key document of the so-called 'Thaw' period. His short stories appear to be unknown in the West, though a slightly longer work, the curious allegorical phantasy *A New Year's Tale* (1960), has been translated.

Konstantin Paustovsky

THE RAINY DAWN

It was night when the steamer arrived in Navoloki. Major Kuzmin went up on deck; it was drizzling and the landing-stage was empty. Only one lamp was still alight.

'Where the devil's the town?' Kuzmin wondered. 'Nothing but darkness and rain.'

He shivered and buttoned up his greatcoat. There was a cold wind blowing from the river. Kuzmin found the chief officer and asked him how long the steamer was going to stay in Navoloki.

'About three hours – depends on the amount of cargo,' answered the chief officer. 'Why do you want to know? You're going on further, aren't you?'

'I've got to deliver a letter from a man I was in hospital with to his wife. She lives here, in Navoloki.'

'Yes, that's tricky,' sighed the chief officer. 'It's as black as pitch out there. Don't miss the siren, or you'll get left behind.'

Kuzmin stepped onto the landing-stage and climbed the slippery steps leading up the steep river bank. He could hear the rain in the bushes. He stood still for a moment, waiting for his eyes to grow accustomed to the darkness. Then he saw a depressed-looking horse and a ramshackle cab. The top of the cab was raised; from beneath it came the sound of snoring.

'Hey, you!' shouted Kuzmin. 'You'd sleep through the last trump!'

The driver turned and clambered out, blowing his nose and

wiping it on the sleeve of his coat. Only then did he suggest that they set off.

'Yes, let's go,' agreed Kuzmin.

'Where to?'

Kuzmin told him the name of the street.

'That's a long way,' moaned the driver. 'At the top of the hill. It'll cost you at least a little bottle of vodka.'

He tugged at the reins and smacked his lips encouragingly. Reluctantly the cab set off.

'Are you the only cabby in Navoloki, then?' asked Kuzmin.

'No, there are two of us, both old men. The rest are fighting. Who are you going to see?'

'A Mrs Bashilova.'

'I know,' said the driver, turning round eagerly. 'Olga Andreyevna, the daughter of Andrey Petrovich the doctor. She came from Moscow last winter and settled in her father's house. Andrey Petrovich himself died two years ago, but their house ...'

The cab clattered and lurched as it climbed out of a rut.

'You keep your eye on the road,' Kuzmin admonished. 'Stop looking round.'

'Yes, the road's not too ...' muttered the driver. 'It's a bit scaring during the day of course, but at night it's all right – you can't see the holes then.'

The driver fell silent. Kuzmin lit a cigarette and settled back into his seat. The rain beat down on to the raised roof. In the distance some dogs were barking. There was a smell of fennel, of wet fences and of the river. 'One o'clock, perhaps later,' he thought. Immediately, from a near-by belfry, a cracked bell chimed one.

'I wouldn't mind spending my whole leave here,' thought Kuzmin. 'The air alone would drive everything away – all that unpleasant episode after being wounded. I'd take a room in a little house with windows looking on to the garden. On a night like this I'd open the windows wide, and lie under a blanket listening to the rain beating on the burdock.'

'You wouldn't be the husband by any chance?' asked the driver.

Kuzmin did not reply. The driver thought that the major had not heard his question, but decided not to repeat it. 'He's obviously the husband,' he reasoned. 'They say she left her husband before the war. Lies, probably.'

'You devil!' he shouted and gave the bony horse a crack with the reins. 'Get a move on, will you!'

'How idiotic that the steamer was late and arrived at night,' thought Kuzmin. And why did Bashilov – his neighbour at the hospital – have to ask him to deliver a letter to his wife personally, when he found out that Kuzmin would be passing through Navoloki? He would have to wake somebody up, and heaven knows what people might think!

Bashilov was a tall, sardonic officer. He was a ready and effusive talker. Before uttering some caustic remark he would always laugh long and soundlessly to himself. He had been an assistant film producer until his call-up, and every evening he would regale his fellow patients with details of famous films. The wounded loved to listen to his stories and would look forward to them eagerly; they were astonished at his memory. In his assessment of people, events and books, Bashilov could be biting and very stubborn: he would laugh to scorn anyone who tried to raise objections. He was so clever at this, with his sly hints and jokes, that the object of his scorn would generally not understand what had happened until a couple of hours later; he would realize that Bashilov had insulted him and would think up some cutting reply – but by then of course it was too late.

The day before Kuzmin's departure Bashilov had given him a letter for his wife. For the first time Kuzmin had seen a confused smile on Bashilov's face. And that night he had heard Bashilov turning in his bunk and blowing his nose.

'Perhaps he's not such a dry old stick after all,' he had thought. 'He seems to be crying, and that means he loves his wife, loves her very much.'

Bashilov stayed close by Kuzmin's side the whole of the next day, and kept on looking at him. He even presented Kuzmin with his officer's flask, and just before Kuzmin departed they had a bottle of wine together which Bashilov had managed to conceal.

'Why are you looking at me like that?' asked Kuzmin.

'You're a fine person,' answered Bashilov. 'You, my dear major, might have become an artist.'

'I'm a surveyor. Surveyors are like artists by nature.'

'Why?'

'They're both vagrants,' answered Kuzmin vaguely.

' "Outcasts, vagrants and poets",' declaimed Bashilov mockingly, ' "always seeking to be what they are not." '

'Where's that from?'

'Voloshin. But that's beside the point. I look at you because I envy you, that's all.'

'What are you envious about?'

Bashilov spun his glass, leant back in his chair and smiled. They were sitting at a wicker table at the end of the hospital corridor. Outside, the wind was blowing, bending the young saplings, rustling in the leaves and raising a cloud of dust. From beyond the river a rain-cloud was threatening the town.

'What am I envious about?' Bashilov repeated, placing his red hand on Kuzmin's. 'Everything. Your hand even.'

'I don't understand,' said Kuzmin and cautiously removed his hand. There was something unpleasant in the feel of Bashilov's cold hand, but not wanting him to notice anything Kuzmin took the bottle and poured out some wine.

'Well, don't understand then!' retorted Bashilov. He fell silent for a moment, and then, lowering his eyes, he added: 'If only we could change places! But that's nonsense of course.

You'll be in Navoloki in a couple of days. You'll see Olga Andreyevna and feel the touch of her hand. That's why I'm envious. Now do you understand?'

'What are you talking about?' said Kuzmin in confusion. 'You'll be seeing your wife as well.'

'She's not my wife!' Bashilov rejoined sharply.

Kuzmin mumbled an apology.

'She's not my wife!' Bashilov repeated. 'She's everything to me – my whole life! But let's talk no more about it.'

He got up and stretched out his hand to Kuzmin.

'Good-bye. Don't be angry with me. I'm no worse than anyone else.'

Now they were driving along a dyke. It had become even darker. The willows were moaning softly and the rain was cascading from the leaves. The horse's hoofs clattered over the planks as they crossed a bridge.

'Yes, it is a long way,' sighed Kuzmin, and said to the driver:

'Wait for me by the house. You can take me back to the steamer ...'

'Of course,' agreed the driver at once. 'Clearly not the husband,' he thought. 'The husband would certainly have stayed a day or so. Must be an outsider.'

They were now driving over cobblestones. The cab began to shake, its metal footboards rattling deafeningly. The driver turned the cab on to the verge and the wheels rolled smoothly over the moist sand. Kuzmin once again became lost in thought.

And so Bashilov envied him. It wasn't really envy, of course; Bashilov had simply used the wrong word. On the contrary, it was he who had begun to envy Bashilov after their chat together. 'The wrong word again?' Kuzmin wondered irritably. No, he wasn't envious, but merely regretful – regretful that he had reached the age of forty without ever experiencing such love as Bashilov. He had always been alone.

'Night-time, the rain beating on deserted gardens, a strange town, the mist rising over the meadows – that's how life will slip by,' he mused incongruously.

Once more he realized he would like to stay in this town. He loved these small Russian towns where, from the porches, you could see the meadows beyond the river, the wide tracks leading up into the hills, the ferries laden with haycarts. He himself was astonished by this love. He had grown up in the south, in a seafaring family. From his father he had inherited a passion for maps, travel and exploration. That was why he had become a surveyor. Nevertheless he considered this choice of profession a matter of chance. If he had been born in another age he would have been a hunter or a discoverer of new territories. At least this was what he liked to think about himself, but he was mistaken. There was nothing in his nature characteristic of such people. Kuzmin was a shy, self-conscious, gentle person. His hair, going slightly grey, gave away his age, but nobody just glancing at this small, slender officer would have thought he was more than thirty.

At last the cab entered the dark town – dark except for one house, probably a chemist's, where a blue lamp shone behind a glass door. The street led uphill, and the driver climbed down from his box to lighten the load for the horse. Kuzmin climbed down as well and began to walk a little way behind the cab. Suddenly he was struck by the strangeness of it all. 'Where am I?' he thought. 'In Navoloki, or somewhere equally remote; I can see sparks flying from the horse's hoofs. Not far away there is this unknown woman. In the middle of the night I've got to give her an important and probably not very happy letter. And just two months ago it was the front line, Poland, the broad, peaceful reaches of the Vistula. Strange, and yet somehow right at the same time.'

They reached the top of the hill and the driver turned into a side-street. Here and there the clouds had dispersed. A star glimmered in the darkness, was reflected for an instant in the puddles and then disappeared.

The cab stopped at a house with a mezzanine.

'Here we are!' the driver announced. 'The bell's by the gate, on the right.'

Kuzmin groped around and found the wooden handle of the bell. He pulled it, but there was no sound apart from the screech of the rusty wire.

'Pull harder!' advised the driver.

Kuzmin gave the handle another tug. In the depths of the house a bell rang, but the house remained quite silent; evidently no one had woken.

The driver yawned. 'People sleep very heavily when it rains.'

Kuzmin waited a little and pulled again, harder still this time. Then footsteps were heard on the glassed-in wooden verandah. Someone came up to the door, stopped, listened, then asked crossly:

'Who's there? What do you want?'

Kuzmin was about to reply, when the driver cut in.

'Open up, Marfa,' he said. 'Someone from the front has come to see Olga Andreyevna.'

'Who's come from the front?' replied the voice behind the door, just as crossly. 'We're not expecting anyone.'

'Maybe not, but there's someone here!'

The door opened a fraction, on a chain. Kuzmin informed the darkness who he was and why he had come.

'Goodness gracious!' said the woman in alarm. 'What a lot of trouble you've been to! I'll let you in at once. Olga Andreyevna is asleep. Come in, and I'll go and wake her.'

The door opened and Kuzmin stepped onto the dark verandah.

'There are some steps here,' the woman warned, speaking now in a pleasant tone of voice. 'Fancy coming on a night like this! Wait here a moment; you might fall and hurt yourself. I'll go and get a lamp – there's no electricity here at night.'

She went off, leaving Kuzmin on the verandah. There was a smell of tea coming from the inner rooms, and of something else, undefined yet pleasant. A cat came out onto the verandah and rubbed itself against Kuzmin's legs, purring. Then it went back inside, as if inviting him to follow.

A dim light flickered through the half-open door.

'Please come through,' said the woman.

When Kuzmin entered the room the woman greeted him formally, with a bow. She was old and tall, with a swarthy face. Trying to make as little noise as possible Kuzmin took off his coat and hat and hung them on a peg by the door.

'Don't worry; I'd have to wake Olga Andreyevna anyway,' smiled the old woman.

'Can you hear the steamer's siren from here?' asked Kuzmin quietly.

'Yes sir, easily. But you're not going straight back again, surely? Sit down here, on the sofa.'

The old woman left the room. Kuzmin sat down on the wooden-backed sofa and, after a moment's hesitation, he took out a cigarette and lit it. He was strangely agitated, and this angered him. He was experiencing the feeling which comes to anyone who finds himself at night in an unfamiliar house, in the midst of another person's life, full of secrets and mystery. This life is like a book which has been left open on a table at page sixty-five; you glance at the page and try to guess the contents of the book.

There was in fact an open book lying on the table. Kuzmin got up and leant over the book. In the other room he could hear hurried whispers and the rustle of dresses. Beneath him lay the following lines, lines which he had long since forgotten:

Even the impossible is possible,
And the distant journey easy,
With the gleam of a girl's eyes
In the distance, beckoning ...

Kuzmin looked up and surveyed the room – low and dark, it too evoked in him the desire to remain in the little town.

Such rooms have an unsophisticated charm all their own – with the lamp hanging over the dining table, the white matt lampshade, the antlers on the wall and, beneath, the picture of a dog sitting by the bedside of a sick girl. Like everything old-fashioned and forgotten, such rooms bring a smile to your lips.

Everything around Kuzmin, even the pink shell ashtray, spoke to him of a long and peaceful life. Again he thought how wonderful it would be to stay here and live as one of the inhabitants of the old house – the unhurried, unceasing round of work and rest, of winter and spring, of rain and sun.

But there were other things too, in amongst the old objects. On the table there was a bunch of wild flowers: camomiles, lungwort and wild rowan. They had clearly been picked only recently. On the table-cloth there was a pair of scissors and some flower stalks. Next to them lay the book of Blok's verse *The Distant Road is Easy*. And on the grand-piano was a woman's small black hat, not old-fashioned but very modern. A watch with a nickel bracelet lay carelessly on the table; it was going quite silently, with its hands pointing to half past one. And always there was the vaguely wistful aroma of perfume, its wistfulness increased by the lateness of the hour.

One of the shutters was open, and beyond it, beyond the vases of begonia, a wet lilac bush glistened in the light falling from the window. Outside, in the darkness, the rain whispered softly to itself, and the metal gutter rang with the sound of heavy raindrops.

As Kuzmin listened to the raindrops it was now, at night in a strange house which he would soon be leaving never to return, that he was struck by the irrevocable nature of each moment in life, a thought which has plagued man for centuries.

'Perhaps I'm getting old?' he wondered and turned.

A young woman in a black dress stood in the doorway. She

had obviously come out to him in a hurry and had not finished doing her hair. One plait had fallen on her shoulder and, with an embarrassed smile but without taking her eyes off Kuzmin, she fastened it to the back of her head with a grip. Kuzmin bowed.

'I'm sorry,' she said, holding out her hand to him. 'I've kept you waiting.'

'You are Olga Andreyevna Bashilova?'

'Yes.'

Kuzmin looked at her and was astonished at her youth and the radiance of her eyes, deep and slightly veiled.

He apologized for troubling her and, taking Bashilov's letter out of his tunic pocket, handed it to her. She took the letter, thanked him and put it on the piano without reading it.

'What are we standing for!' she exclaimed. 'Please sit down – here at the table, where there's more light.'

Kuzmin sat down at the table and asked whether she minded if he smoked.

'Of course not,' she said. 'Perhaps I'll have one too.'

Kuzmin offered her a cigarette and struck a match, revealing an intent face and smooth forehead which seemed somehow familiar to him.

She sat down opposite him. He waited for her to begin questioning him, but she remained silent, looking out of the window to where the rain was still monotonously falling.

'Marfa,' she said, turning to the door. 'Heat up the samovar.'

'No, really!' said Kuzmin in alarm. 'I'm in a hurry, and the cabby's waiting for me outside. All I had to do was give you the letter and tell you one or two things ... about your husband.'

'What is there to tell?' answered Olga Andreyevna and, pulling some camomiles from the bunch of flowers, she ruthlessly began to strip off the petals. 'He's alive – and I'm glad.'

Kuzmin said nothing.

'Don't rush off,' she said simply, as if to an old friend. 'We'll hear the siren. The steamer won't leave before daybreak in any case.'

'Why not?'

'There's a big sandbank, sir, in the river below Navoloki,' said Marfa from the next room. 'It's dangerous to try and navigate it at night, and the captains wait until it's light.'

'It's true,' confirmed Olga Andreyevna. 'It's no more than fifteen minutes by foot to the landing-stage through the park. I'll go with you. You can tell the cabby to go. Who brought you? Vasily?'

'No, it was Timofey,' explained Marfa from behind the door, rattling the flue of the samovar. 'Stay and have some tea, anyway. Otherwise you'll have done nothing but get wet.'

Kuzmin agreed and went out to the gate to settle up with the cabby. For some time afterwards the cabby stayed there, standing by the horse and straightening the breech-band.

When Kuzmin returned, the table had already been laid with blue gold-rimmed cups, a jug of scalded milk, honey and an opened bottle of wine. Marfa brought in the samovar.

Olga Andreyevna apologized for the paltry fare, and then began to tell him about herself – how she intended to return to Moscow, but for the time being she was working in the Navoloki town library. The whole time Kuzmin expected her to ask about Bashilov, but she never broached the subject. He was increasingly embarrassed by this. Back in the hospital he had guessed that all was not well between Bashilov and his wife. But now, after she had put the letter down on the piano without reading it, he had become convinced of it, and was already beginning to feel guilty of somehow not fulfilling his obligation to Bashilov. 'She'll obviously read the letter later on,' he thought. One thing was clear: the letter, to which Bashilov had attached so much significance and for the sake of which Kuzmin had come to this house at such an inopportune time, had lost all its importance and was no longer of any interest here. Kuzmin, instead of helping Bashilov, had only put himself in an awkward situation. Olga Andreyevna seemed to sense this.

'Don't be angry,' she said. 'There's the post, or the telegraph; I can't think why he needed to trouble you.'

'But it's no trouble!' replied Kuzmin hastily, and added after a moment's pause: 'On the contrary, it's a very good thing.'

'What is?'

He reddened.

'What is?' repeated Olga Andreyevna louder, raising her eyes to Kuzmin. She looked at him as if trying to read his thoughts – leaning forward sternly, expecting a reply. But he still said nothing.

'What's a good thing?' she asked once more.

'How can I put it?' he mused. 'It's something special. Pleasant occurrences are so rare in life. I'm talking about myself – I can't speak for anyone else. All the good things in life almost always pass one by. Do you understand?'

'Not very well,' she answered, frowning.

'What's the best way to explain it?' he said, annoyed with himself. 'It must have happened to you as well. You're looking out of a carriage window and you suddenly see a glade in a birch wood with the autumn cobwebs glinting in the sunlight, and you feel like jumping off the train and staying in the glade for ever. But the train moves on; you put your head out of the window and watch as the woods, meadows, horses and country lanes vanish into the distance. You can hear a strange, elusive noise – what it is, you don't know. Possibly the trees, or the air, or the hum of the telegraph wires. Or perhaps it's the sound of the train on the rails. One minute it's there, and the next it's gone, but it's something you remember all your life.'

He fell silent. Olga Andreyevna put a glass of wine in front of him.

'I've always been on the look-out for such simple, unexpected things in life,' he said, blushing as he always did when he talked about himself. 'And whenever I've found them I've been happy. Not for long, but happy nonetheless.'

'And you're happy now?'

'Yes.'

Olga Andreyevna lowered her eyes.

'Why?' she asked.

'I don't know exactly; I just have this feeling. I was wounded near Warsaw and spent some time in hospital. Everybody got letters except me – it was simply that there was no one to write to me. I would lie there and, like everyone else, dream about the future after the war, when I was bound to lead a happy and unusual existence. Then when the wound healed they decided to send me off on convalescent leave and told me where I was to go.'

'Where was that?'

Kuzmin told her the name of the town. She said nothing.

'I got on the steamer,' he continued. 'The usual villages along the banks, the landing-stages. And all the while this nagging sense of loneliness. For goodness sake, don't think I'm complaining; there's a lot to be said for loneliness. And then Navoloki; I was afraid I might sleep through it. I went up on deck at the dead of night and thought how strange that there should be thousands of people, all different, asleep in this rain, in this vast darkness which engulfed the whole of Russia. Then I came here in the cab, wondering all the time whom I would be meeting.'

'But then what are you happy about?' she asked.

'Well ...' Kuzmin suddenly remembered where he was. 'I simply like it here.'

He lapsed into silence.

'Come on, tell me!'

'Tell you what? I've blurted out more than enough as it is.'

'Tell me everything,' she answered, as if she had not heard his last statement. 'Anything you like,' she added. 'It's all a bit strange, though.'

She got up, went to the window and drew back the curtain. It was still raining.

'What's strange?' he asked.

'Still raining,' she said and turned. 'It's strange that we should meet like this. And isn't there something rather strange in this midnight conversation of ours?'

Kuzmin maintained an embarrassed silence.

The blast of the steamer's siren, sounding from somewhere below the hill, pierced the murky gloom.

'Ah, there's the siren!' said Olga Andreyevna, as if relieved.

Kuzmin got up, but she did not move.

'Wait,' she said quietly. 'Let's sit down for a moment before we set off – as they used to in the old days.'

Kuzmin sat down again. Olga Andreyevna also sat down, deep in thought; she even turned away from him. Looking at her high shoulders, her full plaits which she had put up to the back of her head, the smooth curve of her neck, he realized that, if it were not for Bashilov, he would have remained in the little town for the rest of his leave, stimulated by the thought that he was close to this sweet and unhappy woman.

Olga Andreyevna got up. In the tiny hall Kuzmin helped her on with her raincoat. She tied a scarf round her head.

They went out and began to walk down the dark street in silence.

'It will soon be dawn,' she said.

Beyond the river there was a patch of blue, watery sky. Olga Andreyevna shivered.

'Are you cold?' asked Kuzmin anxiously. 'There was no need for you to come with me. I could have found the way on my own.'

'On the contrary,' she answered briefly.

The rain had passed, but raindrops were still falling from the roofs onto the wooden pavement.

At the end of the street lay the municipal park. The gate was open; from it led a number of densely overgrown paths. There was a smell of nocturnal cold and of damp sand. It was an old park, with tall, sombre lime-trees; the blossom was already fading and only gave off a faint scent. Only once did the wind disturb the peace of the park, when everything came to life in a burst of noise, as if there had been a sudden, brief downpour.

The park ended abruptly at a steep cliff overlooking the river; beyond stretched the vast, rain-filled expanse of approaching dawn, the dim lights of the river buoys, the mist – all the melancholy of a rainy summer.

'How do we get down?' asked Kuzmin.

'This way.'

Olga Andreyevna turned on to a path leading straight to the cliff edge and came to some wooden steps which disappeared into the gloom.

'Give me your hand,' she said. 'A lot of the steps are rotten.'

Kuzmin took her hand and cautiously they began to descend. Damp patches of grass showed between the steps.

They stopped at the top of the last flight, from where they could see the landing-stage and the red and green lights of the steamer. Steam was whistling from the funnel. Kuzmin's heart contracted at the realization that he was about to part from this still unknown yet already so familiar woman; and that he would not say a word to her – not one word! Not even to thank her for meeting him, for giving him her small firm hand in its damp glove, for leading him so carefully down the decaying steps and for telling him to bow his head each time there was a wet branch hanging over the railing which might have scratched his face. And he bowed his head obediently.

'We'll say good-bye here,' she said. 'I shan't go any farther.'

He glanced at her; she was looking at him from beneath her scarf with a stern, worried expression. Could it really be true that in a minute's time all this would have receded into the past and become just one more painful memory for both of them?

She held out her hand to him. He kissed it, and sensed the same faint aroma of perfume which he had first noticed in the dark room with the rain falling gently outside.

When he looked up, Olga Andreyevna started to say something, but so quietly that he was unable to make out what it was. It sounded like: 'There's no point ...' but the rest was drowned by the steamer bellowing an outraged protest against the miserable dawn and against its own vagrant existence beset by the rain and fog.

Kuzmin ran down to the river without looking round. As he walked along the landing-stage there was a smell of tar and rope matting. He stepped on board the steamer and went up at once to the empty deck. The steamer was already casting off, its paddles slowly churning the water. Kuzmin went to the stern and looked up at the cliff and the steps – Olga Andreyevna was still there. Dawn was only just breaking and it was difficult to make her out. He raised his hand and waved, but she made no response.

The steamer moved off into the distance, its long wash rocking the buoys and rippling onto the sandy shores. Along the banks the willow thickets re-echoed to the impatient beat of its paddles.

1945/1958

Translated by Roger Cockrell

Vladimir Dudintsev

THE BIRCH-TREE

The six years I spent in the army – two of them in the front line – did not pass by without leaving their mark.

Not that I have become intolerant with others, or lost my characteristic Muscovite friendliness. No, something else has happened to me.

I joined the army in thirty-nine as an eighteen-year-old lad. A non-smoker and without a care in the world, I saw only the bright side of life and never noticed the elderly, preoccupied people with shabby briefcases passing me by. At that time I still hadn't thought seriously about my place in life – probably because I was young, self-assured and unable to see any limits to existence.

I liked military uniform and enjoyed the feel of it as I put it on and, tense with enthusiasm, took my place in the ranks of the conscripts. I passed out of the regimental school as a sergeant, strict and short-spoken. I knew that war was coming, that somewhere my opponent was sharpening his weapons, and I was ready for the encounter.

This may be the moment to recall the occasion of the first Junkers attack in June 1941 when, with my companions, I leapt from the troop train and, dressed only in my shorts and helmet, dashed to safety over the camomile-covered meadows.

But later on, in the confused zig-zag of trenches, I shot and stabbed to death with my bayonet several Germans, as the lemon-coloured lights of the rockets faded into the sky. This was just the first of many such situations. Sometimes my comrades on either side of me would fall, their bodies full of shell fragments.

I saw dead bodies for too long – two years in all. I lay next to them and buried them, and now I no longer respond with panic or grief at the sight of a burial or the sound of a funeral march. I no longer try to think of something else to take my mind off death, as I used to.

But that isn't all. War changed me in another way, too. In thirty-nine I did not believe in the possibility of a man's tears, and took pride in the fact that my manly eyes had never known a single tear.

One winter at the front the battalion CO, Captain Firsov, summoned me to his dug-out; sending everybody out he began to reproach me and accuse me of cowardice. For four nights I had been out with my detachment and hadn't been able to find a single living German – not even one of those whose high-pitched voices carried at night as far as the dug-out.

I tried to justify myself: the Germans had become cautious, we had already captured four of them the week before and they were no longer giving themselves up alive.

'Are you beginning to be afraid, sergeant?' asked the CO. 'You want to get through the war alive, don't you?' He was deliberately refraining from mentioning anything to my credit. 'You want to come through alive, you've decided then? Not if you fight like this, you won't; neither will I. You should be fighting like sergeant-major Badin.' He glanced at the exit.

'Yes, captain?' Badin came down into the dug-out.

'No one called you. Get out.'

Badin disappeared.

Standing to attention I requested permission to go out on patrol the next day.

The CO turned the lamp on me and began to look at me closely, as if I had only just come in. Then he turned the light on himself and said:

'Sit down.' He pushed a map over towards me. 'Today, before it's light, you'll crawl out front, to this square here, and find out all you can for me.'

And as he said this I was busy brushing away the tears with both sleeves.

In hospital, when they made a long, deep incision into my wounded thigh and inserted some rubber tubes, my eyes remained dry. But the next day I parted from my friend Misha Nogotov, who had bullet wounds in his chest; he was carried away on a stretcher, leaving me for ever for some distant hospital. As he went he turned his yellow face with its black, bulging eye towards me and gave me a scarcely perceptible nod, and it was then that I sighed deeply and blinked back the tears.

A year later, in another hospital in Poland, the nurse gave me a little book of Yesenin's verse to read. I read him for the first time in my life, out aloud to the whole ward, and I noticed that I found it difficult to read – I couldn't finish 'Anna Snegina'. I read 'I remember, when I was sixteen, I stood at the garden gate and heard the girl in the white cape tell me gently – no', but I could read no more and buried my head in the blanket despite the entreaties of my companions.

I remembered my own story, which even now is unfinished.

Moscow!

Back in the train I had pinned on the Order of Honour, my two medals for distinguished conduct and my Königsberg and Leningrad medals, and now I was sitting in a taxi being driven along my beloved Krasnoprudny Street. Sitting next to the driver I suddenly sensed a tightness in my chest, and I realized that my heart was too small to contain all the love I felt for Moscow, for this stranger beside me, for life – for which so much blood had been spilt.

I sat there the whole journey with such a smile on my face

and pressed so many cigarettes on the driver that in the end even he, a veteran Muscovite, permitted himself a sly, twisted smile.

And when my home appeared, a five-storey block of flats in amongst the green trees of Sokolniki park, I felt a sharp pang in my chest, something I had never experienced before. 'This way,' I said to the driver and began to look ahead with wide-open eyes – perhaps I would see mother in the street, or by the old gate, or perhaps she would be in the courtyard or at the entrance. The pain grew stronger.

And when, after six lonely years, I embraced her, a sobbing, grey-haired old woman in a neatly darned dress, I felt another sharp pang deep within me.

She took her white canvas purse from the table and the rouble notes crackled in her fingers. I realized she wanted to buy me something special.

While she was laying out the money on the bare table, her face shining and one eyebrow twitching, I undid the straps on my suitcase.

One by one I threw out of the case the bags of flour, rice and sugar which were the rations of a demobilized soldier, and also the special presents from my unit. I found the black cheviot skirt and jacket which were for mother and put them on her bed. Then came the material for the coat, a length of silk which I unwound and, on top of everything, a pair of shoes.

An hour later and mother was dressed almost as she had been in thirty-nine. Although it was the height of summer, I lit the kitchen stove and solemnly burned all her old clothes in the fire. The war was over!

At dinner mother asked me what was still lying at the bottom of my case.

'Nothing much; just odds and ends.'

I didn't tell her what was there and who it was for – you don't generally tell mothers about such things, and I was her only son.

I ate little for dinner, not as much as she would have liked; getting up from the table, I told her that I was going out for half an hour and went off to the barber's. I waited my turn impatiently, but when it came I spent a long time with the barber, because I wanted to see *her* and propose to her – if she had remained true to me. And I wanted mother and the neighbours to understand that this was not just anyone who had returned from the front, but a future husband, still young and honourable. But if she had someone already, then let the medals and sergeant's shoulder-straps, the shining buttons and the hair-style gleam even more brilliantly and hide the things which she would no longer need to know about.

I dashed from the barber's to the metro station. The escalator, smoothly bearing me to my eventual disillusionment, was not fast enough for me and I ran down it; a minute later I was speeding along the roaring tunnel – the first time for six years I had been in an underground train.

At the familiar door I rang the bell twice. Nobody answered. I rang once. A plump young man appeared, humming to himself; he was wearing blue breeches and braces over a white shirt which was undone almost to the waist.

'Does Marya Fyodorovna Sorokina live here?' I asked.

'Come in please,' he said, stepping back into the passage.

I entered in true soldier's fashion, sensing that something was amiss.

'And you are ...?' he asked.

'A friend of hers.'

'Sorokina, you say. There's no one of that name here.' His face took on a sad, affectionate expression and with his head on one side he thrust his hand in the waist of his trousers and slowly began to rub his stomach.

I walked up the passage. He watched me in silence. I said that I had not seen her for six years.

'There are two families living here,' he said behind me. 'Six years, you said? When we moved here in forty-three the flat was locked up.'

'I see,' I said and, saying good-bye to the plump young man, I left – but this time in an unsoldierly fashion. He watched me going down the staircase, his hand still thrust behind his waistband.

If it had not been for the war maybe these six years might have seen the end of my love for Masha. I know that at eighteen I'd been really taken with her. I used to dream about her and be very jealous. In fact we did not even go about hand in hand, but shoulder to shoulder; she used simply to clasp me by one finger and look at me mysteriously.

But when you're at the front, and the girl isn't writing to you, and you haven't a photograph of her, a light infatuation turns into a kind of heavy anguish. You're afraid you might die without ever seeing her again.

She had some friends: there was Tamara, the older one, and Zoya, the little one. Both were like fresh-eyed young lads. If it had not been for Masha I would have loved only them.

These three were inseparable at first. But when Masha and I began our long walks round Sokolniki park, the other two caught on at once and receded imperceptibly into the background.

They had all been in the same year at the technical college.

'I'll go to the girls,' I decided.

When I rang the bell of the flat where Tamara lived, an old man in a black jacket opened the door. His white hair hung down over his cheeks, and in his smooth, yellow hand he held the familiar little brass brazier containing sand. 'Ah, that means Tamara's here,' I thought – the brazier belonged to a large and ancient tomcat which Tamara's mother kept. The cat hated me.

Without waiting to be asked, as in the old days, I walked straight into the semi-gloom of the hall to be greeted by a screech from a huge sand-coloured cat on the chest. It seemed to be saying:

'We've not met for ages!'

'No, not for ages!' I said, mimicking it.

It had become even more bloated in the six years I had been away, and looked like some sea-monster. As soon as it saw me it remembered the old hostility between us and did not let me out of its sight. When I went up to it, it livened up and moaned plaintively, brandishing a quavering paw at me.

'Who do you want, comrade?' asked the old boy with the brazier behind me.

'The owners of this cat.'

'I own it.'

'No, its mistress – Varvara Ilinichna.'

'Ah, you know Varvara Ilinichna, do you? Please come through. Have you any news of them? This is their cat, but its owners, as you can see, have gone away – they went with the factory to Siberia in forty-one. We've lost all track of them.'

'What about Tamara?'

'Yes, completely lost track of them. They set up the factory somewhere or other, and it seems they have no thought of returning.'

'What about Tamara?'

'Tamara Sergeyevna went with them. What would her mother do without her?'

'And Zoya?'

'She went as well. Her father was killed at the front, in forty-one. Yes, killed.'

'And Masha?'

'I don't think I remember her. Liza!' He opened the door, holding the brazier in front of him. 'Do you remember who used to come and visit Tamara Sergeyevna, apart from Zoya?' He went inside and repeated the question. A minute later he came out again, this time without the brazier, his arms flung wide and eyebrows raised.

'No, no one knows,' he said.

I got off the metro at Sokolniki station and wandered home through the park. Evening was coming on; above the sombre ponds the birch-trees hung listlessly in the still air; the straight path, crisscrossed with roots, reminded me of thirty-nine. I saw not myself, but quite a different Vladimir, aged eighteen and without a care in the world, trying to catch his Masha, who kept running away from him.

There are little green benches everywhere in Sokolniki park, but it's not easy to find one free in the evening. I don't know what it's like now, but in thirty-nine Vladimir and Masha always found the benches occupied. There were couples everywhere – with their backs to the path and their heads together.

And so Vladimir stripped away two planks from the shed at home and made a good firm bench for two in the remotest part of the park, in some bushes under a birch-tree. It was here that they came that evening; here that Vladimir, whispering into her ear, kissed her cold cheek and she, blushing crimson, started away from him and looked around her. Then he swore that he would always remember her, but she simply looked at him meekly and affectionately; now and then she shook her head and clicked her tongue reproachfully like an adult, although she was only seventeen.

And afterwards – what wonderful days those were! Twenty-three wonderful days! And then he was called up and joined the army. Six years later I returned in his place.

Once more I saw ahead of me the tall clump of dark green firs. As before, their bristly branches hid the way to our bench.

I tried to find our secret hideout, but without success. So I crawled directly into the mass of needles and battled with them for ten, twenty yards. At last I saw the birch-tree, standing there white and inviolable. But there was no bench under it; even the holes were no longer there. The grass had grown in its unending cycle: withering in the autumn and bursting into life in the spring. It had covered up all traces, so that nobody would remember. But who had found and pulled out our bench?

People can be wounded in many different ways, comrades. I lay down on my back in the grass and flung my arms out wide. Up above me was the dark-blue glow of the evening sky; every little leaf of my birch-tree was alive. Ants were scurrying up and down the trunk.

Suddenly I jumped up.

On the birch-tree, above my head, the following words had been deeply inscribed:

'Leaving with factory. Don't know where. We'll meet again, darling.'

I realized at once how she had managed to get up so high: she had cut out the letters standing on our bench. Then she had pulled the bench out of the ground, so that nobody would be able to destroy what she had written.

I embraced the birch-tree, my eyes welling with tears. No, I bear the war no grudge that it taught me to cry.

1946

Translated by Roger Cockrell

Bulat Okudzhava (b. 1924) is of Armenian and Georgian descent, but writes in Russian; he is best known as a witty and sardonic poet and balladeer (see p. 365). His fictionalized war reminiscences, published in Paustovsky's important anthology *Tarusa Pages* (1961), give an 'anti-heroic', lighthearted but far from unserious account of the war through the mouth of a scared eighteen year old. As a sample of this amiable work we have selected its two opening sections.

Bulat Okudzhava

From GOOD LUCK, SCHOOLBOY!

This isn't an adventure story. It tells how I went to war. How I was lucky and escaped being killed. I really don't know who to thank for that. No one at all, perhaps. So don't worry about me. I'm safe and sound. Some people will be pleased to hear the news, and others, of course, will be sad. But I'm alive. That's all there is to it. You can't please everyone.

A SLOPPY TYPE

In my childhood I used to cry a lot. As a boy I cried less, and in my teens only twice. The first time was one evening just before the war. I said to a girl friend I had then – and I said it with studied indifference:

'In that case it's all over.'

'In that case it's all over,' she agreed with astonishing calm, and promptly walked away. Then I began crying because she was leaving me, and I wiped away the tears with the palm of my hand. The second time I cried was just now: here in the Mozdok Steppes. I'm taking a very important package to the regimental commander. Where the hell can the man be? The sand dunes all look the same. It's night. I've only been at the front two days. But if you fail to carry out your mission, they shoot you. And I'm only eighteen.

Who told me they shoot you? It was Nick Grinchenko, just as I was setting out. He smiled sweetly as he said it.

'Don't give up; if you do, it's the firing squad.'

They'll put me against the wall. But there aren't any walls here. So they'll march me out into the fields ...

And I wipe away the tears. 'Your son showed cowardice in face of ...', that's how the announcement will start. Why did they pick on me to deliver the package? What about Nick Grinchenko? He's a tough, smart lad. He would have found his way there all right. By now he'd be sitting in the warm headquarters dug-out. He'd be drinking tea out of a mug. He'd be winking at the girl radio-operators and smiling sweetly at them.

Suppose I tread on a landmine? They'll find me in the morning. The regimental commander will say to the battery commander:

'What was the point of sending an inexperienced soldier, Lieutenant Burakov? You didn't give him a chance to get used to his surroundings. Your negligence has cost us a good man.'

'Your son was killed in action while carrying out an important mission ...', that's how the announcement would start.

'Hey, where are you going?'

It's me they're shouting at. I see a small trench and someone waving from it. Where the hell do they think I'm going?

'Halt!' shouts someone behind me.

I stop.

'Come here ...'

I go over. Someone drags me into the trench by the sleeve.

'Where were you going?' they ask grumpily.

I explain.

'Don't you know there are Germans over there? Another thirty yards and ...'

They explain. It's one of our advance observation points. Then they lead me to a dug-out, which takes a long time to reach. The regimental commander reads the report and keeps glancing at me. I feel small and insignificant. I look at my rather unclassical legs which are spindly and wrapped in puttees. And then at the soldier's sturdy knee-boots. I suppose I must look ridiculous. But no one laughs. Even the pretty radio-operator looks past me. If I'd been wearing knee-boots and a smart officer's greatcoat ... If only they'd give me some tea. I'd sit at the table made out of a crate and talk to that pretty girl. Obviously, in my present state ...

'Go back to the battery,' snaps the commander, 'and tell your commanding officer not to send me any more reports of this kind.'

He emphasizes the words 'of this kind'.

'All right,' I reply. And I hear the girl snigger. She looks at me and sniggers.

'How long have you been in the army?' asks the Colonel.

'A month.'

'In the army you're supposed to say "Yes, sir" and not "all right", and ... you've got your toes together and heels apart.'

'A sloppy type,' says someone from a dark corner.

'I know,' I say. And I walk out. I practically run.

Again the steppes. It's snowing, and silent. Sometimes it's impossible to believe this is an advance post at the Front, and that there's danger all round. This time I won't lose my way.

I imagine how ridiculous I must have looked with my feet apart, my hands in my greatcoat pockets and forage-cap pulled down over my ears. And the girl was so pretty ... They didn't even give me any tea. When Nick Grinchenko talks to officers, he always half grins. Just a bit. He doesn't argue, he just half grins. Then he gives a really smart salute and says 'Yes, sir,' and I hear him say under his breath, 'Go on, give me orders. I know your type'. And he does, too. But my ankle-boots are good and strong. That's a good thing. A heavy, manly foot. It makes the snow crunch. All I need is a fur cap with ear-flaps and I wouldn't look such a misery. Anyway, I'll soon be back. I'll make my report and drink lots of hot tea. I'll have a nap. I have a right to, now.

I've got a sub-machine-gun across my shoulder, two grenades slung on one side of my belt, and a gas-mask on the other. I must look pretty warlike. Somebody once said belligerence was a sign of cowardice. But I'm not a coward, am I? When I was in the third form at school I had a row with Volodka Anilov. I was the first to shout out 'All right, let's fight it out!' and then felt terribly scared. So we went behind the school building. The other boys crowded round. He hit me first on the arm.

'So that's your game?' I cried, and punched him in the shoulder. Then we kept shouting insults at one another, neither of us wanting to be the first to attack.

Suddenly I wanted to laugh and said: 'Listen, I'm going to let you have it in the kisser ...'

'Just you try,' he said, putting up his fists.

'Or you'll bash me. There'll be blood anyway. What's the difference?'

He suddenly calmed down. We shook hands according to the rules. But we weren't friends again after that.

Am I a coward?

These were the dunes where we stopped yesterday.

'Everyone is here,' said Lieutenant Burakov.

'Where are we?' they asked him.

'It's the advance line.'

Like the rest of us, he was the first time at the Front. That's why he spoke so pompously and proudly.

'Then where are the Germans?'

'The Germans are over there.'

'Over there.' We could see dunes covered with occasional patches of withered scrub. Then it struck me I wasn't the least bit scared. And I was surprised how easily the lieutenant had determined the enemy's position.

WAR

I've got to know you, war. I've got large welts on the palms of my hands. And a noise in my head. I feel sleepy. Are you trying to make me forget everything I'm used to? Are you trying to teach me to obey unquestioningly? The shouts of the officer – run, do it, bellow 'yessir', get down, crawl, learn to sleep on your feet. The swish of a mortar shell – bury yourself in the ground, dig it up with your nose, with your hands, with your feet, with the whole of your body, not feeling frightened while you do it, not thinking about it. The mess-tin full of barley soup – secrete gastric juices, get ready, stuff yourself full, wipe your spoon clean with grass. If your comrades are killed – dig a grave, cover up with earth, fire mechanically into the air, three times ...

I've learnt a lot already. Pretending I'm not hungry. Pretending I'm not cold. Pretending I'm not sorry for anyone. I only want to sleep, sleep, sleep ...

Like an idiot I've lost my spoon. An ordinary spoon. Aluminium. Tarnished, with a jagged edge. Even so, a spoon. A very important tool. I've nothing to eat with. I drink my soup straight from the mess-tin. How about porridge? I've adapted a piece of wood. A splint. I eat my porridge with a splint. Who can I ask for a spoon? Everybody guards his spoon. None of them is an idiot. But I have a piece of wood.

Sashka Zolotarev is making notches on a stick. To remind him of the casualties.

Nick Grinchenko's lips curl into a nasty smile.

'Don't fret, Sashka, there'll be enough girls left for all of us.'

Zolotarev is silent. I am silent. The Germans are silent. Today.

Lieutenant Burakov goes about unshaven. It's for show, I'm sure of that. No order to open fire. There's a parley going on. There goes our commanding officer making a round of the mortar crews. Meantime the mortars are in the trenches, in a hollow. And the trenches have been dug in accordance with army regulations. But we don't study the regulations.

Gunner Gavrilov comes over. He sits down. He looks at the cigarette I've rolled. 'What are you smoking your head off like that for?'

'Why?'

'The wind's blowing the sparks about. It's dark outside. They'll be seen,' he says, and looks round.

I stub out the cigarette against the sole of my boot. Sparks fly all over the place like a firework. And all at once a six-barrel mortar on the German side responds. The shell lands with a crump somewhere to the rear of us. And Gavrilov crawls over the snow.

'I —ing well told you so!' he shouts.

Bang after bang. Bang after bang. Closer and closer ... My mates run past me to their mortars. While I stay sitting on the snow ... It's my fault. How will I ever face them again? Here comes Lieutenant Burakov. He's shouting something. And the shells keep raining down.

Then I get up and start running too and shouting:

'Comrade Lieutenant! Comrade Lieutenant!'

The first mortar grunts. It gives you a comforting feeling. Just as though we'd found strong, cool-headed friends. Then the shouting dies down. Now all four mortars are firing somewhere into the sky from the hollow. And only the telephonist, skinny young Gurgenidze, gives a screech of delight.

'A hit! A hit!'

I do what I am supposed to do. I drag a box of mortar shells out of the shelter. How strong I am. And I'm not a bit afraid. I drag over the boxes. Rumbling, shouting and an acrid smell of explosive. Everything's confused. God, what a fight! A real massacre! Clouds of smoke everywhere. No, I'm making it all up. Not one shell has been aimed at us. It's us making all the noise. But I'm the culprit. And everyone knows. And they'll all be waiting for me to tell them I'm sorry.

It's already getting dark. My back hurts. I can hardly manage to pick up the snow and swallow it.

'All clear!' shouts Gurgenidze.

I'll tell the battery commander everything. Let them see I'm not trying to hide anything.

'Comrade Lieutenant.'

He's sitting on the edge of the trench and running his finger over the map. He looks at me and I understand; he's waiting for me to own up.

'It's all my fault ... I just didn't think ... Do what you like with me ...'

'And what am I supposed to do with you?' he asks thoughtfully. 'What have you been up to?'

Is he joking? Or has he forgotten? I tell him everything. I get it off my chest. He looks at me in astonishment. Then he shrugs his shoulders.

'Listen. Go and have a rest. What are you talking about, your cigarette? We merely launched an attack. We had to start firing. Go on, go away.'

I go away.

'See you don't fall asleep. Or you'll freeze,' he calls after me.

1960–61

Translated by John Richardson

As could be expected, poets quickly responded on a personal rather than rhetorical level to the miseries and challenges of war. Ilya Ehrenburg (1891–1967, see also p. 74), known primarily as a novelist, from time to time produced a certain amount of carefully wrought and emotionally saturated verse, some of the best of which relates to the War. Boris Slutsky (b. 1919), like Ehrenburg also Jewish, went through the War as a 'political officer', and much of his best verse, sometimes bitter but always laconic and understated, relates to this experience. Scarcely published until the 1950s, he has been a prominent figure in the literary world of the so-called Thaw. He has dedicated himself to the memory and publication of the young writers, his own contemporaries, who died in the War: 'Answer' (to what question?) seems to refer to them. Typically, its ballad-like simplicity keeps a sting in its tail.

Nikolai Zabolotsky (1903–58, see also pp. 145, 402), the most important of these three poets and possibly the greatest writer to emerge from Russia after the Revolution, lived through the war years in different circumstances: prison-camp and exile in eastern Siberia and Central Asia, an experience that both saved him from a soldier's death and permanently broke his health. In those six years he was able to write only one poem, but on his release his poetic muse (half-identified here with the 'oriole') came back to him. He was always a philosophically inclined poet, and his best work – particularly of the 1930s and late 1940s – allies an almost eighteenth-century grandeur of abstract vision with certain strangenesses of perception and diction that ruffle the classically smooth surface of his verse. 'In this Birch Wood' (1946) must be one of the earliest reflections on the age of atomic warfare in any country's literature.

*

Ilya Ehrenburg

POETS GRIEVED FOR THEM

They wanted each other for a long time,
But when they met they did not recognize each other
In heaven where there is no grief.
It was not in Eden but on earth
Where every step is grief, grief, grief,
That I wanted her as one can want in love,
Knew her as one can know oneself,
Called her in blood, in dust, in sorrow.
And the day came and the war ended.
I came home and she came towards me,
And we did not recognize each other.

1945
Translated by Anne Stevenson

Boris Slutsky

ANSWER

After the fight
Let's shake our fists:
We've had our drinking
And our feasts.
No, states prepared
For history
And my comrades
For prophecy.

Today it sounds
Banal at best:
In five countries
Our corpses rest;
A soldier's grave
A plywood plaque
Are all the profit
Dreams win back.

For fates (yours, mine)
For glory (ours)
For that fine line
We sought for hours
Because our rhymes
Need no forgiving
Let us, the dead,
Drink to the living!

1956
Translated by Keith Bosley with Dimitry Pospielovsky

Nikolai Zabolotsky

IN THIS BIRCH WOOD

Oriole sing an empty song
in this birch wood
far from trouble,
where the pink stare of daybreak trembles
and the transparent avalanches
of leaves cascade from high branches:
the song of my life.

Fly over us, spy glade out,
take a too tiny to be seen
wooden flute
and visit my morning –
in the fresh hours of the morning –
and at my human door
sing matins virtuous and poor.

But still we are soldiers and men;
and an atomic explosion
flings up houses, a white whirlwind
on the boundary of mind
the war flaps its banners round
like a mad windmill in the wind.
Why are you silent my friend?
Hermit in the forest, O bird.

Flying through bombardment
where black rushes line the stream
and high over ravines

or death and his ruins
silently wandering
into battle my friend –
there is a fatal cloud
low and loud
over your head.

The sun will rise beyond the great rivers,
sunken-templed I shall drop with the killed
in the morning's dark moment.
Machine-guns cry out like the wild
raven, shake and grow quiet;
in my torn heart
your note will start.

Above the birch wood
above my birches
where rosy avalanches
of leaves drop from high branches,
where the fragments of a flower
grow cold under the rainshower
century beyond century
will solemnize eternal victory.

1946
Translated by Peter Levi and Robin Milner-Gulland

Stalin, de-Stalinization, Thaw

Since the Second World War the major public events to which Russian writers have responded have been the death of Stalin in 1953 and 'de-Stalinization' (1956 onwards). The very name 'Thaw', often used to designate the period of the second of these events, comes from a literary work (the title of a 1954 novel by Ehrenburg).

Though such subjects are clearly still delicate in the USSR, poets in particular have made an effort to come to grips not merely with Stalin's deeds and personality but with the manner whereby he held a great nation in physical and spiritual thrall. Slutsky (see also p. 65) finds this experience of Stalin crystallized in a momentary encounter. Pavel Antokolsky (b. 1896) belongs to the senior generation of Soviet poets, and his sombre poem is distilled from the experience of surviving the entire Stalin age as an active – though always honest and fastidious – writer. His verbally precise, lucid and restrained verse is strongly imbued with a sense of community with the Western European and Russian classical heritage, and has links with the 'Acmeism' of Akhmatova (see p. 117).

Boris Slutsky

GOD

We were all under God
And in his steps we trod.
No *deus absconditus* –
He often appeared to us.
Alive. Making a speech.
There was nothing you could teach
This God: he had it over
The one they call Jehovah
Whom he hurled from His place
Burned to cinders, ignored,
Then yanked from the abyss
And gave Him bed and board.
We were all under God
And in his steps we trod.
Once as I took the air
God in five cars went by.
His mousegrey escort were
Hunchbacked in terror: I
Could see their trembling fear.
It was both late and early.
Dawn glimmered in the skies.
He peered out, cruel, wise
With his all-seeing eyes
All-penetrating gaze.
We were all under God.
Ours were the steps he trod.

1955
Translated by Keith Bosley with Dimitry Pospielovsky

Pavel Antokolsky

All we who in his name
Have won renown
And passed in peace the time
That now is gone

All we, his fellows, who
Kept silence while
Out of our silence grew
The greatest ill

Who of nights could not sleep
And locked our doors
When he from our own group
Made murderers

We who dispensed sweet reason
Bear the bloodshed
Of jails, the trials for treason
Upon our head.

Let our contemptuous
Sons cast the same
Stigma on each of us:
Ours is the shame.

These truths need not be weighed
In any balance.
We hate him who has died
Less than our silence.

1956
Translated by Keith Bosley with Janis Sapiets

The chief contribution made by Ehrenburg (see also p. 65) to Russian literary consciousness of the Thaw was probably not so much the novel that gave the period its name as the multi-volume memoirs *Men, Years, Life* of 1960–66. A work of considerable literary power, it gave Ehrenburg the chance to repay intellectual debts, disburden himself of topics about which he had long kept silent and give a coherent apologia for his curious, cosmopolitan (and to many, suspect) public career. To a new Soviet generation it also opened up important areas of twentieth-century 'modernist' cultural history, Russian and Western, that had been almost forgotten in Stalin's USSR. The extracts we give are from the last volume, *Post-War Years*, where he evokes the memory of friends for whom in different ways the Stalin age proved fatal.

Ilya Ehrenburg

From MEN, YEARS, LIFE

The months of which I am about to write are probably amongst the most painful in my whole life; I interrupted my work on the book for a long time trying to summon up the courage to embark on this chapter. I should have been glad enough to omit it altogether. But life is not like a set of galley-proofs; what you live through cannot be deleted on second thoughts. Fifteen years have passed since then. I do not want to reopen old wounds that are healing and I shall leave out certain names as I find the role of prosecutor distasteful. In any case, there is much that I myself do not know, so I shall confine myself to a brief and unadorned account of my own experience.

I realize now that the start of the events which I intend to recount is bound up with the tragic death of Solomon Mikhoëls and, before going further, I shall speak of him. I had met him a long time ago, in the twenties, but did not get to know him well at that time; it was only during the war years that I really began to understand him and grew very attached to him. There was a period when he often came to see us at the Moskva Hotel; on some days he would lustily complain about things or play the fool, on others he would sit in silence, his arms and legs hunched up. He was a great artist and art was his natural element. I shall always remember his King Lear. He was unrecognizable; in real life he was short and his face was by no means kingly, it was rather that of a slightly puckish intellectual with a prominent forehead and pouting lower lip. But on the stage his tall, tragic Lear was superb in its grief and wrath. Mikhoëls's talent was recognized by actors of different schools of thought. I remember with what admiration Kachalov, Meyerhold and Pitoëff spoke of him. He had never been a nationalist; his feeling for the Russian language made his friend Aleksey Tolstoy often remark: 'I can't understand why Solomon won't play in the Russian theatre.' But Mikhoëls's special love was the Jewish theatre. People who did not even understand Yiddish were amongst its regular audiences, for Mikhoëls and Zuskin acted so expressively that everyone was entranced by the adventures of some small-town Jewish Don Quixote or the misfortunes of Tevye-the-Milkman.

During the war Mikhoëls was the animating spirit of the Jewish Anti-Fascist Committee. No one at the time could spare a thought for art. In the little towns of the Ukraine and Byelorussia the Nazis were murdering Sholem Aleichem's classical characters – and girl-guides. Mikhoëls and the poet Feffer were asked to go to America. In 1946 several Americans told me that in one town where they spoke the platform gave way under the weight of the people who rushed it in order to get closer to the Soviet emissaries. Those two raised millions of dollars for Soviet field-hospitals and children's homes.

After the victory thousands of people went to Mikhoëls for help, because they saw him as the wise rabbi, the defender of the oppressed.

And then Mikhoëls was killed.

At the time we were told that he had gone to Minsk with Golubov-Potapov on some assignment for the committee which awarded the Stalin Prizes: he was supposed to be judging a production nominated for the award. One evening he was invited to some people and, accompanied by Golubov-Potapov, was walking along a street in the suburbs when they were either set upon and killed by bandits or, according to another account, run over by a lorry. In the spring of 1948 either version was credible, but six months later both began to be doubted. When Zuskin was arrested everybody asked themselves how did Mikhoëls really meet his death? Not long ago a Soviet paper published in Lithuania reported that he had been killed by Beria's agents. It is not for me to hazard a guess why Beria, who could quite easily have arrested Mikhoëls, should have had recourse to such a criminal ruse; certainly it could not have been out of respect for public opinion; it can only have been that it was his idea of fun.

I went to the funeral service at Mikhoëls's theatre. His mutilated features had been made up with grease-paint. There were speeches. I remember Fadeyev's in particular. A crowd stood outside in the street and many people wept.

On the evening of 24 May a commemorative meeting was held. I made a speech but cannot remember what I said. I felt very bitter.

Still I did not foresee what was to come.

In September 1948, at the editor's request, I wrote an article for *Pravda* on the 'Jewish Question', Palestine and anti-Semitism. Here are a few extracts:

> Obscurantists have for ages past invented lies representing the Jews as a special kind of creature, unlike other human beings. They said that the Jews led a life apart, isolated from the rest of the community, not participating in the joys and sorrows of the people amongst whom they lived. The obscurantists claimed that the Jews felt no attachment to any country, that they were eternally rootless. The obscurantists stated that the Jews in every country were bound together by mysterious ties.
>
> ... Yes, the Jews did lead a life apart, isolated from the community – when they were forced to do so. The ghetto was not an invention of Jewish mystics but of Catholic religious fanatics. In the days when a religious fog obscured men's sight, there were fanatics among the Jews just as there were fanatics among Catholic, Protestant, Greek Orthodox and Muslim believers. But as soon as the gates of the ghetto were thrown open, and the fog of the medieval night lifted, the Jews of every country were absorbed into the common life of the peoples.
>
> Yes, many Jews left their native land and emigrated to America. But this was not because they had no love for their homeland; they

emigrated because oppression and insults made them strangers in that land. Was it only the Jews who, at various times, sought refuge in other countries? Did not the Italians, the Irish, the Slavs in countries under the yoke of Turks and Germans, the Armenians and the Russian dissenters also do so?

... There is little in common between a Tunisian Jew and a Jew living in Chicago who speaks and thinks as an American. If there is a tie between them, it is far from a mystical one: it is the tie forged by anti-Semitism. The unspeakable atrocities committed by the German fascists, the mass murder of the Jewish population which they proclaimed and carried out in country after country, the racial propaganda, beginning with humiliation and ending with the crematoria of Maidanek, yes, all this did create the feeling of a strong common bond between the Jews of different countries: the solidarity of the oppressed and the outraged.

... There are, of course, both nationalists and mystics among the Jews. It is they who drew up the Zionist programme, but it is not they who drove the Jewish population to Palestine. This was done by the ideologists of race-hatred, those adepts of inhumanity, those anti-Semites who uprooted the Jews from their long-established homes and forced them to seek in distant parts not so much happiness as the right to human dignity ...

In my article I quoted what Gorky and Lenin had said about anti-Semitism, and I also quoted Stalin: 'Anti-Semitism, as the extreme form of racial chauvinism, is the most dangerous survival of cannibalism.'

A newspaper article is not a testament, there is much one cannot say in it. Now, as I near the end of my memoirs, I should like to state my beliefs on what is often called the 'Jewish Question'.

As a child I heard talk of the Dreyfus affair and Jewish pogroms. I knew that Lev Tolstoy, Chekhov and Gorky were repelled by the way the Russians were set against the Jews. Some years later I read in the illegal newspaper an article about this by Lenin. My father said that anti-Semitism was a survival of fanaticism and ignorance, and I shared that view.

As the reader knows, I was born in Kiev, my mother-tongue is Russian. I know neither Yiddish nor Hebrew. I have never prayed in a Synagogue, nor yet in an Orthodox or Catholic Church. I have admired and still admire certain works of art which, for the believer, have a religious connotation but for me connote human thoughts and feelings: the Book of Job, the Song of Songs, Ecclesiastes, the Gospels, including the Apocrypha, the Apocalypse, Chartres Cathedral, the Acropolis, Andrey Rublev's icons, Fra Angelico's paintings, the Hindu goddesses at Ellora and the frescoes in the ancient Buddhist monastery of Ajanta. These things mean to me not dead, religious canons but living art. I spent my childhood and early youth in Moscow and my comrades were Russians. When I worked in the illegal organization we called each other by aliases, and I was not interested to know whether any of my comrades were Jews. Then I found myself in Paris. I met two wonderful people: one of them, Apollinaire, was of Polish origin, the other, Max Jacob, was a Jew, but for me, they were both Frenchmen. I was very devoted to the Italian Modigliani; he once told me that he was a Jew, but for me he was forever associated with the anxiety of the pre-war years and with the art of the Italian Renaissance; certainly not with Yahveh.

I love Spain, Italy and France, but all my years are inseparable from Russian life. I have never concealed my origin. There were times when I did not give it a thought, and others when I said wherever I could: 'I am a Jew,' for to my mind solidarity with the persecuted is the first principle of humanitarianism ...

What makes me one with all Jews are the pits in which the Nazis buried old women and children, the rivers of blood that have flowed in the past and the cruel weeds that later sprang from racist seeds, the persistence of prejudice and intolerance. In the speech I made on my seventieth birthday I told my listeners that so long as there is a single anti-Semite in the world I shall declare with pride that I am a Jew. It was not nationalism that dictated those words but my respect for human dignity. I still believe that anti-Semitism is an ugly survival from the past and that it will disappear like all other racial intolerance; but what I now know is that to cleanse minds of age-old prejudice is going to take a very long time.

To go back to the days of which I was speaking: at the end of 1948 the Jewish Anti-Fascist Committee was dissolved, the newspaper *Einigkeit* closed down and the type set up for *The Black Book* was distributed. Not long after, authors who wrote in Yiddish – Peretz Markisch, Kvitko, Bergelson, Feffer and others – were arrested.

In January 1949 the press announced 'the discovery of an anti-patriotic group of drama critics'. No one can say why the campaign was opened with so minor an issue as theatrical criticism. Perhaps some disgruntled playwright had complained to Stalin at a propitious moment, or it may have been quite by chance: it does not matter into what part of a pool you throw a stone, the ripples will spread.

The first article in the campaign posed the question: 'How can A. Gurvich form an idea of the national character of Russian Soviet man?' Two days later I came across another article in which 'gurviches and yuzovskys' were referred to, without capitals. The circle of 'cosmopolitans' was widened to include certain poets and film directors who were thus brought in to join the critics. A fortnight later 'rootless cosmopolitans' hiding their identity under pen-names were unmasked.

Many of my friends were appalled by what was going on. I remember conversations with Obraztsov, Konchalovsky, the architect Rudnev, with Fadeyev, Vsevolod Ivanov and the sculptress Lebedeva. There should be no need to remind readers that all forms of racism, including anti-Semitism, were absolutely contrary to the traditions of the Russian intelligentsia and to those high ideals of internationalism which were

Lenin's legacy and on which the Soviet people was reared.

The persecution of 'cosmopolitans' was not an isolated phenomenon. Large numbers of people were arrested who, through no fault of their own, had been taken prisoner by the fascists, or had not had time to be evacuated from overrun territory, or had voluntarily returned from exile abroad, or had been 'repressed' in the thirties, or had relatives in foreign countries. Beria's arbitary operations were truly comprehensive.

As for myself, from the beginning of February 1949 I was not allowed to publish anything. My name was deleted from the critics' reviews. These symptoms were quite familiar, and every night I expected the front-door bell to ring. The telephone was silent; only close friends rang up to inquire how I was. There were also those who 'checked': the more cautious of our acquaintances would ring up from a call-box to find out whether I had been arrested and on hearing my voice would put down the receiver.

In March 1938 I used to listen anxiously to the lift: in those days I had wanted passionately to live; like many others I had kept a suitcase ready packed with two changes of underwear. In March 1949 I gave no thought to underwear and awaited the outcome almost with indifference. Perhaps it was because I was now fifty-eight and not forty-seven; I was tired and beginning to feel old. Or perhaps because it was a repeat performance, which, coming after the war and the victory over fascism, seemed utterly intolerable. We went to bed late, in the small hours: the idea that they might come and wake me up was too horrible. Once the bell rang at two o'clock in the morning. Lyuba went to open the door. Simonov's wife had sent their driver to find out if her husband was with me.

At the end of March a friend of ours dropped in and shouted with pleasure: 'So it isn't true!' He told us that the day before, at a lecture on literature, a speaker who at the time held a rather responsible position had announced in the presence of over a thousand people: 'I can give you some good news: Cosmopolitan Number One and enemy of the people Ilya Ehrenburg has been exposed and arrested.'

I wrote a short letter to Stalin saying that for the last two months I had been denied all journalistic work and that the day before So-and-so had announced my arrest; that in fact, however, I had not been arrested and I wished to have my position clarified. All I asked was that an end be put to the uncertainty. I took my letter to the Kremlin sentry-box.

The next day Malenkov rang me up. I remember the conversation clearly. 'You wrote to Stalin. He asked me to ring you up. Tell me, how did all this start?' 'I've no idea. I should like to ask you that.' 'But why didn't you let us know sooner?' 'I spoke to Comrade Pospelov, that was all I could do.' 'Strange, Comrade Pospelov is a very reliable man but he never said a word to us.' (Some years later Pospelov told me that this was not true; that he had passed on what I had told him but his words had produced no effect.)

Immediately the telephone came to life again: various editorial offices said that there had been a 'misunderstanding', that my articles would be published and would I write some more.

A. M. Efros and L. N. Chernyavsky were with me at the time. G. M. Kozintsev, who had flu, lay on the sofa. He jumped up wrapped in a blanket. Everyone started talking excitedly.

It is easy to be wise after the event. In the spring of 1949 I did not understand anything at all. Now that we know a little I believe that Stalin used a technique of heavy camouflage. Fadeyev told me that the press campaign against the 'unpatriotic critics' had been launched on Stalin's instructions. But a few weeks later he summoned the editors and said: 'Comrades, the divulging of literary pseudonyms is inadmissible, it smells of anti-Semitism.' Rumour attributed the arbitrary measures to those who carried them out while Stalin was thought to have been a restraining influence. By the end of March he apparently decided that the job was done.

The *Schadenfreude* of our country's foreign enemies made me feel the more bitter. Here was the Soviet people that for thirty years had fought for the ideas of October against the Interventionists and the Whites, against fascist invasion, against pogromists and racists: the people had no hand in the writing of the newspaper articles I have described, they worked from morning till night and never turned aside from the path they had chosen.

Several years later, a journalist in Israel came out with some sensational disclosures. He said that while in prison he had met the poet Feffer who, he alleged, had told him that I was responsible for the arrest of the Jewish writers. This calumny was taken up by several Western papers. Their single-minded line of reasoning was: 'He has survived, so he must be a traitor.'

I was in wretched form and could not work. Then I was told that I must go to Paris for the World Peace Congress. The defence of peace seemed to me a splendid thing but I did not feel I had the strength to go. It would have been torture to find myself abroad in the state in which I was. I was asked to write a speech and submit it for approval. Faced with a blank sheet I began to write about what was stirring me most deeply. This passage occurred in the speech: 'There is nothing more odious than racial and national arrogance. World culture has arteries which cannot be severed with impunity. The peoples have learnt and will continue learning from one another. I believe it is possible to respect distinctive national features while rejecting national exclusiveness.' I was summoned to Grigoryan, who held a rather high position, and he pressed my hand and thanked me. My speech, typed out on good paper, was lying on his desk, and against the passage I have quoted were the words 'Well said!' in a handwriting that looked to me painfully familiar.

We flew to Paris in the middle of April. It was cold in Moscow and there were white patches of snow in the little wood near Vnukovo airfield. Lyuba said that in Paris I should be able to rest and relax, to which I replied: 'Yes, of course.'

Elsa Triolet was at the airport. She said she and Aragon would come to pick me up that evening and we would dine together. We were taken to the embassy where the ambassador gave a survey of the political situation. I tried to listen but could not, and I suddenly realized I was ill: I was bathed in sweat and was sure I was running a temperature. Of all idiotic things to happen! Later I was taken to an hotel on the right bank, near the Salle Pleyel where the congress was to be held. I could neither understand nor see anything – my fever must be raging. Suddenly the taxi-driver, an elderly Frenchman, said: 'What frightful heat.' I stared: 'Oh, do you feel hot too?' It was his turn to be surprised: 'Why, it's 86 in the shade, all the papers say there hasn't been such a hot April for a hundred years.' I was overjoyed: this meant that I was not ill after all. Then I saw what I had failed to notice before: on the café terraces men were sitting in their shirt-sleeves drinking beer or lemonade. But my head was still not very clear.

The Aragons took me to the noisy Restaurant Méditerranée; it was crowded; people were telling one another how they had spent their Easter holidays. Acquaintances came up to the Aragons, there were jokes and laughter. Then Louis and Elsa asked me in Russian: 'What is meant by "cosmopolitans"? Why are pen-names violated?' They were my own people, I had known them for a quarter of a century, but I could not answer their questions. When Cocteau came up and started some urbane social chatter, I forced myself to smile. Huge *langoustes* slowly waved their great antennae. People at neighbouring tables were laughing. It was insufferably hot.

Back at the hotel I quickly undressed and put out the light hoping to sleep but soon realized that it was no use. I tossed and turned, switched on the light, and then for no particular reason put on my clothes again, sat down in an armchair and gave rein to my imagination: what could I think up to make them send me home tomorrow? I reviewed all the possible variants: fall ill, say that I shan't be able to speak, or simply that I want to go home. I sat up till the morning. The image of Peretz Markisch as I had seen him for the last time rose before me. I recalled phrases from newspaper articles and kept on saying to myself stupidly: 'I must go home.'

I have said that in this chapter I wanted to recount the most difficult time I ever had to live through. I hardly think I have succeeded, for how can one really convey such things? Let me add only this: the most terrible experience of all was that first night in Paris when, in the long narrow hotel room, I realized the price a man has to pay for being 'true to men, to the century, to fate' ...

★

'How did you spend your last evening in Paris?' Fadeyev asked me. With old friends, I said. 'While I was being pestered to death by an American who wanted everything explained to him ... Ah, my friend!' He broke off: 'Let's have some cognac.' I glanced at him: he looked mellow and sad, his expression was quite unlike that he usually wore at meetings and conferences.

It is said of Fadeyev that he was greatly talented and intelligent, that he had an iron will and that Stalin had thought highly of him. That is all quite true, but in his case 'talent' stood for far more than a writer's natural gift: for him it meant the capacity to make hundreds of corrections on a single page of manuscript, it meant inner torment, a spiritual make-up utterly unsuited to the kind of public activity in which he engaged so unflaggingly and devotedly. All our writers and, I feel sure, all the leaders of the peace movement were familiar with his glance – clear and cold – with his erudition, his remarkable memory, his ability to give depth and brilliance to a phrase by Stalin or Zhdanov and to endow it with the qualities of a literary polemic and the incontrovertibility of law. But the Fadeyev I want to speak about is less well known.

I first met him a long time ago, in the days when he was one of the leading spirits of RAPP.* From time to time we ran into each other in Moscow, and, later, in Madrid and Paris. I liked his book *The Nineteen* but I did not understand, or rather did not know, the man. And in 1940 when I had talks with him I regarded him as a boss rather than a fellow-writer. For his part, as he confessed on one occasion recalling the past: 'I took you for someone very remote from us. In Madrid I said to the army people who were sticking up for you: "He may be willing to die for our cause but he doesn't want to live with us, and what's more, he wouldn't know how to."'

After the war we began to look at each other more closely. In Penza, during the Belinsky celebrations, we spent a whole evening talking. Later we met again in Moscow and discussed books and the destiny of the writer. It gradually dawned on me that Fadeyev was not quite what he had seemed at first, but it was only during the five or six years that we worked together in the peace movement that I really got to know him. We talked in planes and in railway carriages, and in such towns as Oslo, Vienna and Prague. He would come into my room at night and talk and talk and talk. That is what made me start writing about him after describing the Paris congress.

It would be too much to say that we became friends; we were too unlike for that, which may also have been the reason why Fadeyev was at times more open with me than with people closer to him. He evidently still had a lingering feeling that I was someone remote and he spoke very frankly about things. He had many friends (by which I do not mean the lickspittles who toadied to the man in power, but people who

* All-Russian Association of Proletarian Writers – editorial note.

were sincerely attached to him), yet there seemed to be many questions which he did not discuss with his friends. 'There's nothing anyone can tell me about loneliness,' he said once. He was on familiar terms with a number of people who called him 'Sasha', but he and I always addressed one another formally by name and patronymic.

It is not easy to tell Fadeyev's story: his was a very complicated nature and it is clear that much must have escaped his notice. Besides, the events are too recent. I do not want to indulge in speculations and shall confine myself to quoting extracts from my notes and some of his own words from memory in order to show his attitude to certain things, to dispel the myth of 'the man of iron' and to give some help to the future biographer of a man who played an important part in the history of our literary life.

Fadeyev worked in the literary field for thirty-five years, yet all there is to show for it are two complete and two unfinished novels, a few short stories and some hundreds of articles. 'They won't let me write,' he would complain. 'It's the Writers' Union, the struggle for peace, conferences, meetings, congresses all the time.' And, indeed, the duties involved in directing the writers' organizations and his work in the peace movement took up a great deal of his time; yet he did it of his own free will and was under no compulsion, and, when in the last years he was relieved of some of his functions, instead of welcoming it he felt extremely annoyed. He worked tirelessly inside the peace movement, going into every detail. By chance I have kept a few of the notes he passed to me at some of the meetings. They are full and precise: asking me to have a talk with Nenni; anxious about the length of an American delegate's speech, calculated to last an hour and a half, and suggesting that I should ask him to shorten it; putting forward ideas for broadening the movement.

It has also been said that Fadeyev wrote so little because he drank so much. But Faulkner drank far more and yet wrote dozens of books. It must have been something different that obstructed Fadeyev.

I once told him that of all his writings I liked best *The Nineteen*, his first novel written when he was twenty-three. 'That's quite natural,' he said. '*The Nineteen* is based on personal experience. Of course a sense of one's responsibility can be inspiring but there are times when it's a hindrance.'

For twelve years he would take up his *Posledny iz Udege* (*The Last of the Udege*) almost every year, replanning and correcting it, but in the end he considered it a failure.

When he began writing *Molodaya Gvardiya* (*The Young Guard*) he was no longer twenty-three but forty-four. The story of the young people of Krasnodon moved him deeply for it brought back his own youth, and although he always chose to regard himself as a realist there was a good deal of the romantic in him.

(The fate of *The Young Guard* is closely linked with what we call the 'personality cult'. The novel was written and published, it had a great success and was awarded a Stalin Prize. One of Fadeyev's friends, S. A. Gerasimov, made a film of it. And that is when the storm broke. Stalin had not read the book, but the film made him very angry: here were youngsters left to their fate in a town seized by the Nazis. Where was the Komsomol organization? Where the Party leadership? Stalin was told that the film-director had followed the text of the novel. Sharp criticism of *The Young Guard* followed in the press. Fadeyev replied in a letter to *Pravda* accepting the criticism as well deserved and promising to make suitable changes in the book. When I met him he said he was not altering the text but was writing additional chapters about old Bolsheviks and the role of the Party leadership. After a short pause he added: 'Of course, even if I do succeed, the novel won't be the same. Still, it may be that I'm too easily swayed by enthusiasm for partisan activities. Times are hard and Stalin knows better than you or I.')

The reason I have mentioned *The Young Guard* is because it sheds light on Fadeyev's attitude as a novelist to reality. When he was planning the novel he went to Krasnodon, where he questioned hundreds of people in an attempt to reconstruct the events and the personal appearance of his characters; he was tremendously disappointed when he could not get a clear description of several of them. This shows the extent to which the rules he set himself were those of the chronicler rather than of the poet. Stendhal's *Le Rouge et le Noir* grew out of a newspaper report on an ambitious young man's crime; what the writer did was to make use of the plot without letting his interpretation of Julien Sorel depend on 'facts'. Stendhal never elaborated the description of his characters' personal appearance; he left that to the reader's imagination. Zola on the other hand said that he 'lacked imagination'; he studied the details of the kind of life he wanted to depict or, as we say, 'collected material'. For the first time in his life when he was writing *Nana* he visited a brothel – armed with a notebook. Fadeyev's teacher was Lev Tolstoy: when he wanted to bring out the nature of one of his characters, he stressed some particular physical trait. But, whereas the realism which Tolstoy gave to Karenin's ears is such that from that detail alone we seem to know him better than we know our close friends, Fadeyev wanted to put down every single feature of every one of the young Krasnodon heroes.

I remember a talk we had in a plane. Fadeyev said he had come to the end of the road and went on to describe the fate of his unfinished novel *Chornaya Metallurgiya* (*Ferrous Metallurgy*): 'In fifty-one Malenkov sent for me and said: "There's a new invention in metallurgy which will revolutionize the whole thing. A magnificent discovery. You'll render the Party a great service by describing it." At the same time he told me about the unmasking of a group of saboteur geologists. I got down to work. I made long trips to the Urals and didn't hurry over the writing. I'd got some hundreds of pages written and was beginning to see it as a real novel, the one thing for which I could feel answerable. And then it turned out that the "invention" was a swindle which had cost the State hundreds of millions of roubles, and that the geologists implicated had been victims of calumny and they were rehabilitated. So the novel was a total loss.' I was astounded: 'What do you mean? I've read extracts from it in *Ogonyok*, it's splendid stuff. Make a few alterations. Get them to invent something else. It's not metallurgy you're writing about, it's people.' Until that moment I had seen Fadeyev really angry only twice before. Usually very self-possessed and cool, he went red in the face and shouted in a high-pitched voice when roused. Now in the plane he began to shout: 'It's all right for you. When you describe an engineer in love, you don't care what he's doing at the factory. But my novel's based on *facts*.' When he had calmed down he said quietly: 'All there's left is to do away with the manuscript, and myself as well – I shall never start on another book now.'

It is not, of course, to take issue with the late Fadeyev that I have described his dependence on reality. He was a true writer, and a very self-critical one. Yet this capacity for self-criticism is not enough to account for the long time he took to write *The Last of the Udege* and *Ferrous Metallurgy*; this was bound up with the whole pattern of his life, with his contradictions, with the conflict between the partisan and the disciplined soldier. 'Many writers feel hurt and resent me,' he once said to me. 'I can understand them, but it's hard to explain.' 'Tell them', I suggested, 'that the person you hurt most is the writer Fadeyev.'

In his early youth he had been a partisan in the Far East and later he took part in putting down the Kronstadt mutiny. He was seventeen when he joined the Party, and twenty when the Chita organization sent him as a delegate to the 10th Party Congress. For him Trotsky and the 'Workers' Opposition' were not pages in the *Short Course** but living memories. In the lives of some writers political struggle was no more than a passionate episode lasting a few months or years; for Fadeyev politics was his entire life's work.

I remember a small meeting of the 'active group' of the World Peace Council. It was held in Prague, in a suburban villa where Joliot-Curie was staying. We were discussing our further activities: the success of the Stockholm Appeal had gone to our heads; we talked about the need to collect signatures. Fadeyev had come with a resolution demanding that the five Great Powers should sign a peace pact. After listening to various speeches he proved with great brilliance that everything the others had advanced would in effect be covered by this Five Power pact: economic difficulties, violations of national sovereignty, the fear of war and of a lapse into savagery. The idea was not his own, but he presented it so ably that the small room in which some ten to fifteen people were gathered rang with loud applause as though it were a public meeting. Joliot-Curie suggested having Fadeyev's speech printed and circulated to all the national committees.

In the summer of 1956, when I was in Paris, Joliot-Curie invited me to his house. We talked for a long time about the 20th Party Congress and about all the things that in those days gladdened and interested us intensely. Then Joliot-Curie said: 'Fadeyev – he's shown his extraordinary will-power in this too. It's a great loss for us. He was brusque at times and I've had some difficult moments with him. But I've always admired his intelligence. It was his way of thinking in political terms that won me over. Bernal and I reason as scientists. You I always see as a writer. And not you alone. Take d'Astier: many people think of him as a politician, but he's a poet, although I believe he doesn't write poetry. But talking to

* *History of the Communist Party of the Soviet Union (Bolsheviks). A Short Course.*

Fadeyev I've often thought that his true calling was politics.'

I cannot, naturally, share this last opinion. I know not only Fadeyev's books, I also knew their author and realized that he could not be seen apart from his art. But Joliot-Curie was right when he said that Fadeyev thought in political terms. It was this that determined the dual character of his judgements and gave rise to the contradictions which people who had suffered from them mistook for hypocrisy.

It was a matter of faith with Fadeyev that Stalin was an able statesman who knew exactly what ought to be done and could see far into the future. There were, however, moments when things got too much for him: in Penza he spoke to me about Meyerhold's fate, and later, a short time before Stalin's death, he recalled Yakir and Stern, saying over and over again: 'They misinform him.' In the late forties, though many things shocked him, he still tried to find an explanation: 'It's an evil tide, but Stalin has it under control.' His faith was not unmixed with fear. He once said half in jest: 'There are two people I'm afraid of – my mother and Stalin. I fear them – and I love them.'

He would say about a book: 'Of course it shows talent. But try to see what I mean: it can't be judged on its literary merits alone. It must also be seen from the point of view of the State, and from that angle the book's harmful.'

I have said that Fadeyev's teacher was Lev Tolstoy; this was obvious to everybody. Long sentences with a number of subordinate clauses were (or had become) natural to him. He could not write in any other way. Sometimes, when he had to telegraph a report on a World Council meeting or a talk with some leader, he would ask me to help him; he would seat himself at a table – his handwriting was very clear – and say: 'You dictate – you know how to put this sort of thing into short sentences.'

But Tolstoy's influence went deeper than the mere technique of writing. In Penza Fadeyev went to great lengths trying to convince me that all one could learn from Chekhov was the art of observation: 'What could he teach? And, anyway, he didn't try to teach. But Tolstoy recognized the true purpose of literature, he was a real teacher. Today, of course, we have different ideas, but I'm still full of admiration for the novel which is now looked upon as a failure. Tolstoy wrote *Resurrection* so that good should triumph over evil.

'And take Dickens. Didn't he champion good in his best novels? Naturally, without the inspiration behind it this would be no more than dull didacticism. You can't turn a hack writer into anything that's worth a hundredth part of Tolstoy, but it's the duty of genius to serve good and humanism. In our age that means subordinating oneself to the task of building Communism.'

This was the bridge linking the writer to the literary functionary: the bridge and at the same time a chasm.

In 1929, when Fadeyev was still one of the RAPP leaders, he published an article entitled *The Highway of Proletarian Literature* in which he called for an approach to the novel as he himself saw it. The categorical tone of his pronouncements was not surprising: in those days the RAPP people attacked not only the 'right-wing fellow-travellers' but even Mayakovsky. The title, *The Highway of Proletarian Literature*, is not unusual in itself: the Romanticists, the Realists, the Naturalists and the Symbolists each regarded their path as new and as the only correct one; it is its ultimate fate that was unusual. RAPP was disbanded; a lot was written about the need for diversity in literary trends, but at the same time a close watch was kept on writers to see that they all followed a single literary road; individual paths were looked upon as deadends. Yet the road, or to use Fadeyev's expression, the highway was far from straight, its zigzags determined not only by important political events but also by Stalin's preferences, his moods, his attitude towards various writers. In 1929 Fadeyev imagined that he was laying out a new road. I do not know how long this illusion survived, but in 1949, annoyed by a critic, he said to me: 'He thinks I'm fault-finding, but I'm nothing more than a traffic-controller.' This, of course, was said in anger. He was not laying out a new road, but neither was he a mere traffic-controller. At times he succeeded in evolving theories that went beyond the accepted formulas. For instance, at one point he gave this definition of Socialist Realism: it ought to show people not as they are but as they should be. This view may be closer to romanticism than to the realism of the past century, but in that formulation there is both vision and breadth.

In Fadeyev's entourage there were always critics able to seize upon his ideas and reproduce them in their reviews. I remember Fadeyev at a writers' meeting accusing one such critic of perfidy: 'There's an Oriental story about the scorpion and the frog. The scorpion pursued by enemies begs the frog to carry him across a stream. "You'll sting me," says the frog. "Why should I kill you? Death threatens me unless I can get across to the other bank." He persuades the frog. They have almost reached their goal when the scorpion stings the frog and they begin to sink. "Why did you do it?" asks the dying frog. "I don't know, it's my nature," the scorpion replies.' The critic who happened to be sitting next to me said in a loud voice: 'It wasn't the scorpion's nature that did it, he just didn't trust the frog.'

In 1928 Fadeyev sharply attacked Mayakovsky's poem 'Khorosho' ('Good'). In 1938 he called it 'an historic event'. It was not his response to poetry that had changed but his entire approach to literature, and in his speeches he now began to refer to 'State policy'. He was a courageous and disciplined soldier who never forgot the commander-in-chief's prerogatives.

I remember a talk we had after Fadeyev had been inveighing against the 'aloofness from life' of certain writers, among whom he had named Pasternak. We happened to meet in

Gorky Street close to where I live. Fadeyev insisted on taking me to a corner café where, after ordering brandy, he said without preamble: 'Would you like to hear some real poetry?' And he began to recite from memory verses by Pasternak, going on and on, and only interrupting himself from time to time to say: 'Wonderful stuff, isn't it?'

He was devoted to poetry, but even more devoted to his own line of conduct, and it was not his fault but his misfortune that during a quarter of a century, as for millions of his contemporaries, his loyalty to 'the idea' was inextricably bound up with Stalin's every word, whether just or unjust. Undoubtedly Fadeyev knew that Babel was no 'spy', that Zoshchenko was no 'enemy', that Stalin's dislike of Platonov and Grossman was unfounded, but he also knew that for many millions of courageous and self-sacrificing people Stalin's word was law. 'I was wounded twice during the Civil War,' Fadeyev told me at our last meeting. 'The doctors said the wounds were bad, but I was young. And how can one compare a scrap of metal with what one has had to suffer later on?'

Sometimes when talking to me in a confidential mood he would break off with some inconsequential remark like: 'D'you know the painter I really like? Renoir.' And, seeing my amazement, he would add, 'though I must confess I'm colour blind,' and give one of his unforgettable laughs.

He seemed stern, but I often noticed how his look could soften. He tried to help writers who had fallen on bad times. At the beginning of 1938 he showed me several poems by Mandelstam which he wanted to get printed in one of the magazines. He did not succeed. Ten years later he said to me: 'D'you remember Garry? He was pretty hard on your book *The Second Day*. Well, he's back from concentration camp now. He's written an interesting short novel, it reminds me in a way of *The Death of Ivan Ilyich*. He's rather hard up. I'm going to try to get it published.' But next time we met he said glumly: 'Nothing doing about Garry.'

With every passing year his gloom deepened, and his eyes took on a glazed look. He drank heavily and more frequently, mostly in the company of people quite outside the world of letters, evidently seeking oblivion.

In March 1953, soon after Stalin's death, I came across an article in *Literaturnaya Gazeta* in which Fadeyev sharply attacked Grossman's *Za Pravoye Delo* (*In a Just Cause*). This puzzled me because I had several times heard him speak well of this novel, which he had managed to get published. It had aroused Stalin's displeasure and there had been some scathing reviews of it. But Fadeyev had continued to defend it. Grossman had made a few changes in the text. And now suddenly Fadeyev had come out with this article.

The announcement about the rehabilitation of the doctors appeared: changes were obviously in the air. Fadeyev came to me without ringing the bell, sat down on my bed and said: 'Don't be too hard on me ... I was frightened.' 'But why after his death?' I asked. 'I thought the worst was still to come,' he replied. He afterwards repeated this more than once, driven by some need to do penance. A year later I ran across L. S. Faktor, an interpreter who always accompanied Fadeyev at difficult political talks with the French. 'There's something wrong with Fadeyev,' she said. 'He came to me several times in a terrible state because he'd written so harshly about Grossman's novel.' Late in 1954, at the Second Congress of Writers, Fadeyev spoke about the novel *In a Just Cause* and his own article about it, and made the public admission: 'I infinitely regret having shown such weakness.'

Fadeyev was physically extremely tough. He ate a lot and drank a lot; he could run a distance of five miles; he spent whole nights at meetings without showing any sign of fatigue. It was only in the last years that his nerves began to give way. In December 1952 he wrote to me: '... I am, alas, still unwell and shall probably have to stay another three weeks in hospital. A stranger looking at you and me would almost certainly put me down as exceptionally strong and you as rather ailing. Actually it's you who enjoy robust health. But mind you take good care of it. Everything depends on one's nerves and there's always a limit. You've never learnt to relax, but you ought to try.'

At our last meeting he said he was ill. 'I've got pain in my legs, I can't walk'; 'I've told you, the novel has gone by the board'; 'As a matter of fact, things are bad.' I did my best to cheer him up by saying that the sickness would pass, that he was ten years younger than I and would live to write several more novels. But he shook his head: 'The engine's stalled.'

Two months later I had a telephone call: 'Fadeyev has committed suicide.'

As always happens in such cases there was a good deal of speculation about what had made him do it; all the good and the bad things about him were recalled. The reasons must have been many: Fadeyev never spared himself throughout his life; so long as the harsh winter prevailed he held out, but once people smiled again he began to ponder on what he had lived through and what he had written, and everything must have suddenly revealed itself to him in a new light. That was when the engine stalled.

Looking back at the post-war years I always see Fadeyev's figure. He was a big man who stood out in any gathering. And everything about the man was big too: his ruthlessness, his tenderness, his faith and his tragedy.

1966
Translated by Tatiana Shebunina with Yvonne Kapp

A poet of the younger generation whose name is particularly associated with the opening-up during the Thaw period of themes previously avoided is Yevgeny Yevtushenko (b. 1933; see also pp. 167, 337). His 'personal memoir' of his experiences and thoughts, called in English *A Precocious Autobiography* (written on a visit to France in 1963, and received with misplaced hostility in the USSR), is naturally very different from Ehrenburg's, but it contains several memorable scenes that help to make it a *sui generis* literary work, despite the smell of midnight oil about its construction. Particularly notable is the description of Stalin's funeral, a moment that has passed into Soviet legend. The end of our extract can be interestingly compared with Yevtushenko's poetic treatment of the same event (see pp. 342–3).

Yevgeny Yevtushenko

From A PRECOCIOUS AUTOBIOGRAPHY

On 5 March 1953 an event took place which shattered Russia – the death of Stalin. I found it almost impossible to imagine him dead, so much had he been an indispensable part of life.

A sort of general paralysis came over the country. Trained to believe that Stalin was taking care of everyone, people were lost and bewildered without him. The whole of Russia wept. So did I. We wept sincerely with grief and perhaps also with fear for the future.

At a writers' meeting, poets read out their poems in Stalin's honour, their voices broken by sobs. Tvardovsky, a big and powerful man, recited in a trembling voice.

I'll never forget going to see Stalin's coffin.

I was in the crowd in Trubnaya Square. The breath of the tens of thousands of people pressed against one another rose up in a white cloud so thick that on it could be seen the swaying shadows of the leafless March trees. It was a fantastic and a fearful sight. New streams poured into the human torrent from behind, increasing the pressure. The crowd turned into a monstrous whirlpool. I realized that I was being carried straight towards a traffic light. The post was coming relentlessly closer. Suddenly I saw that a young girl was being pushed against the post. Her face was distorted by a despairing scream which was inaudible among all the other screams and groans. A movement of the crowd drove me against the girl; I did not hear but felt with my body the cracking of her brittle bones as they were broken on the traffic light. I closed my eyes in horror, I could not bear the sight of her insanely bulging, childish blue eyes, and I was swept past. When I looked again the girl was no longer to be seen. The crowd must have sucked her under. Wedged against the traffic light was someone else, his body twisted and his arms outflung as on a cross. At that moment I felt I was treading on something soft. It was a human body. I picked my feet up and was borne along by the crowd. For a long time I was afraid to put my feet down again. The crowd closed tighter and tighter. I was saved by my height. Short people were smothered alive. We were caught between the walls of houses on one side and a row of army trucks on the other.

'Get the trucks out of the way!' people howled. 'Get them away!'

'I can't. I've got no instructions,' a very young, fair, bewildered police officer shouted back from one of the trucks, almost crying with desperation. And people were being hurtled against the trucks by the crowd, and their heads smashed. The sides of the trucks were running with blood. All at once I felt a savage hatred for everything that had given birth to that 'No instructions' shouted at a moment when people were dying of someone's stupidity. For the first time in my life I thought with hatred of the man we were burying. He could not be innocent of the disaster. It was the 'No instructions' that had caused the chaos and bloodshed at his funeral. Now I saw once and for all that it's no good waiting for instructions if human lives are at stake – you must act. I don't know how I did it, but working energetically with my elbows and fists, I found myself thrusting people aside and shouting:

'Form chains! Form chains!'

They didn't understand, so I began to join neighbouring hands together by force, all the while spitting out the foulest swear words of my geological days. Some hefty young men were now helping me. And now people understood. They joined hands and formed chains. The strong men and I continued to work at it. The whirlpool was slowing down. The crowd was ceasing to be a savage beast. 'Women and children into the trucks!' yelled one of the young men. And women and children, passed from hand to hand, sailed over our heads into the trucks. One of the women who were being handed on was struggling hysterically and whimpering. The young police officer who received her at his end stroked her hair, clumsily trying to calm her down. She shuddered a few times and suddenly became still. The officer took the cap off his tow-coloured head, covered her face with it and burst out crying.

There was another whirlpool farther ahead. We worked our way over, the tough boys and I, and again with the help of curses and fists made people form chains in order to save them.

The police too finally began to help us.

Everything quietened down.

'You ought to join the police, Comrade, we could use fellows like you,' a police sergeant said to me, wiping his face with his handkerchief after a bout of hard work.

'Right. I'll think it over,' I said grimly.

Somehow, I no longer felt like going to see Stalin's remains. Instead, I left with one of the boys who had been organizing chains, we bought a bottle of vodka and he walked home with me.

'Did you see Stalin?' my mother asked me.

'Yes,' I said discouragingly, as I clinked glasses with the boy.

I hadn't lied to my mother. Stalin was really what I had seen.

*

That day was a turning point in my life and therefore in my poetry as well.

I realized that there was no one to do our thinking for us now, if indeed there ever had been. I realized that we needed now to do some hard thinking ... A feeling of responsibility, not only for myself but for our whole country, came upon me and I felt its crushing weight on my shoulders. I don't mean that I instantly became aware of the full measure of Stalin's guilt. I still continued to idealize him to some extent. Many of Stalin's crimes were as yet unknown. But one thing was clear to me – that a great number of problems had come to a head in Russia and to opt out of trying to solve them would itself be criminal. So I thought about poetry – both my own and Russian poetry in general.

Perhaps more than any other, Russian poetry has always had a strong civic sense. Russian poets have always been the spiritual government of their country. Pushkin, who could convey the subtlest overtones of feeling, also wrote biting polemical verse. He also wrote:

> While we are still alight with freedom
> And while our hearts to honour live,
> My friend, let's to our fatherland devote
> The noblest upsurge of our spirit

– a whole revolutionary programme for the young progressive Russia of the time, and a programme still for the young Russians of today. Russia's tyrants had good reason to fear her poets. They were afraid of Pushkin, then of Lermontov, then of Nekrasov. Nekrasov once made up a slogan:

> You may or may not be a poet
> But a citizen you must be.

Even Blok, with all his magic powers as a lyricist, would give up his preoccupation with the enigma of woman to speak in a prophetic voice about his country. Finally in Mayakovsky this tradition received its gigantic revolutionary embodiment: 'I want the pen to be equated with the bayonet.'

To a Russian the word 'poet' has the resonance of the word 'fighter'. Russia's poets were always fighters for the future of their country and for justice. Her poets helped Russia to think. Her poets helped Russia to struggle against her tyrants.

So when, after Stalin's death, Russia was going through a difficult moment in her inner life, I became convinced that I had not the right to cultivate my private Japanese garden of poetry. And the great Russian poets came to my help, their example making me believe that civic poetry can be more intimately lyrical than any other if it is written with single-minded generosity. To write only of nature or women or world sorrow at a time of hardship for your countrymen is almost immoral. And it was a time of hardship for the Russians.

The doctors who had been arrested in connection with the 'plot' were freed.

The news stunned the general public who, by and large, had believed in their guilt. The trusting Russian people were beginning to understand that it could be dangerous to trust too much.

I saw the vulture face of Beria, half hidden by a muffler, glued to the window of his limousine as he drove slowly by the kerb, hunting down a woman for the night ... The same man would turn to the people and make them moving speeches about communism.

The bullet lodged in Beria's head was an act of justice – but how belated! Unfortunately justice is the train that's nearly always late.

Rehabilitated prisoners, back from remote concentration camps, were beginning to appear in Moscow. With them arrived the news of the gigantic scale of the injustices committed.

The people were thoughtful, tensed. The tension was felt everywhere. It could not be relieved by the speeches of Malenkov, a man with a womanish face and a studied diction who addressed them on the coming improvements in food, tailoring and haberdashery.

'Suppose we do gorge ourselves on cream buns and put on

new suits, where shall we go in them?' The worker who lived next to us was amused.

What the people wanted was that someone should speak to them openly and seriously about how they were going to live. They had never reduced the notion of 'living' to food, housing and clothing. For them 'living' had always included 'believing'.

There was something very important that needed saying to them, but I couldn't understand yet what that was and felt utterly lost and confused.

But perhaps this confusion existed only in Moscow, in the welter of political events which were chasing and lashing one another on. Perhaps in the depth of Russia there was peace and spiritual balance. I took the train to Zima Junction. I wanted to escape from my own brooding and misgivings. But it was my own thoughts and misgivings I recognized in talking with the engineers and agronomists who sat next to me in the train. And when I arrived in Zima, I found them again in the first questions put to me by my two uncles – one was the head of the local car pool, the other a locksmith. I had come home to find the answers to the same questions. In Moscow and in Zima people were thinking about the same things. The whole of Russia was one pondering mind throughout all the thousands of miles between the Baltic and the Pacific.

The image of the 'simple Soviet man' is the creation of our press. This 'simple man' has been sung, filmed, staged, proudly mentioned in political speeches. But I saw how far from being simple he really was ...

1963
Translated by Andrew R. MacAndrew

A succinct and moving comment on his times, as well as on his and his fellow Thaw poets' role within them, is made by Yevtushenko in a short poem of 1960.

Yevgeny Yevtushenko

TALK

You're a brave man they tell me.
                                        I'm not.
Courage has never been my quality.
Only I thought it disproportionate
so to degrade myself as others did.
No foundations trembled. My voice
no more than laughed at pompous falsity;
I did no more than write, never denounced,
I left out nothing I had thought about,
defended who deserved it, put a brand
on the untalented, the ersatz writers
(doing what had anyhow to be done).
And now they press to tell that I'm brave.
How sharply our children will be ashamed
taking at last their vengeance for these horrors
remembering how in so strange a time
common integrity could look like courage.

1960
Translated by Peter Levi and Robin Milner-Gulland

Though Yevtushenko's writing is above all associated in the minds of most readers with the late fifties and early sixties, neither his civic conscience nor his muse has dried up since then, as some Westerners have assumed. The next poem by him, like the one by Slutsky that precedes it, deals with the tragic losses of post-Nazi-invasion and post-Stalin Russia on a personal and everyday level – through the image of the women left as survivors in a depopulated city or countryside.

Boris Slutsky

OLD WOMEN WITHOUT THEIR MEN

There were many old women, not many old men;
What bent the old women broke the old men;
They died with their fingers clenched hard on their ribs
As their wives, like hurt animals, fussed over the
  funerals,
Jerked open closets, brushed out best suits,
Spent too much money for the solid oak coffins
Where they laid out their husbands, alone, for the last time,
Resting big hands like stones on their lapels.
– Soon there were tenements full of old women,
Whole blocks full of widows who prayed by themselves,
Heard thieves in small noises, gabbed about death
As if death were a person, a friend they had tea with.
Gaunt Anna Petrovna, sad Mary Andrevna!
They got up like sailors, early in the morning
To comb out their thin slats of Hindu-black hair.
To roll their old beads in their stiff, blunt fingers.
They undressed early, too, punctual as soldiers,
But lay without sleeping, lay thinking and sifting,
Turning over old lovers, old duties, old habits,
As if nothing could waken them out of their
  sleeplessness,
And all the dead mouths of their lives, of their years
Chattered in a streetcar's
                    empty rattle.

1961
Translated by Anne Stevenson

Yevgeny Yevtushenko

A hundred miles from the Capital City of Hope,
and the Hotel Ukraine and the Hotel Budapest,
and the cafés of the young
and the sturdy auxiliary police
and the big cars of the ambassadors
and the hard currency shops
and the gravity of the ministries
and the levity and charm of layabouts
and the crosswords in the newspapers
and the quiet security checkings
and the roar Kill the ref!
and the peace congresses
and touring musicals on ice,
as still as stillness like a paradise
runs the river Ugra,
(it cooks itself pancakes)
– there the whole world runs to its own time.

A hundred miles from the Capital City of Hope
is a village without bridegrooms or brides,
with three cottages falling to pieces,
and three old women in three cottages,
and one old man boasting and talking on:
like one samovar for three women.

The three old women fish and mow grass,
they say, Be careful you don't ever die,
we shall bring water and mow grass,

just keep talking you damned old man,
from the heart and as well as you can.

The old man says, I've ploughed my piece.
The old man says, I've talked enough.
Moscow and war took my children,
the grass is sprouting on my roof,
I am confused in my mind;
and what gossip can I talk, old women?

He stares at the ceiling,
he is no gossip,
he lies like a prophet.
And the roof which is heavy with goosefoot
totters above the jut of his beard.

The sunday fisherman from the Capital City of Hope
has finished visiting the natural world:
It's wonderful our Russian hay-making!
He pushes the sweat off his forehead:
'Well ladies, where's your old tsar?'
'Our tsar doesn't reap these days my dear,
he has turned his old eyes away from us,
he lies down on a bench, he wants to die;
but what I think of is this my dear,
I was dying once, but then it passed.'

The scythes whistle, they cut easily,
after one wave of grass, another wave.
'And where were you dying? When was that?'
'It was in the captivity my dear.'
Moving in joy, moving in pain,
moving maybe in both at that moment.
'What captivity? You mean the Germans?'
'Oh no, in ours my dear son, in ours.'

The sunday fisherman from the Capital City of Hope
moved awkwardly, stumbled to one side.

'I hope that the old man recovers.'
'God grant he does,' behind him tranquilly.

In confusion the sunday fisherman
from the Capital City of Hope starts his car.
Better give your soul an airing on asphalt.
Better to buy fish in the fish-shop.
Better live happy among the unknowing
who don't comprehend the price of hope.

Flying overhead, God help them,
went big planes, Russian born,
fastidiously lifting their undercarriages
over the weeds on shaggy roofs, in heaven.

c. 1970
Translated by Robin Milner-Gulland and Peter Levi

Leonid Martynov (b. 1905, son of a Siberian railwayman) had already in the 1930s made a reputation for his semi-allegorical, free-verse phantasies; as Yevtushenko recounts, he was silenced for almost a decade after 1946. In 'Echo' he wryly reflects on the public significance foisted upon a rather private muse in the intensely 'literature-conscious' Thaw years.

Leonid Martynov

ECHO

What can have happened? – when I speak
with you alone, I hear my words
repeated again beyond these walls,
and at the selfsame moment resounding
from near-by woods and distant thickets,
in neighbouring human habitations,
sounding in every hearth and home,
echoing wherever humans live.
Not a bad thing, you'll admit, this bridging
of distance – no more an impediment,
no longer muffling laughter or sighs.
Powerful beyond belief is this echo –
and (we must take it) a sign of our times.

1956
Translated by Robin Milner-Gulland

Part Two
Writers in Their Generations

1 Veterans

A number of major writers who had begun their careers in the 1910s and 1920s, and thus had formed the 'first generation' of Soviet literature, survived the Stalin and War years to become an important force in the revival of literature after 1953. Their example and encouragement were of vital importance to the 'new wave' of writers who have emerged in the last two decades.

The two such senior figures, both of whom had fallen more or less silent for considerable periods in the Stalin era, were the poets Anna Akhmatova and Boris Pasternak. Old friends with one another, and among the last survivors of the pre-1917 middle-class intelligentsia, they were in other respects rather different figures. Akhmatova (1889–1966) lived in Leningrad, held herself aloof from literary life, but was scurrilously criticized for her intensely personal lyric verse in 1946. Her fervent admirers included a number of undemonstrative but technically fastidious and 'classically orientated' poets (e.g. Berggolts, Kushner, Brodsky, q.v.). Her own later verse continually returns to and develops themes of love and parting that she had made very much her own, and seems more and more haunted by the figures and episodes of her distant past. The greatest expression of this mood is her long, allusive *Poem without a Hero*, but it equally memorably informs lyric works such as the cycle *Sweetbriar in Bloom* and the fourth 'Northern Elegy', with its astonishing virtuoso build-up of emotion towards the end.

Anna Akhmatova

From THE SWEETBRIAR IN BLOOM

You are with me again, autumn my friend! I. Annensky

Someone may still be lolling in the South,
Pampering himself in a garden of Eden.
Here it is very north at the year's end.
And I have chosen autumn for my friend.

I live as in a strange house which, like a dream,
Is half familiar. I may have died here.
The mirrors are keeping something to themselves
These long dark evenings of the year.

I move between trees, between black, squat firs
Where the heather is like wind. If
I look up I see a tarnished splinter of moon
Glimmering like an old notched knife.

What of my last not-meeting with you?
I have blessed it and brought it here with me,
The pure, the bitter, ice-bright flame
Of what I know must be my victory.

1946–56
Translated by Anne Stevenson

Anna Akhmatova

From NORTHERN ELEGIES

Memories have three epochs.
And the first is like yesterday.
The soul is under their blessed vault,
and the body is in the bliss of their shadow.
Laughter has not died down and the tears stream,
the ink stain is unwiped on the table,
the kiss is imprinted on the heart,
unique, parting, unforgettable ...
But this does not last for long ...
The firmament is no longer overhead, and
  somewhere
in a dull suburb there is a lonely house,
where it's cold in winter and hot in summer,
where a spider lives and dust lies on everything,
where passionate letters burn to ash,
portraits change stealthily,
and people come to it as though to a grave,
and wash their hands when they get home,
and shake off a quick tear
from their tired lids, and sigh heavily ...
But the clocks tick, one spring
replaces another, the sky turns pink,
names of towns change,
and eye-witnesses of events die,
and there is no one to cry with, no one to reminisce
  with.
Those shadows pass from us slowly

which we no longer call upon,
whose return would be terrible to us.
And once awake, we see that we have forgotten
the very road that led to the lonely house,
and choking with shame and anger,
we run to it, but (as in a dream)
everything is different there: people, things, walls,
and nobody knows us; we are strangers.
We got to the wrong place ... Oh God!
Now comes the most bitter moment;
we realize that we could not contain
this past in the frontiers of our life,
and it is almost as alien to us
as to our neighbour in the flat,
and that we would not recognize those who have
   died,
and those whom God parted from us
got on splendidly without us –
even better ...

1953
Translated by R. McKane

Pasternak (1890–1960, see also p. 421), though from first to last an unapologetic individualist, always played more of a public literary role than Akhmatova – this of course culminated in the publication (so far, in the West only) of *Doctor Zhivago*, and the award of a Nobel prize (1958). He guided and encouraged a wide circle of young poets, both well known (Voznesensky, Yevtushenko) and obscure (Aygi). While Akhmatova's lucid poetic voice remained recognizably the same over fifty years, gaining only in transcendental and allusive overtones, Pasternak continually sprang surprises; the early 1940s marked a major and self-confessed stylistic break in his work, which in general saw a progression from the 'difficult', Futuristic-influenced early work, saturated with unexpected imagery, to a more publicly orientated, orderly, discursive and limpid manner. In his last two decades he developed an influential theory of art and history, of an interest that goes beyond its usefulness in the exegesis of his own work. To illustrate this side of his talent we give a 'programmatic' poem characteristic of the later Pasternak, as well as the second of three letters to Stephen Spender in which he comments on reviews of his novel and explores the nature of the relationship between art and life; its language is Pasternak's own expressive if sometimes imperfect English.

Boris Pasternak

In everything I want to reach
the inmost kernel:
in work, in life's constant quest,
in the heart's trouble;

to sound the depths of passing time,
its secret causes,
its origins, foundations, roots
and its quintessence;

and always clinging to the thread
of fate and history,
to live and think and feel and love
and make discoveries.

If only I could find a way,
after a fashion,
in eight lines I'd write down the forms
of human passion,

its lawlessnesses, sins, escapes,
the hunt that follows,
its sudden, its unhoped-for flights,
its knees and elbows.

I should set down its inner law,
all that's essential,
and say over again its names
and their initials.

I'd make a garden of my poems.
In compact lines,
in Indian file the limes would flower
with trembling veins.

And breath of rose and breath of mint
would fill my verses,
and meadows, sedge and new-mown hay
and thunder's curses.

So Chopin once in his Études
planted the marvels
of living groves and graves and parks
and Poland's farmsteads.

The torment and triumphant play
the poet knows
are strings drawn tight across the arc
of the bent bow.

1956
Translated by P. France

Boris Pasternak

LETTER TO STEPHEN SPENDER

August 22, 1959.

It is, as I said last time, a great pleasure, honour and a thrill for me to write you. But I am aware of the onus that will fall on the person you will choose and entrust with my letter to find out the sense of its gibberish and to transform it in the English shape when using it to literary purpose.

I have no other debts to Mr Edmund Wilson than to pay him gratitude and admiration. Each critic's right is to comment the impression produced on him by a work of art in the manner he likes it or is accustomed to. I am asked to write brief prefaces, introductory accounts, preambling editions, selections, performances of Bloch (for Italy), of Tolstoy and Lermontov (for America), of Chekhov (for India).

I am no explorer, no erudite. I have read very little in my life, and what I have read, I have it for the most part forgotten. I shall write all them short on the many topics, conveying only my general subjective idea on the matter, just so as Mr Wilson does on my behalf.

If I say, for instance, Chekhov's singularity as a playwright and the chief merit and value of his plays consisted in his having inscribed man in a landscape on equal terms with trees and clouds; that as a dramatist he was against the over rating of the social and the human; that the conversational texts of his plays are not written in obedience to any logic of interests, passion, characters, or plots, but that the cues and speeches are taken and snatched out of the space and the air they were spoken, like spots and strokes of a forest or a meadow only to render the true simultaneous resemblance by the subject of the play to life in the far broader sense of a unique vast inhabited frame, to its symmetries and dissymmetries, proportions and disproportions – to life as a hidden mysterious principle on the whole.

If Chekhov should live and have read these words, would he ever consent? Why should Mr Wilson's liberty and licences be less than mine?

Only I don't esteem accessories and details of such importance. Rather their comparative *indifference* has a special deliberate meaning, being one of them means of my language, the real tongue of my thought.

When we take the great novel of the last century in its essence, extolled and idolised, for instance, by Henry James. When we examine the greatest, Dostoevsky, Tolstoy, Dickens, Flaubert. When from the fabric of a *Madame Bovary* we gradually, one after another, subtract characters, their development, situations, occurrences, the plot, the subject, the content ... The second-rate diverting literature will leave no remainder after such a subtraction. But the name creation (or, for example, David Copperfield) lets remains the *cardinal*: the characterisation of reality as such; almost as of a philosophic category; as a member or link of our mind's universe; as life's perpetual companion and surroundings.

For this characterisation of reality of the being, as a substratum, as a common background, the nineteenth century applied the incontestable doctrine of causality, the belief that objectivity was determined and ruled by an iron chain of causes and effects, that all appearances of the moral and material world were subordinate to the law of sequels and retributions. And the severer and more inflexible was an author in showing such consequences (of characters and conducts) the grater a realist he was esteemed. The tragic bewitching spell of Flaubert's style or Maupassant's manner roots in the fact that their narratives are irrevocable like verdicts or sentences, beyond recall.

I also from my earliest years have been struck by the observation that existence was more original, extraordinary, and inexplicable than any of its separate astonishing incidents and facts. I was attracted by the unusualness of the usual. Composing music, prose or poetry I was driven by definite conceptions and motifs. I pursued certain favourite objects and themes. But the top pleasure consists in having hit the sense or taste of reality, in having been able, in having succeeded in rendering the *atmosphere of being*, the surrounding whole, the total environment, the frame where the particular and depicted thing is having been plunged and floating.

But curiously enough, while pondering over the distinctive notes or features of *life perception* (of recognised *existence*) for the purpose of evoking the same sensations through art's expressive attempts I come to results if not diametrically opposed to the tendencies of the named masterpieces so at least to quite different observations than those of our predecessors and teachers.

If I had to represent a broad, a large picture of living reality, I would not hope to heighten its sense of *extant objectivity* by accentuating the fixed statistics of ἀνάχη;* of natural laws, of settled moral regularity.

To attain a true ressemblance between the imitative efforts of art and the truly tasted and experienced order of life it would me not suffice to put my representation in a vivid instantaneous motion. I would pretend (metaphorically) to have seen nature and universe themselves not as a picture made or fastened on an immovable wall, but as a sort of painted canvas roof or curtain in the air, incessantly pulled and blown and flapped by a something of an immaterial unknown and unknowable wind.

Whether it was the scarce and sparse knowledge of the different physical waves as external impellents to our sub-

* Mistake for ἀνάγκη, necessity.

jective sensual date; or as an aftertaste of the legend of world creation; whether it was a kind of feeling derived from the notion of life's being placed in the narrow space between birth and death, but always my sense of the whole, of the reality as such was that of a reached sending, of a sudden unawaited coming, of a welcomed arrival and I always sought to reproduce this trait of being sent and launched, that I thought to find in the nature of the appearance.

That is the only thing I could not oppose, but add to any allegorically directed detailed criticism: that behind and above all stressed and pointed trifles (even on their sharpened magic) and besides the importance of described human lots and historical events there is an effort in the novel to represent the whole sequence of facts and beings and happenings like some moving entireness, like a developing, passing by, rolling and rushing inspiration, as if reality itself had freedom and choice and was composing itself out of the numberless variants and versions.

Hence the not sufficient tracing of characters I was reproached with (more than to delineate them I tried to efface them); hence the frank arbitrariness of the 'coincidences' (through this means I wanted to show the liberty of being, its verisimilitude touching, adjoining improbability).

It is too bold and silly to send you this incorrect pell mell unread, unrevised. Only the hurry wherewith I do it does it justify.

Yours etc.

1959

The veteran Soviet writers who made a new name for themselves after Stalin were chiefly poets (and *Doctor Zhivago* is a 'poet's novel' through and through). As well as those presented in this section, one might mention names such as Semyon Kirsanov (Mayakovsky's late disciple), V. Lugovskoi, P. Antokolsky (see p. 71) and A. Tvardovsky (better known as editor of the journal *Novy Mir*) as having made a significant contribution to Thaw literature. Prose writers for some reason played a less significant role, with the important exception of memoirists such as Ehrenburg (see p. 74), Paustovsky (see p. 31) and Valentin Katayev (*The Grass of Oblivion*, 1968). Well-known pre-war novelists such as K. Fedin, M. Sholokhov and L. Leonov could not match their earlier successes. However, two masters of the Soviet short story, each of whom considerably expanded the stylistic possibilities of Russian prose, lived into the post-war period: one was Platonov (see pp. 17–18), the other Mikhail Zoshchenko (1895–1958).

Zoshchenko was the modern master of a pithily colloquial diction (*skaz*) based on semi-literate speech – pointed and very funny in the original, notoriously hard to emulate in translation. His unpretentious little tale *Adventures of a Monkey* occasioned a *cause célèbre* when in 1946 Zoshchenko (together with Akhmatova, q.v., p. 117) was subjected to severe public attack. The modern reader may boggle at the cultural atmosphere of a period in which so lighthearted a work should be taken violently to task for supposedly comparing 'Soviet man' unfavourably with a monkey; yet many of Zoshchenko's stories are more than the merely humorous sketches they seem on the surface, and they conceal a bitter or profound 'subtext'. Let the reader decide for himself if this may be true of the following work.

Mikhail Zoshchenko

ADVENTURES OF A MONKEY

In one of our southern towns there was a zoo. A small zoo containing one tiger, two crocodiles, three snakes, a zebra, an ostrich and one macaque, or let's call him a monkey for the sake of simplicity. And of course various bits and pieces – birds, fishes, frogs and suchlike insignificant oddments from the animal kingdom.

At the start of the War when the Germans bombed that town they scored a direct hit on the zoo. It blew up there and then with a great deafening bang. To the amazement of all the animals.

In the process the three snakes were killed, all at the same moment, which perhaps isn't that much of a tragedy. And sadly enough the ostrich too.

But the other animals weren't hurt. As the saying goes, they got out of it with nothing worse than a good fright.

Of all the animals the macaque, I mean monkey, was the most scared. The blast knocked his cage over. The cage toppled down. Its side-wall was broken. And our monkey tumbled out of his cage right onto the zoo pathway.

He fell onto the path, but he didn't lie there frozen like human beings who are used to military action. Just the opposite. He climbed straight up a tree. Then he jumped onto a fence. Off the fence into the street. And he skithered away as if he'd gone crazy.

He raced along and was no doubt thinking as he did so: 'Hey, if they're chucking bombs about I'm all against it.' So he ran along the streets of the town as fast as his legs would carry him.

He ran through the entire town. Ran out onto the high road. And ran along this road straight out into the country. Well, he's a monkey after all. Not a human. He doesn't understand what's what. Didn't see any sense in staying in that town.

He kept on running and finally got tired. Tired out. Climbed up a tree. Consumed a fly to keep his strength up. And a couple of worms for good measure. And went to sleep on the branch right where he was sitting.

And at the moment a military vehicle was coming along the road. The driver spotted a monkey in a tree. Amazement. He crept up on him quietly. Chucked his greatcoat over him. And popped him in his car. This is what he thought: 'Better give him to one of my friends than let him die here of hunger and cold and goodness knows what.' And the long and the short of it was, off he went with the monkey.

He got to the town of Borisov. He went about his business. And left the monkey in the car. Told him:

'Just wait here for me, honeybunch. Shan't be a moment.'

But our monkey had no intention of waiting. He clambered out of the vehicle through a broken windowpane and went off for a walk through the streets.

And there he went, nice as could be, strolling along, taking a walk, tail in the air. The passers-by of course were amazed and wanted to catch him. But he wasn't so easy to catch, being lively and agile and quick on his pins. So they never got him, but only tired him out with useless running around.

This thoroughly exhausted him and naturally he felt like a bite to eat.

And where could he eat in the town? There wasn't anything edible in the streets. He couldn't go into a café with that tail of his. Nor into a co-op. Specially as he didn't have any money. Nor any concession. Didn't have any ration cards. Horrible to imagine.

All the same he did go into a co-op. Felt there might be something worthwhile there. And inside they were issuing vegetables to the populace: carrots, turnips and gherkins.

Into the shop he jumped, and what did he see? A great big queue of people. No, he wasn't going to get into line. And he wasn't going to elbow people out of the way to push through to the counter. He raced right over the heads of the customers to get at the salesgirl. Jumped onto the counter. Didn't ask the price of a pound of carrots. And then he just beetled off, as they say. Raced out of the shop happy with his purchase. Well, he's a monkey after all. Doesn't understand what's what. Didn't see any sense in going hungry.

Of course a great noise and hubbub and rumpus broke out in the shop. The customers began shouting. As for the salesgirl who was weighing out the turnips, she nearly passed out from the surprise of it all. And you really would get a shock if instead of some ordinary normal customer a sort of hairy thing with a tail starts leaping around in your immediate vicinity. And furthermore doesn't hand over any money.

The customers rushed out into the street after the monkey. And he ran along chomping up a carrot as he went. Didn't understand what's what.

Right up in front the kids were belting along. The grown-ups behind them. And at the rear there was a policeman blowing his whistle as he ran.

And suddenly a dog jumped out from goodness knows where. And it joined in the hunt for our monkey. It wasn't just yelping and barking, at that, but really trying to get its teeth round him.

Our monkey started running all the faster. Running and no doubt thinking: 'Hey, I reckon I was wrong to leave the zoo. Life's more peaceful in a cage. I'll certainly be on my way back at the first opportunity.'

And he ran for all he was worth, but the dog kept up with him and was on the point of catching him.

And then our monkey leapt onto some fence or other. And when the dog jumped up to grab him by the foot at least, he whacked the carrot across the dog's nose with all his might. And he hit so hard that the dog howled and ran home with an injured nose. It no doubt thought: 'No thank you, citizens, much better I should lie quietly at home than go catching your monkey for you and experience such extreme unpleasantness.'

Briefly then, the dog ran away and our monkey jumped off the fence into a garden.

And while this was going on there was a young lad called Alexander Popov cutting wood in the garden.

Chopping wood, he was, when suddenly he saw a monkey. And as it happened he was very fond of monkeys. All his life he'd been dreaming of having some monkey like that around the place. And suddenly one's presented to him on a plate!

Alex threw off his coat and with it he covered the monkey, who'd taken refuge in a corner on a step-ladder.

The boy took him indoors. He fed him up. Gave him tea to drink. And the monkey was quite happy. But not absolutely. Because Alex's grandmother took an instant dislike to him. She yelled at the poor monkey and even wanted to hit him. All because when they were having tea and granny put down a half-eaten sweet on her saucer the monkey took this sweet of granny's and stuffed it in his mouth. Well, he's only a monkey after all. Not a human being. If a person takes something it wouldn't be under granny's very eyes. And *he* goes doing it when granny's right there. And of course almost reduced her to tears.

Said granny:

'It's really very unpleasant to have some kind of macaque with a tail living right in your own house. He'll be giving me a fright with that subhuman face of his. He'll jump on top of me in the dark. He'll go eating my sweeties. No, I absolutely refuse to live in the same house as a monkey. One of the two of us must be placed in a zoo. Have I really got to move into a zoo myself? No, much better for him to be there. And I'll go on living in my own house.'

Alex said to his granny:

'No, granny, no need for you to move to the zoo. I'll guarantee the monkey doesn't eat anything else of yours. I'm bringing him up like a person. I'll teach him to eat with a spoon. And to drink tea properly. As for jumping, I can't tell him not to get up on that light hanging down from the ceiling. He *could* jump off there onto your head of course. But don't you be scared if it does happen, that's the chief thing. Because it's only a harmless monkey who got into the way of jumping around when he was in Africa.'

Next day Alex went off to school. And asked his granny to keep an eye on the monkey. She began thinking: 'Whatever next, am I going to start looking after all kinds of monstrosities?' And with these thoughts in mind granny went and fell asleep on purpose in her easy chair.

And thereupon our monkey climbed out of doors through an open top-window. Down the sunny side of the street he wandered. No way of knowing, but perhaps he wanted to have a stroll, or maybe he'd decided to take another look into the shop so as to buy himself something there. Not for money – the other way, for free.

And at that moment an old man was walking along the street: a disabled worker called Gavrilych. He was on his way to the public bath. And in his hand he was carrying a little basket with his soap and clean underwear.

He caught sight of the monkey and at first couldn't even believe his eyes when they registered that a monkey it was. He thought it was all imagination after his having drunk a pint of beer.

He looked at the monkey in amazement. And the latter looked back at him. Maybe thinking 'What sort of twit with a basket is this?'

Finally Gavrilych realized it was a real monkey and not an imaginary one. And then he thought: 'Go on, I'll catch him. I'll take him to the market tomorrow and sell him there for

100 roubles. For that sort of money I can drink ten pints of beer straight off.' And with such thoughts in his head Gavrilych began trying to catch the monkey, calling to him, 'Pussy ... pussy ... pussy ... come on, puss!'

No, he knew it wasn't a cat, but he didn't know what language to use. And only afterwards did he realize that this was the highest creature in the animal kingdom. And thereupon pulled a sugar-lump out of his pocket, showed it to the monkey and said ultra-politely:

'Dear little monkey, wouldn't you like to taste a lump of sugar?'

He answered: 'Yes, please, I'd be most grateful ... ' That's to say he didn't really say anything at all since he couldn't talk. But he simply went up and grabbed the sugar-lump, and began eating it.

Gavrilych took hold of him and put him in his basket. And it was warm and snug in the basket. And our monkey had no intention of jumping out of it. Maybe he was thinking 'OK, so this old blockhead is going to carry me in his basket. Quite fun really.'

First of all Gavrilych thought of taking him home. But then he took against the idea of going home at all. And he went with the monkey to the public baths. He thought: 'Better still if I drop into the baths with him. I'll give him a good wash there. He'll be really clean and nice. I'll tie a little bow round his neck. And that way I'll get more for him in the market.'

And so he got to the bath-house with his monkey. And they settled down for a wash.

And it was warm or even hot in the baths – just like Africa. And our monkey was very happy with the atmosphere. But not entirely. Because Gavrilych lathered him with soap and the soap got into his mouth. Of course that doesn't taste nice, but hardly bad enough to scream and scratch and refuse to be soaped. Anyhow our monkey began spitting it out, but the soap got into his eye. And that drove the monkey clean out of his mind. He bit Gavrilych on the finger, tore himself away from his hands and leapt crazily out of the bath-house.

He leapt into the room where people get undressed. And there he frightened all and sundry. After all nobody knew it was a monkey. All they could see was something round and white and covered in foam. It hurled itself first of all onto the couch. Then onto the stove. From there onto a box. From the box onto someone's head. And onto the stove again.

Some of the clients got nervous and started shouting and running out of the bath-house. And our monkey ran out too. And went down the stairs.

Down below there was a ticket-office with a little window. The monkey jumped up through this window, thinking things'd be quieter there, and (most important of all) there wouldn't be so much hustle and bustle inside. But inside the ticket-office sat a fat ticket-lady, who drew in her breath with surprise and let it out with a scream. And out of the office she ran with a shout:

'Help! I think a bomb's gone off in my office! Give me some valerian drops!'

Our monkey had got fed up with all this shouting. He leapt out of the office and set off at full speed along the street.

And once again he was racing down the street, wet through, people were running after him. Kids in front, grown-ups next, a policeman behind. And after the policeman came our aged Gavrilych, half-dressed and carrying his shoes in his hand.

But hereupon the dog jumped out again from goodness knows where – the very same dog that had chased him the day before.

When he saw it, our monkey thought: 'Well, boys, now I'm for it.'

But this time the dog didn't chase him. The dog only gazed at the running monkey and felt a great pain in the nose, and actually turned away. Probably it was thinking: 'Can't get enough spare noses to make monkey-chasing worth while.' And even though it turned away it barked crossly – as much as to say 'Run away if you like, but don't forget I'm around!'

And at that moment our lad Alexander Popov got back from school and couldn't find his beloved monkey at home. He was extremely sad. Tears actually appeared in his eyes. He thought that now he'd never again see the splendid monkey he adored.

And so his frustration and sorrow drove him out onto the street. Along it he walked, sad as could be. And suddenly he saw people running. No, first of all he didn't think they were running after his monkey. He thought they were running because of an air-raid. But then he caught sight of his monkey – soaking wet and covered in soap. He rushed at him and grabbed him in his arms. And hugged him to himself so as not to give him up to anybody.

And then all the hurrying people stopped and crowded round the lad.

But out of the crowd there stepped our aged Gavrilych. And waving his bitten finger at everybody he said:

'Citizens, don't let this kid hold this monkey of mine that I want to sell in the market tomorrow. Yes, it's my very own monkey who bit me on my finger. Just take a look at this swollen finger of mine. And that's evidence I'm telling the truth.'

But at that moment yet another man came out of the crowd: the very same driver as had brought the monkey there in his car. Said he:

'No, he's not *your* monkey, not *yours* either. He's mine because I brought him here. But I'm going off to my army unit again, and so I'll give the monkey to the one who likes hugging it, not the one who wants to sell it cold-heartedly in the market so as to pay for a booze-up. The monkey belongs to that boy.'

And all those present burst out in applause. And Alex

Popov, glowing with happiness, hugged the monkey still tighter. And triumphantly bore him home.

Gavrilych went off with his bitten finger to finish his bath.

And so from then on the monkey went to live with the lad Alexander Popov. He's still there, too. Not long ago I went to the town of Borisov. And I specially went to Alex's to see how the monkey was getting on. Oh, he's having a marvellous time! He doesn't run away anywhere. He's completely house-trained. Wipes his nose with a handkerchief. And leaves other people's sweets alone. So that granny's now completely happy, doesn't get cross with him and doesn't want to move to the zoo any more. When I went into Alex's room the monkey was sitting at table. He sat there as self-important as a ticket-lady in a cinema. And he was eating his rice pudding with a spoon.

Alex told me:

'I've brought him up like a human being, and now all the children and even some of the grown-ups can take an example from him.'

1946

Translated by Robin Milner-Gulland

The 'older generation' of Soviet writers includes not only senior figures like Akhmatova and Pasternak, who began to publish before the Revolution, but a middle age-group of writers born roughly between 1900 and 1920, who came to maturity in the first two decades of Soviet power, and who were in many cases prevented by national and international upheavals from establishing a justified reputation until after Stalin's death. Among those we have already encountered Slutsky, Martynov and Zabolotsky. Some remained almost totally unknown until recently, and as a representative of such figures we may choose the excellent poet Arseny Tarkovsky (b. 1907, first book published 1962), whose son Andrey is, incidentally, the outstanding contemporary Soviet film director (his artistic credo appears to owe much to his father's example). Arseny Tarkovsky's work is deeply concerned with questions of culture and language; strong emotion is offset by a controlled, rather 'classical' verbal texture.

Arseny Tarkovsky

THE STEPPE

Earth engulfs itself; thrusting
Its head up into the sky
Now with grass, now with a man
Patches holes in memory.

Grass under the horseshoe rests
Soul is in its box of bone:
In the steppe only the word
Is erect beneath the moon.

The steppe lies like Nineveh;
Boulders at each barrow-head
Slumber like protector kings,
Sleep tipsy on lunar lead.

The word is the last to die.
But the sky shifts on until
Once again the continent's
Tough shield yields to water's drill.

Burdock's eyelash will take breath
Saddle of grasshopper be bright
Rainbow-like a steppe bird will
Scratch away the webs of night.

Shoulder high in smoky milk
Adam out of paradise
Will restore to birds and stones
Speech wherewith they may be wise

Into roots he will inspire
Ecstasy of being aware
He who yet awhile in dreams
Formed afresh their quivering names.

1961
Translated by Keith Bosley with Dimitry Pospielovsky

Arseny Tarkovsky

TAURUS, ORION, CANIS MAJOR

O mighty architecture of the night!
The angel-labourer described a dome
Turning full circle on the treetops. And
Between the column-trunks there were descried
Dark spaces, as in an old church
By God and man forgotten.
                                        Thereupon
Rose up my diamond Pleiades.

Sappho binds seven strings to them
And speaks
        'My Pleiades have risen
        And I am in my bed alone, alone,
        Alone and in my bed!'

        Further down and leftward
In the warm nectarine afterglow of evening
Have risen – victims at a sacrificial altar –
The golden horns of Taurus.
                                        And his eye
Glowing among the Hyades, as if it were
Another Tablet of the Law.
                                        Time passes;
I am indifferent. For I have patience
And I can wait: till after sacrificial Taurus
That unimaginable wonder rises –
Orion, like a crazy butterfly,
Holding between its wiry legs a font

Where Earth and Sun had baptism.
I shall wait
            till, streaming glassy rays,
Sirius himself
              – his canine head
                Egyptian and sepulchral –
he too shall rise.

Fate has ordained that I should once again
Look on this glittering canvas, –
This heavenly overarch of happiness;
Let other people say what they may say,
I shall live on, shall sift them over starlike,
Shall count them over by the catalogue
Shall read them over by the book of night.

published 1966
Translated by Robin Milner-Gulland

Arseny Tarkovsky

JUST AS TWENTY-TWO YEARS AGO

In memory of M. Tsvetayeva

And every man falls dead, and every blade
Of grass is burnt to ashes or trampled under heel.
And yet above the groans and cries, outweighed,
Another death more strong than grief I feel.

Why in the flames of war, a darting arrow,
Did I not burn? Where lies the end
Of my half-circle? Why hold I, like a swallow,
Life within my palm? Where now is my best friend,

Where my goddess, where the righteous angel of
wrath?
Blood is all around me, before me and behind –
Your bloodless death more deadly by a hundred
times.
The bow of war has flung me far away
From where you are. I shall not be there to close your
eyes.
But what can I say, what can I say?

1941–63
Translated by Peter Norman

In many poems – such as the last of these – Tarkovsky remembers other poets from the 'heroic age' of the 1910s to 1920s. But among Russian writers he seems to stand closest of all to Nikolai Zabolotsky, another figure whose true stature only became apparent in the 1960s – after his death – and whom we may see as the greatest representative of the 'forgotten generation' of Soviet writers.

Zabolotsky (see also pp. 65, 402) moved, like Pasternak, from a highly original, Futuristic, 'difficult' manner (in his first book *Scrolls*, 1929) to a more traditional, civically aware but still individual approach to writing; this change, sometimes considered to have been forced upon him, nevertheless evidently corresponded with inner necessity. He continually returns to 'philosophical' themes, particularly those concerned with Man's relationship to Nature, the metamorphoses between forms of animate (and inanimate) being, and how death may be accommodated or overcome. Like several other 'veteran' Soviet writers, he feels the presence of figures from the past: we end our section with the strange poem 'Good bye to Friends', a 'guided tour to the grave', in which he evokes the almost forgotten experimentalist writers Kharms and Vvedensky, close colleagues of his youth, who had died ten years before.

Nikolai Zabolotsky

TESTAMENT

When the years tilt and my life drains away,
when I blow out the candle and set off
into the unmeasured universe of mist and metamorphosis
when million on million generations
fill this whole world with miracles of light,
when they complete this half-constructed work that nature is,
let my ashes be in these waters,
let me be in this wood.

O friend I will not die but be made known
to this world in the musk breath of flowers,
and many-centuried the oak will knot my soul alive
into its root, sadly and austerely;
I will be the mind's shelter in its leaves,
and in those big branches my own thoughts be cherished and
  live,
above you in the dark wood
    a common consciousness.

And I shall be a slow bird through the sky
  above your head, distant descendant,
    the pale sheet-lightning bursting above you,
      the pouring rain of summers glistening in grass.
        There is no light as bright as existence.
        The wordless grave is an empty languor.
        I have lived out my life and not seen peace.
        There is no peace.
        My presence. Life's presence.

I was not born when I looked out first
from the cradle to the world,
I thought first when the hard crystal sensed,
because the raindrop fell on it,
disintegrating rays of light.

I have not lived on earth without meaning,
and it is sweet to strive out of darkness
for you to hold me, distant descendant,
on the palm of your hand and to finish
what I did not finish.

1947
Translated by Peter Levi and Robin Milner-Gulland

Nikolai Zabolotsky

When the day's light is dying far away
and lowers itself on houses in a cloud of dark,
the sky over my head begins to break into music
like an atomic thing, enormous in motion.
And one vision continually wears me down:
in an unknown cranny of the universe
there might exist the same garden and the same
   darkness,
and the same stars, that incorruptible beauty:
and a poet standing disturbed in his garden who
   might be
asking with an agony of weariness for what reason
should I, whose years are finishing, confuse him
   with my nebulous vision.

1948
Translated by Peter Levi and Robin Milner-Gulland

Nikolai Zabolotsky

THE TALE

In this world where our person plays an unclear role
you and I shall grow old like the old king in the tale;
our life is burning down, the glimmer of patience
in protected places; inevitable fate
encountered in silence.
One day ropes of silver will overshadow your temples
   and then
I will tear up these notebooks and abandon my poem;
let my soul be lapping as if it were a lake
at the underground gates, where purple foliage
clear of the surface shakes.

1952
Translated by Peter Levi and Robin Milner-Gulland

Nikolai Zabolotsky

GOOD-BYE TO FRIENDS

In broadbrimmed hats and long overcoats
        with whole notebooks full of your poems
long, long ago you crumbled to ashes,
        like leafless lilac branches.

In that country no shape is ready-made,
        all is mingled, dislocated, broken,
        the only sky is the heap of the grave
        and the moon's orbit does not move.

And the noiseless insect assembly sings
        in another and indistinct language,
        and the man-beetle welcomes his friends
        with a small lantern in his hand.

        Is it peaceful for you, old comrades?
Are you easy? Do you forget everything?
        Now your brothers are ants and grasses
and roots and heaps of dust and sighs.

Your sisters are the pinks and lilac nipples,
the chickens in the woodshavings, you cannot
remember the language of your brother,
who has no place yet in the country where

light you disappeared like shadows
in broadbrimmed hats and long overcoats
with whole notebooks full of your poems.

1952
Translated by Peter Levi and Robin Milner-Gulland

2 The 'New Generation' in Poetry

The senior and middle generations of Soviet writers have been somewhat under-represented in this anthology in order to leave space for a fuller (though obviously far from exhaustive) presentation of the most characteristic voice of 'today' in Russian literature – that of the younger writers, born since the mid-1920s, who emerged into literature during the 1950s and 1960s. They have rejuvenated the Soviet cultural scene not merely with their treatment of modern (and sometimes previously 'taboo') subject-matter, but more fundamentally with an infusion of lyricism, wit and phantasy, with a certain amount of technical experimentation (particularly as compared with Russian writing of the mid-1930s to mid-1950s) and with a new respect for their readers' aspirations, intellect and taste. Like the new prose writers, they have displayed a pervasive though not overbearing ethical preoccupation.

The 'new wave' first manifested itself in poetry, and became a fact that could not be ignored from about 1956. Its appearance was linked with a boom in the popularity of poetry-readings, large and small, unprecedented since the days of Mayakovsky: much of the 'new poetry' seems clearly angled towards verbal recitation rather than to persual on the page, and is rhetorical in a not necessarily pejorative sense. On the merits of the 'new poets' there are sharp divisons of opinion in Russia; many of them may rouse not only the ire of 'conservatives' with real or supposed heterodoxy, but also the hostility of cultivated 'traditionalists' of all shades with an arguable tendency towards technical sloppiness and 'lack of culture'. But their freshness, honesty and modernity have won for the better known among them an immense readership, ready to snap up editions running into tens, even hundreds, of thousands on the day of publication.

★

It is of course too soon to tell whether any of the 'new generation' will establish a permanent place among the honoured names of Russian poetry, but it is clear that as strong a candidate as any for such a place would be Andrei Voznesensky (b. 1933). Trained as an architect, he was modestly published in the important annual miscellany *Day of Poetry* in 1958; his reputation rose meteorically in the early 1960s. His creative range is impressively wide: his intense and highly personal scrutiny of the world does not preclude his sometimes handling public themes. He has brought into Russian literature a degree of 'expressionistic' virtuosity unseen since the early years of Pasternak and Mayakovsky, and not infrequently ventures into surreal phantasy. Capable of turning the theories of advanced science into his own metaphors (cf. 'Antiworlds'), he is continually aware of man's vulnerability in the machine age. Nevertheless any atmosphere of pessimism or catastrophism in his work is offset by its own formal qualities – its ebullient wit and sound-play, only echoes of which can be captured in translation. For some of his views on literature, see pp. 397–8.

Andrei Voznesensky

ANTIWORLDS

The clerk Bukashkin is our neighbour.
His face is grey as blotting paper.

But like balloons of blue or red,
Bright Antiworlds
                    float over his head!
On them reposes, prestidigitous,
Ruling the cosmos, a demon-magician,
Anti-Bukashkin the Academician,
Lapped in the arms of Lollobrigidas.

But Anti-Bukashkin's dreams are the colour
Of blotting paper, and couldn't be duller.

Long live Antiworlds! They rebut
With dreams the rat race and the rut.
For some to be clever, some must be boring.
No deserts? No oases, then.

There are no women –
                    just anti-men.
In the forests, anti-machines are roaring.
There's the dirt of the earth, as well as the salt.
If the earth broke down, the sun would halt.

Ah, my critics; how I love them.
Upon the neck of the keenest of them,
Fragrant and bald as fresh-baked bread,
There shines a perfect anti-head ...

... I sleep with windows open wide;
Somewhere a falling star invites,
And skyscrapers
like stalactites
Hang from the planet's underside.

There, upside down,
below me far,
Stuck like a fork into the earth,
Or perching like a carefree moth,
My little Antiworld,
there you are!

In the middle of the night, why is it
That Antiworlds are moved to visit?

Why do they sit together, gawking
At the television, and never talking?

Between them, not one word has passed.
Their first strange meeting is their last.

Neither can manage the least *bon ton*.
Oh, how they'll blush for it, later on!

Their ears are burning like a pair
Of crimson butterflies, hovering there ...

... A distinguished lecturer lately told me,
'Antiworlds are a total loss.'

Still, my apartment-cell won't hold me.
I thrash in my sleep, I turn and toss.

And, radio-like, my cat lies curled
With his green eye tuned in to the world.

version of 1962
Translated by Richard Wilbur

Andrei Voznesensky

HOMELESS

We're hoboes,
                    hoboes travelling light,
lucky to borrow
                    a bed for the night,
careless about tomorrow.

Spiritualists
                might steal here for their trysts;
this hideout has more echoes than a church,
it's full of other people's lives;
the place rocks
                    with chromos and priests ...
Come on!
            let's raid the icebox.

Not for us the song of the gas stove,
let the telephone ring – it's not for us.

We're closest, aren't we, when we're most away,
embraced
            by ghostly strangers in the dark,
whose kisses scald and stay.

My dearest, what a sorry tune!
We're émigrés on foreign soil,
condemned in a cold and heartless town
to hide the deepest things we feel.

Shame on fat-bellied bureaucrats!
but what's the scandal, what's the crime

that we should keep each other warm?
The orators tell dirty lies,
but whom, I ask, do we two harm?
Shopkeepers, why are you disturbed by us?
Fear for yourselves, who think love dangerous.

Dreary cellars of our buried life!
Shall we burn up the wallpaper when we wake?
        attack the pictures with a knife?
smash every piece of china into bits
        for love's departing sake?
'Be careful with that dish, it isn't ours to break.'

1965
Translated by Stanley Kunitz

Andrei Voznesensky

SKETCH FOR A POEM

I

On the twenty-second a woman threw herself from a lift that had stalled;
It doesn't matter where –
just that it was in Moscow;
A guillotine blade,
the lift rose
Up toward her head.

I run up the stair;
blood stains everywhere;
or have I gone mad?
Blood leads to the door;
My ribbed heels grind blood there
into the floor –
blood,
her blood ...

'Darling, stay alive, stay calm
If you can, stay alive; if you can't, still stay
Alive.
An ambulance is on the way; if only by some miracle, stay
Alive.
What a bastard I've been,
Darling, if you pull through,
I won't again let go of you ...
If only ...'

II

'Forgive me, dearest, it happened this way:
The deadend seemed deader
Than ever today,
The deepest sadness, sadder.

I know the end will come
In the dark shaft where I lie,
Where those who love love not enough,
          and no one hears you scream,
And the bastards let you die.

A net of iron encircles all,
Dearest, and you are close by; but it keeps me from you.
Even if I sliced my heart, this net is so fine,
I could not get through.

Perhaps, my love, you're not to blame.
The guiltless are guilty, all the same;
We thrash in a loveless bed as against a net
And want the world to perish in fire.

Suicide is no solution.
What's done is done; but must it be said
That to get attention
I must sever my head?

Don't look for me. My Mother
Will tell you I've gone to Alma-Atá or some place or other;
Be nicer to the next woman in your life,
Don't let that woman slip through your life.'

III

The wounds have opened –
          the blood drains –
                    something more has opened.

Deeper, fresher,
more vulnerable,
more terrible than veins.

Feelings depart,
husbands depart –
cannot be stopped.

Enchantment drains
like water into the soil:
You're here one moment, then you're gone.

All beings are
blood vessels of blue,
green, or brown,

And flow into each other –
exchange existence
through their essence:

Blue flows into you,
I am turning brown,
and you and I

Incessantly flow
into other things,

Flow into what nights,
what sweeping views
of other universes?

Stop it! You say,
but it can't be stopped.

Highways flow,
cities are dough,
houses dissolve

And someone's big ears
sag like an elephant's trunk.
Great, now it's worse!

Now
all things flow. All things – all
fading one into the other.

Ellipsoid, squares sprawl.
Brass bedsteads
ooze out into overcooked macaroni.

Prison bars dangle down like pretzels or shoulder braid.

Henry Moore,
pink-cheeked English sculptor,
rushed along the green baize
of his new-mown lawns.

His sculptures, resplendent as billiard balls,
Either puffed out like sore cheeks, or assumed
the delicate contours of pelvic bones.

'Stay as you are!' howled Moore. 'You are beautiful – stay!'
They would not.

A small flock of smiles flitted by along the streets.

In the world arena two wrestlers panted,
Locked in an embrace, one black, one orange;
Chests glued together, they resembled in profile
an upright pair of pliers.
But horrors!
Ominous black spots began to show through the
orange.

The ooze had begun:

The orange wrestler deftly twisted his rival's ear
and howled with pain himself –

He held, now grafted onto the other, his own ear.

The Royal Castle of the Georgian Kings
        was sliding down the wrinkled skin of the plateau,
                a dim tear
                        of compassion for humankind ...

They let Buggins, the accountant, out of jail;
He almost got back to his office,
        but didn't;
                with all the reshaping,
                        it, too, had reformed.

Back home, out of matches,
        he ran down one flight
                to borrow some.
Found Mrs Buggins bouncing on his neighbour's bed.
'What are you doing here?'
'I'm not sure myself; maybe I leaked through the ceiling, who
  knows?'
Perhaps it's true:
        On her skin,
                as in hot asphalt,
                        five fingers with a seal-ring had left their
                          print;
                                and, with them, a foot.

A rainbow,
        attached as if with nails,
                hung radiantly down
                        like the cable strands of the Crimean
                          Bridge.
The chief of the Igogo-jo tribe sought new means of moving
                                        from feudalism to capitalism.

Everything flowed down,
        down to one level,
                down to sea level.

The sculptor, gone mad, rushed about,
modelling, shaping,
giving objects their ideal contours
understandable only to him;
But as soon as they were free
of his fingers,
They returned to their original shapes,
deflating like hotwater bottles
or rubber syringes.

Above the flood, the lift rested, a pontoon perched in the water.
Up and down –
It went like a pump handle.

Up and down –
Pumping the planet's blood.

'Be sure always to hide matches from children.'
But the places to hide them now are hidden.
Up and down!

Phrases have lost all power. Wordsgetgluedtogether.
Consonants have dissolved.
Only vowels remain;
And they cry: 'A-e-i-o-u! A-e-i-o-u!'

Now I'm the one who's screaming;
And they prop me up, tuck a thermometer under my armpit.
Terrified, I look up at the ceiling;
It is square.

P.S.

I've fallen, deep within my dream,
To the bottom of a giant shaft;
The lift speeds along within the shaft
Against my head, Damoclean.

Light leaps out around the lift,
Escaping from a square eclipse;
The voices bubbling there inside
I slowly begin to recognize.

These are the passengers I begat:
Buggins, the bath maid with her pail,
Old Moralizer, now retired;
And all those others – oh, my pets,

I gave you life and gave you hell,
Gave you the stupidest things to say;
And now, my grateful family,
You are racing down
To do me in.

I thrash in the cage, my voice grows thin.

My sick brain now begins to see
That all the trouble lies with me;
So what? – with me!

But when the lift comes crashing down,
I shall be happy in my grave
That you are gone, and being gone,
That you, at least, may still be saved.

1965
Translated by William Jay Smith

Andrei Voznesensky

AUTUMN IN SIGULDA

Hanging out of the train, I
Bid you all good-bye.

Good-bye, Summer:
My time is up.
Axes knock at the dacha
As they board it up:
Good-bye.

The woods have shed their leaves,
Empty and sad today
As an accordion case that grieves
When its music is taken away.

People (meaning us)
Are also empty,
As we leave behind
(We have no choice)
Walls, mothers, womankind:
So it has always been and will be.

Good-bye, Mother,
Standing at the window
Transparent as a cocoon: soon
You will know how tired you are.
Let us sit here a bit.

Friends and foes, adieu,
Good-bye.

The whistle has blown: it is time
For you to run out of me and I
Out of you.

Motherland, good-bye now.
I shall not whimper nor make a scene,
But be a star, a willow:
Thank you, Life, for having been.

In the shooting gallery
Where the top score is ten,
I tried to reach a century:
Thank you for letting me make the mistake,
But a triple thank-you that into

My transparent shoulders
Genius drove
Like a red male fist that enters
A rubber glove.

Voznesensky may one day be graven
In cold stone but, meanwhile, may
I find haven
On your warm cheek as *Andrei*.

In the woods the leaves were already falling
When you ran into me, asked me something.
Your dog was with you: you tugged at his leash and
called him,
He tugged the other way:
Thank you for that day.

I came alive: thank you for that September,
For explaining me to myself. The housekeeper, I
remember,
Woke us at eight, and on weekends her phonograph
sang
Some old underworld song

In a hoarse bass:
I give thanks for the time, the place.

But you are leaving, going
As the train is going, leaving,
Going in another direction: we are ceasing to belong
To each other or this house. What is wrong?

Near to me, I say:
Yet Siberias away!

I know we shall live again as
Friends or girl friends or blades of grass,
Instead of us this one or that one will come:
Nature abhors a vacuum.

The leaves are swept away without trace
But millions more will grow in their place:
Thank you, Nature, for the laws you gave me.

But a woman runs down the track
Like a red autumn leaf at the train's back.

Save me!

1961
Translated by W.H. Auden

Yevgeny Yevtushenko (b. 1933, see also pp. 98, 337) came into the public eye earlier than his friend and coeval Voznesensky, with the journal publication of the long poem *Zima Junction* – a key Thaw work – in 1956; he had published sporadically since the age of sixteen. A master of platform recitation, he has probably had more impact on the outside world than any other living Russian poet; his diatribe against anti-semitism 'Babiy Yar' must surely be the world's best-known poem of the 1960s. Inevitably he has attracted hostility in a number of quarters: some of it, Eastern and Western, maliciously based, some more seriously directed at the over-facility of his poetic manner. But whether or not he publishes too much, he is an uncommon master of the telling line, the rhetorical barb, or the catching of a generation's mood. Less experimental in technique than Voznesensky, he nevertheless owes much (particularly in the ingenuity of his rhymes and assonances) to representatives of the 'modern movement' such as Mayakovsky and Kirsanov. He has written competent, though little-known, prose and is at present engaged on a novel.

Probably the most influential side of his talent as far as his poetic contemporaries are concerned (and to a large extent he 'blazed the trail' that Voznesensky, Rozhdestvensky, Tsybin and many others have followed) is its more intimate, 'humane' aspect, with its trust in spontaneous human emotion and the worth of individual experience. The following poem is a moving 'programmatic' expression of this impulse.

Yevgeny Yevtushenko

PEOPLE

No people are uninteresting.
Their fate is like the chronicle of planets.

Nothing in them is not particular,
and planet is dissimilar from planet.

And if a man lived in obscurity
making his friends in that obscurity
obscurity is not uninteresting.

To each his world is private,
and in that world one excellent minute.

And in that world one tragic minute.
These are private.

In any man who dies there dies with him
his first snow and kiss and fight.
It goes with him.

They are left books and bridges
and painted canvas and machinery.

Whose fate is to survive.
But what has gone is also not nothing:

by the rule of the game something has gone.
Not people die but worlds die in them.

Whom we know as faulty, the earth's creatures.
Of whom, essentially, what did we know?

Brother of a brother? Friend of friends?
Lover of lover?

We who knew our fathers
in everything, in nothing.

They perish. They cannot be brought back.
The secret worlds are not regenerated.

And every time again and again
I make my lament against destruction.

1961
Translated by Robin Milner-Gulland and Peter Levi

Women poets have been prominent among the 'new generation' of Russian writers; they have broadened the impact of the 'feminine voice' that was first heard in modern Russian literature with Akhmatova and Tsvetayeva, and in the 'middle generation' with Olga Berggolts (see p. 357) and Margarita Aliger. The leading contemporary poetess is undoubtedly Bella Akhmadulina (b. 1937, wife first of Yevtushenko, then of Nagibin), famous or notorious for the intricate, sometimes rather obscure phantasies woven in her severely classical quatrains, but a writer with profundity as well as superficial sparkle. She is hard to represent adequately in translation; the same alas goes for her contemporaries Novella Matveyeva (whose fanciful ballads to guitar accompaniment are enormously popular), Yunna Morits (b. 1937) and Natalya Gorbanevskaya (b. 1936). They share an unassuming, but subtle, ironic and rather sophisticated sureness of touch and delicacy of feeling.

Bella Akhmadulina

VOLCANOES

Extinct volcanoes are silent:
Ash chokes crater and vent.
There giants hide from the sun
After the evil they have done.

Realms ever denser and colder
Weigh on each brutal shoulder,
But the old wicked visions keep
Visiting them in their sleep.

They behold a city, sure
Here summer will endure,
Though columns carved from congealed
Lava frame garden and field.

It is long ago: in sunlit hours
Girls gather armfuls of flowers
And Bacchantes give a meaning sign
To men as they sip their wine.

A feast is in progress: louder
The diners grow, more heated and lewder ...
O my Pompeii in your cindery grave,
Child of a princess and a slave!

What future did you assume,
What were you thinking of and whom
When you leaned your elbow thus
Thoughtlessly on Vesuvius?

Were you carried away by his stories?
Did you gaze with astonished eyes?
Didn't you guess – were you *that* innocent? –
Passion can be violent?

And then, when that day ended,
Did he lay a knowing forehead
At your dead feet? Did he, didn't he,
Bellow: 'Forgive me!'?

published 1962
Translated by W. H. Auden

Bella Akhmadulina

POETRY DAY

What loyal dunce dreamed up this celebration?
What fool's excitement named it Poetry Day?
There in the street of my own obliteration
The crowd is gathering for the holiday.

O glorious hour, your revellers are gay;
I hear their voices and their throbbing feet,
Yet work in silence through a sober day
And will not drink your wine or eat your meat.

The heart of the throng is full of trust and confusion,
But great simplicity is in its soul.
How can it know the truth from the illusion
Or choose between the great man and the small?

Illiterate swaggerers boast; the innocent listen,
Swayed this way and that way without knowing
  what they do.
But I cherish a hazy desire, half hope, half
  compassion: –
That holidays leave a saving residue,

That not for nothing do people fly to the poets,
That not for nothing do poets shriek aloud,
And the eyes of boys and girls ignite with ignorance
In the terrible, beautiful innocence of the crowd.

1962
Translated by Anne Stevenson

Yunna Morits

MORE ABOUT THE DEVIL

To D. Zhuravlev

The organs addressed themselves to god
Like Pushkin to Anna Kern – brilliantly,
And people in churches cleansed themselves
Of vile thoughts and depravity.

And in that squalid paradise,
In the realm of foolish love,
A mediocrity was named god,
And they mocked mankind from above.

And the devil burst out of paradise,
He descended into the duped world,
But still exercising his contempt,
He chastised, scoffed and whistled.

And he revealed that there was no god,
No actual god, that is,
But how deep, o arrogance,
You plunged him into the abyss!

... The centuries flew swiftly by,
But there was no change:
He offered his ideas
And took your freedom in exchange.

The living flame of revelation
He held laughing in his paw
And this miserable genius
Turned into a pot-house bore.

1961
Translated by Daniel Weissbort

Natalya Gorbanevskaya

Turn the sky over,
lower it into the sea,
the silent into the voiceless.
Help the sea to rise,
lift the sea into the sky,
sea-blue into sky-blue,
height and depth
bring into balance.

Balance yourself and the world,
the world and the ladybird,
the wavelet and the wave
that drags you under to the bottom.
And go down to the bottom, softly
banging the moist doors behind you.

1964
Translated by Daniel Weissbort

Natalya Gorbanevskaya

One of Three Poems to Iosif Brodsky

We shall remember
– smoke rises from dry grass.
We shall remember
– millstones grind to a stop.

We shall remember
each footstep, each sigh,
the blood, the blood-flecked sweat
and blood's heavy burden.

The flame leaps through the grass
and reaches the trees,
and the one who lies in the leaves –
his time has come.

A fanfare sounds in the dark,
a blade is drawn across the pane:
we shall remember,
we shall remember all.

1964
Translated by Daniel Weissbort

If – as some commentators have felt – there is a distinctive 'Leningrad school' among the younger poets, it would seem to be characterized by a certain formal restraint and respect for cultural traditions, traceable, no doubt, to the effect of Akhmatova, for so long Leningrad's presiding literary genius.

Iosif Brodsky (b. 1940) published little in Russia (he is now living abroad) though his verses in memory of Eliot appeared in *Day of Poetry*. (His deep love of English literature is also shown in a long *Elegy for John Donne*.) Powerful metaphysical notes are heard in his poetry, whose tightly controlled verbal texture nevertheless has an 'incantatory' quality evident when Brodsky reads it himself. He is one of the outstanding poetic talents – some would say the greatest – to emerge from post-Stalin Russia.

Iosif Brodsky

The night-black sky shone brighter than his legs;
he could not drift into dissolving dark.

That evening, sprawling by an open fire,
we caught our first sight of the raven steed.

I have seen nothing in this world more black –
the very colour of his limbs was coal.
His body was as black as emptiness,
blacker than night, from mane to trembling tail.
His flanks, which bore a blackness set apart,
had never known the saddle's bruising mark.
He stood unmoving, and he seemed to sleep.
But terror stalked the blackness of his hooves.

So black was he that shadows made no stain;
they could not dye him darker than he stood.
He was as black as any midnight dark
or any needle's fierce unfathomed heart –
as black as the dense trees that loom ahead,
as the tense void between the nested ribs,
the pit beneath the earth where a seed lies.
I know that here within us all is black –

and yet he gleamed still blacker to our gaze!
It was no more than midnight by my watch.
He came no closer by the slightest step.
Unplumbed obscurity lurked at his loins.
His back had wholly vanished from our sight;

no single spot of light now lingered there.
The whites of his two eyes struck like twin blows.
Their pupils were more terrifying still,

with the strange leer of eyes in negatives!
But why then did he interrupt his flight
to watch beside us till the morning dawned?
Why did he stand so close against the fire?
And why then did he breathe the blackness of that air,
and crush the brittle bones of fallen leaves?
Why did he blaze black light from those great eyes?

– He sought to find a rider in our midst!

1961
Translated by George Kline

Iosif Brodsky

VERSES ON THE DEATH OF T. S. ELIOT

I

He died at start of year, in January.
His front door flinched in frost by the streetlamp.
There was no time for nature to display
the splendours of her choreography.
Black windowpanes shrank mutely in the snow.
The cold's town-crier stood beneath the light.
At crossings puddles stiffened into ice.
He latched his door on the thin chain of years.

The days he leaves to us will not declare
a bankruptcy of Muses. Poetry
is orphaned, yet it breeds within the glass
of lonely days, each echoing each, that swim
to distance. It will splash against the eye,
sink into lymph, like some Aeolian nymph,
a narcissistic friend. But in the rhyme
of years the voice of poetry stands plain.

With neither grimace nor maliciousness
death chooses from its bulging catalogue
the poet, not his words, however strong,
but just – unfailingly – the poet's self.
It has no use for thickets or for fields
or seas in their high, bright magnificence.
Death is a prodigal, it piles
a horde of hearts upon a wisp of time.

Used Christmas trees had flared in vacant lots,
and broken baubles had been broomed away.
Winged angels nested warmly on their shelves.
A Catholic, he lived till Christmas Day.
But, as the sea, whose tide has climbed and roared,
slamming the seawall, draws its warring waves
down and away, so he, in haste, withdrew
from his own high and solemn victory.

It was not God, but only time, mere time
that called him. The young tribe of giant waves
will bear the burden of his flight until
it strikes the far edge of its flowering fringe,
to bid a slow farewell, breaking against
the limit of the earth. Exuberant
in strength, it laughs, a January gulf
in that dry land of days where we remain.

II

Where are you, Magi, you who read men's souls?
Come now and hold his halo high for him.
Two grieving figures gaze upon the ground.
They sing. How very similar their songs!
Are they then maidens? One cannot be sure:
pain and not passion has defined their sex.
One seems an Adam, turning half away,
but, judging by his flow of hair, an Eve ...

America, where he was born and raised,
and England, where he died – they both incline
their sombre faces as they stand, bereft,
on either side of his enormous grave.
And ships of cloud swim slowly heavenward.

But each grave is the limit of the earth.

III

Apollo, fling your garland down.
Let it be the poet's crown,
pledge of immortality,
in a world where mortals be.

Forests here will not forget
voice of lyre and rush of feet.
Only what remains alive
will deserve their memories.

Hill and dale will know him.
Aeolus will guard his fame.
Blades of grass his name will hold,
just as Horace had foretold.

Thomas Stearns, don't dread the sheep,
or the reaper's deadly sweep.
If you're not recalled by stone,
dandelion will make you known.

Thus it is that love takes flight.
Once for all. Into the night.
Cutting through all words and cries,
seen no more, and yet alive.

You have gone where others are.
We, in envy of your star,
call that vast and hidden room,
thoughtlessly, 'the realm of gloom'.

Wood and field will not forget.
All that lives will know you yet –
as the body holds in mind
lost caress of lips and arms.

12 January 1965
Translated by George Kline

Iosif Brodsky

ÉTUDE

I embrace these shoulders and I look
at what looms up beyond the back
I see the proffered chair grow pale
against the iridescent wall.
The light bulb with its keener glare
shows up the shabby furniture
and makes the corner couch aglow
its brown leather appearing yellow.
The table is empty, the floor flickers
the stove is dark, a landscape has
frozen in its dusty frame: it seems
only the dresser lives and dreams
and quickens my unmoving stare.
If here a ghost has ever been
then it has left this house and gone.

1962
Translated by Keith Bosley with Dimitry Pospielovsky

Among other notable contemporary Leningrad poets are the slightly older Gleb Gorbovsky (see p. 402) and two – both born in 1936 – who contrast with each other: Aleksandr Kushner and Viktor Sosnora. Kushner, a careful 'traditional' craftsman, seems to hark back both to the Russian Symbolists of the turn of the century and to certain post-Symbolists such as the 'clarist' Kuzmin. Sosnora is technically more flamboyant, and perhaps the nearest Leningrad poet to Voznesensky (though in no way imitative). Published since 1960, his work first tended to show a witty, lighthearted, impressionistic face to the world; in the later 1960s it became darker, with surrealistic and apocalyptic overtones. In a cycle of poems on *The Owls* he has created a sinister bird-image fit to stand beside Ted Hughes's *Crow*. He has become absorbed in history (cf. 'Kitezh'), and his harsh, concrete, unsentimental vision of it probably owes something to a harrowing war-time childhood. He uses an idiosyncratic register of diction that hovers – without being a pastiche – between the Old Russian and the contemporary language.

Aleksandr Kushner

Never to tire of looking
At the square-shaped glow
Behind the mother and child,
That is the window:

A window of sparkling rivers,
Tree clumps glittering,
Sheep and cripples straggling,
Land beyond land.

The narrow roadway winds ...
We must write so as to
Bring groves to the eye
At the bright window,

To make hillsides of wild vine
And the domestic sort
Keep company
Shimmering in accord,

As too the far country
And this dull lodging –
And wind the distance tight
As the watchmaker his spring.

1966
Translated by Daniel Weissbort

Aleksandr Kushner

October. Mist and rain
Spread through clearing and glade.
Already love asks no return
But hides in the heart.

And we, in melancholic mood,
Walk in the forest silently,
Our small secrets hid
In one large mystery.

1966
Translated by Daniel Weissbort

Viktor Sosnora

NIGHT IN NOVOROSSIYSK

The world was at peace.
Night.
Fires like grains of rice.
Night.
Over Novorossiysk
night.
Inexpressibly black
night.
And the sea – bilberry.
Glass.
The searchlight – cyclopean
blue.
Five fishermen – five capes
in a boat.
Well, will the storm part their elbows?
Five fishermen.
Five capes – a banner.
The motor fights like a wild boar.
In the searchlight beam glimmer
five faces –
five blue
plaice.

published 1965
Translated by Daniel Weissbort

Viktor Sosnora

THE TALE OF THE CITY OF KITEZH*

And I shall make my way back to Kitezh, that city where I was
brought up.
Then I shall dive to the dark depths whose guardians swing the
gates,
and this return will be thought of as hostile by the guards,
and worthy of suspicion.
I shall go to my wife, to the halls of my dwelling, speaking
'What of my herds?'
'The guards have slaughtered them and used
the hides for shoe-leather.'
Speaking, 'What of our son?'
'The guards killed him, his body quartered.'
Speaking, 'What of our daughter?'
'Ten times ten guards and forty raped your
daughter.'
And I shall ask my wife, 'What of you?' 'What of my
liegemen and retainers?'
and she will say, 'Your servants kept their peace,
and, fearing suspicion, your liegemen joined the guards.
As for myself – I am wed to the ruler.'

* Kitezh is a legendary town often mentioned in Russian popular tales and epics. According to these old stories, during the thirteenth-century Mongol invasion, rather than submit to worldly degradation and corruption, the heroic city chose to sink to the bottom of a lake. Under the water, the stories ran, lay a purer existence than that which was found on land. It was said that during the summer solstice a chosen few could sometimes hear the ringing of the bells from its vanished churches and see the lights of the lost city burning beneath the waters. (Translator's note)

Thus will I turn back to Kitezh which I ruled in the past,
where my servants and liegemen held the walls
and the Mongols could take neither us nor our city,
where every first man was a hero, and every second man
immortal.

I spoke these words: 'Sword-bondsmen, speak the truth:
Are we to give our freedom to the foe, or must we sink?'
Then we roasted alive ten times a hundred hundred bulls
and many times this number of protesting boars
and when the last carcass was burnt, the crawling smoke
obscured the sun.
Then we sank down at midnight. To the bottom. Utterly.
There remained only cranberry bogs and the songs of serfs,
serf-songs of the immortal City of Heroes.

So I must turn back to Kitezh, to that City of Heroes.
How time has changed the servants of my realm!
The deep ends of the marshes hold no lights.
The days have gone wan. The mares do not neigh.
No grain is harvested, no meat is roasted.
Their noses are like twigs, spineless, blunt as the snouts of fish,
the scimitar-shaped whiskers ossified,
human jaw bones collapsed into toad's cheeks:
Thus have my realm's servants changed.
Yet I must turn back to Kitezh, there where loyalty
was once held high as the grain deities.
No one awaits me in that city; he who awaited played me
false.
I shall take with me the heads of twelve onions,
which will make up thirteen with my own head.
It seems that in this age the onion
is the last growth which will bring tears.

Then shall I come to the Overlord, speaking
'Are you truly supreme? Do you rule all?'
'The guard alone is supreme

And I rule a little myself. I have, in a way,
the people's support – dictated by the guards.'

And I shall leave upon the square – let them weep for a while –
my onion, this simple remembrance of nature,
in this land, ruled for centuries by optimism,
where all was transient
where for the slightest tear heads were removed like shoes,
where for the slightest tear heads were sliced off like warts
the guards cried! The people cried, all of them!
The Overlord himself, a mighty ruler with a star upon his
chest,
swallowed tears instead of spittle and flew into a rage.
And yet they did not overlook my execution,
or to bury the twelve onion heads in the nearest pit.

Sometime, after, much, much later,
twelve onion heads will sprout over the city
and my head will sprout up as well, a warning
that mine was not to be the last beheading.

But it is said no one has ever seen the city of Kitezh.
That may well be so, no one has seen it.
Indeed, that may well be.

1960–62
Translated by John Statathos

We end this section with a poet unlike any of the others represented, one whose vision of the world is personal, hermetic and allusive to the point of obscurity: Gennady Aygi (b. 1934), a Chuvash who came to Moscow in 1953, sat at the feet of Boris Pasternak in the last four years of the latter's life, and has written in Russian since *c.* 1960. His poetry has scarcely been published in the USSR (save for translations into Chuvash), though he is known in Eastern and Central Europe. Fragmented in texture, free in form, saturated with an intense private symbolism relating to childhood, to the fields and forests of his remote homeland, to transcendental speculations, his work owes more to the 'alogical' painting of Malevich and the Futurist writings of Kruchonykh than to any more contemporary Soviet sources.

Gennady Aygi

CHILDHOOD

Yellow water
where the cattle live –
distant, and cold, and *a priori*,

and there, like drum-sticks,
knowing no end
the alphabets of wild children:

O Straw, Wood-Splinter, Shiver of Glass,
o Linear Scythian Winds,
and, like a cheerful brawl in basements
Paper, Paper, and more Paper.

o midshipmen of straw,
o damp letters imprinted on the fingers!

HERE AND NOW – THIS SEEMS TO CUT
BUT ONLY ME, NOT YOU!
CUTS – THROUGH PICTURES AND DRESSES
AND THROUGH BIRDS' CLAWS!

Cows' hooves are bright, unbelievable,
something of sailing into a bay,
something of the dance,

and at once, like clattering rails,
bright, broad, unmerciful,
those participants embracing us –
arms, sisters, necks and mothers!

Let us enjoy ourselves again, enjoy ourselves,
fall asleep again and pass onward
not yesterday, not today, not tomorrow, a-a-a-ah!

THROUGH CHILDREN'S CRIES,
THROUGH DAMP LETTERS,
THROUGH PICTURES AND DRESSES
AND THROUGH BIRDS' CLAWS!

1960
Translated by Robin Milner-Gulland

Gennady Aygi

DAWN: WILD ROSE IN FLOWER

To K.E.

In the thicket of suffering
and I stir:

and I hear the long
'Le dieu a été'
of Kierkegaard:

resembling an echo! –

o it is stirring! ... and:

not even scarlet:
the spirit of scarlet:

as if in everything – that constitutes pain
like the repository of a world
similar in thoughts:

it paints without colour but sharp as if cutting:
in transfiguration – no knowing how often! –
purification:
not of the scarlet, even
but of its spirit! –

and the un-human:
'le dieu *a* été'
(†):
quietly ... – as if in
the thicket of suffering:

anew and anew:

–́ –́ :

/oh ! two last syllables:

a flute should have played:

friend for you ! /

The phrase of Kierkegaard – in the original 'Gud *har* varet' – is from his *Philosophical Fragments, Philosophiske smuler.* (Author's note)

1969
Translated by Robin Milner-Gulland

3 The 'New Generation' in Prose

The so-called 'young prose' was slower to become an evident force in post-Stalin literature than the 'new poetry', though some of its representatives are older than the chief poets; indeed, certain 'middle generation' writers who did not become popular until the Thaw seem to belong spiritually with the 'young prose' (e.g. Yury Dombrovsky, author of a remarkable novel set in the late thirties – *Keeper of Antiquities* – Yury Nagibin – see p. 316 – Vladimir Tendryakov and, at least at the outset of his career, Aleksandr Solzhenitsyn). The prose of the new generation has been less flamboyant than the poetry, its formal explorations more tentative; but one senses that its possibilities are still being developed – particularly among the 'village' writers (cf. p. 426). Characteristic of the 'new prose' is a reaction towards modesty of scale and precision of aim after the rather overblown and hollowly tendentious novels of the Stalin era. The story and the short novel are the dominant forms; the influential predecessors seem to be Chekhov and Hemingway rather than more radical experimentalists, though steps towards re-invigorating the heritage of Daniil Kharms (1905–42) – whose miniature tales ('happenings') recall Kafka – have been taken by the almost unknown and unpublished Vladimir Kazakov (b. 1938).

Among dominant themes are the contradictoriness and complexity of the individual's experience, his inadequacies when faced with the larger demands of society (cf. the stories of Vladimir Tendryakov, too long to be satisfactorily represented here), while the social doctrine that 'ends justify means' is frequently and firmly rebutted (as in Pavel Nilin's novel *Cruelty*, hinging on a tragic suicide). A 'populist' concern to explore the roots of Russian peasant life is found in the work of certain of the newer writers, and of course characterizes some of Solzhenitsyn's best work: see his *Matryona's Home*, p. 451.

*

Vasily Aksyonov's (b. 1932) position as a prose writer is perhaps comparable to Yevtushenko's as a poet: he is particularly popular as an articulator of the younger generation's outlook on life, and has caused some stir in conventional circles by his uninhibited employment of slang and colloquialisms. Several of his tales have been translated into English, including the amusing *Halfway to the Moon*; a bittersweet, throwaway humour informs much of his work. Son of Yevgeniya Ginzburg (author of *Into the Whirlwind*), Aksyonov trained to be a doctor and did not begin to publish until 1959. For some of his views on literature, see pp. 390–91.

Vasily Aksyonov

SURPRISES

Tapes! L. Sokolov gets them. Gerka knows everything.

What do you get if you marry a hedgehog to a snake? Answer: two yards of barbed wire.

Her name is Lyudmila Gordon. Ah-ha!

The modern style of 'bebop' is linked with the name of the fabulous Charlie Parker.

Tatyana, you're a femme fatale.
And you're just a babbler!
She's an idiot.

Komsomol on Monday. With a telling-off for yours truly – how to swallow it?

The Marble Hall. A 0-00-04.

Gerka's the drinks man, the girls will bring the food. The medics will cart along the music, I shall provide the spirit of mutual understanding.

I feel fed up.

Constable and Turner are like the impressionists, but they lived much earlier.

The English have fine artists, great writers, but their composers? I don't know of a single one. Find out about them.

Blok wrote that to understand lyric poetry you have to be 'a bit that way yourself'.

Ring up Sokolov about those tapes.

Kirill, let's get lost during the interval!
?
To 'The Wages of Fear'?
!

Mikhail lay with his feet on the divan reading his old notebook which had unexpectedly turned up in the drawer of his writing desk. It looked as though his mother had not touched his papers at all during these last three years. Mikhail lay wriggling the toes of his bare feet and smiling. It had been a good time. Both when they were all together, and when he was alone with a girl, and even sadness had been happy. You'd be walking along alone feeling bored, storm clouds piling up on the horizon, and suddenly there'd be a breath of a particular kind of wind, or the smell of wet leaves on the boulevard – and you'd feel like dashing away and running, running, running. And you'd run like a madman (it's a good job they haven't lit the street lights yet), bound into a telephone box, take out this very same notebook and, when you heard someone answer, you'd start reading poems in a deep voice, looking out with a glassy stare at the dark contours of Leningrad, and you'd feel as you got colder that the sea was just over the way. Now it's all somehow different. Time has passed, youth has gone. Now it's young manhood. Mature young manhood, ha ha ha. And so three years later you sit down at your old writing desk and find everything there just as it was then. It stands there like a monument to your past. Isn't it a bit early for you to start building yourself monuments? But still, it's very nice that everything is just as it was. That's very understanding of Mum.

Mikhail laid aside the notebook and let his eyes run around the room. The open suitcase and the soles of his bare feet were reflected in the mirror, which was still hanging in its old place. He had flown in to Leningrad several hours earlier. In his ears he still had the roar and whine of that unbelievable journey. The plane from Pevek to Magadan, another from Magadan to Khabarovsk, a third from Khabarovsk to Moscow and yet a fourth from Moscow to Leningrad. Twenty-four hours of roar and whine. The incredibly violent technology of the twentieth century had hauled him across the whole continent and dropped him down on this old divan which unemotionally and hospitably had received its master into its lap: mummy's little boy Misha, stylish young Michel, twenty-fifth on the list for the Faculty basketball team. It was as if these three years had never been. How could this decrepit old furniture know about those three years? Old, pre-Revolutionary, faded, battered junk. It should all have been thrown out long ago and replaced with modern stuff. Old and intimate friends, our life's onlookers! Dear, good monuments of our youth!

The telephone rang. It was very understanding of his mother to have left even the telephone here. A long time ago Mikhail had asked for the telephone from his father's study to be transferred to his room. He had explained that he needed it for 'artistic consultations'. At that time he and Kirill were writing a film scenario together. And it really was very convenient: without getting up from the divan he could chatter away to Kirill or Lyudmila Gordon or to the whole town, whoever he liked.

'Hallo!'

'Mate!' shrieked Kirill into the earphone.

'Man, is that really you?' asked Mikhail in astonishment.

'Of course it's me, mate.'

'Good God, it is you!'

'That's right.'

'It really is you, you old bastard!'

'Not gone off your head after all that flying around then?' Kirill asked solicitously in his surprisingly child-like voice.

'I'm sorry, mate, the last letter I got from you was from the Urals, that's why I got a shock just now.'

'Last letter!' laughed Kirill, 'that was over a year ago, and you didn't answer it, of course.'

'I did answer it. Three months later. We were spending the night in Ust-Maya, and I scribbled you off a whole masterpiece of the epistolary style.'

'Some answer! I got it six months later. The boys sent it on to me from the Urals.'

'Why the hell didn't you answer?'

'I was just going to.'

They burst out laughing. Mikhail could just imagine his plump, voracious, untruthful friend shaking with laughter. At last Kirill got his breath back.

'Listen, mate. Antonina Sergeyevna told me yesterday that you were bringing your old carcass back and I've already planned everything.'

'You've already planned everything!' said Mikhail in admiration.

'Everything to the last detail. We're all going to get together at my place at eight. I'll try to get all the old crowd here, all those who are in town at the moment, that is. There are one or two little surprises for you.'

'Let's hear about them now.'

Kirill was silent for a moment.

'You'll see for yourself. And so, milord, quite informal, just a dinner jacket! Eight o'clock sharp. We'll make it seem like old times, eh?'

After Kirill, Gleb Pomorin rang up. It turned out that he already knew about the gathering at Kirill's.

'I'll come along to your place right away and we'll go together,' suggested Mikhail.

'OK, come along. Only I don't live at the same place now.'

'Where then?'

'Do you remember Tatyana's address?'

'Tanya's house? How could I forget it. What? You're living

there now? Since when? Two years? You've already got a son? Well, how about that, real old-timers!'

Mikhail hung up and began to put his shoes on. He had a strange feeling, almost like envy, although he had never been interested in Tanya, and never ... No, once at a party he had tried to kiss her, but only for the fun of it. In those days he used to think that all the girls were in love with him. He had got his face slapped and been very put out. But five minutes later he was kissing Lyuda on the balcony. And Kirill was shooting at them with a water-pistol. Everyone seemed to have gone a bit mad that evening. He would have to look Lyuda up, but that could come later.

Mikhail dressed meticulously (he didn't want them to think he had gone wild up in the North), had a few words with his mother ('Yes, Mum, of course, I'll get back before they raise the bridges. You're quite right, I've grown up, become more serious. All right then, tomorrow you can get the whole family together, I'll put up with it!'), went out into the street, watched the taxis driving off from the taxi-stand for a moment, filled his lungs with Leningrad air (oh yes, that's Leningrad air all right!) and walked off along the avenue.

'I love this town'– he thought –'and I'll go across it on foot.'

It was somehow strange to be walking, he could not understand why for a while and then he realized: his hands had nothing to carry. He had lost the habit of walking along with his hands free and not carrying anything. He walked for a long time until he came out on the bank of the canal where Tanya's house loomed up. He set off towards it; it was pleasing to bang his heels down on the old flagstones – and then he saw Tanya. She was striding along towards him, pushing a pram in front of her. In the pram, standing up and staring straight ahead of him like a sea-captain, was the Pomorin offspring. Tanya was very stylishly dressed, just as she used to be. Mikhail stopped and Tatyana went past without paying any attention to him.

'Well hullo there, Ma!' he said.

She started and turned round.

'Mishka!'

And rushed to kiss him.

'And she never used to let me get anywhere near her,' he thought as he kissed her.

'How about introducing me to Gleb junior?' he asked.

'Vanya, this is uncle Misha,' said Tanya.

'Ooooh,' said the infant menacingly.

'He's just trying to frighten you. He tries to frighten all new acquaintances at first.'

Mikhail offered the little boy some chocolate.

'You're out of your mind!' shrieked Tanya. 'He's only got three teeth and you give him chocolate.' She looked at the label – 'I'll have it.'

They sat down on a stone bench and ate chocolate and chatted.

'Well, how's life?'

'What can I say? Like everyone else's.'

'And Gleb?'

'He's studying as an external student. He finishes next year. You won't know him. He's quite different, not at all like what he used to be. I had a lot of trouble persuading him to leave the workers' hostel. You see, you didn't even know he used to live there. Only when I' – she drew a shape in the air with her finger – 'it was only then that he came to live with us. There's not much room, and we shout at each other, most likely because of it,' she ended thoughtfully, looking away.

'But Tanya, did you and Gleb really use to ...?'

'Yes. He used to write me poetry.'

'Who didn't use to write you poetry? I did too.'

'You only used to make fun of me. In your poems too. You know you never felt anything serious for me. It's true, Mishka, isn't it? Go on, be honest about it.'

'Of course, nothing serious,' said Mikhail.

Gleb appeared, sturdier and unrecognizable. For a couple of minutes he and Mikhail thumped each other on the shoulder and made inarticulate calf noises. Then Tanya's mother came out and bore Vanya off. He waved his hand in goodbye to Mikhail. The Pomorins, husband and wife, looked sidelong at Mikhail. He dutifully displayed rapture. He knew that one was supposed to show oneself enraptured over children.

'So you did put that tie on after all?' Tanya asked her husband tartly. 'Yes, I did,' said Gleb dourly, looking at her.

The second surprise really took Mikhail aback. It was Lyudmila Gordon in a very full blouse which even so could no longer hide anything. Lyuda opened the door of Kirill's flat to them and seeing Mikhail she at once went scarlet. The Pomorins went in first and Lyuda and Mikhail looked at each other in silence for a minute or so, both red-faced. Then Mikhail went up to her and kissed her on the cheek.

'You see how ugly I've got,' said Lyuda.

'Idiot, what could be finer than that? I'd sooner you told me who I ought to have done to death in a duel before it was too late!'

'Him,' Lyuda nodded her head towards the inner depths of the flat from where could be heard the tones of Kirill's excruciating tenor.

'So that's it,' thought Mikhail, 'so he wasn't just shooting at us for fun with his water-pistol that time.'

Radiant, shining, sleek and polished from top to toe, Kirill zoomed into the entrance hall like a bolt of lightning. He at once threw himself upon Mikhail and hugged him with friendly intensity. And at once he hugged away a feeling of aversion which had begun to well up in Mikhail.

'So what do you think of my monster?' he cried, with a wave of his hand towards Lyuda. But when they stepped aside to let Lyuda pass in front and followed her into the room, Kirill squeezed Mikhail's shoulder and whispered: 'Mate.'

It was as if there was a flood of something vast and moist

(a bit like music or a waterfall) when Mikhail came into the room and everyone's attention focused on him. Old friends, acquaintances, girls, the whole crowd. They had all married each other and were expecting children. And he was the one they were all fond of. They had all come because of him. He would have to watch himself or to cap it all he would burst into tears. There were about twenty people in the room, certainly no less. Old friends from the Arts Faculty, artists, Laszlo Kovacs was there for some reason or other, but of the medics only Sasha Zelenin – and the 'just girls' too: Sima, Klara and that other one ... what's her name? I can only remember that I met her in Odessa, and she was diving with an aqualung.

They all flocked round Mikhail and began to kiss him. They kissed him and thumped him and tugged at his suit (what cloth, boys, Mishka the gold miner's arrived!). Someone stuck a glass in his hand. Mikhail came round to find himself kissing some completely unknown girl.

'This, by the way, is my wife, Nina,' said Sasha Zelenin, looking dazed.

'Is she now! Well, never mind!' shouted Mikhail, pushed Sasha off with his elbow and kissed his wife a second time. All round there was a roar of laughter. There could be no doubt about it, it really was Mikhail who had arrived, that very same Mikhail they all remembered and loved.

At first everything went like old times. Some of them were dancing. A couple of records got broken. Languidly Kirill exuded witticisms. Borka, as always, at once got drunk and the aqualung girl led him out on to the balcony.

'They're obviously man and wife,' Mikhail thought with a certain irritation and he took off his coat and stood on his hands and then did a backwards somersault. He did it to show that he was the same person they all knew and loved, young, free and a bachelor ... But somehow after he had done it he felt awkward. He put on his coat and looked around for

Sasha's wife, Nina. She smiled at him in the way people smile at children.

And only at table did it begin to be apparent that the party was not working out. It was a gay, lively party, there was a lot of music, a lot of wine, clever remarks flew back and forth and new jokes, and people were beginning to get light-headed, but – there was something lacking. And in the gaps between the general laughter Mikhail could hear quite different things from all sides.

Lyuda: But where can you get a good one? No, Misha, I'm sorry, I mustn't have even a drop.

Tanya: If you'd waited six months longer I'd have passed on Vanya's pram to you.

Zelenin: We're working with a heart-lung machine now.

The aqualung girl (softly): You ought to be ashamed of yourself, you just can't behave. Just you dare. (Loudly): Klara, so you've decided to buy that Finnish bedroom suite then?

Kirill: The book's coming out early next year. They've promised to make it a pretty big edition.

Gleb for some reason was sitting away on his own and listening to Sasha with a vague look in his eyes.

'Gleb,' Mikhail called to him. 'Here's to you,' and raised his glass. Gleb smiled his shy dreamy smile – the old Gleb.

'Will you recite something new?' asked Mikhail. Gleb shook his head in a way that ruled out any further request. This was unheard of: in the old days after three glasses you couldn't stop him, he just went on reeling it off.

'Was it rough going up in the North, Misha?' asked Sasha Zelenin.

'He's the one I like best,' thought Mikhail, 'him and all those medics.'

'Quiet, friends!' shouted Kirill. 'Now Mishka's going to tell us about the North. Tell us about the bear meat, Misha, about the ice floes, about the crude metal ores, about the criminals and about the raw liquor.'

Everyone began to clamour.

'Tell us about the meat!'

'Easy does it,' thought Mikhail and said in a deep voice:

'Meat. Give me some sausage.'

That's him. Our good old Mishka.

'Liquor. Pour me some cognac.'

Just the same, young, gay bachelor ...

The party had just not come off. That became especially clear after supper. The company split up into small clusters and everywhere the talk was about theses, or books, or pictures, about Finnish furniture or about looking after new-born infants, or about the accommodation problem. Only when Mikhail came up to them the conversation stopped and they said:

'Michel, tell us about the meat.'

'About the gold.'

'About the ice floes.'

'About the criminals.'

'About the liquor.'

And they laughed in anticipation. And for a while it seemed that everything was going well. Kirill sat down at the piano and they sang – songs from old films, Okudzhava, parodies, all the old things.

'Let's go and have a chat, mate,' said Kirill and took Mikhail out on to the balcony.

The dark contours of the town against the background of the pale-green sky reminded him of a mountain range. And the lights of its windows were just like the mountain villages. Down below, right beneath the balcony a tram screeched wildly. It came from the islands and was full of young people.

'Oh tram! I love you because you don't have pneumatic doors. There aren't many like you left now.'

'I can see you're a bit put out,' said Kirill. 'Whatever you may say, you've broken with all this, haven't you?'

'You bear along my love, you old boneshaker. You drag

it along from the islands from where the yachts put out, where the canoes are laid out on the shore like cigars, where the asphalted forest rustles, where the stadium rumbles and roars; through the whole town you drag it past the dark houses, each like a complete poem in itself, you pull it over the Neva, youngster, so proud and confident in yourself as if you couldn't possibly fall off into the water, and winding your way around the centre you drag it still further into the smoky, noisy outskirts.'

'It's time for us to change our ways, mate. All that was splendid, our youth. It's pleasant to remember the past, but we're twenty-six now ...'

'You're business-like and haphazard all in one – look, over there you've scattered something as you go. A heap of silver and phosphorus. Or are you saluting me in farewell? You're such a ... such a ... such a ... I could weep over you, bearer of my love, because I haven't seen you for three years, because I've drunk too much today.'

'Yes, yes, Mishka, our time is beginning now. We're at the age when we have to take up active positions in life. And now bonds of friendship are especially valuable.'

'That's true,' mumbled Mikhail, 'quite true, quite true.'

The tram went out of sight round the corner. A new one had already appeared from the direction of the islands, but it was another sort of tram altogether. Everything suddenly became clear to Mikhail.

'Listen, mate,' he exclaimed, 'you've hit the nail on the head. You've put into words something which I've been thinking for some time now.'

Kirill grinned contentedly.

'We always did speak the same language.'

'That's right, we're just that age,' continued Mikhail. 'It feels as if you're coming up to some kind of barrier. If you can get over it, everything will be changed and you yourself will become different.'

'Haven't you got over the barrier yet? Think about it. Maybe you've passed it already.'

'I don't know. I doubt it,' said Mikhail thoughtfully. The conversation gave him a great deal of pleasure. He was fond of serious and not altogether clearly defined discussions.

Kirill put his arm round Mikhail's shoulders.

'Look old chap, I came back a year earlier than you and now I think I'm firmly on my feet. I've got a book of essays coming out soon. I'm known all over. I think I'll soon get on to — '(he named a well-known newspaper).' It'll be easier for you from now on. We all help each other here. It's the law of friendship. It's great, Mishka,' he gulped with gladness and excitement, 'you and I, we'll get going nicely now. We could get moving on that scenario of ours. What about it?'

'Yes, of course, why shouldn't we?' mumbled Mikhail.

He couldn't even imagine himself sitting down to that scenario again.

He covered all the long route home on foot.

'Why didn't I tell Kirill that I was going to go back there?' he thought. 'We've always been quite frank with each other. Lyuda came out on to the balcony, that's why I didn't tell him. If only I'd written her even one letter from the North, perhaps everything would have been different. No, that's stupid, nothing could have been different. Once something has happened, that means that it couldn't have been different. Gerka's gone crooked and he's in prison; and Gleb, a first-class production worker, is an external student and Tanya's husband; Sashka Zelenin is a specialist surgeon. Could it really have been any different? Kirill is a journalist, an essay writer, an optimist and Lyuda's husband. Everything has changed and it's not a question of jobs at all. And me? What's happened to me? Have I got over the barrier?'

He reached home, unlocked the door with his own key, took off his shoes and noiselessly, like a cat ...

'Mishenka, what is it you've dropped there?' shouted his mother.

... went through into his own room. He collapsed on to the divan. The open suitcase stood near it as before. His old note-book lay on the table. Mikhail put his hand into the suitcase and pulled out his notepad, full from cover to cover with what he had written up there in the North.

Endless volcanic hills. From the aircraft it all looks like a countless herd of camels.

Not a day without a line. Stendhal.

Mine-surveyor Ivanov, enrichment engineers Petrov, Sidorov, excavator operator Burokobylin took upon them-selves the tasks of ...

In an atmosphere of enormous enthusiasm over their work the miners of the 'Zolotisty' mine ...

I call heroes not those who are great in thought or strength, but only those who are great in heart.

... Where there is no greatness of character, there can be no great men, there are only idols, fashioned for the vulgar crowd. Romain Rolland.

How long can meetings go on for, Zhenka? One's patience just explodes.

Don't get hysterical. Better to get up and say something yourself and put some life into them.

What's that? Now I will say something. (Half a page torn out.)

Can a vegetarian fall in love with a woman? Answer: yes, if the woman is neither flesh nor fowl.

In response to the noble initiative of the toilers of the Indigirsk administration, the collective of the 'Buranny' mine ... I shall burst with rage at language like this. But if you write in any other way about it – it gets cut.

I have never kept a diary and I never shall. This is the first and last entry, whatever may happen. What has driven me to take up my pencil now? Because I'm still alive, God almighty! Igor won't ever be tempted to take up a pencil again. In any case, he wasn't ever particularly inclined to. He was given to liquor and to that well-known beauty, 'petrol-pump Mashka'. I wonder if he thought about her at the last moment? God, I'll never forget it! Will any of those who get out of here ever be able to forget it? Once in Leningrad we lit candles and began to chatter about what way of crossing into the other world each of us would pick if he had the choice. I said 'plane crash', and everyone agreed with me. Because it would be dramatic. What rubbish! What did we know about plane crashes? But I've seen one, seen one – and I'm still alive, how's that for luck!

I was sitting beside Igor. It was just as if we were hanging in the middle of cotton-wool. The boys in the fuselage didn't give a damn about the fog. They could hear the noise of the engines and they knew it was Igor at the controls up front. They were stretched out on the sacks. Some were asleep, some just nattering. I don't know whether something had gone wrong with the instruments or something happened to Igor, but suddenly, right in front of our nose, something grey and enormous loomed up and bore down upon us serenely. I saw Igor's mouth and his frantic eyes. He pulled me close up to him and screamed, 'We're done for! Get into the tail fast, Mishka!' and flung me out of the cabin. While I was rolling about among the sacks, I heard the boys cursing. The plane all but stood on its end. We were all tossed into the tail in a heap and I only saw someone's bulging eye and a mouth with a stopped tooth in it. At the last moment the man next to me was sick in my face.

Igor did everything he could, but it was too late for him to do anything. Now, when the remnants of this cursed fog are hanging like shreds of wool here and there around the tops of the volcanic hills, I can see where we crashed. We went right through a corridor on into a canyon. How did it happen? Friend Igor, sleep in peace, the inquiry won't be able to reach you now.

All of us have broken bones and we are scattered over the hillside. I have only a broken leg, I think. By the morning eight people had crawled to the wreckage of the aircraft. Then Kostya and I dragged Sidorov and the Georgian here, I don't know his name. I think he's dead. No, he just moved. How many died instantaneously I don't yet know. I have seen only Igor and the radio-operator. And us, the survivors? We've eaten almost all we had. No means of communication. Nothing left to burn. We are lying together in a heap in a makeshift shelter made from pieces of the aircraft. The fourth day. And how the sun is blazing over this white landscape. No, I don't curse this land. I love it, although ... it has smashed my bones.

Even so, I have done something here, me, Mishka, the newspaper man, known to all the drivers on the Kolyma route. I have seen real people here and written stern things about them in harsh language, but at least I have written about them. And if I stay alive, I shall write about them again, but not like I used to. And if not? I'll write now until my last breath. And in summer, when this hillside is covered with bilberries ... No, we're going to live, boys! Now I'll shake you all awake and show you – look, over there along the bed of that frozen stream two dog sleighs are running.

Kostya fires into the air.

They're Orochi, I recognize them from their clothing.

1964

Translated by Bernard Johnson

Andrei Sinyavsky (b. 1925) established a reputation as a literary critic before beginning to write a series of tales in the late 1950s and to publish them abroad pseudonymously as 'A. Tertz'. If Aksyonov's 'fantastic realism' sometimes deliberately blurs the borderline between everyday reality and the author's imagination, Sinyavsky carries this process further, into sometimes shocking grotesquerie. Such effects do not always translate well, and the more straightforward satirical humour of *The Icicle* (unfortunately too long to be included in its entirety) makes a good introduction to 'Tertz'. This series of tales came to an end with the notorious court case against Sinyavsky in 1966 and his consequent imprisonment; he now lives in France, and his recent work – a collection of *pensées*, and a reflective 'mosaic' made up from his letters from prison-camp – marks a new stage in his writing.

Andrei Sinyavsky ('A. Tertz')

From THE ICICLE

A Winter's Tale

AUTHOR'S NOTE

I write this story as a castaway tells of his distress. Sitting on a piece of wreckage or stranded on a desert island, he throws a bottle with a letter into the stormy sea in the hope that the waves and the wind will bring it to people who will read it and learn the truth long after its poor author is dead.

But the question is: will the bottle ever reach its destination? Will a sailor haul it up by the neck with his strong hand and will he shed tears of pity on the deck of his ship? Or will the seal gradually be corroded by brine, the paper eaten away and the unknown bottle, filled with bitter sea-water, dash against a reef and come to rest motionless on the bottom of the ocean?

My task is even more difficult. Though I have no scientific or literary experience, I want my work to be published and accorded recognition. Only in this roundabout way can I hope to reach you, Vasily. Oh, Vasily! Believe me when I say that I want not money or honours, but only your understanding. I need no readers except you, though my story will pass through many hands perhaps before it happens to come your way.

What else can I do? The sea of life is vast and the bottle is such a tiny thing, and it will have to drift thousands of miles before it reaches its destination.

Forgive me, Vasily! I do not have your address. I do not even know your surname: I had no time to ask and, when I thought of it, it was too late. But I know that, like me, you live adrift in the waves of space and time, and I hope that some day you may go into a second-hand bookshop and happen to see my battered book on the shelf.

Will you remember me? Will your heart miss a beat and will the shadowy images of the past come to life? Will you stretch out a hand of friendship and help?

Vasily, I ask only one favour: find Natasha. You see, she must live somewhere quite close to you. Don't be surprised that she is also called Natasha, though she is completely different from the other Natasha. But I think that their names happen to be the same. Would you believe it, she is also called Natasha! And if you don't recognize her from my description, I hope that your heart will tell you who I mean ...

So I beg you, Vasily, find Natasha and marry her as soon as possible, while you're still alive, before it's too late. Marry her without fail, even though she may be older than you and have children – and I believe you have a family too. But never mind. Leave your wife and marry Natasha, as I tell you. You see, this is the only chance of meeting her and if we let it go by, we shall again lose sight of each other ...

Don't frown, Vasily. I shall explain everything in a moment, I shall put it all down just as it happened and I shall try to do a good job of writing. Let's hope it comes out in a large edition – it's more likely to reach you like that. It's all right, you needn't worry – I've read a lot of novels and stories and I have a fair idea of how it's done. And the main thing is that I have the time. If it comes to that, what's to stop me becoming a famous writer during the rest of my long life?

And as you follow the story, Vasily, keep a close watch on yourself. Perhaps something will stir in you and you will help the wretched castaway ... And, as you sit with Natasha in some beautiful arbour, you will take her sadly by the waist and say in the words of the poet:

Do not sing, my beauty,
Songs of sad Georgia:
They bring to mind
Another life and a far shore.
Your cruel songs, alas,

Bring back the steppe at night
And the face of a poor girl
Far away in the moonlight.
Seeing you, I forget
The dear, doomed wraith,
But you sing, and once again
I picture it before me.

Incidentally, this was written by the Pushkin you know so well. But you were wrong when you said that Pushkin was shot. He was killed in a duel, by a pistol. I know this for a fact, believe me.

One more thing: should you read my tale of woe to Natasha? Much better read her Pushkin, and love her as I loved her. And be happy.

This is all I ask of you.

I

Natasha and I were sitting on a bench in the Tsvetnoi Boulevard. We were quite alone. It was icy underfoot and no one ventured out on to the boulevard, except Natasha and me – because we were in love and were not worried about falling and hurting ourselves.

'Disgusting,' I said, 'it's enough to drive you mad. If the weather doesn't change by tomorrow and if we don't have snow, I shall refuse to see the New Year in. Have you ever known anything like it at the end of December? Nor have I. It's all these atomic tests and the arms race. Cold in summer and rain in winter. We've had it.'

I was going to develop my idea about fall-out in the atmosphere, as a result of which there would be a new ice-age and we should all grow shaggy hair and start breeding mammoths, but Natasha interrupted me. She said that in early childhood she had once seen it snow in the middle of June. This, she assured me, had happened when they were on holiday in the country near Saratov in 1928.

This tale struck me as absolutely fantastic. It was all quite impossible for the simple reason that Natasha was then only two and could not have remembered her snow-fall. Our memory has a limited capacity. And then there was a lot of detail about insects, butterflies and grandmother ...

'You're pulling my leg,' I said angrily. 'Or have you been deceiving me about your age? I bet you were born in twenty-three, not in twenty-six.'

I said this just to tease her, of course. I was a little annoyed because I thought that I knew her inside out. We had been friends for long enough and by this time we had told each other everything we remembered about ourselves, including things one normally tries not to remember and talk about. Although we were not yet married and were not living together, it was now a whole year since I had got her to leave Boris for good, and I met her every day or every other day. And now I suddenly learn that Natasha's life was more eventful than I had supposed. Before she had learned to walk, for instance, she had been playing with matches and had set her hair on fire, and it had burned with a yellow flame – all of which she remembered well.

I was older than her, more intelligent, and more widely read, and I was not one to give any points away. So I started an argument about vague recollections and pressed her all the harder as my chances of winning diminished.

'No, I remember ...' she kept on saying.

'Well, so do I ...' I replied.

And I rummaged in my childhood memories, hoping to turn up something long since forgotten. This was probably the psychological cause of the physical changes which came over me that evening and which were shortly to alter the whole of our lives.

Now, many years later, I find it difficult to say exactly how it happened. Perhaps I had been prepared for it by the whole course of my previous development and had been predestined, as they say, to go through all the things that I subsequently underwent. I don't know, I don't know ... At that moment, at any rate, I was not thinking about this at all, but was simply battering at the gates of memory, trying to force them open and remember the past. Then some fateful barrier suddenly gave way and I hurtled headlong into an abyss with an almost physical, and unpleasant, sensation of falling. I fell down and down and down, at a loss to understand what was going on, and, when I came to, my whole surroundings were different and I was not quite the same.

I was in a long ravine which was hemmed in by ranges of bare mountains and flat-topped hills. The bottom was covered with a crust of ice. Trees, also bare, grew along the edge of the ice, at the foot of the sheer cliffs. There were not many of them, but the hollow moan of the wind showed that the forest was not far away. There was a smell of corpses. Rotten branches glowed in large numbers. Though they were probably not rotten branches but bits of the moon which had been torn to pieces by wolves and was now waiting for the moment when its bones would again grow white, luminous flesh and it would rise into the sky to the envious baying of the wolves ...

But before I had a chance to wonder about the meaning of all this, I was charged by a monster with a gaping mouth. It moved its unseen legs at enormous speed and I guessed that it had not four, or even five legs, but at least as many as the fingers and toes on my hands and feet. Smaller than a mammoth, it was nevertheless as hefty as the largest bear and, when it was close up, I could see that it had a transparent belly, like a fish's bladder, in which tiny humans, swallowed alive, were tossing up and down in the most terrible way. The monster must have been so greedy that it swallowed its victims without chewing them and they went straight to its stomach, still writhing and jumping.

Of course, I am only giving a rough idea, in my own words,

of what I felt. At the time, there were no words at all in my head, only conditioned reflexes and various religious throwbacks, as they are now called, and, in my terror, I muttered vows of such a nature as I can't bring myself to put down on paper.

But I remember that, at that moment, these nonsensical vows had a definite effect and the monster relented, moving off along the cliffs without touching me and throwing up, by way of warning, a shower of electric sparks. I suppose it is only because these sparks appeared to my clouded mind as 'electric' that I realized I had been passed by a harmless trolleybus and I was restored to my lost sense of the actual moment.

As it now appeared, I was still quietly sitting on the bench with Natasha, who had noticed nothing, as calm as ever at my side, and the big city, blanketed by the night, was roaring and moaning round about, like a storm-stricken forest.

'If the weather doesn't change,' I said, feeling oddly ill at ease, 'and if it doesn't snow tomorrow, I shall refuse to see the New Year in.'

But I risked no more exploration of my brain. I had been terribly shaken by this trick which my memory had played on me. Trying to keep calm and not to worry I silently breathed in the familiar air with its stench of petrol fumes and shimmering haze of putrescent light from the street-lamps, which faintly resembled moonlight and was undoubtedly of very real electric origin. I kept looking rather anxiously at the houses, the street-lamps, the trees, and the trolleybuses, which every now and then scurried past the houses and the trees, and it was all so real, so like itself and unlike anything else. I also noticed a large woman who was walking over the curved ice-crust of Tsvetnoi Boulevard, swaying like a ballerina as she went.

She was a good way away from us, and it was impossible to tell her age or make out her features. But her figure, heavily built and swaying merrily, somehow suggested to me that she was an old woman who really had at one time danced in the ballet and had even had a success with Admiral Kurbatov in the role of Odette. I had no idea how this knowledge came to me, since I had never seen the woman in my life before, and I imagined it was the result of pure deduction. I had no desire to check my hunch, but I could not rid myself of a feeling that as soon as she came up to the next but one lamp-post, which she was now approaching, the ballerina would have an accident. To be more precise, I felt that she would slip at the very spot foreseen by me and I even wondered whether to give her a warning, but curiosity prevented me and I watched her progress with bated breath. And when she reached the place and fell down, throwing her short arms in the air, I felt a twitch of conscience somewhere deep down, as though I had myself given her a push.

Natasha and I ran to help her to her feet. Frightened out of her wits, the old woman just wouldn't get up and kept falling down again with her wet bottom on the icy ground, saying that she couldn't stand on her right leg because the main bone was broken. In a fearful whisper she told us that, as she fell, she had heard a splintering and crunching sound. There was a smell of good port wine from her toothless mouth.

As we struggled with this wheezing heap of flesh, the whole situation at last became clear to me. The old woman was obviously making herself out to be in a sorrier state than she was. There could be no question of a right leg, because she had lost it in an accident thirty years ago and had it replaced, in secret, by a magnificent artificial one, which was now the real object of her concern. I would have sworn, however, that this remarkable contraption, built of aluminium in Berlin at the expense of Admiral Kurbatov, had not been damaged in the slightest, or even scratched during her fall.

'Up you come now, Susanna Ivanovna, you'll get radiculitis,' I said sternly to the morbid old girl and finally, to make an impression, I even shouted at her. Soon, however, she was pouring out her gratitude and, reassured as to the sterling quality of German aluminium, she thanked me with typically French effusiveness. It did not strike her as odd that, although we had never met, I addressed her by name. She took it all for granted and repeated over and over again that she was happy to meet such a kind young man who no doubt remembered her from her unforgettable performance of Odette on the stage of the Mariinsky Theatre in St Petersburg.

'Ah, if only I were nineteen again,' she exclaimed, and, putting the tips of her ragged gloves to her toothless mouth, she blew me a kiss. Only with great difficulty did we manage to say good-bye, telling her to walk with the greatest care on her shaky legs ...

Natasha laughed a great deal and, of course, quizzed me about how I had come to know this Susanna Ivanovna. I had to invent a vague story about some magazine or other having printed an old photograph of the ballerina when she was young and which had once made a great impression on me during my teenage craze for the history of the Russian theatre. Natasha said she was terribly jealous and with wonderful charm she tried to show it on her face. Then she played the fool and cuddled up to me – she was very affectionate that evening. I did my best to reciprocate ...

But I could not get Susanna Ivanovna out of my mind. I kept thinking that the old woman was in for some sort of trouble. No, it would be nothing to do with her legs – I was sure of that. Other ways by which she would die, and soon, sprang into my mind. For some reason I figured that it would happen in two months' time from cancer of the womb. And my head was swarming with all kinds of other presentiments.

When we were absolutely frozen, Natasha asked how we would get back: on foot or by trolleybus? It took me a long time to decide. I had no worries about myself, but walking with my Natasha meant almost carrying her, rather as one carries a bagful of eggs from a shop. I tried not to think about eggs breaking.

We went by trolleybus: it really was very slippery.

II

It did in fact begin to snow a bit the next day and the pavements and roadways were covered by a thin blanket. By nightfall one had the illusion that some sort of winter had arrived, bringing cleanliness and order, and, overcoming my ill-temper, I agreed to see the New Year in with Natasha and Boris at a party given by some people I didn't know. It was clear to me that Boris, as the ex-husband, had been asking her to do him this favour for some time. Natasha had been pestering me now for two weeks:

'He's very cut up, you know. It's all right for you and me, but he's in a bad way. Perhaps his only pleasure in life is seeing me now and again. Just seeing me and nothing more. He even suggested that you come with me. And it's in somebody else's place, on neutral ground. They're all strangers to each other ...'

I couldn't see why Boris was so ready to put up with my presence. In his place I should never have done such a thing. But anyway, I couldn't care less about his feelings and I didn't want to refuse Natasha anything – as though I sensed already that it would all soon come to an end.

'All right! To blazes with your Boris and your philanthropy!' I said to Natasha about an hour before midnight. We went off to these people we didn't know, taking a couple of bottles of wine for decency's sake.

As always at these scratch parties, when a random assortment of people come together by chance, time dragged slowly and everyone was bored. After shouting out a few toasts and kicking up a bit of a rumpus in honour of the New Year, we all somehow collapsed and became uneasily subdued. Every one of us had probably waited impatiently for this moment and had been looking forward to it for a week, or even a month, and now here we all were at the festive table and it suddenly turns out that we have absolutely nothing to do and it would be far better to go home and make an early night of it. But, since so much anticipation had gone into the occasion, nobody left and we all sat waiting, staring at each other with sleepy eyes as though we thought that at any moment now one of us would get up and do something to make all our hopes come true.

An exuberant and handsome man of Caucasian origin, with a rakish moustache above his sensual mouth, tried for half an hour to relieve the tedium by telling funny stories about people in lunatic asylums. But when he at last realized that neither his stories, already nauseatingly familiar to everyone, nor his overdone Eastern accent were raising even the faintest of smiles, he stopped grimacing and guffawing, sank into moody silence and pouted his red lips, which were weak and effeminate.

A test-pilot was chatting with his wife, in an exaggeratedly matter-of-fact way, about things to buy for the house, as though they had no chance to discuss this topic elsewhere. For the single men there was nothing for it but to smoke like fiends. The single women, who were uniformly ugly, took it in turns to go to the lavatory, forcing Natasha and me to get up every time and let them through between the table and the sofa.

It was a sheer waste of time for everyone except, perhaps, Boris. Huddled in a far corner, he never once took his imploring love-lorn eyes off Natasha. It was a sickening spectacle. Natasha, sitting at my side with downcast eyes and looking like death, played up to him. I didn't try to get to the bottom of this relationship and drank glass after glass, without eating.

My drunken gaze was willy-nilly drawn to the Christmas tree, on which they at last lit the candles, and I asked for all the other lights in the room to be switched off, so as to give them full scope. They flickered cheerfully with a wonderful spluttering noise, creating round about the festive atmosphere we needed, and gradually, with the exception, perhaps, of Boris, we all fell under their spell and crowded round the tree, which was like some lavishly decorated domestic altar. For a few minutes a festive spirit settled on the house – the spirit, perhaps, which we had sought in coming here and for whose sake it is sometimes worth putting up with the company of people you neither know nor like.

But the candles gradually burnt down and my feeling of unease, which had been partly dispelled by drink and had almost completely disappeared at the sight of the tree, now came back. I watched anxiously as the candles, which had lit up cheerfully all together, now burnt out at different intervals and, I would have said, with different shades of expression. I suppose this depended on the length of the wick and other technical details of their manufacture, but, for reasons everybody will understand, I was interested and disturbed by another aspect of the business.

I don't consider myself a pessimist, but I must say in all seriousness that, if one thinks closely about the essence of life, it is clear that everything ends in death. There's nothing peculiar about this and it would even be undemocratic if any one of us were to survive and keep on living. But, of course, we would all like to, and when one thinks that even, say, a Leonardo da Vinci had to die, one feels quite helpless.

It wouldn't be so bad if there were some equality about it or if it were a matter of some iron law. If, for example, we all left this life in organized fashion: in large collective units and in a definite order, according, say, to age-group or nationality. One nation comes to the end of its allotted span and off it goes to make way for the next one. Then, of course, everything would be much simpler and the inevitable departure would be less upsetting and nerve-racking. On the other hand, the chief complication in your existence, and hence its piquancy, is that you never know for certain when it will come to an end, so that you always have the possibility of going one better than the next man and outliving him – even if only by an extra month or so. It is this that gives our life its interest, its risks and fears, its stock-exchange atmosphere and great variety.

And so, looking at the candles, which had changed places in my drunken mind with the assembled merrymakers, I observed their different ends with interest and suspense.

Some burnt out as gaily as they had lived and even gave a generous spurt of flame, brighter than before, at the end. Others started economizing half-way through, as if they knew what was coming and hoped to put off the end as long as possible. But this didn't always help them and an occasional thrifty wick would suddenly choke in its own wax a good two inches from the bottom.

There were others which only grasped the full horror of the situation at the very end and began to dart from side to side in their tin holders, casting outsize reflections on the walls and ceiling, entirely using up all their vital juices and gases, and which then suffocated in their own prematurely decomposed remains, their death agony being a most unseemly spectacle.

I now understand that I made a great mistake getting absorbed in this game of my overheated brain. But a second, and even graver mistake, which had an effect on my existence just as irreversible as the evening on Tsvetnoi Boulevard, was that I gave in to the temptation of picking out the candle which seemed most suitable and guessing from it the length of my life and the date of my death.

And what do you think happened? While all the candles round me gradually went out, I lived on and on as a humble little flame, and, when the room had gone quite dark, I still went on smouldering all by myself, having outlived everybody else, much to my astonishment, by at least ten years.

Someone got up to switch on the light. But I said we should

go on in the dark until the last candle had completely burnt out. And, not taking my eyes off it, I counted off the years to which I was entitled: one, two, three, four, five, six ...

Altogether, counting in the age already reached, I got to eighty-nine and, as I did so, a sister, or it may have been an ordinary nurse, came into the almost dark room and leant over the head of my bed.

A spark of life still smouldered in me. I was dying slowly and quietly, in full possession of my faculties, and I just couldn't make it. Other people round about were snoring and rambling quietly in their sleep. There was a smell of disinfectant and excrement and the nurse, sitting on a hospital stool, was waiting patiently for me to release her. She was very sleepy and yawned out loud, crossing herself, scratching her head, and throwing reproachful glances at me. From time to time she checked whether I had died or not, but, well aware as I was of her good reasons for trying to hurry me up, and of my own thoughtlessness in the matter, I just hadn't the physical strength to tell her in words, or make her understand by some gesture, that she could go away. I simply looked at her apologetically and I was overcome by shame and despair in the presence of this good woman, the only person left in the whole world who still had the slightest connection with me – shame at still being alive. I felt so bad that I got up, quickly blew out the candle-end, and switched on the light.

My drinking companions, male and female, looked at me questioningly with bleary eyes, as though I had done them, too, some wrong and it was my duty to lighten their presence in my company. Someone, yawning, suggested a game: charades, for instance, or forfeits. And again they all gave me an impatient look, as though I were the master of ceremonies here and it all depended on me. Pulling comic faces I brushed the cobwebs of fear and shame from my face.

'Listen, everybody! Listen, everybody!' I shouted, and snapped my fingers like a light-switch. 'You are about to witness a performance by the celebrated clairvoyant and mind-reader! The past is revealed and the future is foretold! Will anybody in the audience step up?'

Of course, nobody at first believed in my gifts, and, indeed, I was myself doubtful. But when I began to fire off facts and dates and various out-of-the-way details in the life of the test-pilot, and he said I was right every time, they were all delighted, and astonished, and, interrupting each other all the time, bombarded me with questions …

I would look rapidly at the diagram of somebody's face and immediately give the date of birth, amount of salary, number of identity card, how many abortions … I preferred figures, because nowadays they tell us more about real life than anything.

'And do you foretell the future as well?' asked a girl student from the Institute of Light Industry.

'A bit,' I said evasively. 'For instance, at your exam next week you'll get top marks in Marxism–Leninism. You needn't bother to prepare: you'll be asked about the 5th Party Congress and the fourth law of the dialectic.'

She clapped her hands and said gleefully that she would mug up nothing except these two questions.

'How can you know that?' asked the handsome Georgian. 'Why should we believe you?'

'Wait a week and check up,' I said, slightly offended.

But they couldn't wait and wanted proof there and then of my ability to foretell future events, and I suddenly had an idea:

'All right,' I said, 'let's wait one minute. In a minute's time I promise you that a bedbug will appear on the wall. You see the engraving over there? A Giorgione, I think. It'll go round in a circle and crawl away to the left under the next frame …'

And soon, just as I had said, the bedbug appeared. It crawled out from under a sleeping Venus and, having made the promised circle, wandered on to another girl – one with a broken pitcher. The women shrieked. Somebody said that there was no bedbug – that it was only suggestion on my part. Others said that it was a trained bedbug and that I had surreptitiously let it out from my sleeve. And the sceptical Georgian Apollo said:

'What of it? A bedbug is nothing at all, anybody could see that coming. Let him tell us when we'll have communism in the whole world ...'

I let that one go by. The Georgian was an agent-provocateur. Looking at him out of the corner of my eye, I could see real female breasts growing rapidly in the space between his collar-bones and his diaphragm. I could soon clearly see his young and girlish, but fully formed bosom. However, he kept his moustache and other masculine attributes which, in combination with the breasts, gave him the appearance of a real hermaphrodite.

I didn't know what to make of this at first, and I thought it might be the effect of my drunken state and I was glad of an explanation which would make it possible to hope that all the odd happenings of the last few days had also been due to some harmless and simple cause. But this hope was short-lived. It was not wine and vodka drunk in large quantities, but other forces that had taken hold of me and given me a distorted image of the surrounding world.

After the Georgian, all the other guests began to change as well. The outlines of their bodies and faces began to waver, reminding one of the oscillating blips on a radar screen. Each line broke up and became blurred, giving birth to dozens of breathing shapes. Many of the women grew beards; people with fair hair went dark and then bald, again grew a new crop of hair; they became covered with wrinkles and then grew young again – so young that they were like children with bandy legs, large heads, and vacant eyes. These, in their turn, began to grow, their bones set and they became fat or thin.

All the same, each of them kept some likeness to the original form, so it was not too difficult for me to identify them and talk with them, though I could no longer be certain about their past or future.

Up to now I had known which one of them was a thief, a bigamist, or secretly the daughter of a runaway White-guardist, but at present everything was all mixed up and in flux and I had no means of knowing where one person ended and another began. When a young engineer by the name of Belchikov turned to me politely and asked me to guess the year of his birth, I almost blurted out on the spur of the moment the preposterous reply, contradicting all the laws of nature: 237 BC!

This reply came to me involuntarily and automatically, under the influence, evidently, of the changes which had taken place in Belchikov. An ancient fireman's helmet gleamed fleetingly on his head and under his loose-fitting worsted suit there were white sheets in which he had very unskilfully draped his large torso, leaving his legs bare under the trousers. But of course it was not the trousers, but the helmet and some other more elusive features which suggested to me that Belchikov had been born in 237 BC.

Fortunately I didn't say this aloud. The helmet dissolved into thin air, the sheets billowed, and out stepped a woman of great beauty, no longer all that young, but still completely serviceable – and without drapes. I saw straightaway that she was a prostitute and also, probably, of fairly ancient origin. She moved her whole body invitingly, but I had no time to feast my eyes before the frivolous creature disappeared, giving way to a priest – or it may have been a eunuch. He quivered for a couple of seconds and turned back into a prostitute, but a different one this time and less attractive than the first one. And so it went on: monks and prostitutes changing places and trying to outdo each other, different every time in price and quality, until at last they achieved the status of engineer Belchikov again. He was standing in front of me, politely repeating his question:

'Can you guess when I was born, please?'

Before he had time to change from an engineer into something else, I said quickly that he was born on 1st March 1922, in Semipalatinsk, and that he shouldn't pester me any more with silly questions, adding, for all to hear, that his parents had kept a butcher's shop employing one assistant in Semipalatinsk and were not, as he liked to write in questionnaires, poor peasants. He blushed and took fright, and in his fear he began to tremble and hastily change shape.

All his previous transformations had seemed to take place in the past, in ancient times, or at least in no period later than AD 1922. Now, however, these courtesans of his carried on their activities, and austere ascetics cancelled them out and expiated them, at a different and higher stage of historical development, probably foreshadowing the inner conflict in Belchikov's further evolution. Calculating the possible limits of their fleeting existences, I realized that we had come to the middle of the twenty-fourth century. But they went on flitting by, suggesting by their behaviour that even in the splendid future we shall not completely rid ourselves either of the humbug of priests or of the frailty of women, though it will all, of course, assume new social forms and be quite different in appearance ...

I hasten to say that I am not trying to make a theory of this or to take sly digs at anybody. I am perfectly well aware that every man, even a Leonardo da Vinci, is the product of economic forces which are responsible for everything in the world. To this I would only add that the individual, the character, the personality – or even, if you like, the soul – also have no part in life and are only reflexes of our vision, like the spots we see when we press our eyeballs or look at the bright sun for a long time without blinking.

We are used to seeing people against a background of air, which looks empty and transparent, while the human figure appears to be of great firmness and density. Now, we are wrong to attribute the unvarying density and sharpness of outline of the human silhouette, which comes out particularly well in the bright light of day, to man's inner world and to call this his 'character' or 'soul'. In fact there is no soul, but only a gap in the air through which mutually unconnected psychic substances rush in nervous gusts, changing according to age and circumstances.

When I say that whores and priests occupied a prominent place in Belchikov's life, I am far from wanting to hurt the good man's feelings. I am simply pointing out a situation common to all. It wasn't the engineer Belchikov himself, but the person using his name at the moment, or rather the indefinable empty space at present filled with his substance, which at other times gave refuge to completely different and constantly changing substances. Why this happens, I don't know – perhaps to preserve some historical balance.

Anyone who looks closely into himself will easily detect the most unexpected lapses into past and future states, the urge to steal, for instance, or to kill, or to sell oneself for money. I must say that I have sometimes felt even worse impulses in this thing called the soul, and so will you, unless you cheat and abjectly shy off. The main thing is not to be hypocritical, and then you will see that you have no right to say: 'He is a thief,' and 'I am an engineer,' because, in fact, there is no such thing as 'I' and 'He' and we are all thieves and prostitutes, or even worse perhaps. If you think you are not, then you are just lucky for the time being, but we all were in the past, even if it was a thousand years ago, or we all certainly shall be in the future, as our sweet memories and bitter presentiments never cease to tell us ...

I later got the upper hand of my art of seeing further than our nature permits. I learnt to check and control myself and to treat people as if they really were confined to the strict limits of their own personalities and biographies. But at the time I felt myself surrounded not by a score, but by at least a couple of hundred, moving faces. Frightened of falling into an abyss 500, 1,000, or 10,000 years deep, I kept my eyes on the move. The horror of Tsvetnoi Boulevard and my descent into the age of fossil trolleybuses, the shame and disgrace of my recent death, imposed caution, but my eyes still darted hither and thither and there was nothing that seemed stable to them, or could be taken at its face value.

And then, in search of support, I turned to Natasha, though I knew beforehand that this was wrong. Natasha, after all, was also human and she might develop a moustache, not to mention similar characteristics of an even more basic nature. I was not quite clear about the events in store for us and, to be on the safe side, I had avoided looking at her too closely, because I guessed that this was not something to be taken lightly ...

All the same, trying to find a resting-place for my eyes, I did look at her and was at first relieved to see no moustache, beard, or other monstrosity which might have ruined her looks. But then, her head was not quite all there. Only force of habit made me think it was, but the more I looked, the more clearly I saw that her skull was grimly missing right down to her neck and the tip of her chin. Yet her body did not fall or slip down, but remained upright in the chair and her fingers straightened invisible hair, performing pirouettes in mid-air.

It was with much trouble and visual adjustment that I reconstituted Natasha's true appearance, fitting her head and face together again, just as a restorer mends a broken vase. But I didn't want to think of fragile vessels cracking and smashing to bits, if one drops them on the pavement, hits them with a lump of ice, or, say, accidentally lets a hard object fall on them from some height. In general I tried to think as little as possible about what had happened, because Natasha was too frail for all this and might once more fail to stand up to a sudden collision with my unstable consciousness.

'Let's go home, Natasha,' I said quietly, feeling tired and somehow apathetic. My sense of irreparable loss was so great that I scarcely heard Boris, who suddenly spoke from his corner:

'I say, sorcerer, darling of the gods,' he said with a leer, 'try and guess what I was doing last Sunday between ten and eleven!'

These were the only words he spoke and the whole of his pent-up envy, jealousy and shame was concentrated in this question from the corner. He didn't even spare Natasha and named the day and the hour right to her face – 'last Sunday between ten and eleven' – so as to make the sneer even worse and also to try out in practice the range of my powers.

Another time I would have beaten him up on the spot and probably done a lot of other silly things. I might, in my temper, have given up Natasha and returned her to Boris, saying in disgust exactly what I thought of her. But I now knew more about her than he could imagine. Among all our troubles, both present and imminent, it didn't seem to me to matter very much that Natasha had been unfaithful to me from ten to eleven – half-past ten, to be exact – last Sunday ...

Not looking at her, or replying to Boris, I said softly and slowly, as though nothing had happened:

'Let's go home, Natasha. Let's go, please.'

She got up at once and walked across the room with me, her warm hand in mine. I was grateful for this sign of true affection. What did I care if she was sometimes unfaithful to me, giving in to the pleas and cajolery of her ex-husband? She did it out of pity and force of habit. But she loved only me, she loved me for all she was worth and while she still could ... That's something to be valued in our troubled times.

In the lobby I was buttonholed by the test-pilot who pressed me up against the hat-rack and said he wanted my advice. He asked me in a whisper, out of earshot of his wife, when approximately his end would come. He was worried about whether or not to start a family, and whether it was worthwhile buying a refrigerator.

That night I had sworn never to tell anybody the date of their death in case their sense of the romantic was impaired and they got down-hearted and lost their healthy spirit of adventure. But now I had to make an exception. Death was all in a day's work for a test-pilot and not an object of idle curiosity. So I told him, as man to man, that he had five-and-a-half years to live and would then be vaporized while doing a record speed in the region of the Pacific Ocean, without even realizing the technical reason for such a sudden exit.

He was enormously pleased to hear this. Five-and-a-half years seemed a very long time to him. He hadn't reckoned with anything like this, thinking it would all happen much sooner. He could now buy a refrigerator, and enjoy himself with his wife unhindered by contraceptives. He was as pleased as Punch.

'And now own up, old chap,' he said hoarsely, shaking with laughter and slapping me on the shoulder, 'may as well admit it, that bedbug of yours was trained, wasn't it, like you train a dog? Some leg-pull that was! Come on, let's have the secret, I won't tell anyone ...'

This pilot readily believed me when I predicted his death in a rocket in five-and-a-half year's time, but it was beyond his understanding that one could predict the crawling of a bedbug over a wall. . .

1961

Translated by Max Hayward and Ronald Hingley

Two much younger Leningrad writers, Andrei Bitov and Maya Danini, are here represented by 'psychological', impressionistic stories concentrating on their characters' inner lives rather than outward action. Bitov (b. 1937) has already made himself a considerable reputation since 1963, but Danini has published only one book, of which 'Quick Money' is the title story.

Andrei Bitov

THE JUBILEE

During the night, as usual, he woke up and, lying on his back, examined the ghostly reflection on the ceiling. And, as always, he thought he could still understand this reflection and rejoice in it, and sense the mystery of it almost exactly as in childhood. It was really funny that even now, if he didn't look at his parchment-like chest and arms and didn't move, and so didn't feel how weak he was, but just lay there calmly and coolly and looked at the ceiling, he could imagine he was still a child. When the blanket hardly weighed on him at all and he did not feel hot, and he was alone and there was that reflection on the ceiling, he experienced the very same sensation that he had had as a child. And if he looked at the ceiling like that, and then shut his eyes, it seemed as though he could move about the room and turn the bed round – now he was lying with his head to the window, now with his head to the door; and after that, now he was lying facing the room, now face to the wall, while in fact he was lying and lying away on his back and not moving a muscle. And if you twist yourself about like that you don't really realize that you're lying down at all. And then mother would come, young, with her hair piled up on her head, and quietly stroke his hair and forehead, and he could feel this without waking up. The sensation was so definite this time, almost abrupt, in fact, that he opened his eyes and slowly turned his head to have a look; it wasn't that he was frightened, but it was so strange to feel her touch so definitely and abruptly. All the same, he turned his head – the books and the dark mass of the table were drowned in the darkness – and trembled: flowers, there were flowers everywhere – baskets of them – some looked white and others dark, standing in a row on the floor with a row above them on the stools.

He grew cold, but not very cold, and he was struck by the thought that he had died. For the flowers were – for him. He was lying there, he wasn't cold, or hot, or in pain – somehow he couldn't feel anything. They had all left and turned off the light.

THE WRITER BORIS KARLOVICH VAGIN DIES IN HIS 71ST YEAR

After your jubilee – it isn't even original, thought Boris Karlovich.

It began about a week ago with that phone call. And then the visit. The representative tried and tried to talk him into it. Boris Karlovich was wearily trying to refuse – the representative felt this and went on pressing him harder and harder. Actually Boris Karlovich had heard about this jubilee earlier. Now he realized that even then he had feared it and just because of this hadn't thought about it. Boris Karlovich couldn't have cared less about this jubilee, rather as though it was someone else's jubilee, but the fact that it was his jubilee instilled him with fear. To return suddenly from that measured life away from society, the life he had led for so long and which in its own way was so dear to him, to a completely different life – it was ridiculous. Moreover he didn't know the new people. At any rate Boris Karlovich couldn't understand this cheerful young representative at all.

The celebration seemed to Boris Karlovich now just as ridiculous as if, for instance, he decided to put on the short trousers he had worn as a boy. However, it wasn't the trousers which frightened him, but that tight, stiff best suit which had been hanging for years in the rarely used cupboard and which he would have to put on. And the fact that there would be a lot of those loud and cheerful people there; they would speak and push and eat a lot. And of course they were doing this for some purpose or other, but what it was and why – Boris Karlovich couldn't understand that either. And languidly and timidly he went on refusing, so that the representative suddenly became completely confident and something satisfied and flat appeared in his eyes. And Boris Karlovich wanted, wanted now more than anything else, this perfectly pointless conversation to be over. And he suddenly felt that it was much easier to agree, because the jubilee was still a week off, while the conversation was now. That the way out was – to agree. And he felt so relieved that this strange man had gone and that there was a week ahead of him, a marvellous week, because he suddenly felt what time was. And how simple it had been.

For two days he felt the relief, he was kind and affable; and everyone at home discussed among themselves what happiness it was that all this injustice was coming to an end and what a joy it would be for the old man.

On the third day all the fuss got the better of Boris Karlovich and he was in a bad temper about the fuss, and the people at home said it was natural for the old man to be getting a bit nervous, it was quite understandable, and they were considerate and tactful with him. But Boris Karlovich was becoming nervous because he realized it wasn't far off now – and he was angry at himself because of this. He was angry at the people at home for their consideration and tact, and they became even more considerate and tactful. 'I've a good mind to go away,' he thought. But he would have to dress, get to the station, catch a train ... and then the exclamations of his daughter-in-law – 'How glad we are to see you! What a surprise!' And then that mild, reproachful tone about whyever hadn't he given anyone any warning and that he'd come all by himself and didn't value his health. And there would be a general commotion. Everything would somehow be different from usual. He didn't go. And the consideration and tact of the people at home so exhausted him, he felt so weary, that he grew calmer.

And his even-temperedness and calm didn't leave him from then on, and all the people at home were glad. And he was pleased that he had calmed everyone down and that it was so easy to stop them worrying about him. Then his granddaughter and her husband visited him and they went away completely charmed by the old man. And when they said good-bye he kissed his granddaughter on the forehead, which he didn't usually do.

And there were phone-calls, invitations, suggestions. Boris Karlovich agreed to everything but put everything off till after Friday, until after the jubilee: you see, I'm very busy. It even gave him some strange sort of pleasure to postpone everything until this mysterious Saturday, which was after the Friday, and see this Saturday turning into an unimaginable lump. Then he amused himself by putting off certain things until the day of the jubilee, and the fact that it would then be impossible to fit everything in tickled his sense of humour, and he laughed straight into the phone; he was such a dear, kindly old soul.

It was the day after tomorrow. That was ever such a lot of time – the day after tomorrow. And it was tomorrow. And it seemed that there was even more time left, because really time was very short.

And it was night. There was the reflection on the ceiling. And astronomically it was today, although actually you could still say to yourself: tomorrow.

He didn't fall asleep again. It didn't irritate him that he couldn't fall asleep. He lay on his back looking at the striped reflection, and it grew pale and melted, and it was the dawn of the day on which he could no longer say to himself: tomorrow. It was easy while he was alone. And he realized that as long as he was alone it still wasn't tomorrow.

Well, I'll go along to this jubilee, he reflected. Lord, what is there to worry about ...? If they don't realize that it's quite unnecessary, the simplest thing is to agree and go along. It'll take a lot less effort. When all's said and done I haven't got that sort of strength, for resistance. So it's even better to go.

A sunbeam made its way in and then the door opened a little, quietly, and Masha, the maid, squeezed clumsily into the room. Even more persistently than the sunbeam, her appearance announced the arrival of tomorrow. Boris Karlovich was on the point of shutting his eyes and pretending to be asleep, but somehow he didn't do this and Masha saw that Boris Karlovich, Karlych, was awake. 'Now she'll start saying what they've taught her,' thought Boris Karlovich gloomily, imagining how she would begin to dance attendance on him. He always thought that good, conscientious Masha hadn't learnt a thing. She'd only learnt how to show that she was doing everything she had been taught. 'Now she'll begin to dance attendance on me and nurse me,' thought Boris Karlovich, but he heard something quite different:

'Can you let me off a bit early today ...' said Masha, lowering her eyes, and all the time rubbing, rubbing her hands against her apron.

The effect this had on him was a surprise to Boris Karlovich himself. He suddenly thought pitifully that in fact, in fact, nobody wanted him at all ... he was angry with himself for this and said:

'No, today you've got to dust the books.'

Then he got angry at the books – what have they got to do with it? – and said:

'You know very well what day it is today.'

Masha went out. But the sentence 'You know very well what day it is today' put Boris Karlovich out of joint once and for all. He was ashamed of those words. He knew Masha would come back again in a minute on some pretext or other. And in fact she did appear again in the room, noiselessly and clumsily, somehow it seemed even more clumsily than it was because she didn't make any noise.

'Perhaps you'd like some coffee ...'

How repulsively healthy she was, thought Boris Karlovich testily.

'No, I'll get it myself,' he said. 'I'll do everything myself. Go on now, go away.'

Masha looked at Boris Karlovich in bewilderment and her face grew rounder and rounder.

'Go away with you, you ought to be ...' Boris Karlovich felt he was weakening and turned away so as not to see Masha.

Immediately after this he heard her pattering along the corridor and then back along the corridor again, and then she banged the door.

Oh, to get it over with as quickly as possible, thought Boris Karlovich.

He stayed in a bed a little longer.

This is no good, he said to himself, I'll have to get ready. I'll get up in a minute, grind some coffee, have a drink ... The first few things he had to do were clear to Boris Karlovich, but everything after that was packed closely together and it was impossible to tell what would come next. I'd better have a look anyway and see what they've got about me in the paper.

He got up, dressed, took the paper from the table – it had long ago been put there for him – and went into the kitchen. But the coffee had already been ground and the steaming coffee-pot was on the gas stove. He felt disappointed, as though the thing he had wanted to do most of all was to get the coffee ready himself. And of course, the coffee wasn't made the proper way.

He went out of the kitchen and forgot to take the paper with him.

He went into the study. Everything was in its proper place. He moved the ink-stand a fraction. And moved it back again to its previous spot. He had a look at the books. They certainly do need a dust, he thought. He moved his finger across the spines. What does the dust matter, he thought.

'I'll have to get ready,' he said to himself again. 'After all, it's today now ...'

And then he finally realized that *suddenly* it was Friday. Up to now it had been a long way off, even on Thursday it had still been a long way off – it hadn't been. And now, suddenly, here it was.

Well then, better go out for a spot of fresh air, thought Boris Karlovich, and the idea pleased him greatly. 'Heaps of time, I can go out for a good hour.'

At that moment the phone rang. Boris Karlovich answered it and stood listening for a long time. And suddenly he laughed.

'You know what,' he said, and giggled, 'we can do that right away, today.' He giggled again. 'Come to the jubilee today. We'll talk about it there.'

Still laughing a little he forced himself to put on his coat. His hat fell behind the table and it took him a long time to pick it up.

He went downstairs and made for a little public garden.

In the centre of the garden was an open space round which there were seats, and in the middle was a sand-pit. Boris Karlovich chose a seat in the shade, sat down and began to watch the children. They were very young, quiet children; there was no shouting. Boris Karlovich liked the children. And on the seats were grandmothers and nannies, warming themselves in the sun, talking, calling their children, and everything was quiet here too.

A very fat boy with slanting eyes was squatting on all fours near the sand-pit and clinging on to a toy lorry. Opposite him a slender, agile boy was pulling the lorry towards himself. Beside them stood a little girl who was even younger. She seemed to be all dressed up, in a sweater and little trousers. The fat boy was whining protractedly. The other one was trying to find the best way to get the lorry from him. And the little girl was standing over them holding a spade and looking now at one, now at the other.

She wants to hit the fat one with the spade, thought Boris Karlovich.

The little girl was taking her time.

Finally she couldn't resist any longer, scooped up some sand and sprinkled it over the beret of the fat boy who was crouching on all fours.

I almost guessed it. That's just the same as hitting him, thought Boris Karlovich, gladdened. I understand it. I know all about this sort of thing.

The little girl was pouring sand on the fat boy.

No reaction from the fat boy.

He's so fat he can't cry, thought Boris Karlovich.

Someone on one of the seats shouted at the little girl.

But she wasn't doing it from spite: what a vivacious little face she had. She simply wanted to know what would happen, since he was such a fattie. Or perhaps she didn't like him being so fat.

The little girl realized play-time was about to end and there was no time to scoop up any more sand, and she hit the fat boy several times on his beret with her spade. The fat boy still didn't cry.

There, I was absolutely right – she wanted to hit him with the spade.

A large-breasted, perspiring nanny angrily ran up to the fat boy. She pulled him out of the sand like a radish and stood him up on the path.

'Sitting again!' she said. 'What did the doctor tell you? You're to walk!'

Fatty moaned wearily; he didn't want to go away, and walked with difficulty along the path, prodded on from behind by his nanny. When they were going past him Boris Karlovich noticed that despite his plumpness the boy had a really fine, expressive little face and that the nanny was pinching his hand, but so that no one else could see.

'Walk! Walk!' – said the nanny, and returned to her soldier.

The little girl in trousers was taken away by her young parents, and she pulled the lorry with sand along behind her; while bringing up the rear came the slender little boy whom nobody seemed to be interested in, gazing sadly at the lorry.

Then he returned and joined a little boy playing with an aeroplane. Within a minute he had taken possession of the aeroplane. The boy ran about, holding the plane in his outstretched hand: the boy glided, the boy ascended, the boy got into a spin.

Boris Karlovich felt as though he was holding the plane and it was he who was gliding and ascending. He could even feel the little plane in his hand. And he realized how he could become one with this little bit of iron.

Yes, I understand everything about this sort of thing, thought Boris Karlovich again.

Then he thought that now it would be necessary to bring them up and hope that they would be different. That they would be able to live like human beings a little bit longer than only while they were children. Yes, anything for that, he thought. For if not for that, then for what?

A little girl appeared with a puppy. She walked proudly past the sand-pit and sat down on a seat. The slender little boy dropped the plane and gazed at the puppy. The girl looked at the boy proudly and sat on the seat like a grown-up.

Yes ... who wouldn't agree that a puppy is better than a sand-pit ...? That's obvious, thought Boris Karlovich.

But the puppy got tired of sitting with the girl and it ran up to the sand-pit. Everyone began to pat it. The girl fidgeted jealously on the seat, could not resist it any longer, and ran up to take hold of the puppy.

The puppy again ran off to the sand-pit.

The girl got cross and began to shake the puppy and get angry with it.

There's something grown-up about her, thought Boris Karlovich.

But now her elder sister appeared, reprimanded her, took hold of the puppy and set off home. The little girl, disappointed, went after her.

Boris Karlovich could imagine how she had secretly taken the puppy and secretly run out on to the street, and realized what this independent walk with the puppy meant for her. And he was angry at the elder sister – *she* was grown up, but the other one wasn't.

And Boris Karlovich noticed that the same young man had already walked past him three times, looking down and glancing at him. Still in a benign mood Boris Karlovich looked at him amicably and thought about him in the same way: a fine young fellow. Then, catching his glance, the young man approached Boris Karlovich, blushed and said in a constrained voice:

'Excuse me for just coming up like this, I wouldn't have done it, but I, er, if you'll excuse me ...'

'Yes,' said Boris Karlovich, realizing what was coming and tensing.

'Well, you're Boris Karlovich Vagin!' said the young man.

'Mm-m-m,' mooed Boris Karlovich, somehow unsure of himself and startled.

'I so much wanted to get to know you. Your books ...'

Boris Karlovich felt ashamed. Burningly, painfully ashamed as one is only in childhood.

'Very well then, yes,' said Boris Karlovich.

'I very much wanted to ...'

Boris Karlovich felt even more embarrassed. But at that moment he remembered something and rejoiced because of what he had remembered.

'There you are,' he said gaily. 'Come to my jubilee today.'

Contented, the young man went away. Boris Karlovich sighed with relief.

I can't understand it, he thought with a feeling of hostility, and then he noticed that the young man was coming back. What else did he want ...? Boris Karlovich shut his eyes and pretended to be asleep.

Strange, he thought. I did all that so long ago ... And what was it that suddenly happened to them all? There's Sasha, for instance ... He was a better writer than I ever was. They didn't remember him. What's the point of it all? I don't need anything like this now. None of it's mine – it's all theirs. How is it they don't understand this? And my life – that's theirs too. And they won't let me be. Lord, they don't even understand that you've got to have mercy on old people! That they ought to leave you in peace at least some day. That this need ... What more do they want of me? Everything'll be left to them as it is. The collected works and everything – I don't want anything of all this.

Four hours away, he thought – time to be going already.

He chased away these thoughts in fear and dozed off.

When he opened his eyes the fat boy, and the nanny, and the soldier had all gone.

There were some new children.

The sun had moved on, and his seat had come out of the shade. The warmth fondled and embraced. Boris Karlovich even thought it had grown less sultry. It was getting warmer and warmer. A woman was walking along the path clutching two long bread rolls to her breast. When she drew near to Boris Karlovich one of the rolls slipped out of her grasp. Boris Karlovich's heart missed a beat as always happened when he dropped something himself. The woman bent down for the roll and the second one slipped out of her hand. It seemed to Boris Karlovich that there were a great number of rolls and they were all slipping, slipping ... everything swam before his eyes. Boris Karlovich knew that he ought to get up and go into the shade. But to get up was the last thing of all that he wanted to do. 'Tomorrow' – he thought – 'it isn't today yet ...' Above all he wanted to close his eyes. He closed them. Then he wanted to rest his head back. He put his head back. His head immediately started spinning round. The sun beat against his eye-lids. Pink, everything was pink. Smooth. His arm slipped down, rucking up his sleeve. Boris Karlovich felt how hot his watch was getting in the sun. He wanted to settle himself down more comfortably so that everything was in its only rightful place. His arm, and his head, and his legs. And suddenly Boris Karlovich felt that he was comfortable. So comfortable that there was no need to change anything again at all.

'Ask the old gentleman what time it is,' someone said on the next seat.

Boris Karlovich's heart jolted in his chest. 'Four more hours!' he wanted to shout. And suddenly his heart broke off, galloped away and began to jump down somewhere. Into the cool. He felt cool. His heart was jumping down, as though it was going down a staircase. He felt as though he was a little boy again, a very little boy of the last century. And now the little children were running down the slope and yelling. There he is, there's Borya. They're running, turning head over heels on the sand and leaping into the water, the water. The water embraces you with coolness. Everything seems somehow to grow numb inside you. Water up to your ankles, your waist, your chest ... on to your throbbing, burning heart.

'Grandpa, Grandpa, what time is it?' asked the boy insistently.

And from the neighbouring seat some strange voices were shouting:

'Vova! Vova!! Come back!'

May 1960

Translated by Martin Dewhirst

Maya Danini

QUICK MONEY

Pasha walked through the market, peering into the shops and booths and wondering what to buy Nelya for a present. There was a lot she liked and a lot she wanted to buy: that enamelled pail, so nice and white like an eggshell, and those rubber boots, but she realized she liked these things because she didn't have them herself, whereas they meant nothing to Nelya. Nelya was educated now, a doctor, so what would she want with rubber boots? And she lived in Zaporozhye, in a big house with running water, so a pail was unnecessary.

The thing to do would be to buy that cashmere scarf that Nina Valinova was selling; that was what Nelya needed. Pasha had inquired about it ages ago: Nina was asking forty roubles.

She was so darned *prof'table*, that Valinova, such a *swindler*, as Pasha called her, paying off an old score, for the Valinovs had carved a plot out of her land and built a house on it, while Pasha stayed on in her adobe shack. And that was why Pasha called the Valinovs *prof'table*, but then that scarf of hers, she had tumbled to it right away, it was worth forty roubles, well worth it. Pasha held it up to the light to make sure there were no holes in it and she wasn't selling used or moth eaten stuff.

The scarf was a new one, Pasha liked it, but she didn't let on that she liked the scarf. She handed the scarf back to Nina indifferently and said:

'It's too dear.'

She put on an expression of indifference so that Nina

wouldn't put on an expression of indifference and so she wouldn't think Pasha would pay anything she asked.

Pasha always haggled. Even if she knew quite well she'd get nothing off, nevertheless she haggled long and stubbornly, adding a copeck at a time, angrily throwing the thing down and making as if to go away, but she didn't go and she'd say:

'Wear it yerself, then, and watch out, for the last time I'm offering you thirty-five. You won't take it? I'm going!'

But she didn't go. She would pick the thing up again, turn it round and round and find a wee little hole in some corner or other, or not even a hole but a dropped stitch, and she'd seize on that stitch and say the whole scarf would fall apart because of that stitch and that's why they were selling it, else they'd be wearing it theirselves, because Pasha knew a thing or two and you couldn't pull a fast one on her.

She had seen Nina with the scarf at the market on Sunday and there and then had told her precisely what she thought of her, because you could never have a real barney with your neighbours at home and she didn't feel like kicking up no stink at Baybuga any more, she'd had enough of that, and then she caught Nina one beautifully on the raw so that she yelled:

'I'll let you have it for thirty-seven, are you gonna take it? I'll give it you 'cos you're so poor, for a sack of sunflower seeds, eh?'

Pasha was already leaving; she didn't want Nina's scarf.

Pasha sold sunflower seeds and never gave way, not even for a little boy, not even when he begged:

'I haven't got a kopeck, miss, give us a few!'

Pasha didn't give him any and wouldn't look at him. Sometimes she stayed silent, or else she would say:

'Seeds are no good for you, they'll give you appendicitis.'

Pasha liked using expressions that she had picked up from her daughter while the latter was studying.

Oh, how proud Pasha was of her daughter! She told everyone about her, even those who knew Nelya anyway:

'Ever since her childhood she's been every bit as proud and stubborn as what I am. Just to get the coal she'd dress up to beat the band, then tie her scarf on straight, tidy herself up, powder her nose – and away she'd go.'

Pasha had another daughter, Nadya, who had married a driver, Tyurin. Tyurin was such a quiet fellow and very small, like a boy, but Pasha suspected he had a *slut* somewhere and was *carrying on* with her and driving her about, while Nadya, the fool, sat at home making dressing gowns. She never dreamed of seeing where Tyurin was gadding about to or who he was *carrying on* with. Pasha, on the other hand, went herself to sell seeds near the office and kept watch to see who Tyurin took into his cab, and one day she saw him settle a strange woman inside and the moment she saw it she threw herself in front of the lorry and shouted:

'Oh, you gadabout, now I've caught you, oh you fallen woman, I'll do for you.'

But the woman didn't understand and Tyurin didn't understand. For a long time he couldn't get a word out and then it seemed to dawn on him and he shouted:

'It's the new transport manager, Mum! It's the new transport manager ...'

That night he got drunk, came home late, and, as Pasha related it, went and ripped every last stitch on hisself to shreds and stripped to the buff, so blinkin' *plastered* he was, so blinkin' *plastered*! And she sighed.

Before that Pasha had told Tyurin they should build, and she had hoped he would start bringing some limestone home like all the other drivers, but Tyurin had no intention of building, he was such a *stick-in-the-mud*.

And now Pasha lost all hope.

She couldn't build herself, even though she had the money, because where? Stones she could buy, timber she could buy, and get transport for everything, hire a lorry – even though they'd got their own lorry, as you might say, with Tyurin. Yes, their own lorry, you might say …

Pasha loved the market, Pasha spent all her days at the market. 'Doing the market,' she called it. It was still dark when she arrived, took her place, exchanged greetings with everyone she knew, priced everything, and then went to the gate to wait for the lorries from Nikolayev and Sem Kolodezei.

When the lorries arrived, Pasha ran after them and stood by their sides till the drivers started unloading.

She was waiting for sunflower seeds. The people from those distant parts didn't charge too much for their sunflower seeds, but Pasha haggled just the same. Peremptorily:

'Come on now, matey, let me have 'em.'

Complainingly:

'Pity a poor old woman with no roof over her head.'

And threateningly:

'Oh, you swindler, you, you should have the police on you!' And she got her way. They let her have them. Then she would try them, sniff them to see if they were mouldy and pour them from hand to hand. She pinched the sack to make sure they were all nice round ones, that no husks had been added, and then she'd start counting out the money. Smoothing each rouble out with her fingers, she re-counted the money several times, then forced the seller to count it too, all the while watching him sharply, with suspicion, to make sure he didn't pull God knows what cunning trick on her. Then she'd set about extracting the small change from her pocket and invariably stopped about twenty copecks short. With her it was always a case of 'absolutely the last copeck to m'name, even if I has to walk home'. Until the seller gave up in disgust:

'Ugh, to the devil with you, old woman!'

And walked away. Pasha was content.

She took up her place and opened her sack – not the one

she'd just bought but another she'd brought with her, with roasted seeds, then she rolled back the neck of the sack and took out her glass.

Pasha cherished this glass even more than money. If she had lost it she would have been inconsolable for the rest of her life, because there was no other glass like it in the world.

She had seen it in a cashier's booth in a shop and the moment she caught sight of it she just stopped and stared.

The glass was inside the booth and held some withered snowdrops.

Pasha moved closer and started to study the glass. It was cut glass, ordinary to look at, but with an extra-thick bottom and sides. It was a reject. Pasha looked at it and couldn't even bring herself to speak to the cash girl inside. The bottom of that glass was a goldmine, that's all Pasha knew, a goldmine.

'It must be stuffy sitting in there, real hot,' said Pasha, 'and your lovely little flowers are dead. You should chuck 'em out.'

The cash girl sighed.

'Stuffy and how. Work, work, work, haven't even got the strength to breathe.'

'Where'd you get that glass from?'

'Yes, it's a fright,' said the cash girl carelessly.

'What you need is a dinky little vase in there. You're still young, you know.'

The cash girl smiled, patted her hair, looked at herself in a fragment of mirror and sighed.

Pasha meanwhile kept on talking.

'Young, yes, you're young. Lots of boy friends I 'spect.'

The cash girl laughed and it occurred to Pasha that she'd turned the conversation the wrong way, but so passionate did she feel that suddenly she just blurted out:

'Let me have that glass, will you?'

Just like that. And how sorry she was that she'd said it. The cash girl got angry. It's a well-known fact that cashiers are busy people, no time to make conversation.

Pasha waited till the other customers had gone, then went up to the booth again – so crushed and pitiful – and said:

'Child of my heart, take pity on me, an old woman, and give me the glass, I've broken mine.'

But the cash girl didn't like it when people whined. She used to get beggar women in emptying sacks of coppers and changing them for larger money, and she was so tired already of changing this money and so fed up with old women, so distrustful of them, that of course she didn't give the glass to Pasha, nor would she sell it, nor would she exchange it.

Pasha went away and came back an hour later with some flowers: she had picked up some abandoned snowdrops in the market place and brought them back.

Pasha put the flowers down in front of the cash girl and stepped back, but it so happened that the cash girl didn't like flowers because her husband was jealous and used to think she got the flowers from soldiers and holiday-makers; and so she didn't like accepting flowers.

Pasha stood humbly to one side and bowed to the cashier and smiled, while the latter kept wondering what the old woman could want with the glass. And suddenly she remembered that she had bought some sunflower seeds from the old woman at the market place and it irritated her when she realized.

And for a long time afterwards Pasha had trouble with that cashier. The cashier told everyone what she had realized and now everyone in the shop knew Pasha and smiled contemptuously whenever she appeared, but Pasha knew how to take care of herself.

One day she went to see the watchman after dark and after giving him a rouble managed to exchange the glass for an ordinary one. For a long time afterwards she feared the cashier would kick up a fuss, that she'd even come to Baybuga and bawl her out and even bring a vigilance squad along, but the cashier evidently couldn't be bothered. Pasha merely avoided standing near the shop with her seeds. But the shop was right next to the cinema. People always bought seeds there in the evenings, and then Pasha even decided to go away to Zaporozhye to see Nelya and wait it out for a month or two.

How nice it was for Pasha at Nelya's, how peaceful it was. And for three days Pasha didn't go out, for three days she couldn't stop admiring the flat. It was so beautiful in there, so luxurious. Pasha picked up all the things and put them down again, envied Nelya and pitied Nadya for not having such things.

For three days she had a holiday, for three days she made the most delicious borshch and meat ravioli for Nelya, but on the fourth day she got bored and went out to the street to sit on the bench and get to know the neighbours.

She sat next to a girl who was shelling sunflower seeds. The girl said she worked at the stocking factory, was herself 'from Lenin's Way – the kolkhoz', had come here to work and wasn't doing at all badly.

The girl was throwing seeds into her mouth without bothering to spit the husks out. She already had a whole beard of sunflower seeds. The seeds had made her front teeth uneven, but, gaptoothed as she was, she made short work of them and it was impossible even to see how she could shell and chew them, so swiftly did the seeds fly into her mouth.

Pasha told her how Nelya was such a good daughter to her, and told her about Nadya too and about Tyurin, and that Nadya wasn't happy but Nelya would be. Nelya was going to marry a doctor, and not just any old doctor but some sort of *chief doctor*. She talked and talked and all the while the girl was eating sunflower seeds, and apart from what she was saying she also thought to herself: 'My, how they love sunflower seeds here, goodness they really love 'em!' And she fingered the glass in her pocket.

All night long Pasha couldn't sleep and she kept thinking: 'If only I could get a lift down to Sinelnikovo, that's the place for markets.' As she thought about it, she tried to hold herself back and she calmed herself: 'I don't need no seeds, what do I want with seeds? Where can I sell 'em here? Nelya's a doctor, everyone knows her, everyone respects her, what will they say – that her mother's a market woman?' She thought of this and yet she still remembered that she could buy seeds in Sinelnikovo and not sell them here but hide them. And then take them home with her to Baybuga and sell them there in the winter-time.

Pasha didn't travel to Sinelnikovo but went to the local market instead. The entrance was jammed with farm wagons and hooting lorries. Pasha was shivering, but she knew the sun would soon take the chill off; and how the cucumbers would glisten in their carts, and the radishes and early tomatoes! What a warm glow of joy this would bring her! And already there came a smell of squashed tomatoes and meat in sacks. For Pasha these were familiar, homely smells. She warmed up by elbowing her way through the queues for the cashier's office, where people stood to pay for a place and scales. She didn't need any scales but she stood there, sizing up the sacks by eye and guessing their contents: spuds, cucumbers, nuts. She was feeling the sacks with her eyes, feeling and pricing.

They certainly charged for their sunflower seeds here, they certainly did.

And no wonder, what a market! Stand there from morn to night, they would, selling away. And maybe only the leftovers would be knocked down a bit, so that everybody could leave at the same time.

Suddenly she caught sight of a youth with a sack. He was standing to one side and looked as though he was preparing to steal instead of sell. Pasha knew those sort of people, she had a practised eye. She knew he was too shy to trade; he was a stroke of luck that had turned up in her path, the sort of luck that rarely happens. She knew the lad would even implore her to take the sack, but the question was: what was in it?

And Pasha went up to the youth.

He had apples, soft apples, the like of which it was impossible to buy in Zaporozhye at that moment. Pasha looked at the apples and felt them, while the youth explained for some reason that he had just come from Moldavia and that one of their tyres had just burst ... Pasha didn't even hear the price, but she already knew she would buy the apples, that this was luck, a rare stroke of luck. She knew she would buy the apples and at the same time reassured herself that Nelya needed the apples: 'I bet she never lays eyes on a bit of fruit.' And she bought the apples.

Buying was one thing, but what next? She couldn't even lift the sack. Three quarters of a hundredweight. Not to speak of carrying it away ... And Pasha joined the queue for scales. She sold the apples quickly, though it didn't give her much pleasure. She hurried and hustled, but while she was selling she spied out some big fat sunflower seeds. These seeds, the size of a fingernail, were all nice and stripey and long-looking, like beetles. Exactly like beetles, and they wriggled like it too. Pasha gazed at them with admiration. She scurried home quickly and hid the seeds from Nelya, and she rejoiced to herself and also worried. She was afraid that someone had seen her at the market, but then she comforted herself that nobody went to the market so early. And the whole time she was thinking of how she would come home and start selling the big fat sunflower seeds. How people would fall over themselves to get her sunflower seeds. And Pasha day-dreamed, picked up her glass and filled it with seeds. They settled airily; not many fitted into the glass. Pasha cheered up completely, went outside and treated the girl from Lenin's Way to some sunflower seeds. The girl took the seeds, but said she didn't like big ones, big ones were often empty, and she herself preferred little ones that were full.

Pasha herself knew that big ones were often empty, but then not everyone knew how to shell sunflower seeds the way this girl did.

And Pasha laughed. She went home, rolled back the neck of the sack, filled her glass and sank its bottom into the seeds.

Automatically she turned the glass upside down and then filled it again.

How nice it would be to go round to the cinema now and stand there for half an hour ...

But she didn't go to the cinema.

All night Pasha tossed and turned, she even wept without tears. She got an idea that everything ached, that she needed treatment, that maybe she had cancer.

She groped under the bed with her hand, fumbled at the sack of seeds, then groaned again so that she even woke Nelya. Waking Nelya upset her because Nelya had to get up early, didn't she, and wouldn't get enough sleep, and what's more it would have to be explained what was wrong with Pasha.

Pasha wanted to go out into the street, but Nelya was sleeping too lightly after being disturbed. Pasha said to herself that she was going out into the street to stretch her legs, but at the same time she put on her market things: scarf and anorak, old skirt, socks and galoshes. She moved about the room quietly, like a person who's up to no good, but nonetheless Nelya woke up:

'Where are you off to, Mum?'

'Sleep, my child, I'm just going to stretch my legs ... Maybe I'll be gone a while though, so don't expect me in the evening.'

And she hurried off so that Nelya wouldn't ask anything else.

She walked down the street and still didn't feel any better, but then she thought: 'I think I'll take a trip to Sinelnikovo, yes, that's what I'll do.'

And the moment she said it she felt relieved and cheerful. And she said to herself aloud: 'Ooh, my, ha, ha!' And she set off fast, as fast as she could go. Jumping onto a bus, she got out to the main highway. There she was immediately picked up by a tip lorry, climbed into the cab, even smiled at the driver and almost winked at him:

'Give us a ride to Sinelnikovo!'

She thrust her head out of the window and breathed deeply and easily. The wind rushed into her lungs and Pasha even felt that some colour had come into her cheeks.

All of a sudden she remembered that as a little girl her mother had sent her to the shop for some curds, or 'cheese', as they called it at home. Pasha played games with herself as she ran and kept repeating to herself: 'Cheese, seeds, cheese, seeds, cheese, seeds ...' Arriving at the shop she forgot: was it cheese or seeds she was supposed to buy? And when they asked her it was:

'Cheese! No – seeds ... Cheese ... No – seeds.'

And seeds she bought when it should have been cheese – in other words curds for cheese ravioli. When she got home she got a thrashing from her mother.

'Cheese, seeds,' repeated Pasha aloud, and gave a laugh. The driver looked and thought: 'Funny old bird.'

Pasha showed the driver her lovely glass, winked and advised him to drink from such a glass – then he'd never get drunk, but better still he shouldn't drink at all because else they'd take his licence away. The driver grinned and wagged his head from side to side:

'Funny old dear, you are, and you know all about drivers too.'

'Well, me son-in-law's a driver.'

'Oh yes, and does your son-in-law drink out of that glass?'

'No, he don't drink at all,' sighed Pasha.

'What then, beats his wife?'

'No, he don't beat his wife neither.'

'You then?'

'Just let 'im try, I'd wallop him to kingdom come.'

'Lawks, what a woman ...'

They chatted the whole way and got to know one another. Pasha was in a good mood and talked her head off. Breezily and cheekily, like a young thing, and posh, like the holiday-makers. For instance, she didn't just ask the driver what his name was, but 'what's your initials?'. And she discovered that his name was Nil.

And when they arrived Pasha was already so excited she jumped out of the lorry like a young girl that a driver feels flattered to give a lift to. She jumped down and decided not to pay. He didn't need buttering up. She said to him:

'Me son-in-law don't drink and I don't advise you to neither. Thanks a million for the ride,' and then slammed the door and walked off.

Moving off, she listened to see if he would shout at her to pay. Perhaps he'd swear after her as she left? But he didn't shout and he didn't swear. And Pasha was content.

Goodness, what a market it was! There were sheep bleating, geese gobbling, horses neighing. A warm haze lay over the market, bright dust stood in the air. Pasha was so hungry she could have eaten everything that was on sale. She bought some cooked lard, white bread and some heated sour milk, and then some raw eggs and swallowed three on the spot. When she cut into the lard it just melted on the knife and spread on the bread of its own accord. It was light, pink lard, and like the bread it had the aroma of fresh wheat – so the piglet had been well fed. Pasha decided to buy some more lard. She took six pounds and the woman left, while Pasha went on eating and didn't bother to pack the lard away. She ate so heartily that one old fellow came up and asked how much it was. She said she wasn't selling, she needed it herself, but she did a deal and sold it. And all day she had such good fortune, such luck, such pleasure – and money, money! But in the evening a gentle fatigue stole over her and she fell asleep on a cartload of hay. And she slept, oh she slept – so well that she couldn't remember when she had slept better. But in the morning she was wakened by some sort of push and she started. She sensed at once that something was wrong: she made a grab for her sock at the knee and realised that the money was gone. A whole handkerchief-full. Bulging, uncounted – so much ... She rolled off the hay and banged her leg on the cart, but didn't notice the pain and set off at a run, looking around her: there was nobody about. Nobody! And then Pasha gave a shout and yelled so that it was not just a shout, but a roar and a bellow mixed up with a groan and a wail. She ran along the rows of stalls and looked at random under counters and boxes. People gathered round her and she gave voice, she shrieked – in front of them all, in a special (for all of them now) sobbing wail. And she fell on her stomach across a trunk, so hard that she even knocked herself and realized the pain, and rocked back and forth, back and forth.

They pitied her and questioned her, but she didn't reply and only yelled, and then she grew calm and they left her. She seated herself, pulled the scarf from her head, combed her hair, wiped her face with the scarf, and just then she felt the glass in her pocket – it clinked ... She thrust her hand in and cut herself. She herself had broken the glass. Now Pasha wept silently and hopelessly. The glass couldn't even be glued together. Couldn't possibly be glued together ... And there wasn't even any change in her pocket – they'd pinched everything, everything ... And how was she to get home?

She wandered along the road, dejected and distraught, wandered along and was even scared to stop a lorry. She was hungry, and there was nothing to eat. She walked and walked and thought: 'Even if I begs a free bus-ride the conductors are scared of the inspectors.' Now, all of a sudden, she had become timid. And Pasha went on walking along the side of the road.

It was already hot and hard to walk, but she kept on; then she felt completely exhausted and sat down.

She fell asleep shivering and slept with her head flung back, her mouth open, and in such a strange position that a driver who was pouring water into his radiator noticed her: with the old girl lying there like that, maybe she was dead? He went up to her and all of a sudden recognized that funny old bird who had talked about the glass. He recognized her by her scarf and anorak, but the face he didn't recognize, even when he woke her. It was a swollen, an old face.

'Old lady!' he roused her. 'Come on, you funny old thing, I'll take you again for free.'

Pasha was still half asleep and hardly recognized Nil, and she didn't seem all that pleased to see him. She got up and walked a few steps, holding on to her heart, groaning and blowing her nose in her handkerchief. She only just managed to climb into the cab and flopped down heavily into the seat, then started to cry and tell him how her money had been stolen. She bored Nil to death with her stories, warmed to her misery and talked and talked, and it seemed now that she was enjoying her misery, and Nil thought: 'The old lady'll be talking about this till her dying day.'

But Pasha was weeping and showing him the glass and weeping, and suddenly her feelings carried her away to such an extent that she said to him:

'Sonny boy, child of my heart! A good man, you are ... Like my son-in-law Tyurin, he's a good man too! I think I'll send him a telegram – he'll send me the money at once, that's the sort of man he is, the same as you are, child of my heart ...'

And she wept and wept. Consoling herself with her tears, she was, consoling herself with tears.

1965

Translated by Michael Scammell

The humble 'journalistic sketch' provided a literary jumping-off point in their time for writers as considerable as, for example, Chekhov and Zoshchenko, and can still provide a vehicle of more than evanescent interest for sharp or gentle satire and unusual reflections of Soviet *mores*. 'In the Compartment' was published in the monthly journal *Novy Mir*; its author, Vladimir Voynovich, was born in 1932 and is well known as an author of amusing, truthful and biting stories of contemporary life.

Vladimir Voinovich

IN THE COMPARTMENT

(*An Episode*)

Once I was travelling from Moscow to Leningrad on some business of great importance to me. I was travelling in a two-berth compartment. Not from any inclination for luxury – simply because the booking office had no other tickets. The business I mention was not only important but also pleasant, and so I decided I could justifiably permit myself the extravagance. Later I regretted this. Now I recall it with a smile. But at the time it was ...

When I got into the carriage I was in a good mood. I wanted to do or at least say something nice to each person I met, and everyone without exception seemed at that moment to be wonderful. Even the travelling companion in my compartment at first sight aroused in me no suspicions. She was a blonde of about thirty, but still fairly young-looking, with large, apparently sad eyes and dimples in her cheeks. She was dressed in a dark-blue suit, with a white starched blouse beneath the jacket. A diamond-shaped college-badge revealed that my companion was a person of education.

'How d'you do,' I said, carrying my suitcase in front of me as I came in. 'We'll be sharing this compartment.' In reply to this I heard:

'A man?' she asked sharply, emanating cold hatred at me.

I became rather embarrassed. Somehow I had never before had occasion to doubt that I belonged to that half of mankind.

'Well, don't I look like one?' I mumbled.

'Unfortunately all too like one,' she said quietly and distinctly.

At first I was nonplussed, but then decided that she was simply joking, and tried to put myself in a joking mood too. I asked: 'And is that good or bad?'

'And what do you think yourself?'

I thought a bit.

'You're right. It's simply awful. I understand the whole tragedy of my position, of course, but what's to be done? Am I really to blame that I was born into this estate?'

'You mean I am to blame?'

'Good heavens no,' said I, putting my suitcase under the seat. 'But still, I think ...'

'I am not interested what you think.'

'I see. But I would like to say that when you were buying your ticket the chances of finding yourself next to a man or a woman were roughly equal. However, if my presence embarrasses you, you can swap places with someone.'

'Why should I be swapping places? This is my compartment.'

'And mine too,' I reminded her.

'But you're a man,' she said, and at once corrected herself: 'Although of course if it's permitted for a man to be alone with a woman ...'

'It depends on which man with which woman.' I couldn't contain myself and went to ask the attendant whether she couldn't find me another place.

No other place was to be found. Nobody wanted to swap. I returned to the compartment and reported this to my companion.

'Well naturally,' she said and turned away towards the window.

We fell silent. But sitting opposite each other was somehow difficult. I decided to have it out with her.

'I must say, you're a strange woman,' I said.

'Certainly,' she said very proudly, 'when a woman behaves as she's meant to ...'

That finished me. I went to the attendant, collected some sheets and began to make my bed. She was looking out of the window and from time to time glanced at me with an expression which implied that I was doing something indecent. Suddenly she asked: 'I see that in other compartments there are men and women travelling together. What are they – all husbands and wives?'

'Sorry, I haven't checked their marriage certificates.'

'Well you ought to have done. Strange women are travelling with strange men, and it doesn't worry anyone. It's simply incomprehensible.'

I was silent. To give her a chance to make her bed and lie down I took my cigarettes and went out of the compartment, closing the door behind me. On my return I found her in the same position and the same place.

'Well, aren't you going to bed?' I asked.

My question provoked a burst of disapproval.

'Bed? I'm not the sort of person you think I am.'

'As you like,' I said, and shut the door.

Like a cat, she threw herself at the door and pulled it wide open.

'Forgive me, but all the same I'm going to shut the door,' I said, and at once did as I promised.

'No, you're not,' she said, and opened the door.

'Yes, I am,' I said, and again pushed the door away from me.

'No, you're not,' she said, and pulled the door back again.

'Yes, I am.'

'No, you're not.'

The duel lasted for an interminably long time. A passenger who passed by with a towel round his neck stopped, as if wondering whether or not he should rush to the aid of the woman. Evidently he soon realized that the woman could look after herself, and silently, shaking his head, he carried on.

I was the first to lose patience.

'Listen,' I implored, 'maybe you think that after shutting the door I'm going to throw myself on you?'

'I don't think anything.' She was breathing heavily.

'Then forgive me, but I want to sleep.' Once again I grasped the door handle.

Instantly she launched a counter-attack. Her mouth was wide open, a mad gleam blazed in her eyes.

I could resist no longer; I was tired. I said to her: 'Permit me to shut the door. I give you my word that I shall make no assault on your honour. I have absolutely no need of you.'

'Of course not,' she hissed, 'you naturally prefer women who allow themselves ...'

'My dear girl ...' I said.

'I'm not your dear girl.'

'My non-dear girl,' I corrected myself, 'get this straight, I'm tired and want to go to sleep. But I'm not in the habit of sleeping with the door open.'

'One's habits should be left at home.'

I washed my hands of her and just lay down. For a long time I couldn't sleep. The light from the corridor shone straight in my eyes. I turned away towards the wall. I lay there cursing the moment when I had agreed to take the ticket for the two-berth compartment. But then I thought that after all one should always see the funny side of things. And I also thought what it would be like if my companion was made the director of our entire life. She would be able to do a lot of re-organizing on the principle of separating men from women. At present we have separate bath-houses, toilets and hostels. These divisions could be extended for a start to cover cinemas, shops and public transport. On one tram, say, there would be a 'W', on the next an 'M'. Separate stops, too, divided by impenetrable partitions. Then one could go further. One could divide towns and villages into men's and women's. And in the process of mastering the cosmos it would be possible to solve the whole question once and for all by settling the representatives of the different sexes on separate planets. With this horrible vision I went to sleep. And I dreamt about the universe and a multitude of round planets. On some there was a 'W', on others an 'M'.

Several times I woke up in a fright, always to see the same picture. She was sitting, chin on hands, exhausted, sleepy, and her eyelids kept closing. But as soon as she noticed that I was awake she would put herself on her guard, straighten up, and hold her arms out in front of her, prepared for the worst.

When I woke for the last time it was already light. Outside the window the rain-soaked platforms of suburban stations were flashing by.

My travelling-companion was unrecognizable. She sat exhausted, crumpled and pale. Beneath her eyes were dark, bluish circles. One might have thought she had spent the night goodness knows how. It seemed as though she could no longer react to anything, but I only had to move for her once again to give a start and take up her defensive posture. I began to pity her. I thought that if the energy she spent on the defence of heaven knows what could be usefully applied, then much good would be done for society. I even wanted to tell her this, but at that moment the attendant came in and began to collect the bed-linen. The train was approaching Leningrad.

1965
Translated by Peter Reddaway

The doyen of the new prose literature is Yury Kazakov (b. 1927); he first appeared in print in 1953, but has published rather little. A fine creator of atmosphere, drawn particularly to the remote northern provinces of Russia for his settings, he writes with a lyricism and subtle understatement that have led to his general recognition as the truest contemporary heir to Chekhov. His 'heroes' (if that is the word) are often inarticulate, reprehensible or disadvantaged, but may be gifted with more-than-compensatory inner talents; the eponymous Arcturus is, literally, an underdog, whose spiritual triumph is no mere exercise in sentimental anthropomorphism. One of the few Soviet authors to write convincingly and subtly about love, Kazakov is a true moralist – which does not mean he moralizes. For some of his views on literature, see pp. 394–5.

Yury Kazakov

ARCTURUS THE HUNTING DOG

No one knows how he came to be in town. He arrived in spring and stayed. He troubled no one, forced himself on no one and took no one's orders – he was free.

It was said that the gypsies had left him behind when they passed through the town in spring. Strange people, gypsies! By early spring they are on the move, some by train, some by boat or raft, while others trundle along the roads in their wagons and look daggers at the cars and lorries shooting past them. A southern people, they yet wander about in the remotest parts of the north. Dark, handsome, wearing earrings and bright clothes, they suddenly appear encamped on the outskirts of a town; they hang round the market, fingering the goods and haggling, they go into houses, they tell fortunes and swear and laugh – then, as suddenly as they came, they vanish, never to be seen again. The world is wide, and they dislike returning to a place where they have been before.

So it was that many people thought the gypsies had abandoned him.

Others said that he had floated down on the ice during the spring floods. There he had stood, alone, motionless, black against the swirling, drifting, white and pale-blue ice, while overhead the swans had flown and cried 'Clink-clank! Clink-clank!'

People always wait impatiently for the swans. And when they see them at last, at dawn, rising from the flood waters with their great spring call 'Clink-clank!' their blood runs faster and they know that spring has come.

Among all this movement of rustling, crackling, booming ice and calling swans, he stood, his tail between his legs, uncertain, wary, sniffing and listening. When the ice floated near the bank, he got excited, jumped clumsily, fell into the water but quickly scrambled out on to the bank and, shaking himself, disappeared among the piles of stacked timber.

In this way or in some other, he appeared in spring, when the days were filled with brilliant sunshine, ringing streams and the smell of bark, and stayed in the town.

What his past had been, one can only guess. He must have been born on the straw under some porch. When her time came, his mother – a thoroughbred Kostroma retriever, short-legged and long in the back – her belly swollen, hid under the porch to carry out her great task in secret. They called her but she wouldn't answer, she wouldn't eat, wholly concentrated on herself, sensing that what at any moment was about to happen was the most important thing in the world, more important than even hunting, more important than people – those people who were her masters and her gods.

Born blind, like all puppies, he was at once licked all over by his mother and put close to her belly which was still straining with birth pangs. And while he lay, practising his first breaths, brothers and sisters kept joining him. They moved about, whimpered and tried to whine – all were like him, smoky pups with naked bellies and short quivering tails. Soon it was all over. Each found a teat and was quiet. Now there was only the sound of sniffing and sucking and his mother's panting. And so their life began.

In time, they opened their eyes and were enthralled to discover an even greater world than the one they had lived in until then. He, too, opened his eyes, but he was never to see the world. He was blind. A wall of thick grey film covered his pupils. His life was to be hard and bitter. It would indeed have been terrible had he realized that he was blind. But he could not know this. He took life as it came.

Somehow it happened that no one drowned him or otherwise did away with him, as might have been the kind thing to do to a helpless pup which was no use to man. He lived on and suffered great hardships which prematurely tempered and toughened him, body and soul.

There was no master to feed and shelter him, to look after him like a friend. He became a homeless dog tramp, sullen, awkward, distrustful: his mother, having weaned him, soon lost interest in him as in his brothers. He learned to howl – a howl as long-drawn-out and melancholy as that of a wolf. Always dirty, often ill, he rummaged in the rubbish dumps outside the restaurants and, like all the other homeless, hungry dogs, was kicked and swilled with buckets-full of dirty water.

He could not run fast: his legs, his powerful legs, were almost useless to him, for all the time it seemed to him he might be running into something sharp and hostile. When he fought with other dogs – and the greater part of his life he spent fighting – he snapped and threw himself at the noise of breathing, snarling and growling, at the sound of his enemies' pads on the ground – and he often snapped and threw himself at empty space.

The name his mother gave him at birth is unknown (every mother, even a bitch, knows her offspring by name). To people, he was nameless ... Neither is it known whether, left to himself, he would have stayed in town or gone off to die somewhere in a ravine, praying in anguish to his canine god. As it happened, man took a hand in his destiny and everything changed.

That summer I was living in a small northern town on the bank of a river. Along the river sailed white steamers, dirty brown barges, rafts and broad beamed rowing boats with tar-stained hulls. A jetty, smelling of matting, ropes, damp rot and fish, stood out from the bank. Scarcely anyone ever landed at the jetty except people from near-by collective farms on market day or sad-faced officials in grey raincoats who came to the timber mill.

Around the town, on low, gently sloping hills, stretched the vast virgin forest: the timber, which floated down the stream, was felled in the upper reaches of the river. Here and there in the forest were wide meadows and enclosed lakes with huge ancient pines along the shore. The pines were always quietly murmuring. But when the cool damp wind blew from the Arctic Ocean, chasing the clouds, the pines hummed threateningly, dropping cones which thudded on the ground.

I took a room on the outskirts, at the top of an old house. My landlord, a doctor, was taciturn and always busy. His house had once been full of people, but his two sons had been killed in the war, his wife had died and his daughter moved to Moscow, so now he lived alone and did nothing but look after his patients; they were children. He had a passion for singing. He sang every aria you could think of, his voice – the thinnest possible falsetto – quavering in ecstasy on the top notes. He had three rooms downstairs but he seldom went into them. He slept and had his meals on the verandah. The rooms were gloomy and smelled of dust, medicines and old wall-paper.

My room looked out on a neglected garden overgrown with currant bushes, raspberry and burdock; nettles grew along the fence. In the morning, sparrows hopped and chirruped on the windowsill while thrushes flew down in clouds to peck at the currants; the doctor let them be: he never picked the fruit. Sometimes the neighbour's rooster and hens flew up on the fence. The rooster stretched his neck and sang loudly, his tail feathers quivering as he looked inquisitively round the garden. In the end, unable to restrain himself, he flew down, the hens after him, and they all hastily rooted among the bushes. Cats also prowled in the garden, lying in wait in the burdock and stalking the sparrows.

I had spent about a fortnight in the town, but I could not

get used to the silence, the wooden pavements, the grass growing between the boards, the creaking steps of the stairs, the occasional hoot of a steamer by night.

It was an unusual town. The white night lasted almost through the summer. The quay and the streets were quiet and thoughtful. At night footsteps drummed on the pavement outside – those of the few workers coming off night shift. The steps and the laughter of lovers could be heard by anyone who woke in the night. It seemed as if the walls of the houses were sensitive to sound, and the town, silent and watchful, was listening to every step.

At night our garden smelled of currants and of dew. From the verandah came the gentle snores of the doctor, while on the river the engine of a motor launch throbbed and its hooter sang nasally 'Do-dooo' ...

One day, a newcomer appeared in the house. It happened like this.

Returning from his rounds, the doctor saw a blind dog. Half hidden among the logs, a piece of rope hanging from his neck, he sat shivering. The doctor had already seen him several times. Now he stopped, carefully looked him over, whistled, made noises, and finally picked up the rope and took the dog home.

At home, the doctor washed him in warm soapy water and fed him. As he ate, the dog by habit winced and kept his tail between his legs. He ate greedily, gulping and choking. His head and ears were covered with white scars.

'Now, off with you,' said the doctor, edging him off the verandah when the dog had finished.

The dog stood shivering and refused to budge.

'Hm ...' the doctor muttered, sitting down in his rocking chair. The evening wore on, the sky darkened without ever turning black. The brightest of the stars came out. The hunting dog lay down on the verandah and dozed off. He was so thin that his ribs showed and his spine and shoulder blades seemed to cut through his skin. Occasionally he half opened his sightless eyes, pricked his ears and moved his head, sniffing. Then again he laid his muzzle on his paws and closed his eyes.

The doctor looked at him, perplexed, fidgeting in his rocking chair, thinking of a name for the dog. What should he be called? Or was it better to get rid of him before it was too late? What did he want with a dog anyway? Thoughtfully, the doctor looked up. Low over the horizon, a star blazed with a bluish light.

'Arcturus,' muttered the doctor.

The dog twitched his ears and opened his eyes.

'Arcturus!' repeated the doctor, his heart thumping.

The dog raised his head and uncertainly wagged his tail.

'Arcturus! Come here, Arcturus!' the doctor called, now confidently, masterfully, joyfully.

The dog stood up, approached and gently nuzzled his master's knee. In this way, the never uttered name by which his mother had known him vanished from the blind dog's mind, to be replaced by the new name given him by man.

Dogs, like people, are of different kinds. There are pauper, beggar dogs; free, sullen tramp-dogs; silly, excitable, yapping dogs; cringing, cadging dogs that creep to anyone who whistles to them. There are wriggling, tail-wagging, slavishly ingratiating dogs that dash away squealing in panic, if anyone so much as threatens them.

I have seen devoted dogs; meek, wilful, proud, stoical, crawling, unfeeling, sly and stupid dogs. Arcturus was not like any of these. His feeling for his master was unusual and lofty. It was fervent and lyrical; he loved him perhaps more than life itself. But he kept his dignity and his reserve.

Sometimes his master was in a bad mood, sometimes he was indifferent, often he smelled nastily of eau-de-Cologne. But most of the time he was kind, and then Arcturus was overwhelmed by his love for him, his coat fluffed out and his body tingled; he wanted to jump up and dash along, choking with joyful barks – but he restrained himself. Ears flopping and tail motionless, his whole body relaxed and grew still – only his heart beat loud and fast. And when his master chuckled and played with him, tickling him, stroking him – how delightful it was! The sounds of his master's voice were now long, now short, gurgling, whispering; they were like the mutter of streams and the rustle of trees and yet they were like nothing else on earth. Every sound set off mysterious sparks and smells and ripples in his memory, as a raindrop sets the water quivering in a pool, and it seemed to Arcturus that he had lived through all this before, but very long ago, and he could not remember where or when. Probably he had felt the same happiness when, as a blind pup, he had sucked his mother's milk.

Soon I had the opportunity to get to know him better, and I learned much that was curious.

It seems to me now that he was somehow aware of his handicap. He was a fully grown dog with muscular legs, a black back and reddish-brown markings on the belly and muzzle. He was strong and big for his age, but in all his movements he betrayed uncertainty and strain. His muzzle, his whole body seemed to express an embarrassed perplexity. He knew perfectly well that every living being round him was freer and swifter than he. They ran quickly and surely, walked lightly and firmly, without stumbling or knocking into anything. The sound of their steps was different from his. He moved slowly, cautiously, edging his way along; he was always meeting obstacles; whereas hens, pigeons, cats and sparrows, dogs and people, and many other animals boldly ran up steps, leapt ditches, turned into side streets, flew away and disappeared into places of which he had not the slightest notion. Wariness and uncertainty were his lot in life. I never saw him walk or run freely, calmly, swiftly, except perhaps for a few moments along a wide road or a meadow, or on the verandah of our house ... At least, animals and people were familiar – I am sure that he identified himself with them in some way – but cars, tractors, motor-bicycles and bicycles were utterly incomprehensible and frightening. Steamers and launches at first greatly excited his curiosity. But as soon as he realized that he would never unravel their mystery, he ceased to pay them any attention. Nor did he ever show the slightest interest in aeroplanes.

But, if he could see nothing, his sense of smell was unrivalled by that of any other dog. Gradually he learned all the smells in town and became good at finding his way about. Never once did he get lost or fail to return home. Everything had a smell. There were countless smells and they all made themselves felt, they all advertised their presence. Each thing had its particular smell – nasty, neutral or pleasant. Arcturus had only to raise his head and sniff in the direction of the wind and he at once became aware of the rubbish dumps, the dust bins, houses, stone and wooden fences and sheds, people, horses and birds, as clearly as though he were seeing them.

On the bank of the river, behind the warehouse, there was a large grey stone which seemed almost to have grown into the ground and which Arcturus was particularly fond of sniffing at. The smell of the stone itself was of no interest but in the cracks and fissures the most unexpected and surprising smells lingered for a long time. They remained for days; sometimes weeks, and only a strong wind could blow them away. Each time Arcturus ran by this stone he turned aside and spent a while busily investigating it. He sniffed and got excited, went away and came back again to check up on some additional detail.

He could also hear the faintest sound, such as we could never hear. He would wake at night, open his eyes, prick his ears and listen. He heard every whisper for miles around – the singing of the mosquitoes, the buzzing from the wasps' nest in the attic, the fidgeting of a mouse in the garden and the stealthy movement of the cat on the roof of the shed. The house itself was not, for him, silent and lifeless as it is for us. The house too was alive: it creaked, whispered, cracked, shivered almost perceptibly from the cold. The dew trickled down the drainpipe, gathering at the bottom and falling drop by drop on to a flat stone. From far below came the faint swish of the river. The logs, floating downstream and trapped by the timber mill, rustled, rubbing together. Rowlocks squeaked faintly: someone was crossing the river. And somewhere, in a far away village, the cocks crowed in the yards. Here was life, mysterious and inaudible to us but familiar and understandable to him.

He had another peculiarity. Life had been cruel to him, but he would never come to you, whining and yelping, demanding your pity.

One evening, as it was beginning to get dark, I was walking along a road on the outskirts of the town. It was warm and still, with the warmth and stillness that belong only to calm evenings in summer. A long way down the road there was a cloud of dust and I heard the sounds of moo-ing and of long-drawn-out cries and whips cracking. They were driving the cattle from the meadows.

Suddenly I saw a dog running with a businesslike air towards the cattle, and I knew by its characteristic, strained, uncertain gait that it was Arcturus. He had never before gone beyond the limits of the town. 'Where is he going?' I wondered, at the same time noticing an unusual excitement among the cattle, which were now much closer.

Cows dislike dogs. Dogs remind them of wolves and their fear and hatred of them is congenital. Catching sight of the dark dog running towards them, those in front stopped dead. Immediately a massive yellow bull with a ring through his nose pushed forward. Straddling his legs and lowering his horns, he bellowed, his hide twitching and his eyes showing their blood-shot whites.

'Grishka!' someone shouted at the back of the herd. 'Run on in front, they've stopped!'

Arcturus, unsuspecting, trotted clumsily along the road and was now quite near the herd. Afraid of what might happen, I called him. His momentum took him forward a few more paces, then he pulled up sharply and turned. At that instant the bull snorted, rushed at him headlong and tossed him. Black against the sunset, the dog flew through the air and landed in the thick of the herd. His fall produced the effect of a shell-burst. The cows, snorting, dashed in all directions, their horns colliding noisily. Those behind continued to push forward; there was utter confusion, half hidden by rising pillars of dust. With tense and painful anxiety, I waited to hear Arcturus's dying yelp—but there was not a sound from him.

Meanwhile the herdsmen had come running, cracking their whips and shouting. The road was cleared and I saw Arcturus. He was lying in the dust and looked like a heap of dust himself, or like a bundle of old rags that someone had thrown away. Then he moved, got up and, staggering, limped to the side of the road. An old herdsman noticed him.

'Ugh, a dog!' Cursing, he swung his whip and brought it down with all his strength and skill on Arcturus's back. Arcturus did not squeal. He merely shuddered and briefly turned his sightless eyes towards the herdsman; reaching the ditch, he stumbled and fell in.

The bull stood across the road, pawing the ground and bellowing. The herdsman lashed out at him with the same strength and skill as at Arcturus and he quietened down. The cows also calmed down and the herd moved on, raising dust which smelled of milk and leaving cakes of dung on the road.

I went up to Arcturus. He was dirty, panting, his tongue hung out and I could see his ribs heaving. There were moist weals on his sides. One hind paw had been crushed and was twitching. I put my hand on his head and spoke to him, but he made no response. His whole being expressed pain, hurt and bewilderment. He could not understand why he had been trampled and whipped. In such cases, dogs usually whine. Arcturus was silent.

Yet Arcturus might have remained a house dog and perhaps run to fat and idleness, had it not been for a lucky event which gave a quality of heroism to his later life.

It happened like this. One morning I went into the forest to enjoy the last remaining glow of summer. Arcturus followed me. I drove him away several times. He would sit down at a distance, wait a while and again run after me. I was puzzled by his persistence but soon grew tired of chasing him and ceased to pay him any attention.

It was the forest that amazed Arcturus. In town he knew everything – the wooden pavements, the wide roadways, the planks along the edge of the river, the smooth paths. But here, on every side, he was assailed by unfamiliar things – tall grass, already coarse, prickly bushes, rotting stumps, fallen tree trunks, supple young firs, and dry leaves rustling on the ground. Here, everything caught at him, brushed him, jabbed him from every side, as though in a conspiracy to drive him from the forest. And the smells! The smells! The countless, unfamiliar, frightening smells – faint smells, strong smells, smells of which the meaning was unknown to him! And Arcturus, frightened and confused by all these scented, rustling, crackling, prickly things, kept close to my heels and shivered and snorted.

'There, there, poor Arcturus,' I spoke to him quietly. 'Poor dog! You don't even know that there is such a thing as sunshine, you don't know how green the trees and the bushes are in the morning light, or how the dew sparkles on the grass, or that all around us it's full of flowers – white ones, yellow ones, blue ones, red ones – or that clusters of rowan and sweetbriar berries show red among the grey firs and the yellowing leaves. If you could see the moon and the stars by night, perhaps you would enjoy howling at them. But you can't even tell that horses, dogs and cats are of different colours, or that fences can be brown or green or merely grey, or how brightly the windows flash in the sunset, or what seas of fire flood the river! If you were a normal, healthy dog, your master would be a hunter. Then, in the mornings, you'd hear the call of the hunting horn and voices shouting wildly, as no ordinary people ever shout. You would chase after prey, barking, spluttering, beside yourself, and by this furious chase after a hot scent you would serve your master – there would be no higher duty for you in life. Poor dog! Poor Arcturus!'

Talking soothingly to him, to calm his fears, I continued into the forest. Arcturus gradually recovered his confidence and began to investigate the bushes and stumps; the more he discovered that was new and unusual, the more delighted he was. Carried away by his own important affairs, he no longer kept close to me and only now and then stopped, listened, turning his white lifeless eyes towards me, wishing to assure himself that he was doing the right thing, that I was there behind him; then again he circled through the forest.

Soon we came to a clearing and walked on over moorland. Arcturus was seized with a tremendous excitement. Biting the grass, stumbling over hummocks, he flashed among the bushes, panting, charging, paying no more attention to me than to the sharp twigs. Finally, flinging aside all restraint, he screwed up his eyes, and, crashing through the branches, disappeared in a clump where I could hear him thrashing about and snorting. 'He's scented something,' I thought, stopping to wait for him.

'Woof!' his loud yet uncertain bark rang from the bushes. 'Woof, woof!'

'Arcturus!' I called anxiously.

But at that moment something happened – he yelped, howled and dashed noisily further into the undergrowth. His howling quickly changed to an excited yapping and, from the movement of the branches, I could see where he was forcing his way through. Fearing for his safety, I rushed to intercept him, calling loudly 'Arcturus! Arcturus!' But my shouts seemed only to add to his excitement. Gasping, stumbling, getting caught in the undergrowth, I ran across one clearing, then another, and down into a hollow – as I was coming out of it into an open piece of ground I saw him. Bolting out of the bushes, he hurtled straight at me. He was unrecognizable; his gait was comic, bounding, not like that of other dogs, but he was giving chase excitedly, full of confidence, ceaselessly barking, choking, straining, his voice going up into a thin puppyish whine.

'Arcturus!' I shouted.

He broke his pace and I had time to jump at him and grab him by the collar. He pulled away, snarled and almost snapped at me, his eyes bloodshot; it was only with the greatest difficulty that I managed to calm him and distract his attention. He was thoroughly tousled and scratched and his left ear drooped – he had obviously crashed into obstacles, not once but several times, but such were his passion and excitement that he never felt his injuries.

From that day his life took a different turn. Early in the morning he was off, alone, into the forest and disappeared for the day, sometimes for the night as well, coming back exhausted, battered, with bloodshot eyes. During this time he developed greatly; his chest broadened, his voice deepened, his pads grew hard and strong as steel springs.

How he managed to chase around on his own without knocking himself out, I could not imagine. I wondered if he felt that there was something lacking in his solitary hunting, if perhaps he felt the need of man's approval and encouragement, which are so essential to a normal hunting dog.

Not once did I see him return with his hunger satisfied. Of

course, being blind, he was slow, awkward and uncertain. To him the forest was a silent enemy. It whipped him, lashed his muzzle and his eyes, it struck at him from underfoot and brought him to a standstill. No, he never overtook his enemy. Never did he sink his teeth into its neck. His only reward was the scent itself, the wild, perpetually disturbing and enticing scent, intolerably beautiful and hostile – the one trail, among all the thousands of others, which lured him on and on.

And how, when he came to after his mad race and his magnificent dreams, did he find his way home? What sense of space and topography, what powerful instinct enabled him to make his way back when he found himself miles away in the depths of the forest, helpless, gasping, voiceless, alone with the whispering grass and the damp-smelling gullies?

Every hunting dog feels the need of man's approval. A dog hunts a wild animal and forgets everything else but, even in the moment of greatest excitement, it knows that somewhere there in front is its master, gripped by the same passion, following the same trail and that, when the time comes, it is his shot that will determine the issue. At such moments the master's voice adds to the excitement of the dog; the master too clambers through bushes, runs, grunts, shouts hoarsely, helping the dog to keep to the scent. And when all is over, the dog knows that the master will throw it the scraps and look at it with wild, intoxicated eyes and shout delightedly 'Good dog!' and pull its ears.

In this sense Arcturus was lonely and he suffered. Love for his master contended with his passion for hunting. I often watched him as he climbed from under the verandah, where he liked to sleep, ran about the garden and sat down under the doctor's window, waiting for him to wake up. He had always done this and if the doctor, waking up in a good mood, looked out of the window and called 'Arcturus!' – how that dog went on! Solemnly approaching close to the window, he raised his head, his throat quivering, and stood swaying, shifting his weight from foot to foot. Then he went into the house and a cheerful bustle started up, the doctor singing his arias and the two of them tramping from room to room.

Now too, Arcturus waited for the doctor to awake. But there was something that troubled him. He twitched nervously, shook himself, scratched, looked up, stood and sat down again and began to whimper. Then he ran about in front of the verandah, making ever wider circles; he again sat down, even giving a few short impatient barks, pricking his ears, tilting his head now to one side, now the other, listening for a long time. In the end he got up, stretched himself, yawned, made for the fence and resolutely squeezed through the gap. Soon after, I would see him far away in the field, trotting in his characteristically strained and uncertain way. He was off to the forest.

One day I was walking with my gun along the high bank of a narrow lake. The duck were unusually plump that year; there were plenty of them and in the marshes there were often snipe as well; the shooting was easy and enjoyable.

I picked a comfortable stump to sit on. A light breeze had risen; when it died down there came a moment of perfect, dreamlike silence; then I heard a strange sound. It was as though someone were pulling rhythmically on the rope of a silver bell, and the warm, mellow chimes carried throughout the forest – muffled by the fir trees, louder in the pines and communicating their solemnity to everything. Gradually the sounds grew more distinct and, concentrating, I realized that somewhere a dog was baying. The baying came from the far shore of the lake, from the depth of the pine woods; it was clear, though faint; sometimes it vanished altogether, then again persistently returned, nearer now and louder.

I sat on the stump, turning to glance at the yellow, thinning birches, and the crimson leaves of the aspen sharply visible a long way off against the grey moss. I listened to the silver baying and imagined that, listening with me, were the silent squirrels, the woodcock on the dry ridge near by, the huddled green fir trees, the lake below, and the quivering spider webs. There was something familiar about the beautiful, musical sound, and I suddenly knew that it was Arcturus's hunting cry.

It was the first time I had heard it. It echoed faintly against the pines, and this made it seem as though there were several dogs barking. Once it faltered and died away. The silence continued for many long minutes, and suddenly the forest seemed empty and dead. I could almost see the dog circling, blinking his white eyes, trusting only to his sense of smell. Or had he crashed into a tree? Was he lying, his chest shattered, too weak to get up, bleeding and in anguish?

But the baying started again, louder than ever, and now much nearer the lake. The lake was so placed that all the tracks and paths converged on it – not one went past it. I had seen many interesting sights by the lake. Now again, I prepared to wait. Soon a vixen streaked on to a small meadow, reddish-brown with sorrel. She was a dirty grey and had a thin, matted brush. She stopped, one foot raised, ears erect, listening to the approaching sound of barking. Then, unhurriedly crossing the meadow, she made for the verge of the forest, dived into a gully and disappeared in the scrub. Just then Arcturus too hurtled into the meadow. He was running a little off the trail, incessantly, wickedly giving voice and, as always, leaping high and awkwardly as he ran. Following the vixen, he jumped into the gully, thrust his way into the undergrowth, yelped, howled and fell silent as he stopped to extricate himself from some difficult place, then again gave that low, measured cry, which was like the ringing of a silver bell.

As in some strange scene from a play, the hound and its eternal enemy flashed across the stage and vanished, and once again I was alone with the silence only broken by the distant baying.

The fame of this unusual hunting dog spread quickly through the town and the entire neighbourhood. He was seen on the distant river Losva, in the fields beyond the wooded hills and on paths in the remotest parts of the forest. They spoke of him in the villages, on the quays and the ferries; the raftsmen and the workers from the sawmill argued about him over their glasses of beer.

Hunting men began to call on us. They disbelieved rumours on principle – they knew from their own experience how much faith to put in hunting stories. They looked Arcturus over, discussed his ears and his limbs, his tenacity, his speed and other matters of concern to sportsmen; they probed his shortcomings, and they tried hard to persuade the doctor to sell him. They would dearly have liked to feel his muscles, to have a look at his chest and his pads, but Arcturus sat at the doctor's feet with such a grim and guarded expression that no one dared to put a hand on him – while the doctor, getting red and angry, assured them for the tenth time that the dog was not for sale, it was high time everyone knew it. The hunting men went away disappointed, and others took their place.

One day when Arcturus, worn out by all the running he had done the day before, was lying under the verandah, an old man appeared in the garden. He had lost his left eye and the eyelid had closed over the socket; he had a wispy little Tatar beard and wore a crumpled fur hat with earflaps, and battered hunting boots. Seeing me, the old man blinked, pulled his hat off, scratched his head and looked up at the sky.

'Funny weather these days …' he said vaguely, grunted and fell silent. Guessing what he wanted, I asked:

'You've come about the dog?'

'That's just it!' he brightened up and put on his hat. 'Look at it like this. What's the doctor want with a dog? It's no use to him – but me, I need one. Soon it'll be the hunting season and all that … I've got a dog, see, but it's no good, it's a fool – can't follow a scent, can't give tongue. And just look at this one! A blind dog, imagine! God alone knows how he ferrets them out! By the holy cross, it's fit for a Tsar!'

He sighed, blew his nose and went off into the house. Five minutes later he re-appeared, very red and put out. He stopped beside me, grunted, took a long time lighting his pipe and scowled.

'Did he refuse?' I asked, knowing what the answer would be.

'He certainly did!' he exclaimed in a hurt voice. 'What d'you think of that? I've been hunting since I was a child – see that?' he pointed at his eye; 'that's how I lost it – and all my sons are hunters as well. We must have a dog, see? We need it for our work. But will he let me have it? ... 500 roubles I offered him – what d'you think of that for a price? – but no, nothing doing, he won't let me come near it! Yelled at me, nearly howled, can you imagine? ... It's I who ought to howl! The hunting coming on and no dog!'

He looked vacantly round at the garden and the fence, then suddenly a sly and knowing expression flashed over his face.

'Where d'you keep him, eh?' he asked casually, blinking his one eye.

'You're not thinking of stealing him, are you?' I asked.

The old man was embarrassed, took off his hat, wiped his face with its lining and gave me a searching look.

'God forgive me!' He laughed. 'Don't you put the idea into my head! Is that what you thought? Well, what does he want with a dog? Tell me that!'

He started for the gate but stopped and turned to me with a look of joy.

'That voice, that voice – eh? Understand what it means? As clear as a bell, I tell you.'

He came back close to me and whispered, winking and squinting at the windows of the house.

'You wait, that dog will be mine! What does he want with

a dog? He works with his brains, he doesn't shoot ... He'll sell me that dog, by the holy cross, he'll sell it to me. There's plenty of time before All Saints Day, we'll think of something. And you thought ... Never mind!'

The old man had no sooner gone than the doctor came hurrying out.

'What was he talking to you about?' he asked anxiously. 'What a disgusting old man! Did you see his eye? A real brigand! And how did he get to know about the dog?'

He rubbed his hands nervously, his neck flushed; a grey strand of hair fell over his forehead. Arcturus, hearing his voice, crept out from below the verandah and limped towards us.

'Arcturus!' said the doctor. 'You'd never betray me, Arcturus, would you?'

Arcturus closed his eyes and nuzzled the doctor's knee. Too weak to stand, he sat, nodding, almost asleep. The doctor looked at me happily, laughed and ruffled Arcturus's ears. What he didn't know was that from the very moment when the hunting dog first came with me into the forest, he had already betrayed him.

It would be fine if all beautiful stories had happy endings. And did not our hero, though only a hunting dog, deserve a long and happy life? No one is born without a purpose, and a hunting dog is born to hunt his prey – to hunt him for remaining wild for all time, instead of coming to man and befriending him, as did the first dog who befriended man. A blind dog, unlike a blind man, gets help from no one; he is alone in his darkness, helpless and doomed by nature itself, which is always ruthless towards the weak. If, in spite of this, he lives and passionately serves his predestined purpose, what can be better, loftier than this? But Arcturus was not to enjoy this fate for long ...

August was nearly over, the weather had deteriorated and

I was getting ready to leave, when Arcturus vanished. He had gone off to the forest in the morning and had not returned that evening or the next day or the day after that.

When a friend who lived with you, whom you saw day in, day out, and to whom you often paid little attention – when such a friend goes away for good, all you have left are memories.

I recalled the days I had spent with Arcturus, his diffidence, his confusion, his awkward, slightly crab-like gait, his bark, his habits, his endearing ways, his love for his master, his smell even, the smell of a clean, healthy dog ... I remembered all this and was sorry he had not been my dog; I wished I had been the one who had given him his name – the master he had loved and to whose house he had returned at night when he recovered from the chase so many miles away.

During these days the doctor lost weight, he looked worn and pinched. He had at once suspected the old man and we spent a long time searching him out until at last we found him. But he swore by everything sacred that he had not set eyes on the dog and volunteered to help us search for him.

The news of Arcturus's disappearance spread like wildfire all over the town. It turned out that many people knew him and were fond of him, and all were ready to help the doctor to look for him. All were busy listening to rumours and spreading them. Someone had seen a dog who looked like Arcturus, someone else had heard his baying in the forest ...

Children, whether patients of the doctor's or strangers, roamed about the forest, shouting, firing off guns, looking into every lodge, and coming back a dozen times a day to ask the doctor if his wonderful hunting dog had not come back, had not been found ...

I did not search for Arcturus. Somehow I could not believe that he had lost his way; his sense of smell was too good for that. And he was too devoted to his master to attach himself to some hunter. I felt sure that he was dead. But how had he died? Where? ... There were plenty of places where he could have met his end.

Within a few days, the doctor also realized this. He became listless, he no longer sang, and at night he was a long time getting to sleep. Without Arcturus, the house was empty and quiet, the cats had no one to fear and wandered freely about the garden, and the stone by the river had no one to sniff at it. Useless, it stuck out of the ground, dismal, blackening in the rain, its smells no longer interesting anyone.

The day I left, I had a long talk with the doctor. We tried not to speak of Arcturus. But the doctor mentioned that he was sorry he had not taken up hunting as a young man.

Two years later I happened to be in the neighbourhood and again stayed with the doctor. He was still living alone. There was no sound of claws on the floor, no sniffing, no tapping of a tail on the wicker furniture. The house was silent, and, as before, the rooms smelled of dust, medicines and old wall-paper.

But it was spring, so the impression created by the empty house was not oppressive. The buds were bursting in the garden and there was a din of sparrows; in the grove in the public park the rooks were settling in, making a great commotion; the doctor sang away at his arias in his falsetto voice. In the morning a blue haze hung over the town, the river had flooded its banks as far as the eye could see, and on the flood waters the swans rested at night and took off in the morning, everlastingly calling 'Clink-clank!' while bright launches signalled in their nasal voices and stubborn tugs hooted and hooted. It all looked cheerful.

The day after my arrival I went on an early spring shoot. The woods were full of a golden mist and of the dripping, gurgling, clinking of water. The snow had melted and the bare earth had a strong, sharp smell. There were many other smells as well – the smell of aspen bark, of rotting wood and of damp leaves – but all were killed by the strong, sharp smell of earth.

It was a beautiful evening, the sunset like a sea of fire and the snipe coming in thick flights. I brought down four but could scarcely find them in the dark layer of leaves. As the sky was fading and going green and the first stars were coming out, I started quietly for home along an unfrequented but familiar track, walking round the wide expanse of flood waters which reflected the sky, the bare birch trees and the stars.

As I walked along a low ridge beside one of these stretches of water, I noticed something white, and thought at first it was a last patch of snow, but, going nearer, saw the few scattered bones of a dog. My heart thumped; I looked closely and found the collar, its brass buckle turned green ... Yes, this was all that was left of Arcturus.

By the time darkness fell, I knew what had happened. There was a fir tree, not old but dead, which had a low branch. Like the whole tree, it had dried out, crumbled and broken until all that remained was a bare sharp stick. It was into this stick that Arcturus had run while pursuing a hot scent, forgetful of all but this trail which lured him on and on.

I went on in complete darkness to the verge of the forest, crossed a clearing, my feet squelching in the damp earth, and came out on to the highway, but all the time my thoughts went back to the small mound and the dry fir tree.

Hunters have a curious love of sonorous names. You find the strangest ones among their dogs – Diana and Anthea, Phoebus and Nero, Romulus and Venus ... But surely no dog has ever been so worthy of its resounding name, the name of an eternally undimmed blue star.

1957

Translated by Manya Harari and Andrew Thomson

Part Three
Some Themes

To select certain themes (or bundles of themes) as characteristic of modern Russian writing does not of course mean they dominate Soviet literature quantitatively, or even that other themes have any less significant role to play in it – indeed we have encountered a wide range of subject-matter already in earlier sections of this anthology. But those we have chosen for our final section do seem to us to represent, in their variegated Russian development, areas where Soviet literature of the past generation has made something of a special contribution to modern European literature as a whole – not spectacular, perhaps, but of lasting value; they are all themes that set up particular reverberations among Soviet readers and writers, and so bring us close to the heart of 'Russian writing today'.

1. Childhood, Upbringing, Experience

The 'growing-up story' is popular in the Soviet Union almost to the extent of a literary cliché; yet in the hands of writers as considerable as Vera Panova or Yury Nagibin it remains fresh, and carries the ring of conviction and insight. It would be easy to explain this popularity simply by pointing to the fact that the Soviet Union has undergone so many convulsions that any childhood is likely to have been to a greater or lesser extent dramatic; but more essential, from a literary point of view, is the long-standing tradition of intense interest in, and writing for, children (associated in an earlier generation with names such as Kornei Chukovsky and the dramatist Yevgeny Shvarts). Deep interest in the child's perception of the world was shown by such 'adult' writers as Zabolotsky, while Soviet children's literature was able to keep much of its integrity even in the worst Stalin years.

Fazil Iskander (born in Sukhumi on the Black Sea in 1929) was known for many years primarily as a poet but has lately turned more towards prose. He is one of several writers from other Soviet nationalities – e.g. Bulat Okudzhava, Chingiz Aytmatov – who have adopted the Russian language and extended its flexibility, bringing a new freshness and humour (like a breeze from the south) to modern Russian writing. This story was published in 1966.

Fazil Iskander

MY UNCLE WAS A LAW UNTO HIMSELF...

When the kids from our street used to start bragging about their famous relatives, I kept quiet; I let them really get it out of their systems.

People in the Services had top priority. But a child's imagination made distinctions even amongst them. First place went to the frontier-guards, second came the pilots, and third the Tank Corps; after them, all the rest. The Fire Service was outside the rules of the competition.

The war hadn't started then, and, as though to spite me, not a single one of my relatives was serving in the Forces. But I had my own special trump card, which I made use of pretty successfully.

'And I have an uncle who's a madman,' I would say calmly, for the moment pushing my playmates' over-realistic heroes into the background. Being mad, now that's something unusual, and more important still, unattainable. If you work hard, you can get to be a pilot, or a frontier-guard; at least, that's what the grown-ups went on asserting. They knew the rules of the game. But you can't become a lunatic even if you have Top Marks. Unless, of course, you really over-work yourself. But this couldn't possibly be a threat to us.

In short, you have to be born mad, or have a lucky fall in childhood, or get meningitis.

'But is he a real one?' one of the kids would ask, unbelievingly.

'Of course,' I said, expecting this question. 'He's got papers to prove it. He was examined by professors.'

There really were papers; they were kept in Aunt's Singer sewing machine.

'Then why isn't he in an asylum?'

'Grandma won't have him put away.'

'Aren't you afraid of him, at night?'

'No, we're used to him,' I would say calmly, like an official guide, expecting the next question. Sometimes I was asked silly ones, such as 'Does he bite?' but I paid no attention to them.

'But you're not mad, are you?' someone would be sure to put forward, looking at me penetratingly.

'May be I could be, if I tried,' I would say with modest dignity.

'I wonder who'd come out top ... Fran Gut or a madman?' someone would slip in, and at once dozens of interesting possibilities would suggest themselves. Fran Gut was a famous wrestler in Shapito's travelling circus. He was a negro; that's why we were all fans of his.

Uncle lived on the first floor of our house, with Aunt, Grandma and other relatives of ours. There were two versions current in our family, explaining his not quite normal condition. According to the first version, it happened in childhood, after an illness. This was an uninteresting, and therefore not very plausible version. According to the second, spread by Aunt, and which finally smothered Grandma's recollections, it appeared that he'd fallen off an Arab steed when he was a little boy.

For some reason or other Aunt didn't like his being called a madman.

'He's not a madman,' she used to say. 'He's mentally deranged.'

This sounded beautiful, but incomprehensible. Aunt liked to embellish reality, and she was partially successful. All the same, he was a real madman, even though he was nearly normal.

As a rule he didn't interfere with anyone. He used to sit on a little bench on the balcony, singing some song he'd made up himself. Mainly they were romantic songs without words.

Sometimes, it's true, something would suddenly come over him. He would remember some old offence, and begin to bang doors, and run up and down the long corridor on the first floor. At times like that it was better not to let him catch sight of you. Not that he would actually do anything undesirable, but all the same it was better to keep out of the way. If on such an occasion Grandma was at home, she would very quickly bring him to his senses. She would turn down the collar of his shirt, and with no more ado hold his head under the tap. After a good dose of cold water he'd grow calm again, and settle down for tea.

His vocabulary, like that of contemporary pop songwriters, was extremely condensed. If you shook out a twelve year old's exercise book onto the table, you'd have all the words that Uncle had managed to get by in life with. True, there were some expressions which you obviously wouldn't meet in a twelve year old's exercise book; you wouldn't even meet them in a real book. He used them, like a normal person, in moments of great emotional stress. Only one of them is printable: 'Blast your mother!'

His basic language was Abkhazian, but, when he swore, it was in two languages, Russian and Turkish. Evidently the swearwords had engraved themselves on his mind by reason of their searing intensity. From this you could deduce that Russians and Turks, in moments of rage, express themselves with approximately equal emotional power.

As with all lunatics (and some normal people) he was very strong. At home he did all the jobs that didn't need much intelligence. He emptied the slops, lugged in the fresh water before the days of mains water-supply, carried the shopping bags and chopped the wood. He worked conscientiously, even with inspiration. When a mighty stream of slops, pouring in a steep curve from the upstairs floor, sploshed deafeningly into the drainage pit, the stray cats rummaging in it flew up as if caught by the blast of an explosion.

Grandma was sorry for him, and thought he might strain himself working. Sometimes, when spring-cleaning time came, she would forcibly put him to bed and announce that he was ill. She would bandage his head or his cheek, and he would lie there bewildered and a bit embarrassed because of all the mystification. At last, bored with lying still, he would try to get up, but Grandma would push him back into bed again. To try to make him do any work at such times was impossible. He'd shrug his shoulders and say: 'Grandma won't let me!' He used to call Grandma 'Grandma', although she was his mother. That's how he was ... odd.

Uncle was astonishingly fussy about cleanliness. He was always being held up to us children as an example. Ever since then, whenever I meet a very fussily clean person I can't help thinking that he's not quite right in the head. Naturally I don't mention this to him, I just bear it in mind.

Anyway, Uncle was frightfully fussy about cleanliness. You hadn't to come near him when he was bringing in the fresh water or the shopping bags, or when he was sitting down to eat. And as to his hands, he'd be washing them every ten or fifteen minutes. He'd get scolded for this, because he made holes in the towels, but they couldn't break him of the habit. If anyone shook hands with him, he'd immediately rush to the wash-basin. The grown-ups used to amuse themselves by often shaking hands with him during the day. Some inner tact prevented Uncle Kolya from refusing to shake hands, although he knew he was being made fun of.

He loved sweet things more than anything in the world, and, of all sweet things, fruit-juice drinks were what he liked most. If we were sent with him to the market and we went past the fruit drinks stall, he would touch me with his hand, though he was not usually given to displays of affection, and point to the glass cylinders of fruit-juice syrup, saying shyly: 'Kolya wants a drink.'

It was very pleasant treating a grey-haired grown-up to a fruit juice; in comparison with him you felt like a man of the world, condescendingly kind about his childish weaknesses.

He loved having a shave too. True, this pleasure wasn't granted him all that often. About once a month. Sometimes he'd be sent off to the barber's, but more often Aunt would shave him herself.

He took being shaved very seriously. He would sit not stirring, nor wrinkling his face, while Aunt scrubbed his proudly raised, lathered head mercilessly. At moments like this, you could put out your tongue at him from behind Aunt's back, or shake your fist, and he'd pay not the slightest attention, abandoning himself to the dreamy intoxication of the barber's-shop atmosphere. And this, in spite of the fact that his beard and especially the hair on his head sprouted forth in thick curls, as though they were growing in the virgin lands, and desperately resisted the razor. Sometimes Aunt would ask me to hold onto one of his ears, or to spread out a bit of the skin on his neck. I agreed willingly of course, well aware of the unattainability of such a pleasure in ordinary circumstances. With somewhat exaggerated zeal I would hold on to his large, swarthy ear, turning it in the necessary direction, and examining the bumps of intelligence on his head.

Usually he was like a genial bee-keeper, with a curly beard, but after a shave he would change radically. His face would take on the fastidiously haughty look of a Roman senator in a history book about the ancient world. For the first days after a shave he became withdrawn, almost arrogant, then by degrees the Roman senator retreated into the depths of the beard, and the good natured, democratic, country bee-keeper re-emerged.

I wouldn't go so far as to say that he suffered from megalomania, but when passing the monument in the town square he would get slightly excited, and say, nodding to the monument, 'That's me!' He'd repeat the same thing when he saw the portrait of the person who was given pride of place in the daily or weekly papers. But, to be quite fair, it should be said that he'd identify himself with any man in the place of honour. As, in point of fact, it was almost always the same man who occupied this place, it could be taken, somehow or other, as being a hostile hint, a dangerous cast of thought, generally detrimental to all concerned. Grandma went on trying to break him of this habit, but she didn't get anywhere.

'No, no! You mustn't! The medical commissioners will come for you!' Grandma would say threateningly, prodding the portrait with her finger, and warding uncle off it, as though he was an unclean spirit.

'Me, me, me!' Uncle would answer joyfully, tapping the portrait with a tough finger-nail. He didn't understand a thing. I didn't understand anything either, and the qualms of the grown-ups seemed to me simply stupid.

And Uncle really was afraid of the medical commissioners. The fact was that every now and then the neighbours, from purely humanitarian motives, used to send in anonymous denunciations. Some of them implied that it was against the law for Uncle to live in our house, and that he ought to be in a lunatic asylum like all normal lunatics. Others said he worked night and day, and there ought to be a check that there wasn't some hidden exploitation of man by man going on here.

Round about once a year the medical commissioners appeared on the doorstep. While they were cautiously coming up the stairs, Aunt would manage to get him into a newly laundered shirt, push Grandma's prayer-beads into his hands and, in a threatening whisper, order him to sit still and not stir. Slightly unnerved by their rather unusual duties, the commissioners would apologize and put the necessary questions to Aunt, glancing at Uncle from time to time with discreet curiosity. Aunt would extract Uncle's documents from inside the Singer sewing machine.

'He's got a heart of pure gold,' she would say. 'And physical labour is good for him. That's what Doctor Zhdanov himself used to say. And what does he do, after all? He brings in a couple of buckets of water out of sheer boredom, that's all.'

While she was speaking, Uncle would sit at the table, rigidly clutching the prayer beads, and staring in front of him with an unblinking gaze, just like on an old family photograph.

Before leaving, one of the commissioners, beginning to feel more at home and more daring, would ask Uncle:

'Any complaints?'

Uncle would look questioningly at Grandma, and Grandma at Aunt.

'He's a bit hard of hearing,' Aunt would say, in such a way as to imply that this was his only failing.

'I said, have you any complaints?' the commissioner would repeat more loudly.

'Batum, Batum!' the words seeped reflectively through Uncle's closed teeth. He was beginning to get cross with the whole circus, because he only mentioned Batum in moments of extreme irritation.

'What sort of complaints can he have? He's joking!' Aunt would say, smiling charmingly, as she saw the commissioners to the door. 'He lives here like a lord,' she would add, in a voice growing firmer as she watched their retreating backs. 'If some of those Ethiopian hussies looked after their husbands as well as I look after my invalid, they wouldn't have time to invent all those Armenian jokes!'

This was a challenge to everyone in the courtyard, but they were hidden behind doors, in cowardly silence.

After the medical commissioners had gone, Uncle's Sunday-best shirt was removed, and to spite the neighbours Aunt sent him out to fetch water. Clanking the buckets, he would dash out joyfully, clearly preferring his ancient occupation of water-carrier to any sort of tricks for the sake of the public.

More than anything in the world Uncle disliked cats, dogs, children and drunks. I was probably partly responsible for his dislike of children, though I can't answer for the rest.

Over the years I had carefully studied his likes, dislikes and weaknesses. My favourite pastime was teasing him. Sometimes the jokes were cruel, and now I feel repentant, but what's done can't be undone. The only thing that consoles me is that I had quite a few knocks from him in return.

On damp winter days we would sit in the warm kitchen. Grandma would be busy at the stove, with Uncle sitting beside her on a little bench, and me on the couch reading some book or other. The fire crackles, the kettle whistles, the cat purrs. Finally, this peaceful, mad cosiness begins to pall. More and more often I put down my book and look at Uncle. And Uncle stares back at me with his green, Persian eyes. He looks at me, because he knows that sooner or later I'll be bound to play a trick on him. And, as he knows this, and is waiting for it, I can't resist.

The simplest way of upsetting his calm is to stare at him long and fixedly. Then he begins fidgeting on his chair, lowers his eyes and studies his big hands. But I know perfectly well what he's thinking. Then he lifts his eyes quickly, to see if I'm looking at him or not. I go on looking at him. I even adopt a quiet and relaxed pose. This is meant to suggest to him that I intend going on looking at him for a long time, that it presents no difficulties to me. This begins to worry him, and he says in an undertone: 'That little fool's teasing me!'

He doesn't like making a fuss before he has to. He's saying it just for me. It's as though he was rehearsing the complaint he'll be making later.

I go on staring hard. The poor old boy turns away, but not

for long. He wants to know if I'm still staring at him. Of course I am. Then he covers his eyes with his hands. But even that doesn't help. He has to know if I've left him in peace at last. Thinking that I don't notice, he spreads open his fingers a little and peeps through one of the cracks. I go on looking as though nothing has happened. Then the row starts.

'He keeps on staring at me! I'm going to kill him!' poor old Uncle shouts out, wicked fires sparkling in his eyes. I look down at my book immediately, then raise my head like one whose peaceful activities have been unexpectedly interrupted.

'What *is* it? Do I have to put his eyes out for you?' says Grandma, giving him a little biff on the head, and advising him not to look in my direction if the sight of me irritates him so.

But sometimes, driven to the point of rage by even more wicked tricks, he himself lashes out, seizing a log, or the poker, and then the frightening moment arrives. Especially if neither Grandma nor any strong-armed man is around. 'Please God,' I whisper, 'save me just this time, and I'll never tease him again. I'll always love You, and even pray to You with Grandma. Just save me this time, and You'll see!' But obviously I daren't rely too much on God, because I've let Him down each time. In spite of my fear, my mind works clearly and quickly. If Uncle hasn't already cut off my retreat to the door, I run. But if escape is impossible, the only salvation is to come up to him unexpectedly, and bow low, ready for punishment. 'Hit me!' It's a pretty terrifying moment, facing an armed lunatic, and one in a rage too!

But apparently this pitiful pose, this absolute submission to fate, disarms him. Some inherent nobility prevents him from hitting me. He cools off at once. He pushes me off with disgust and moves away, shrugging his shoulders, puzzled that people can be at the same time so insolent and so grovelling.

I once read a remarkable book, where a spy pretended to be a deaf-mute, but later was unmasked because he spoke German in his sleep. One of our counter-intelligence people fired over his head on purpose, but he didn't even jump. He was a strong personality. But when he was asleep he stopped being a strong personality, because he was asleep. And then he began talking German, and the boy unmasked him. Another boy heard him talking in his sleep too, but he couldn't unmask him, because he'd never worked properly at his German, and didn't realize which language it was. But that's not the main thing. The main thing was that the spy pretended to be a deaf-mute.

Suddenly an inspired thought struck me. It was obvious, Uncle wasn't mad at all! He was a real spy. The only thing that bothered me was the fact that Grandma remembered him from childhood. But I cleared this hurdle very quickly. They must have substituted someone for him, I reckoned. A mad Uncle there had been, but the spies had studied all his little habits and phrases, and then, one fine day, they kidnapped Uncle, and slipped a spy into his place. And he pretends to be fussy about cleanliness on purpose, so that no one will poison him.

I remembered that there was a lot that was suspicious in his behaviour. Sometimes he would scribble things on bits of paper with coloured pencils. He would hide these scraps of paper very carefully. Of course I used to snatch glances at them, but till now they seemed to me to be just the scribblings of an illiterate person. Fantastic, how he'd deceived us! And what about the fishing rods?

Uncle sometimes went fishing in the sea. There was nothing odd about that. Even normal people get enthusiastic about fishing. But the thing was, he had no hooks on his line. And all the time we'd been laughing at him! But maybe inside the rod there was a secret radio transmitter, broadcasting information to enemy submarines! My mind was all aglow. In my imagination, I was already reading banner headlines in *Pioneers' Pravda*. 'Young Pioneer Unmasks Spy! Children, Be Vigilant!'

This was followed by my portrait and the story, beginning with the words:

For some time past, Pioneer So and So (meaning me) had become pensive and sad. His unimaginative parents (meaning my parents) thought that he was sickening for something. In reality, he was considering how to unmask a seasoned spy who for some time had been passing himself off as a mad uncle. Such a step was not easy. But the Pioneer did not lose his head. It was a struggle of nerves.

And so on in the same vein, and even better.

The first thing to do was to steal the fishing-rod and test it. It lay under the bed in Uncle's room. He wouldn't let me get near the bed, all because of this put-on cleanliness mania. But I seized the opportunity when he was sent to fetch water, extracted the rod and line from under the bed, got a file, and began stealthily filing through the jointed lengths of bamboo in the kitchen garden. I filed through every section, but the rod turned out to be empty. I didn't despair at this, but fastened on the fact that the very first section at the bottom of the rod didn't have a proper natural partition; it was broken through, and you could shove in a finger. All was clear! He must be putting his transmitter in here, and then taking it out and hiding it. The crafty old devil! I buried the rod in the kitchen garden, and started thinking what to do next.

I'd have to hurry before he discovered that someone had pinched his rod. And then Aunt went off on some errand, Grandma came out into the yard to sit for a little in the cool, and I could go upstairs. As usual Uncle was sitting in the kitchen by the window, watching the passage to make sure that no stranger got into the house. I went into the kitchen and sat down opposite him at the table. The main thing, I decided, was resolution, and the element of surprise. He'd be thinking that I was going to start teasing him, while in fact ...

'Your career is ended, Lieutenant-Colonel Stauberg,' I said distinctly, and felt the goose-flesh creeping up my spine, like bubbles of soda-water rising to the surface. I don't know where

I got the idea that he was Lieutenant-Colonel Stauberg. Obviously I was relying on intuition, like many counter-spies of genius about whom I'd read, and amongst whom was Major Pronin himself.

'Stop it!' said Uncle by way of answer, in the pathetic voice he always used when he sensed that I was starting to tease and when he didn't want to get involved with me.

Not a tremor showed on his face. 'A man of iron,' I thought, shivering with excitement, and going on with what was prescribed for that particular moment.

'You've not played your part badly, but we've not been caught napping either,' I said, magnanimously paying tribute to my enemy's astuteness. The words formed themselves, precise and firm, giving me confidence in the justice of my case.

'The boy's mad!' said poor Uncle with the first signs of irritation. He always called me 'boy' as though I hadn't got a name of my own.

'Trying to wriggle out of it, the old rascal!' I thought, almost choking with the excitement of my inspiration, and deciding that the moment had come to slip in another hint.

'Fish not biting?' I asked, smiling perspicaciously and looking him straight in the eye. 'Sea's too rough, or the fishing rod's no good, what?'

'Fishing rod?' he repeated, something approaching a thought flickering in his dim eyes.

'That's it, the rod!' I said, realizing that I had got hold of the very link by means of which the whole chain could be unravelled without too much clanking.

'My rod!' he said again, beginning to tumble to what had happened.

'You've been hooked with your own line, Lieutenant-Colonel!' I said jokingly, leaning back in my chair and awaiting the next move.

'My fishing-rod, my fishing-rod! Blast your mother!' he muttered in great agitation, and, the light finally dawning, he plunged for the door.

'Don't move!' I screamed. 'The house is surrounded!'

'Batum!' he shouted and dashed into his bedroom.

I was a bit taken aback. Instead of his having given in with dignity, saying 'This time you outwitted me, Lieutenant ...' he had run to look for his fishing rod, as though that was of any importance.

After a minute he flew back into the room, and everything became a turmoil.

'He's stolen my rod!' he shouted in a fury, trying to grab me.

'A voluntary confession will mitigate your sentence,' I shouted in answer, running round the table, and throwing down chairs in his path, in the well-tried English secret-service manner.

'Thief! My fishing-rod! Blast your mother!' he screamed, getting excited by the scrimmage.

'Name your accomplices!' I screeched in answer, taking a short cut round the corner of the table. This was my salvation, because he didn't know how to put on the brakes, and shot past, just missing me. All the same, once or twice he managed to get in a slap at me across the table, or a jab with his fist as he pursued me.

I knew that wars of nerves could be appalling, but, when one person does the hitting and the other only does the evading the one who hits sooner or later wins.

In the end I jumped onto the couch and, kicking hard, yelled with all my might:

'Grandma!'

She was in fact already coming up the stairs. Apparently the din from our skirmish was audible down in the yard. On seeing her, the poor old boy threw himself at her and started justifying himself. Incidentally, he hardly ever succeeded in this. It's difficult enough for normal people to justify themselves, and no one ever wants to listen to someone like him.

'My fishing-rod, my fishing-rod!' he babbled, having lost the few words he did know in his agitation.

And suddenly I felt sorry for him, and I realized that he would never, ever be able to justify himself properly in life. And I really had smashed up his rod for him. But I lacked the courage to admit that it was I who was wholly responsible. And not only courage. I knew that in such circumstances the grown-ups were used to accepting him as guilty, and I guessed that it would be awkward for them to change their comfortable habits of thought and consider more complex possibilities.

I said that he had attacked me, but hadn't managed to hit me. It was a conciliatory way out, and, unfortunately, the most common one.

I didn't suspect him again of having connections with foreign agents.

And now, however much I've put it off, I have to tell the story of his great love, which, unfortunately, he couldn't keep hidden from those around him. He was in love with Aunt Faina. Everyone knew about it, and the grown-ups discussed his passion with relish, paying little heed to the fact that they were overheard by children who were not quite ready for such matters.

Even now I can't understand why he chose *her*, the grubbiest, most freckled and stupidest woman in our yard. I am far from maintaining that you would find a Shulamith or a Sofya Kovalevskaya amongst them. But nevertheless it was the ugliest and the stupidest that he chose. Maybe he felt the path between their spiritual worlds was the least tiring to tread.

Aunt Faina was a dressmaker. She did all the sewing for our yard. In actual fact she was only entrusted with the alterations of old things, with making children's shirts, shorts and other such trifles.

'Lovely frills and cuffs,' she would say, taking a customer's measurements busily, and pretending to be a real professional. It was obvious she sewed badly, and she was paid very little for her work, and sometimes nothing at all, if they promised to give her some new orders and pay then.

'Thank you, Faina, love, we'll settle later,' they'd say.

'You can't buy bread with thank-yous,' she would answer, with a sad little smile, and a suggestion of offence in her voice, as though she was hurt, not so much by the customers as by those who refused to sell bread for a thank-you.

In her free time, and sometimes while working, Aunt Faina would have a slanging match with her nearest neighbour, a single young woman of no fixed occupation. She was called Aunt Tamara. Sometimes, in the evenings, sailors would come and visit her. They sang wonderful, plaintive songs, with Aunt Tamara joining in. It used to sound lovely, but for some reason we weren't allowed to go in to her. The neighbours didn't like Aunt Tamara, but they were a little afraid of her.

'She fights like a man!' they used to say.

Aunt Faina and Aunt Tamara were always quarrelling. The fact was, they were both redheads. And redheads can never get on with each other, especially if they are close neighbours. They just can't endure one another.

'Here's the Redhead Brigade!' Aunt Tamara used to shout, standing by the washing line, all hung about with clothes-pegs like a bandolier.

'Redhead yourself!' Aunt Faina would answer, with absolute fairness.

'I'm not a redhead, I'm a honey-blonde,' Aunt Tamara would say with a little laugh.

'Sailors come visiting you!' Aunt Faina would go on, getting het up.

'I wonder who'd ever come visiting you!' Aunt Tamara would say acidly.

'I've got a husband!' Aunt Faina would assert. 'Everyone knows my husband, he's an honest man.'

'Oh, blow your husband!' Aunt Tamara would say, somehow making it sound offensive, and, having hung out her washing, she'd retreat to her room.

It was with this same Aunt Faina that poor old Uncle was in love. Now I realize that it was the longest-lasting and most disinterested love that I've ever come across in my life. This kind of holy blindness, which can give men wings or make them mad, was his from birth.

He didn't need anything from his loved one, only to be near her, gazing at her Crimean freckles, the colour of a fresh dab, and listening to her professional mourner's voice.

When she used to come to Aunt's to do some sewing, he would settle down next to her, and look at her with yearning eyes.

'Whatever does he love me so for?' she would say, if she was in a good mood.

Uncle couldn't get through a day without her. Next door to Aunt Faina's room was a little kitchen-cum-outhouse, really a small market booth, bought by her husband on the cheap. All day long she would potter about in this little kitchen, looking out into the yard from time to time, to see who was going where and if she could guess from the expressions on the neighbours' faces whether anything in short supply was on sale somewhere or other. Peering out, she looked somehow scared, as if frightened that while she was busy getting the dinner she might miss something vitally important, or that someone might simply do her in. That's how a bird looks, excitedly pecking at something, and then, suddenly remembering danger, it quickly lifts its head and has a cautious look round.

And so Uncle used to approach this little kitchen from the rear, bend down to the plywood partition and keep watch on her through the crack. He couldn't see anything except what was on the stove, but apparently that was all he needed. He could stand like this for hours, just watching, till she got exasperated, and shouted right across the yard to Aunt:

'Tell him I've got a husband! He's hanging around after me again!'

Aunt would chase him home, scolding him, really mostly for effect. Caught on the scene of the crime, the poor old boy would feel the shamefulness of his passion, and, walking alongside Aunt, would vaguely shrug his shoulders, as if to show that it was stronger than he was.

'Give him some fizz with a double tot of fruit-juice! That'll quieten him down,' advised Aunt Faina.

But apparently a double tot of fruit-juice was too poor a consolation. In an hour or two Uncle would run away from Grandma's watching eye and sneak back to the cherished corner.

In the evening, when Aunt Faina's husband came home from work, she used to tell him all about the day's trials and tribulations, not forgetting Uncle. Her husband, a squinting shoemaker, was a kind and peace-loving man.

'I like everything to be nice and calm. My wife doesn't bother anyone,' he used to say in a low voice, so that no one would take offence – but you could see that he was really trying to protect his wife. Then he would plug the crack constantly made by Uncle in the partition, or fill it up with putty.

The grown-ups often talked about this strange love. Apparently for many of them it was in itself sign enough of abnormality.

They talked in his presence, thinking he understood nothing. But I'm certain he guessed what it was all about. At such moments I noticed an expression of suffering and shame in his eyes, the faintest quivering of his lips, and an involuntary protesting gesture of the hand. As if he wanted to say: 'Leave off! Aren't you ashamed of yourselves?'

He loved her to the end of his days, never once winning the least sign of affection from his cruel sweetheart.

Uncle died soon after Grandma. He missed her very much and kept on asking where she had gone, although she died in his presence. He soon forgot her death, but remembered her alive, because, living, she had surrounded his madness with human warmth and love. After all, mothers do love their helpless offspring more devotedly – they need that protective love more than the others do.

Afterwards Aunt said that just before his death Uncle regained his sanity, as if fate decided at the last moment to show him what it was like to be normal. This would have been doubly cruel, because such a brief flash of insight would only have lasted long enough to make him realize the inhumanity of going from one void to another.

But I think it was only Aunt's imagination. She liked everything to be beautiful, and so she had to do a lot of exaggerating.

I regret now that I never managed to do anything kind for him while he was alive. Apart from offering him the occasional fruit drink, or going with him to the public baths. He loved washing himself. In the public baths he didn't look any different from the others; he was simply shyer, trying to cover his nakedness with a sort of biblical gesture of the hand.

I remember one lovely sunny day. A road along the cliff top. We are on our way to a village about twelve kilometres from the town. Grandma, Uncle and me. In front goes Uncle, and we can hardly keep up with him. He is all hung round with little parcels, his hands clutching suitcases, a samovar on his back. It is early summer. The foliage is still free of dust, and as yet the sun does not scorch, and a little bouncing sea-wind comes to meet us, cooling us, bringing with it the sweet novelty of being on the road. Grandma, smoking a small cigar, taps along with her stick, and in front goes Uncle, the samovar on his back, gleaming in the sun. He sings his endless songs, because he's happy and he feels the living freshness of the summer day, and the enchantment of this little journey.

So life didn't deprive even him of happy moments. After all, he used to sing, and his singing was simple and joyous, like the singing of birds.

1962

Translated by Felicity Ashbee and Irina Tidmarsh

Yury Nagibin (b. 1920) has been publishing since 1940, but gained real popularity only with the Thaw. A short-story writer with some affinities to Platonov and Kazakov, he writes with particular sensitivity on the growth of personality in children and simple people.

Yury Nagibin

THE ECHO

Sinyegorya, the seashore, empty in the early afternoon, a girl emerging from the sea ... It was nearly thirty years ago now!

I was looking for pebbles on the deserted beach. It had been stormy the night before: the waves, hissing, had crept right up the beach as far as the seafront sanatorium. Now the sea had calmed down and withdrawn to its usual limits, leaving bare a broad, chocolate-coloured expanse of sand, shot with blue, that was cordoned off from the land by a little rampart of shingle. This sand, moist and so firm that one's footprints left no mark, was strewn with sugar-lump pebbles, greenish-blue stones, smooth round fragments of glass that looked like sucked fruit-drops, dead crabs, rotting seaweed which gave off a pungent smell of iodine. I knew that big waves throw up some beautiful pebbles on the seashore and step by step I was patiently inspecting the sandflats and the pebbles just washed onto the beach.

'Hey, why've you sat on my shorts?' piped a thin voice.

I raised my eyes. Above me stood a naked little girl, so thin that her ribs showed, and with slender arms and legs. Her long wet hair clung round her face, the water glistened on her pale and scarcely sunburnt body which was bluish and goose-pimpled with cold.

The girl bent down, pulled her yellow and blue checked shorts from under me, shook them and banged them on the stones, then flopped down prone on a sloping patch of golden sand and started to scrape it up along her sides.

'Oughtn't you to get dressed ...?' I muttered.

'Why? It's better for sunbathing like this,' replied the girl.

'Don't you feel ashamed?'

'Mummy says it doesn't count if you're little. She says I shouldn't bathe in my trunks: they get cold afterwards. And she hasn't got time to be bothering about me ...'

Amid the dark, rough pebbles something gave a sudden faint flash, like a tiny, pure teardrop. I took a cigarette packet out of my shirtfront and added it to my collection.

'Oh, do show me ...'

The little girl pushed her wet hair behind her ears, revealing a thin, freckled face, green cats' eyes, a snub nose and an enormous mouth that stretched to her ears, and she began to examine my stones.

On a thin layer of cotton wool there were: a small, pink, translucent oval cornelian and another cornelian, larger but not polished by the sea and therefore shapeless and dull in colour; a few little pebbles with a figured porcelain-like coating; two rather odd fossils – one in the shape of a starfish, the other with the impression of a baby crab; a small circular stone disc and – the pride of my collection – a smoky topaz like a wisp of mist dissolved in dark glass.

'Did you collect them today?'

'Today? All the time I've been here!'

'Haven't got many, have you?'

'You try!'

'Oh thanks!' She shrugged one thin, peeling shoulder. 'Crawl around all day in this heat looking for horrid old stones!'

'You're a silly ass!' I said. 'A silly little ass with no clothes on!'

'Silly ass yourself . . . I suppose you collect stamps too?'

'Well, I do ... what of it?' I replied, challengingly.

'And cigarette packets?'

'I did when I was small.'

'What else do you collect?'

'Well, I used to have a butterfly collection ...'

I thought this would please her and I somehow wanted her to like it.

'Pooh, how disgusting!' She drew back her upper lip, showing two sharp white front teeth. 'Did you squash their little heads and pin them on pieces of cardboard?'

'Not at all, I put them to sleep with ether.'

'It's still disgusting ... I can't bear people killing things.'

'D'you know what else I used to collect?' I said, after a little thought. 'All the different makes of bicycles.'

'You didn't!'

'I did. I used to run round the streets asking all the cyclists "What make of bike's that, guv'nor?" And they'd say Dux or maybe Latvella or Opel. Like that I collected all the makes, the only one I didn't get was a Royal Enfield ...' I spoke quickly, afraid that the little girl would make some sarcastic interruption, but she looked seriously interested and even stopped trickling sand out of her fist. 'Every day I used to run to Lyubyanka Square, once I was nearly run over by a tram, but I still couldn't find a Royal Enfield! You know, it has a mauve badge with a big English "R" on it ...'

'And you never ...' said the girl and gave a laugh with her big mouth. 'I'll tell you a secret: I collect something too ...'

'What?'

'Echoes ... I've collected a lot. There are echoes that sound like glass, some like a brass trumpet, some with three different sounds in them and there are ... oh, there are millions ...'

'Fibber!' I interrupted angrily.

The green cats' eyes seemed to bore into me.

'Want me to show you?'

'All right ...'

'I'll only show you, nobody else. Will they let you? We'll have to climb up on the Big Saddle.'

''Course they'll let me!'

'All right, we'll go tomorrow morning. Where are you staying?'

'On the promenade.'

'We're staying at Mrs Tarakanikha's.'

'I think I've seen your mother. Is she tall, with black hair?'

'Uh-huh. Only I never see my mummy.'

'Why not?'

'Mummy likes going dancing.' The girl shook her hair, which had now dried out and looked somehow greyish. 'Come on, let's have a last bathe.' She jumped up, sand all over her, and ran down to the sea, her narrow heels flashing.

The morning was sunny and windless, but it was not hot. After the storm the sea was still exhaling cold and preventing the sun from heating the air. Whenever a ragged cloud floated like cigarette smoke across the sun and robbed the gravel paths, white walls and tiled roofs of their blinding southern glare, the horizon darkened as if heralding a long spell of bad weather and the cold onshore breeze at once increased.

The path leading to the Big Saddle began by winding past some low hillocks, then straightened out and climbed sharply upwards through a dense, aromatic forest of walnut trees. It was cut by a shallow, pebble-strewn gully – the bed of one of three violent torrents which cascade down from the mountains after rain, roaring and gurgling loud enough to be heard all around, but which dry up before the raindrops have dried on the walnut leaves.

We had covered a good deal of the way when I decided to find out my girl-friend's name.

'Hey!' I shouted at the blue and yellow shorts as they bobbed through the walnut grove. 'What's your name?'

The girl stopped and I caught up with her. The undergrowth thinned at that point and opened out to show a view of the bay and our village – a wretched little huddle of cottages. The vast, menacing sea spread out its waters to the horizon and beyond it hazy, dull-blue shapes piled up one on top of another into the sky. But in the bay the sea pretended to be small and tame, playing a game of drawing a white thread along the edge of the shore, biting it off and then stretching it out again ...

'I don't really know how to tell you,' said the little girl thoughtfully. 'I've got such a silly name – Viktorina. But everybody calls me Vitka.'

'They could call you Vicky.'

'Pooh, horrid! Somebody I know has a mouse called Vicky. I can't bear mice.'

'All right, Vitka it is then. My name's Seryozha. Is it far to go still?'

'Worn out? Once we pass the forester's hut you'll be able to see the Big Saddle.'

But there was still a long way to thread through the walnut grove with its tangy, honey smell. Eventually the path joined a stony track, gleaming white with sand as fine as icing sugar, that led us to a broad, gently sloping hill-side ledge. There in a thicket of apricot trees nestled the forester's hut, the walls coated with plaster made of crushed seashells.

Hardly had we reached the little hut than the silence was shattered by a furious barking. Rattling their chains, which were fastened to a long wire, two huge, shaggy, dirty-white dogs rushed out at us leaping into the air. Strangled by their collars they could do nothing but stick out their pink tongues, wheeze and slobber at the ground.

'Don't be afraid, they can't reach us,' said Vitka calmly.

Half a pace away from us the dogs gnashed their teeth. I could see the mange on the backs of their necks, the ticks on their muzzles swollen to the size of beans, their eyes sunk behind a shaggy fringe. Strangely, no one came out of the hut to call off the dogs. But however hard the dogs strained and pulled at the wire they could not reach us. As soon as I was certain of this I felt wildly elated. Our march was leading us to cliffs and grottoes peopled by mysterious voices and it would not have been complete without some fearsome guardian dragons barring the bold adventurers' way to the secret. And here were the dragons, these overgrown, eyeless, red-mawed dogs!

Once again we set off through the walnut trees along a path that narrowed to a thread. Here the grove was not so thick as below; many of the bushes had withered and the leaves of others had been chewed down to a cobweb by a species of tiny black glistening beetle.

I was tired and annoyed with Vitka – she was striding heedlessly on with her thin legs, straight as sticks except for her slightly bandy knees. But suddenly the wood cleared ahead; I saw a slope overgrown with short brown grass; in the distance a grey cliff reared skywards.

'The Devil's Finger!' Vitka shouted over her shoulder.

The nearer we got to it the higher rose this great rocky spike – it seemed to grow more quickly than we could approach it. By the time we reached its dark, chill shadow it had become monstrously big. It was much more than a devil's finger now; it was a devil's tower, grim, enigmatic, unapproachable. As if answering my thoughts, Vitka said: 'You know, lots of people have tried to climb it but none of them has ever succeeded. Some fell off and were killed, others broke their arms and legs. But one Frenchman climbed to the top.'

'How did he do it?'

'I don't know how, but he did ... He couldn't get down again, though. He went mad up there and then he died of hunger ... All the same he was brave,' she added thoughtfully.

We walked right up to the face of the Devil's Finger, and lowering her voice Vitka said: 'It's here ...' She took a few steps back and shouted, not very loudly: 'Seryozha!'

'Seryozha ...' a mocking, insinuating voice repeated in my very ear. It sounded as though it came from within the depths of the Devil's Finger.

I shuddered and took an involuntary step back from the cliff and the sound floated clearly back at me from the sea: 'Seryozha!'

I froze. From somewhere up above came a bitter, agonized groan: 'Seryozha!'

'What the devil!' I muttered in a strained voice.

'What the devil!' rustled in my ear.

'Devil!' groaned from the sea.

'Devil!' resounded from above.

Each one of these unseen mockers had a definite and rather sinister character: the whispering one was demure yet somehow maliciously ingratiating, the voice from the sea belonged to a man with a grim sense of humour, whilst up above lay hidden an inconsolable but hypocritical mourner.

'Well, what are you waiting for? Shout something!' said Vitka.

And before she had even finished the whisper crept into my ear: 'Well, what are you waiting for?' and clearly, sarcastically: 'Shout!' – and then as though between sobs: '... something ...'

Pulling myself together with difficulty, I shouted: 'Sinyegorya!'

And heard the three-voiced response.

I shouted, spoke and whispered many more words. The echo had extremely sharp ears. Some of the words I spoke so softly that I could hardly hear them myself, but the echo cast them back every time. I was no longer exactly frightened, but every time that invisible man whispered in my ear my spine went cold and the sobbing voice made my heart contract.

'Good-bye!' said Vitka and moved away from the Devil's Finger.

I strode off after her, but the whisper caught me up, rustling its venomous, insinuating word of farewell, the distant sea gave its grim laugh and from above the voice groaned:

'Good-bye!'

We walked towards the sea and soon found ourselves on a rocky outcrop hanging over a precipice. To right and left rose up mountainous spurs whilst below us yawned the abyss. To look down it gave you a feeling of drowning. If the Devil's Finger had crashed through the earth, it would have left behind it just such a vast, fearful hole as this. Down at the bottom was a jumble of sharp rocks like giant's teeth, battered by the dark, inky sea. A bird, its motionless wings spread as though paralysed, was slowly dropping, circling, into the chasm.

There was a feeling here of something unfinished, as if the terrible forces which had wrenched the gigantic stone finger from the bowels of the earth had not yet regained their equilibrium after having gouged this monstrous well out of the living rock, strewn its bottom with sharp chips of stone and made the sea lacerate its gentle tongue on them. The whole rocky mass above and below was precarious, unstable from hidden inner stresses liable to break it all up again ... At the time, of course, I was unable to define that nagging sense of unease which gripped me on the precipice of the Big Saddle ...

Vitka lay down on her stomach at the very rim of the chasm and beckoned to me. As I spread myself beside her on the firm, warm, smooth stone, the sucking, chilling attraction of the abyss vanished and it became quite easy to look down. Vitka leaned over the edge and shouted:

'Oho-ho!'

A moment of silence and then a deep, roaring voice boomed back:

'O-ho-ho-o!'

Despite its strength and deepness there was nothing fearful in this voice. Obviously the cleft was inhabited by a good giant who wished us no harm.

Vitka asked: 'Who was the first woman, do you believe?' And the giant, after a moment's reflection, replied with a laugh: 'Eve!'

'And do you know,' said Vitka gazing downwards, 'no one has ever been able to climb down from the Big Saddle to the sea. One old chap got halfway down and stuck there ...'

'And died of hunger?' I inquired sarcastically.

'No, they threw him a rope and pulled him up ... I think you could get all the way down, though.'

'Let's try!'

'Yes, let's!' was Vitka's immediate and enthusiastic reply and I realized that she meant it seriously.

'Some other time,' I joked lamely.

'All right, come on then ... Good-bye!' Vitka shouted into the chasm and jumped to her feet.

''Bye!' guffawed the giant.

I wanted to go on talking to him, but Vitka dragged me away.

The next echo, in Vitka's words 'as clear as glass', lived in a gorge as narrow as a knife-blade. This echo had a thin, piercing voice. It reduced even a word uttered in a deep bass to a squeak. And there was something even nastier about it: this echo did not stop once it had piped its answer but went on squeaking away for a long time somewhere within its crannies.

We did not stay for long at this crevice and went on. We now had to clamber up a steep slope, parts of which were covered in coarse brown grass and thorns, parts bare and slippery-smooth. At last we reached a ledge strewn with enormous blocks of stone. Each block looked like something – a boat, a tank, a bull, the Head which Ruslan killed in the fairy-tale, a fallen knight in armour, a coastal gun with a broken barrel, a camel, the mouth of a roaring lion, even the broken-up parts of a giant's body – a nose with a wart, the shell of an ear, a bearded jaw, a mighty fist forever clenched, a bare foot, a forehead with a few curly locks above it ... all these petrified creatures, parts of creatures, objects clothed in stone, instantly threw back any word spoken among them as if it was a ball, and reflected every sound sharply and precisely. This was the home of the 'copycat' echo.

But most amazing of all was the echo about which Vitka had told me nothing. We did not walk to it but crawled down a steep slope, clutching at projecting stones, moss and dried bushes. Pebbles showered down under our hands and feet, drawing bigger stones after them and making a continuous rattling noise behind us. When I glanced round I was amazed at the insignificance of the drop which had made our heads spin at the top. From where we were the sea was no longer a smooth sheet: limitless, vast, it merged into the sky, forming with it a single sphere – a dome that reigned over the whole vast panorama. And the Devil's Finger, emphasizing our height, had now dwindled to a little spike.

Vitka stopped at a dark, semi-circular opening that led deep into the cliff-side. I looked in and when my eyes had grown slightly used to the dark I saw a vaulted cave hung, beard-like, with stalactites. The walls shimmered green, red and blue, the cave smelled as musty as a crypt and I involuntarily stepped back.

'Hullo!' Vitka shouted, sticking her head into the cave.

And as if empty barrels were clashing beneath that vault there rang out a deep 'Boom!' Rattling round the corners of the cave, it finally popped out into the open as a low groan, just as if the mountain itself had breathed out.

I looked at Vitka with respectful amazement. Thin, freckled, with her matted greyish hair, sharp teeth at the corners of her lips, with her shining green eyes, she seemed to me at that moment to be as much of a fairy-tale being as the secret world into which she had led me.

'Go on, shout!' Vitka ordered.

I bent down and groaned into the mountain's little black

mouth. And again there came the booming and muttering and an unearthly cold breath puffed at my face. A terrible sense of loneliness suddenly gripped me, loneliness and defencelessness amidst this stony world of cliffs and precipices inhabited by strange wild voices.

'Let's go,' I said to Vitka, betraying my unease. 'Let's get out of here!'

I remember the rest of the way as one long descent. Again we passed by the petrified cemetery, the Devil's Finger, the scraggy, withered walnut trees, the dogs tugging at their chains and snorting with asphyxia, then the other, thicker walnut grove. Our way down stopped at the dry gully which circled the uphill side of the village ...

'Well, was it interesting?' asked Vitka as we reached our street.

I felt myself back in the serene, everyday world and Vitka was no longer the magic ruler of the mountain spirits. Simply a toothy, bony, ugly little girl. And I had played the coward in front of her!

'It was interesting all right ...' I drawled. 'But you can hardly call it a collection, can you?'

'I suppose you'd prefer one you can keep in a matchbox in your shirt?'

'No, I didn't mean that ... just that an echo works for everybody, not just for you.'

Vitka gave me a long, curious look. 'Well, what if it does? I don't care!' she said with a toss of her hair and walked home.

Vitka and I became friends. Together we climbed Temryuk-Kaya and Svadebnaya, where we found a little grotto with an echo that quacked. But Temryuk-Kaya, with all its spurs, great buttresses and sharp thrusting peak turned out to be no good at all ...

We were hardly ever apart. I grew used to Vitka bathing

naked. She was just a chum and I never saw her as a girl. I vaguely understood the reason for her lack of modesty: Vitka considered herself hopelessly ugly. I have never met anybody who so simply, openly and with such plain dignity admitted their own ugliness. Once when she was telling me about a schoolfriend, Vitka happened to say:

'She's almost as ugly as I am ...'

One day we were bathing not far from the fishermen's jetty when a gang of boys straggled down from the high shore. I knew them slightly, but my shy attempts to make friends with them had come to nothing. This was not the first year that these boys had come to Sinyegorya on holiday; they regarded themselves as old inhabitants and would not allow strangers into their gang. Their ringleader was a tall, tough boy called Igor.

I had come out of the water and was standing on the beach drying myself, but Vitka was still frisking about in the sea. She would watch for a wave then jump high and sail through the crest on her stomach. Her little buttocks glistened.

The boys answered casually when I hailed them and were going to pass on when one of them, wearing a red singlet, noticed Vitka:

'Hey, fellows, look – that little girl's got nothing on!'

Then it started – shouts, whistles, howls. To give Vitka her due she paid no attention to the boys' behaviour, but that only threw oil on the flames. The boy in the red singlet proposed standing the girl on her head. The suggestion was greeted with delight and the boy in the red singlet waddled off towards the water. At this Vitka bent down with the agility of a little animal, fumbled for something in the water and when she stood up again she was holding a heavy stone.

'Just you come in the water ...' she said, baring her sharp little teeth, 'and I'll bash your face in!'

The boy stopped and tried the water with his foot. 'It's

cold,' he said, and his ears turned redder than his singlet. 'I don't think I feel like going in ...'

Igor approached and sat down on the sand at the water's edge. The boy in the red singlet understood his leader without being told and lay down beside him. The rest of the gang followed their example. They formed a chain to cut Vitka off from the beach, her clothes and her towel.

Vitka tried their patience for a long time. First she swam far out to sea, came back, dived, wallowed about in the water, then sat on an underwater rock pushing waves over herself with her hands. But at last the cold was too much for her.

'Seryozha!' Vitka shouted. 'Give me my shorts!'

All this time without noticing it I had been drying myself. I had been rubbing my skin so hard that it was burning as though I had been scalded, but I went on and on towelling as though I was trying to rub a hole in myself. In the miserable and shameful confusion which had overcome me I was aware of only one very definite desire – not to get involved in Vitka's humiliation ...

'Seryozha, give your little lady her shorts,' squealed the boy in the red singlet in a put-on falsetto.

Turning on his elbow Igor threatened me: 'Just you try!'

His warning was unnecessary: nothing would have made me move from the spot. Vitka realized that she could expect no help from me. Squirming miserably and covering her narrow little loins with her hand, purple and goose-pimpled with cold, her face twisted, she crawled out of the water and sidled up to her shorts while the boys laughed and whistled. What in her innocence she had always disregarded now appeared to her as something disgusting, humiliating, shameful.

Hopping on one leg and fumbling unsuccessfully to put her other foot through the leg of her shorts she somehow managed to dress, grabbed her towel from the sand and ran off. Suddenly she turned round and screamed at me:

'Coward! Coward! Dirty coward!'

Of all possible words Vitka chose the worst, the most insulting and unfair. Surely she must have realized that it wasn't Igor's fists that I was afraid of? But obviously she wanted to leave me feeling ashamed in front of the boys.

I don't know whether it was just a whim of the ringleader in not wanting to follow the herd, or whether Igor really was intrigued by something about Vitka. Whatever it was he suddenly asked me in a friendly and confiding voice:

'Listen, what's the matter with her – is she crazy?'

'Of course she's crazy!' I surrendered totally to such kindness.

'Then why do you go around with her?'

Without any intention of whitewashing Vitka but simply wanting an excuse for my behaviour I said:

'It's interesting with her. She collects echoes.'

'What?' said Igor, astonished.

In a sickening burst of grateful frankness I told him all Vitka's secrets.

'Well I'm blowed!' said Igor in excitement. 'I've been coming here for three years and I've never heard anything like it.'

'You're not making it up, are you?' queried the boy in the red singlet.

'Want me to show you?'

'Yes – the lot,' said Igor in his bossy voice, acting the leader again. 'You're going to take us there tomorrow.'

It started raining early the next morning. The mountains were covered with bluish-white clouds like soap-suds and the low rumble of the swollen rivers and streams was mixed with the grim roar of the sea, which had turned the same kind of brown as the mountain grass.

But Igor's gang was not to be put off. We started up the now familiar little path, only this time it was cut by a muddy yellow stream pouring down the gully. The walnut grove no longer smelt honey-sweet with a tinge of bitterness but stank of rotting leaves – the reek of wet earth soaked in decomposing matter that gives off an acid, vinegary stench. Walking was difficult as our feet slithered on the wet earth and slipped on the stones ...

At the forester's hut we were met by the usual furious barking from the watchdogs, but in the damp air their barking sounded softer and more muffled and even the dogs themselves seemed less frightening in their wet, matted coats. We could see their eyes, looking like black olives.

Then came the diseased, beetle-ridden walnut thicket. The wind and the rain had stripped off much of its scraggy foliage, and the sullen expanse of the sea was visible through its bare, sad branches.

It was a long time until the Devil's Finger, swathed in clouds, came in sight. Then its peak loomed up, black and unassailably high, and disappeared again. Again its shaft bared itself to its full height only to vanish a moment later in the swirling mist. It was strange – the wind was blowing hard offshore and yet clouds as light as breath on a cold day were simultaneously floating inshore. They slithered along the very ground, covering us with damp vapour, and then suddenly evaporated, settling as dew on the slopes.

At last the Devil's Finger emerged again from the froth of clouds and barred our way.

'All right, let's see your marvellous tricks,' said Igor without a smile.

'Listen!' I announced solemnly, feeling the familiar chilling of my spine. I cupped my hands into a megaphone and shouted 'Oho-ho!'

The only answer was silence. No eerie, insinuating whisper, no guffaw in response from the sea, no moan from above.

'Oho-ho!' I shouted again, stepping closer to the Devil's Finger, and all the boys separately repeated my call.

The Devil's Finger was silent. We shouted again and again –

without the slightest echo in reply. Then I rushed to the chasm, the boys after me, and roared at the top of my voice into the swirling depths. But the giant would not answer either. In embarrassment I tore back from the cliff-edge to the Devil's Finger, from the Devil's Finger to the cleft in the rock-face, back to the chasm and back again to the Devil's Finger. But the mountains would not speak ...

Miserably I tried to persuade the boys to climb up to the cave – we'd be bound to hear the echo there! They stood in front of me as silent and stern as the mountains, then Igor unclenched his lips to say a single word:

'Cheat!'

And swinging round he stalked away, taking his whole gang after him.

I stumbled along behind them, vainly trying to understand what had happened. For the moment I did not mind about the boys' contempt, if only I could unravel the mystery of my failure. Was it that the mountains only answered Vitka's voice? But when she and I had been up there together they had obediently echoed me too. Could it be that she really did possess the key which enabled her to unlock those voices from their rocky caves?

Sad days followed. I had lost Vitka and even my mother blamed me. When I told her the mysterious story of the echo, she measured me with a long, unfriendly, penetrating look and said sadly:

'It's very simple – the mountains only answer people who are decent and honest ...'

What she said revealed a lot to me, but not the riddle of the mountain echo.

It kept on raining and the sea seemed to be divided into two parts: in the bay it was a muddy yellow from the sand carried down by the rivers and streams, whilst out in the open water it glittered in pristine brilliance. The wind howled unceasingly. By day it flung the rain about in grey sheets; at night, always clear with tiny white stars, the wind was dry and bleak, because it always took on some black form – twisting whirlwinds, swaying branches and treetrunks, coal-black shadows careering across the starlit earth.

Occasionally I caught a glimpse of Vitka. She went down to the beach in all weathers and managed to acquire a rich chocolate tan from the rare, meagre spells of sunshine. Every day now, out of boredom and loneliness, I went with my mother to the market where they sold the local produce – vegetables, apricots, goats' milk, yogurt. Once I came across Vitka in the market. She was alone, a plaited basket hanging on her arm. I watched her walking round the stallholders' stands in her blue and yellow shorts, firmly picking out the tomatoes, slapping a lump of meat on to the scales, and I was painfully aware that I had lost a good friend.

On the first sunny morning I was loafing about the garden, picking up the slightly rotten windfall apricots, when someone called me. At the gate stood a girl in a white blouse with a blue sailor's collar and a blue skirt. It was Vitka, but I did not recognize her for a moment. Her greyish hair was combed smooth and tied at the back in a ribbon, on her sunburnt neck was a string of coral beads, buckskin slippers on her feet. I rushed over to her.

'We're leaving,' said Vitka.

'Why?'

'Mummy's bored here ... Look: I want to leave you my collection. It's no use to me, anyway, and you can show it to the boys and make it up with them.'

'I won't show it to anyone!' I exclaimed hotly.

'Please yourself, it's yours to keep. Did you ever guess why it wouldn't work for you?'

'How did you know it didn't work?'

'I heard ... Did you find out why?'

'No.'

'Well you see the most important thing is *where* you shout from.' Vitka lowered her voice confidentially. 'At the Devil's Finger you've got to shout from the seaward side. And I bet you shouted from the other side – there's no echo there. At the chasm you've got to hang over the edge and shout straight at the cliffside. Remember how I made you bend your head down? In the cleft you shout right down at the bottom to make your voice carry further. And the cave always echoes however you shout, but you didn't go there. And by the stones too ...'

'Vitka . . .!' I began penitently.

She pulled a face.

'I've got to run, or I'll miss the bus ...'

'Shall we see each other in Moscow?'

Vitka shook her head.

'We're from Kharkov ...'

'But won't you come back here again?'

'I don't know ... Well, so long.' Vitka laid her head on her shoulder in embarrassment and ran off.

My mother was standing at the gate and followed Vitka with a long, intent look.

'Who's that?' she asked, oddly cheerful.

'That's Vitka, she stays at Tarakanikha's.'

'What a charming creature!' said my mother in a deep voice.

'She's not, she's just Vitka!'

'I'm not deaf ...' Mother glanced again in the direction that Vitka had gone. 'Oh, what a delightful little girl! That snub nose, ash-blond hair, those remarkable eyes, slim feet, delicate hands ...'

'Oh mother, do shut up!' I exclaimed, annoyed by her curious state of blindness: she seemed to be somehow insulting Vitka. 'Did you see her mouth, though!'

'A beautiful big mouth! You know absolutely nothing about these things!'

Mother went indoors. For a few seconds I watched her go, then tore off to the bus station.

The bus was still there. The last passengers, laden with bags and suitcases, were storming the doors. I immediately caught sight of Vitka, sitting on the side of the bus where none of the windows had been opened. Beside her sat a fat dark-haired woman in a red dress, her mother.

Vitka saw me too and grabbed the handle of the window-frame to open it. Her mother spoke to her and touched her shoulder, probably trying to make Vitka sit down. With a sharp gesture Vitka pushed her hand away.

The bus started with a roar and slowly began to roll across the unpaved road, throwing up behind it a trail of golden dust. I walked alongside. Biting her lip, Vitka dragged at the handle and the window dropped open with a bang. I found it easier to think of Vitka as beautiful when she was out of sight: her sharp little front teeth and the dark freckles spattered all over her face spoilt the convincing image created by my mother.

'Listen, Vitka,' I began quickly, 'mother says you're pretty. You have lovely hair, lovely eyes, mouth, nose ...' The bus picked up speed; I started to run. 'And your arms and legs too, it's true, Vitka!'

Vitka just smiled with her big mouth, joyfully, trustingly, devotedly, putting all her sweet soul into that big smile, and then I saw with my own eyes that Vitka truly was the prettiest little girl in the world.

Swaying heavily, the bus started to cross the wooden bridge across the stream – the boundary of Sinyegorya. I stopped. The bridge groaned and trembled, but the front wheels of the bus had already reached firm ground. Through the window again appeared Vitka's head, her ash-coloured hair blown by the wind, and her sharp little sunburnt elbow. Vitka waved to me and threw a silver coin across the stream. The flash of its flight went out in the dust at my feet. It was a local superstition: if you threw down a coin there, you would be sure to come back sometime ...

I longed for the day of our departure to come. Then I would drop a coin too, and Vitka and I would meet again.

But it was not to be. When we left Sinyegorya a month later, I forgot to throw down my coin.

1960

Translated by Michael Glenny

A classic Soviet 'growing-up' poem, which also had considerable political impact as a seminal work of Thaw literature when it appeared in a journal in 1956, is Yevtushenko's account of his return to the town of Zima where he had spent his childhood: in a series of varied encounters the poet reflects the turbulent state of Russia in the years following Stalin's death. It could be argued that this poem remains Yevtushenko's best achievement: its looser, narrative texture suits his discursive style, and as in all his best work the public theme grows naturally out of strongly felt personal experience. Our extracts are taken from the opening and closing parts of the poem.

Yevgeny Yevtushenko

From ZIMA JUNCTION

As we get older we get honester,
that's something.
And these objective changes correspond
like a language to me and my mutations.
If the way I see you now is not the way
in which we saw you once, if in you
what I see now is new
it was by self-discovery I found it.
I realize that my twenty years might be
less than mature: but for a reassessment:
what I said and ought not to have said,
and ought to have said and was silent.

My life has often been by backward glances,
few personal emotions, thoughts or wishes,
and in my life, its even turns and courses,
some generous impulse but nothing finished.
Yet always here these means for a new design,
new strength, touching the same ground
where you first moved bare-footed, kicking up dust.
I rely often on this ordinary thought:
near Lake Baikal my own town waiting for me.

And the wish to see the pines again,
mute witnesses of time and its distance,
of my great-grandfather and of the others
in exile here after a peasant's rising. ...

*

So years went past, one after the other.
I grew up in the small town
acquiring an affection for the forest
and landscape and the quiet houses.
I grew up
          and at hide-and-seek
uncatchable whatever guard you kept
we peered out from the barn through bullet-holes.
There was war at that time;
Hitler not far from Moscow.
                                        And we
– we were children and accepted a lot lightly.

From classroom threats untroubled and forgetful
we tore away out of the school playground
and ran down through fields to the river,
broke open a money-box and ran away
to look for the green stick,
baited our wet hooks.
I used to go fishing, stuck paper kites,
or often wandering by myself bare-headed
sucked at clover, grass polished my sandals,
I knew the black acres the yellow hives
the luminous clouds that dropped still lightly stirring
half out of sight behind the immense horizon,
and skirting around outhouses used to listen
for the neighing of their horses, peacefully
and tiredly fell asleep in old hayricks
long darkened by the rain.

I scarcely had one single care in the world,
my life, presenting no big obstacles,
seemed to have few or simple complications –
life solved itself without my contributions.
I had no doubts about harmonious answers
which could and would be given to every question.

But suddenly this felt necessity
of answering these questions for myself.
So I shall go on where I started from,
sudden complexity, self-generated,
disturbed by which I started on this journey.

Into my native forest among those
long-trodden roads I took this complication
to take stock of that old simplicity,
– like bride and groom, a country matchmaking.
So there stood youth and there childhood together,
trying to look into each other's eyes
and each offending, but not equally.
Each wanted the other to start talking.
Childhood spoke first, 'Hullo then.
It's your fault if I hardly recognized you.
Once when I often used to dream about you
I thought you'd be quite different from this.
I'll tell you honestly, you worry me.
You're still in very heavy debt to me.'
So youth asked if childhood would help,
and childhood smiled and promised it would help.
They said good-bye, and, walking attentively,
watching the passers-by and the houses,
I stepped happily, uneasily out
through Zima Junction, that important town.

I worked things out about it in advance
– and just in case – with these alternatives,
if it hadn't got any better then it wouldn't
have got any worse.
Somehow the Corn Exchange had got smaller,
so had the chemist shop, so had the park;
it was as if the whole world were smaller
than it was when I left it.
And it was hard at first among other things

to see the streets hadn't all got shorter,
but I was walking with a longer pace
ranging the town.
Once I lived here as if the place were a flat,
could find whatever I wanted in three seconds,
cupboard or bed, could move here in the dark.
Maybe the circumstances had altered,
– and mine had been too long an absence,
but now I bumped on everything I used
to avoid, now knocked against it awkwardly,
and unfamiliarly they caught my eye:
the tall fence with the obscene inscription,
the drunk slumped against the café wall,
the women quarrelling in the shopping queue.
All right if this were any old place,
but this was here, and where I was born,
where I came home for strength and for courage,
for the truth and truth's well-being.
There was a driver cursing the Town Council,
two cocks were fighting under somebody's laughter
and drowsy audience the big burdocks
listened dustily, never moving an ear.
The wooden legs of beggars banged on cobbles,
a small boy with a stick was chasing a cat ...
And purposely at first I didn't go
by the directest way, but then later
I started hurrying.
And this was necessary too.
To have drenched my face in freshness,
as I got near to home, near to the gates,
turning the iron ring.
At once from the very first expostulations,
'He's here!' 'Zhenka!' 'Come and eat something!'
from the first embraces, kisses and reproaches,
'And couldn't you have sent us a telegram?'

from, 'We were just lighting the samovar'
from recollections, 'how many years is it?'
just as I thought, all indecision vanished,
and things became peaceful and full of light.
And anxious Aunt Eliza put forward
the strong proposal I should have a wash
since she knew what those trains were like, she said.
Already tureens and kitchen-implements,
already the table dragged to the living room,
and passing among the grey-blue onion shoots
I went off for water from the well,
waking the well with a cossack song –
the well kept the smells of my childhood,
the bucket came up bumping on the sides,
the chain was wet and sparkled in the light.
So I from Moscow, I the important guest,
hair damped down, clean-shirted,
sat in a crowd of radiant relations,
centre of questions, glasses, scurryings.
I'd got too weak for the great Siberian dishes
and now despaired at the sight of their abundance.
My aunt said, 'Have another bit of gherkin.
What do they feed you on in Moscow then?
You're eating nothing at all. It isn't decent!
Here, take a dumpling. Have some aubergine.'
My uncle said, 'I expect that Moscow vodka's
what you've got used to; try some of this.
Go on, go on – I do say all the same
it isn't good for you, not at your age.
Who taught you that? Look, down in one gulp!
Well, cheers, and God grant it won't be the last.'

We drank and joked and chattered excitedly,
until my sister suddenly thought to ask me
was I at the Hall of Columns in March,

and everyone grew suddenly serious.
They spoke of the year and the year's gravity,
the events and worries and the long reflections.
Uncle Volodya pushed away his glass.
'Nowadays,' he said, 'we all behave
as if we were a sort of philosopher.
It's the times that we live in. People are thinking.
Where, what, how – the answers don't come running.
Now the doctors have turned out innocent;
well, why should people suffer in that way?
It's an international scandal, of course it is,
and all that bloody Beria, I suppose.'
Speaking, not capable of rhetoric,
of what stirred up the emotions in those days:
'You live in Moscow; things are clearer there:
tell me about it all, explain it to me.'
He took me by the buttons so to speak
and wouldn't be put off by anybody;
he made himself a home-rolled cigarette
and waited for an answer.
                                        And I think
that I was right, my uncle all attention
as if the truth and I were personal friends,
to answer peacefully, 'I'll tell you later.'...

*

...
It dawned.
                    Everything seemed younger.
Night dissolved away to nothingness,
it got a little colder for some reason,
masses took on their authentic colour.
Some rain blew down, not enough to notice,
and he and I wandered along together.
Somewhere else, driving around,
Pankratov, complacent in his jeep,

the ponderous didactic president;
and happy with his stick of birchwood
walking among the dew's heavy sprinkle
the sly boy: stubborn, with bare feet.
Nothing exceptional. Not cold; not hot.
It was a day like any other one
but such a crowd of pigeons in the air;
I was someone good, young, going away.
I felt sad and clean
and sad perhaps because
of having learnt something
and not yet knowing what.
I drank some vodka to my friends
and strolled through Zima Junction one more time.
It was a day like any other one:
the trees their brilliant shivering foliation
luminous green against the ground.
A few boys throwing rubbish at a wall,
a queue of lorries stretching, women at market
among the cows and different sorts of fruit.
And sad and free on and on
I passed the last house, climbed into the sun,
and for a long time stood on the hill-top
looking across at the station buildings
and farmhouses and barns.
And the voice of Zima Junction spoke to me
and this is what it said.
'I live quietly and crack nuts.
I gently steam with engines.
But not without reflection on these times,
these modern times, my loving meditation.
Don't worry. Yours is no unique condition,
your type of search and conflict and construction,
don't worry if you have no answer ready
to the lasting question.

Hold out, meditate, listen.
Explore. Explore. Travel the world over.
Count happiness connatural to the mind
more than truth is, and yet
no happiness to exist without it.
Walk with a cold pride
utterly ahead
wild attentive eyes
head flicked by the rain-wet
green needles of the pine,
eyelashes that shine
with tears and with thunders.
Love people.
Love entertains its own discrimination.
Have me in mind, I shall be watching.
You can return to me.
Now go.'
I went, and I am still going.

1956
Translated by Robin Milner-Gulland and Peter Levi

Boris Balter (1919–74) grew up in the south of Russia, and is one of the several Soviet writers who have brought a fresh 'tang of the sea' into modern literature. He became widely popular in the early 1960s for his somewhat nostalgic and lyrical stories; the short novel *Good-bye Boys* has appeared in English.

Boris Balter

DISCOVERY

I was drinking mineral water. Three yards away stood a small boy, licking an ice-cream from all sides. There was thoughtlessness for you. When he spent his money on an ice-cream he didn't think he would want a drink. Now he did want a drink; that was why he was looking at me, carefully working his tongue.

I pointed to a glass and nodded to him. He was unconvinced, or maybe didn't understand, anyway he popped the last of the ice-cream into his mouth.

'Want a drink?' I asked.

He nodded.

'Can you drink two glasses?'

He nodded again.

'Or three?'

'Get on Mister, what do I want three for? I can't drink three. Give me some cherry juice Missis,' he said. The woman behind the counter was already pouring orange juice into a glass.

'You'll have orange. It won't do you any harm,' she said.

'That's it. Have some orange and wash it down with cherry,' I urged.

Good deeds ennoble mankind; the people around smiled and nobody jumped the queue. The little boy drank and looked at me over his glass. Pressed under his arm were fishing-rods, and a bucket containing pied gobies hung from his bent elbow.

That boy won't forget the mineral water and he won't forget me, I know from experience. He will certainly remember those two glasses when he thinks back to his childhood, as everyone does. I couldn't help passing my hand over his bare back and feeling his hot skin and the thin bones of his spine with my palm.

I strolled along the sea-front. It's surprisingly simple to make a person happy, even with only eight copecks. Nobody could make *me* happy any longer, not with all the money in the world. That was the sad difference between the boy and myself. I looked at the harbour tightly choked with vessels and listened to the early evening hum of the sea-front as I discovered this truth.

I had lived a week already in this big seaport. What had I been doing there? Discovering truths. But what had brought me to this town was a journalistic assignment on the theme 'Cement – the bread of builders' and a desire to avoid the sympathy of my friends.

Even on the trams people hurry for places. While I was searching for my place in life. A strange occupation for a man well past forty. But what could I do, having already lost one place in the historic transition from war to peace? Not long before the war I had been persuaded that the army needed me and that I should make my life's career a military one. It might indeed have been a life's career. But I wasn't killed in the war. And after the war more officers were left than the army needed in peace-time. It was suggested I should exercise my own judgement and choose a new life's career. From the individual's point of view I was unjustly done by. But what does the individual signify compared with the interests of the State? I wrote two stories. Things went well for my heroes. Knocked off their perches by the sharp turns of history, they easily got to their feet again, with my assistance. I wasn't any better off for this. I behaved like a man with something to say but for whom the time had not yet come to say it. Others lived like that too. But I decided not to live that way any longer.

In childhood a brilliant future had been forecast for me. The future had long since become the past, and I hadn't noticed the process.

To look at I had always given the impression of a very successful man, completely self-confident and at ease. I saw I gave the same impression even now, on the sea-front. Anyway, women eyed me with some interest, and I irritated men. Foreign sailors wandered along the front. They were noticeable in the crowd not only by their uniforms but also by a certain apartness.

Two *druzhinniki* came towards me. There were a lot of *druzhinniki* standing about and sauntering along the front. Just like any other boys. I had seen their like in factories and on beaches, in town parks and restaurants. But their red armbands somehow subtly changed them. It was at once obvious that these boys in their red arm-bands were performing Civic Duties.

In my time I had been very fond of medals. I had worn 'Prepared for Labour and Defence of the Soviet Union' and 'Voroshilov Marksman', 'Prepared for First Aid in Defence' and 'International Organization for Aid to Champions of Revolution'. To get each of them you had to achieve certain standards. The medals were awarded with pomp at ceremonies and meetings. I had particularly liked the 'Voroshilov Marksman' medal because it looked like an order. All my shirts had holes from medals. The medals had exalted me in my own eyes. I and the medals had been inseparable, I merged with them.

Beside the sea-wall, opposite a restaurant entrance, stood a Negro sailor. He wore a white beret with a blue pompon. When the *druzhinniki* walked past him, he drew himself up, placed his hand to his head and guffawed. Like all Negroes he had dazzlingly white teeth.

Someone touched my arm. A girl stood half-turned away from me and, not looking at me, said:

'Take me into the restaurant.'

'Are you talking to me?'

'Yes ...'

Now she looked at me and gave the ghost of a smile.

'Leave me in my far-off place. I am constant, innocent,' I said. I didn't think the girl would know Blok.

'Don't worry,' she said. 'I won't pester you. They won't let me into the restaurant by myself, and I'm hungry. Just take me in. I won't even sit with you.'

'Thank you,' I said. 'Come on.'

We went past two *druzhinniki* standing in front of the restaurant entrance. In the doorway the girl looked back and waved to someone.

She kept her word. I sat alone at my table. The Negro followed us into the room and the girl went off with him. They sat in a corner. The Negro guffawed. He nodded to me, guffawed again, clasped his hands together and shook them. The girl also looked at me, with very bright, very beautiful and very impudent eyes. But perhaps that was only how it seemed to me because I felt offended; perhaps her eyes were not impudent but simply bold.

The room looked like a tavern with its low ceiling and walls decorated in a variety of colours. On the low, semi-basement windows, however, hung tulle curtains, and an enormous reproduction of Ayvazovsky's picture 'The Ninth Wave' gleamed down from the wall. The room was full of tobacco smoke and the hum of speech in many languages. I remembered the New Songs tavern back in the twenties with the owner at the bar and the tarts sitting brazenly on the knees of fishermen and sailors. On the demand of the town *komsomoltsy* the tavern had been closed and the tarts were rounded up from all the ports and sent off in goods-wagons to distant building projects. I was political leader of such a wagon, and when I climbed up to the girls, they showered me with obscenities, of which 'eunuch' was the mildest. But I sat down beside them on the planks and told them how beautiful they all were and what a splendid life lay ahead of them. I was eighteen then and that was my first serious komsomol job.

A man came up to my table. The bleached vest under his crumpled and excessively wide-shouldered pea-jacket revealed a prominent collar-bone. He sat down, saw some cigarettes on the table and took one. Then he wandered off among the tables again, closely scrutinizing the clientele, and I already knew that he would choose my table. Not because I was sitting alone, but for the same reason the girl had turned to me. And even before he said 'Can you treat me? Long-distance helmsman – years ago of course,' I was resigned to listening to a long seaman's yarn the whole evening.

I looked at him and smiled. He held a cigarette and matches in his hand and looked at me. He despised me, my prosperous appearance, and didn't even try to hide it.

'Stingy? You're still earning,' he said.

'I'm working out how much I can spend.'

He lit his cigarette unhurriedly. Then he said:

'Nonsense. Only 200 grammes. Been getting drunk quickly lately.'

I didn't have to call the waitress – she was already standing by the table looking at the helmsman. It seemed to me he purposely took no notice of her.

'Another 200 grammes,' I said.

'You're not to give him more than 100 grammes.'

The waitress went away and the helmsman said:

'Jilted sweetheart – can't forgive me.'

My fears proved groundless. He was not going to tell me a story. He sat absorbed and silent. A band was playing on the stage; a heavily painted woman blew moaning tones from a saxophone, and veins swelled with tension on her exhausted neck. The waitress returned bringing some plain herring besides the vodka. She poured a glass for the helmsman herself.

'We've got some crab already,' I said.

'It's all right, don't worry – the herring's not on the bill.' The waitress was stout and no longer young. She was flat-footed and had a homely appearance. The helmsman sat absorbed and silent until she went away. He drank slowly, upper lip slightly raised, revealing his teeth. His head was small and active, his neck wrinkled like a tortoise's. Wrinkled rather from spareness than from age. He placed his half-empty glass on the table and immediately refilled it.

'Taganrog's a terribly difficult mooring,' he said, and gazed a long time at his glass before raising it. I realized he was drunk. He had already been drunk when he sat down at my table. Various fragmented memories arose in his head, but he couldn't connect them into a single whole.

The Negro and the girl were dancing between the tables. Her face touched his chest, and her high-raised hands lay on his shoulders. When they turned about the girl's face could be seen round his broad back.

'I hate racists,' the helmsman ground his teeth. 'In Havana I had a black woman fond of me.'

The girl heard him and gave a slight smile.

'That'll do, old man – you don't have to,' I said.

He withdrew his hand from the neck of the carafe, only to grip it again tightly in his fingers.

'What's to be done? The years go by, and we're still no happier.'

His gaze was wholly conscious and sober. He got up and walked along the aisle without saying good-bye and without looking at me. I no longer existed as far as he was concerned. Too bad. I felt like shouting 'All men are brothers.' But two *druzhinniki* appeared at the doorway and I didn't.

The restaurant was packed with foreign sailors. The Negro and the girl were dancing near my table. The sailors exchanged loud words; what they meant I didn't know and couldn't guess.

I don't know what people look like when they're making

great discoveries. Archimedes is said to have discovered his law in the bath. But I sat under Ayvazovsky's picture with my elbows propped carelessly on the back of a chair. As I sat there I discovered a truth: the fewer the misfits the better off the State. All my life the good of the State had been my prime concern. I simply couldn't allow myself to be a failure. There was just one small thing. I had to grasp the nature of the discrepancy between my past and my present.

The girl lazily moved her feet. Her cheek lay on the Negro's chest. She was looking in my direction; I was certain her eyes didn't see me. I sat beneath a raging sea, my elbows propped nonchalantly on the back of a chair, and no doubt I looked, as always, completely at ease and completely successful.

1962
Translated by Antony Wood

As a coda to this section we give a short poem by Yevgeny Vinokurov (b. 1925), whose compact, precise and formally traditional work has been held in considerable esteem by the writers of the new generation.

Yevgeny Vinokurov

A man walked alone in the world.
Raised his collar, drew the flap across.
At a corner, stooped,
Lit up,
        back to the wind.

He went into a park. Greenish pond.
Mooring line in freshly painted boats.
Whistling, he snapped off a twig,
Banged it, for some reason, against his leg.

On the plank stage, he spat into the water,
Lazily, without malice.
Nothing had happened; it was just
He saw in a flash that
                              life had passed him by.

1962
Translated by Daniel Weissbort

2 Art and Heritage

Theorizing about the purpose and proper nature of art has been something of a national Russian vice in the last couple of centuries; but at least it has been carried on more in the realm of practical experience than of abstract aesthetics. The early years of the Soviet Union were particularly fertile in vigorous but generally constructive debate linked closely with literary practice. For a decade and a half the Soviet government declined to come down positively in favour of any one aesthetic policy, while reserving its right to do so; when in the 1930s it finally did so, this narrowed the permissible area of such debate but did not obliterate it. The 'Socialist Realist method' (note that it is not considered a 'theory', still less a 'style') was promulgated as official policy for the newly founded Writers' Union in 1934; it implies general adherence to Communist Party positions, and an avoidance of 'formalistic' experimentation or 'art-for-art's-sake' hermeticism, but in itself is hardly the restrictive force in Soviet literary life that it is generally reckoned to be in the West (rigorous if rather unpredictable State censorship is another matter). In the post-Stalin era discussion of the social function of literature, its possible varieties and evolutionary potential, has been energetically resumed – not on a very exalted aesthetic level, but immediately and involvingly. The Soviet Union, usually for better if sometimes for worse, is a country where literature matters (and the virtual absence of any equivalent to a 'colour-supplement culture' gives so-called 'serious literature' a role of high importance in the entire educated population*).

Closely bound up with the problem of the nature of art and its purpose are considerations of the Russian national (and supra-national) artistic heritage. The violent nature of the ostensible break between an old culture and a new, Soviet culture was bound to bring about, if not a full-scale nostalgic reaction, at least a sensitive re-examination of the extent to which revolutionary iconoclasm might lead not to the heightened cultural level envisaged by early Bolsheviks such as Lunacharsky, but to a new philistinism. (A clearcut example is the destruction associated with anti-religious campaigns of the mid-1930s and early 1960s, arousing the indignation not only of believers.) An associated area of concern is that of language: its potential richness and frequent actual degradation, a symbol if not actual agent of some of the grimmer happenings in Soviet cultural history.

*

No recent writer has shown himself more fiercely concerned with the problem of Russia's cultural continuity than Aleksandr Solzhenitsyn (b. 1918). Before he became a household name in the West as well as the East, and began to devote himself exclusively to the longer genres, he composed a series of miniature prose works (*krokhotki*) of which some are little more than anecdotal, but most raise sharp questions about Russia's artistic heritage and destiny. We give two of these here (and three more in our subsequent section: see p. 409). These are followed by two poems: one, referring to a (happily still-standing) gem of Russian seventeenth-century architecture, by Olga Berggolts, a Leningrad poetess (b. 1910)

* Perhaps the only 'lower' (though hardly 'escapist') form of literature extensively cultivated in the USSR is science fiction, which has attained high quality in the work of the Strugatsky brothers.

whose restrained, Akhmatovian verse sometimes reveals bitter pathos; the other an evocation by Vladimir Kovshin, a contemporary poet who has contributed to several 'unofficial' journals, of that most moving Russian early-summer festival, Trinity Sunday.

Aleksandr Solzhenitsyn

THE CITY ON THE NEVA

Angels, lamp in hand, bow down around the Byzantine dome of St Isaac's. Three fluted golden spires greet each other across the Neva and the Moyka. Lions, griffins and sphinxes keep watch over treasures or doze and dream. Victory's team of six leap over Rossi's cunning crooked arch. There are hundreds of porticos, thousands of columns, horses rearing, bulls straining ...

How fortunate that nothing else can be built here! – no pastry-cook's sky-scraper wedged into the Nevsky, no five-storeyed box slapped down by the Griboyedov Canal. The most eminent and incompetent architect of the lot could not with all his influence get a construction site near the Chornaya or the Okhta.

So alien to us – and yet our greatest glory – this magnificence.

How delightful it is now to stroll along these avenues! But other Russians, clenching their teeth and cursing, rotted in the sunless bog to build all this beauty. The bones of our forefathers caked and fused and petrified into palaces – yellow, brown, red and green.

It is awesome to think that perhaps our own shapeless and wretched lives, our explosive disagreements, the groans of the executed and the tears of their wives, will all be clean forgotten. Will from this, too, come perfect and undying beauty?

1958–60

Translated by H. T. Willetts

Aleksandr Solzhenitsyn

A POET'S ASHES

What is now the village of Lgovo, and was formerly the ancient town of Olgovo, stands on a cliff high over the river Oka: the Russians of those distant times took a liking to the water, which was fast-running and good to drink, and also to the beauty of the place.

Ingvar Igorevich, who was delivered miraculously from the knives of his brothers, built here, for his soul's sake, the monastery of the Assumption. On a clear day you can see a long way from here, over the rolling water-meadows, and more than twenty miles away on a hill as high as this stands the tall bell-tower in the monastery of St John the Divine. Batu Khan was superstitious and spared them both.

This place took the eye of Yakov Petrovich Polonsky. He liked it more than any other, and gave orders that he should be buried here. We cannot help imagining that our souls will hover over our graves and gaze on the broad and peaceful countryside.

But the domes have gone, the churches have gone, only half of the stone wall is left, and the holes have been stopped with board fence and barbed wire. Looming over the ancient ruins there are watch-towers, those hideous scarecrows that we know so well ... and in the gateway of the monastery – GUARD-HOUSE. A poster with the caption 'Peace among the Nations' shows a Russian worker with an African child in his arms.

We pretend to know nothing, and one of the warders, off-duty and wearing a singlet, explains to us:

'Used to be a monastery here. Second biggest in the world. The biggest was in Rome, I think. Moscow only had the third biggest.

'The place was a children's settlement once, and the boys, of course they know no better. They made a mess of all the walls and smashed the ikons. Then a collective farm bought the two churches for 40,000 roubles – for bricks, to build a six-row cow-shed.

'I got taken on myself. They paid fifty copecks for whole bricks and twenty for halves. Only the bricks weren't easy to pick out – it was all chunks of brick and mortar. A vault was found under the church, and there was a bishop lying there. Nothing left of him but his skull. But his robe was still in one piece. Two of us tried to tear it off, but we couldn't ...'

'Yes. Well, according to the map the poet Polonsky's grave should be somewhere here. Can you tell me where it is?'

'You can't get to Polonsky. He's in the prohibited area. You can't get to him. And anyway, what's there to see? Just a broken down memorial. Wait a bit though.' The camp-guard turned to his wife – 'Didn't they dig Polonsky up?'

His wife, cracking sunflower seeds on the porch, nodded: 'Of course. He was taken off to Ryazan.'

The camp-guard couldn't help laughing. 'Got his release, eh ...'

1958–60

Translated by H. T. Willetts

Olga Berggolts

UGLICH: THE 'WONDER' CHURCH

Came forth the church – so beautiful
in each particular that men
gave it its name that cannot fail:
'Wonder' it has been called since then.

Its trinity of towers soars
so straight, so strong and so majestic
that it reflects the further stars
when to daylight the dark has yielded
and in the tempest
                    is cloud-gilded.
But time has passed – three centuries
have changed the seasons of the heart
and choked with weeds the Wonder has
in pride and silence come apart.
There a birch tree bursts up from under
the floor, there, there the rafters fall.
We meant no malice to the Wonder:
we did not tend it, that is all.

... Structures will yet be built, I know,
where at the mere touch of a button
a host of northern lights will glow
and cosmic conflicts be forgotten.
Restore the Wonder? – just you try
without the ancient riddle: guess
how stone on stone could firmly lie –
was it through truth, love, faithfulness?

I did not learn this yesterday.
I cannot touch it up with lies.
May its three towers
crash on me
their loveliness that never dies.

1962
Translated by Keith Bosley with Dimitry Pospielovsky

Vladimir Kovshin

Trinity Sunday. Pealing bells
echo across the drizzling rain.
An aged woman wanly smiles
watching the pigeons peck her grain.

And stamping prayers into the crush
like a cross in spun gold inlaid
the good priest's open features flash
through candle points that wink and fade.

And Trinity, and rain, and gold
Russia and God, heads lost in smoke
and (what the guidebooks leave untold)
the prattle of a farmyard cock

the brow, the candles and the prayer
the multitude that swoons and steams
all is so novel and so clear:
Russia and Moloch and the prayer
Russia, the candles and the dreams.

1965
Translated by Keith Bosley with Dimitry Pospielovsky

Among the poets deeply concerned with the Russian linguistic heritage, its use and misuse, is Naum Korzhavin (sometimes known by his original name of Mandel, b. 1925). Published only in recent years, he is recalled in Yevtushenko's *Autobiography* as the only poet openly to write and recite verses against Stalin in his lifetime, and to get away with it: 'the authorities evidently thought him insane'.

Vladimir Soloukhin (b. 1924) is unusual among contemporary Russian poets in his predilection for Whitmanesque free verse. He is well known as a journalist; his most original prose works take the form of extended investigations into the peasant roots of his native Vladimir province and into its folk heritage of icon-painting (translated into English as *A Walk in Rural Russia* and *Searching for Icons in Russia* respectively). A rather 'populist' respect for the way of life of simple people imbues his work.

Bulat Okudzhava (see also p. 57) is an unusual and important contemporary poet. He ranges from impulsive lyricism, through satirical broadsides, to whimsical poetic jests, but always avoids the over-solemnity and stolid pretentiousness that haunts too much run-of-the-mill Soviet poetry. In representing him, however inadequately, we can at least make a bow in the direction of the interesting 'vernacular' art of balladry, whose leading practitioners (Okudzhava, Aleksandr Galich, Novella Matveyeva and the brilliant actor V. Vysotsky) raise their sardonic, nostalgic or pathetic songs to the level of true poetry – broadcast through countless guitars and tape-recorders, though not very often reaching print. With their topical allusiveness, their touches of pastiche and parody, their frequent gipsy lilt, such ballads have proved particularly intractable to translation. The poem we print here leaves us in little doubt of its serious intent, despite its typically ironic and imaginative garb.

Naum Korzhavin

To love and not to 'die of loving',
To live and not 'delight in living'.
I do not like words that pretend too much.
Nature is more than any such invention.
You cannot love more strongly than you love
And there is nothing loftier than life.
The purpose of pretentious words may be
To hide your impotence before simplicity.

1950
Translated by Daniel Weissbort

Vladimir Soloukhin

WORD

This morning I was finishing a poem
And for a long time worried over a word that wouldn't come.
I took words and tested them:
For weight,
For taste,
For smell,
For colour,
For strength,
For shades of taste, of colour and of smell
(Almost imperceptible shades, but in this lies
The whole charm and point
Of our unusual trade),
For sharpness,
Like blade of knife or axe,
I tested words on my finger.
No use!
Today, not one word served me.
Everything in the world dropped out of sight: all aims, all tasks,
Aspirations, interests, joys, cares, plans, people,
One task remained, one single thing:
To find the word and set it in its place,
As without it the poem wouldn't live.
Besides, I started feeling, all other
People, living in the world, were in absolute need of this word,
That they were missing precisely
It alone,

Although they possibly did not suspect this.
But otherwise what sense was there
In sleepless searching for the word,
In the so-called throes of creativity,
And in the whole poetic trade?

Suddenly, through the party wall
(Our wooden, village house is derelict and shaky)
I heard a conversation between the eighty-year-old blacksmith Nikita
And his daughter Marya, who had come to rouse him.
– Get up! – she said. – Your breakfast's on the table.
I've got to get off to work. It's already past eight, get up!
– Wait, – answered blacksmith Nikita. – Don't disturb me.
I am dying. –
Then I remembered that this was the third day the blacksmith had been ailing,
And I realized that it was serious. And she did too.
– Wait, I'll bring you some milk ... Hang on, I'll warm it up right now.

(Wait? Wait to die?)
I'll bring you some hot milk ...
And so, blacksmith Nikita uttered that word
Which was for him, at that moment, the most important and necessary:
'Dying.'
Should I ask him
How long he looked for the word?
How many words he ran through first,
Before he found that unique one, compelling you to shudder,
Magnificent in its simplicity?

Should I ask
What torment of creativity he had to suffer?
How he tested them, the words, choosing

For taste?
For colour?
For smell?
For weight?
For strength or sharpness?
By what complex means,
As a result
Of what desperate endeavour,
Did he come to the word most important to him?

Needless to say, that morning
I did not finish my poem after all.

1960
Translated by Daniel Weissbort

Bulat Okudzhava

A PERSONAL MATTER

The waiter Ivan Afanasyevich detests the clatter of dishes.
It's all the same to him: whether they're pewter, silver or gold.
And the guests' uninhibitedness is transformed into malice,
and his buoyant coiffure is dishevelled.

The chef Anton Andrianych detests every sort of comestible,
All he wants is a morsel of bread and a herring ...
But his good lady predicts him a death from starvation,
prepares him various dainties.
He won't have a sniff of them.

She takes him rare dishes as if the whole thing were a party,
but the dumplings get cold, the ragoût is left to go bad;
prone and untouched lie the fish in cream sauce –
like French grenadiers in the Muscovite snows.

Major Sergeyev detests the ringing step of parade-grounds:
he'd really like people to shuffle around in their slippers;
but even he marches out briskly when over his head
he smells a storm brewing.

I, the hereto undersigned, what do *I* detest? Words.
Words that don't mind getting threadbare in speeches,
words that go straight to the head of the speaker,
words that cry out for resounding enunciation.

These words are always smiting their own copper breasts,
pursing pink lips in order to bray like a trumpet,
words that are desperately anxious to fool me
(though I'm an old hand and won't be so easily fooled).

Oh, there is nothing that anyone here couldn't do.
One's all for one's country: body and soul and the lot.
And all these people are splendid, indeed, I'm practically
God ...
Ah yes – the above-mentioned facts: *that's* a personal matter.

published 1967
Translated by Robin Milner-Gulland

We have already touched upon the fact that the first three decades of the twentieth century were notable years in Russia for the investigation of the nature of literature as an aesthetic and social phenomenon, and that interest in these questions has revived since 1953. Our anthology would be incomplete if it did not move away from belles-lettres at this point in order to present some notion of contemporary Soviet views of literature. We have indeed anticipated this in Boris Pasternak's late letter expressing some of his aesthetic views (p. 124).

Though literary scholarship suffered – like other branches of intellectual life – under Stalin, certain representatives of the senior generation of critics and theorists have lived to make important contributions in the 1950s and 1960s. Their doyen is undoubtedly Viktor Shklovsky (b. 1893), coeval of Mayakovsky, brightest star of the trail-blazing 'formalist' movement in the 1920s, who after many years working primarily in the cinema has returned to literary topics and in his eighties continues to write as fluently and wittily as ever. The scholar who laid the foundations for the modern understanding of Old Russian literature and culture, Dmitry Likhachev (b. 1906), should also be mentioned: in a remarkable article printed in *Novy Mir* (1969) on *The Literature of the Future as a Subject of Study* he drew up a penetrating scheme of the tendencies of modern literary development. In the 'middle generation' the most brilliant literary theorist is Yury Lotman (b. 1922), who more than anyone has been responsible for bringing a distinctive brand of modern 'structuralist' poetics into Soviet literary analysis.

To represent these and similar leading critical theoreticians with excerpts would, however, scarcely do them justice, while complete articles would unbalance our anthology by directing it in too specialized a direction. Instead we have chosen to limit ourselves to a substantial extract from one critical work by a writer of the younger generation: Vladimir Turbin, who teaches Russian literature at Moscow University. His book *Comrade Time and Comrade Art* occasioned controversy when it appeared in 1961; but it seems to be a classic statement of a 'liberal' Soviet aesthetics, approximately the sort of position represented by the journal *Novy Mir*, building firmly on nineteenth-century 'progressive' thinkers such as Belinsky in traditional Soviet fashion, but eschewing the utilitarian dogmatism and fixed habits of thought characteristic of 'Stalinist' criticism. It is of course a popularization rather than a work of rarefied scholarship, and perhaps of all the more interest to us because of that.

Vladimir Turbin

From COMRADE TIME AND COMRADE ART

It seems to us that there has been some sort of hitch in the development of art. The pessimists prophesy gloomily: 'It's getting out of date.' They are depressed: 'No new geniuses, no one who can create either a tragedy on the scale of *Hamlet* or a painting anywhere approaching a Raphael.'

And indeed there won't be any 'Hamlets' or 'Sistine Madonnas' – they have already *been.* They are masterpieces, but it doesn't follow from this at all that the criterion of the value of every subsequent work of art must be its degree of similarity to them. They were too dissimilar from everything that had preceded them. Why should all subsequent works have to be similar to them?

A new art is being born. 'It's ugly.' 'It's crude.' Once upon a time the novels of Chernyshevsky, and later the verses of Mayakovsky, seemed to be just this. New art brings with it new ideals and puts forward new hypotheses.

But we weary ourselves with questions which have already been answered by Belinsky!

> Civilization is to be prized only when it fosters enlightenment and thus entails the good – the only purpose of man's being, of the life of nations and of the existence of humanity. We too shall have railways in time and, I dare say, the air post, and our factories and mills will attain efficiency and the national wealth increase; but shall we have a sense of religion, shall we have a sense of morality? That is the question! We shall be carpenters, locksmiths, factory-owners, but shall we be human beings? That is the question!

If you discard the idealistic terminology of the great thinker you uncover the disputes of the present day.

And we gloomily go on repeating: 'We don't need art, we'll get on all right without it!'

Or we try to look on the bright side of things: 'What do you mean, we don't need it? Even astronauts will need a branch of lilac!'

And art has to be shielded not so much from its detractors as from its defenders. A branch of lilac! Art is brushed aside into the category of innocent pastimes which incidentally 'widen man's mental horizons'. Something like a quiz in the Sunday number of an illustrated magazine or the Big Wheel in the Park of Culture. And in the papers you see portraits of aged professors of physics playing 'cellos on their days off. The fragrance of the lilac!

It's impossible to discern the ideals of art through lilac clusters and whispering foliage. Art didn't come into the world for the assuagement of our souls. It has never abased itself to the point of simply 'drawing' or 'reproducing' the lilac; it has revealed something new in what has apparently been studied exhaustively and conclusively, once and for all. It has experimented. It has armed men with the methodology of creation.

No doubt each of us, taken separately, can get on fine even without art. Worse things happen than that.

Some people happen to spend their whole lives a long way from the sea, not even once having had occasion to admire it. And moreover such a person, Ivan from Morshansk or Pyotr from Kobelyaki, turns out to be no worse but, quite the reverse, a good deal better than Andrei, who lives by the sea.

But you can hardly infer from this that the sea isn't really any use to anybody and humanity wouldn't have lost anything if our planet had consisted merely of one big continent. There does exist a link between Ivan and Pyotr and the sea. Each year it's becoming clearer and clearer, but nonetheless it's a complex, multi-stage, indirect link. It can't be perceived directly, in everyday life, but its invisibility doesn't make it any the less strong.

It's more or less the same with art as well.

If you haven't read a single poem or seen a single painting, you can still be a first-class engineer, virtuous father and loving husband – a person who is moral in the broad and in the narrow, everyday, meaning of the word. And, on the contrary, there are immoral actors and poets who behave in an extremely unpraiseworthy manner in their ordinary life – people who live on the very shores of the sea and all the same are lesser men in all respects than the stay-at-homes in Kobelyaki.

And what follows from this? Absolutely nothing ...

Although one thing does follow from it: in our arguments about the place of art in social life absurd things begin to happen at the point when, without realizing it, and instead of discussing *the full range of the historical experience of humanity*, we fix our eyes on the *everyday experience* of Ivan, Pyotr and Andrei, naïvely (and outside art triumphant naïvety presents a sorry spectacle!) identifying the part, the unit, with the enormous whole. As a result ... Nothing, apart from waffle about a nice branch of sweet-smelling lilac.

You want to warn people in good time against mistakes like that.

'Artistic forms of thought precede scientific forms of thought.' But this doesn't mean of course that when an engineer begins to draft the contours of a crank he must at all costs listen to a Beethoven symphony, or that a physicist ought to play a passage on his 'cello before he sets off for the laboratory. The engineer can do his work all right without Beethoven. It's something else that is important: but for Beethoven there wouldn't *be* the achievements of contemporary technology! The music of the great composer, establishing the ideal of all-embracing thought, lit a beacon in front of science by which it will have to orientate itself in practice eternally. And the natural sequence of events, accurately formulated by Tsiolkovsky, remains incontrovertible: 'implementation is preceded by thought, precise computation – by fantasy'.

The problem of the future of art should be put broadly, without a shadow of pragmatic narrowness: nations consist of Ivans, Pyotrs and Andreis, but the fates of nations are not identical with the fate of each individual citizen.

Thus I do not dispute the right of anyone at all to spend his entire life in Kobelyaki, and I do not in the least doubt the spiritual excellence of people who do not experience the need to commune with art or the sea. But I believe that, if two thirds of the surface of the planet is covered by the ocean, its existence is worthy of study and research; it is inexhaustible, it has a definite bearing on the climate of the continents.

We 'shall be human beings', of course. Moral people, too, if the morality of a man is measured first and foremost by the degree of his participation in collective production. And art has helped and will help us to rise to the peaks of morality. Art was. Is. And will be.

Originating in concord with technology and science, art has never broken with them. The links were external too: a temple or palace belongs equally to the architect and engineer, and in our times the development of the industrial arts – the cinema and television – is timidly getting under way. But the main thing is that these links were also links in depth, internal links. 'Poetry and science are identical,' asserted Belinsky, 'if by science one understands not only the schematic outlines of knowledge but also awareness of the thought concealed within them. Poetry and science are identical when they are considered not as one or other of the manifestations of our soul but as all the fullness of our spiritual being, as expressed by the word "reason".' It is creativity which unites the artist, scholar and engineer. And how right Pushkin was when he spoke the famous words: 'Inspiration is as necessary in geometry as in poetry.' It is therefore high time to turn our attention to the special and unrepeatable creative character of the art of our days.

From century to century the artistic ideal changes. The aspiration to display the intellectual perfection that has been achieved, as shown by the artists who sculpted Venus and depicted generals and civil servants expressing their thoughts in magnificent iambs – this aspiration loses its point and relevance with the course of time. A citizen of our sceptical and analytical century cannot be satisfied with stories about the adventures of our fellow-countrymen narrated in sonorous iambs, and there comes, to take over from the heroes of Pushkin and Shakespeare ... Vasisualy Lokhankin, a parasite and idler who somehow or other has acquired the gift of the lofty style, a figure who gradually parodies the style of the art of the past.

On the other hand perfection which appeared on the horizon of art as something established and secured gives way to a perfection which is *creatable* and *achievable*. The Venus was a harbinger of the far-distant *end* of cognition; but with time art enters a period of searching for ideal *means* of cognition. Art lives by seeking the *ideal dialectic*; it constructs hypotheses of new, unattainably powerful epistemological methods.

'Here is the complete triumph of the dialectic!' – these are the silent words on the lips of the white marble Venus.

'That's what you've got to do for the complete triumph of the dialectic!' roars the multi-voiced orchestra of contemporary art.

Its creative character is not in the 'content' and not in the 'form'. It is impossible to disunite form and content; in a magnet, even when you have grimly sawn it in two, you can't separate the north pole from the south. Pound the magnet dust, and each particle will still be bipolar. In a work of art it's the same: each of its 'cells' or 'fractions' possesses content and ideology. And artistry in a work is not opposed to the work's social importance, as though it served merely as a decoration or embellishment. The composition of a work of art, its style, images, poetics – all this, everything that is created, bears the imprint of the inquiring, experimenting thought of the composer, sculptor or poet, and all this is an emanation of the powerful dialectic, which is so vitally necessary to society. Artistry *is* the social nature of art.

And even if we do not have perfect pitch, we can distinguish the various melodies amid the sounds of contemporary art:

> Reconstruct your creative imagination. Take it to pieces. We shall not eternally pay anxious attention to the speeches and feats of literary heroes! It would be wiser to see by what power poets have learnt to create them ...
>
> Do not stuff classical iambs into the mouths of a turner or dairymaid; simply show the worker and peasant how a thought is born and clothes itself in a word. Acquaint them with the secrets of language creation. Become improvisors!
>
> Time! The lyric has been foretelling its relativity for forty centuries, and physics has confirmed that it was correct. Let us perfect ourselves, let us, in competition with physics, depict the very movement of man's thought, as it perceives the relativity of time ...
>
> Standing on the threshold of new times, let us try to embrace at a glance the entire history traversed by the human race! Writing historical novels is, without doubt, a worthy occupation. But what if one were to bring together nineteenth-century St Petersburg and ... Ancient Egypt? Contemporary America and Babylon? October 1917 and antiquity?
>
> Space! Since olden times painting has demonstrated the conversion of three-dimensional space into two-dimensional. It has manoeuvred freely with space. And have we not had enough now of painted photographs? Is it not time for the brush of the artist to tell men of the secrets by means of which they can grasp the dialectic of space? To create on their canvases a magic and really real world without parallels, without absolute straight lines ...?

And colour! To penetrate into the great secret of the spectrum. To break up any smugly absolute conceptions of colour. To demonstrate its transformation ...

And movement! How little we know about it! But cine-montage will proclaim the approach of new methods for the cognition of movement!

Television! The transmission of pictures over a distance – the dream of the magi and seers in their garden sheds come true! The hypothesis of new means of communication. The vision of distant transformations in biology.

Everything taken separately – for the complete cognition of time, space, movement. Everything taken together – for the union of art with science, with physics and mathematics. For the collaboration of form and formulae. For the perfection of research into the processes of human thought and its methods, its explorations ...

You get used to this music. You want to understand it.

'Small' art – the applied and decorative arts – lives alongside 'big' art.

A clock, made in the form of the bronze statue of Peter the Great. A pipe with the head of Mephistopheles. An unassuming box in the shape of a sputnik.

Nameless skilled craftsmen have portrayed both the Russian Tsar and the legendary dweller in the underworld. But why did they repeat what had already been done by their 'serious' colleagues? They can't have presumed to surpass Falconet and Goethe!

No. And, if we wish to make the acquaintance of the clever Devil, we don't examine the pipe – we re-read *Faust*. And, if we want to have a look at the memorial to the Emperor, we go to Leningrad. But all the same we take pleasure in looking at the bronze clock and unreflectingly admire the smoke rising out of the head of the Wooden Devil. In unsophisticated trinkets we sense something related to 'real' art. They contain something which only they, only these common-or-garden trinkets, have the power to comprehend – an artistic image is embedded in them.

Where are they then, the content and the image? It's simply impossible to maintain that the craftsmen have created an 'image of Peter' or an 'image of a sputnik', if at the same time you claim, for example, that some still-life or other showing a shot bird on a kitchen-table, surrounded with grasses and vegetables, reproduces the 'image of a goose' or the 'image of a grouse'. And perhaps what we grew used to calling an 'image' at school – 'the image of the Tsar' or 'the image of the Devil' – isn't really an image at all, but only one element in it? But the artist has given us ...

He has given us some link between objects which we know are not linked with one another: there's nothing in common between a monument in a public square and a clock, between a pipe and the malicious mentor of Dr Faust, or between a sputnik speeding through the heavens and a little box for pins. Phenomena have been selected deliberately, just because they are so extraordinarily different from one another. But they are aligned or, as it were, equated with one another. A transformation has occurred. The awe-inspiring and magnificent has become homely, inoffensive and cosy; the tragic has turned out to be – entertaining.

There is a story by Chekhov called *The Pipe*. It's about an old shepherd. The clever old boy has been looking at nature and reflecting on it for years. And he shares his most cherished idea with a chance passer-by, speaking fervently and without haste: 'How much good there is, oh Lord! The sun, the sky, the forests, the rivers and living beings – and all these created, fitted, moulded to one another. Everything has its own task and knows its rightful place ... In everything there's reason.' And any real craftsman is like a wise shepherd of this kind. He too tries to remind people that all things that exist are 'fitted, moulded to one another', and that 'in everything there's reason'.

He *depicts* various things. But he wants to *express* – jokingly, with a scarcely concealed grin on his face, having just a little fun at the expense of the explorations of the human mind – a complex system of thoughts and feelings. What he's trying to do is to play a highly tuneful symphony on a shepherd's pipe. With intentional naïvety he shows how the most complex thoughts can intertwine with one another.

But if one is to speak of feelings, emotions ... Do not seek them in what is depicted and do not demand of a meerschaum Mephistopheles that it sparkle with the wonders of psychology. But feelings and emotions do inspire the work of the applied artist, filling him both with good-natured astonishment at the complexity of the simplest things in the world, and with delight in them, and perhaps with a gentle, wry good humour at the very possibility, when one has lapsed into false profundity, of going off in search of complexities when in fact there are none. Objects we know well become deformed; ideas occur to us, fanned by feeling, and feelings are aroused in us to which our thought responds.

Applied art speaks of the hidden 'rational nature' of life. And it may well be that it doesn't contain 'the image of the devil', but that its value lies in the *image of the mutual connection between phenomena*, of a miraculous metamorphosis – for instance, the movement from the sublime to the ridiculous. Thus the image is first and foremost the revealed or assumed system of links and relationships between the aspects of reality which are depicted.

But something even more complex overlays what is *depicted*: that which is *expressed*. A whimsical movement of thought, some conjecture, notion or assumption flashing through the craftsman's consciousness is expressed in his finished article: 'For all you know they'll go and find something in common between a clock and a statue forged to last for centuries!' The childlike naïvety of art has grown greater still in the craftsman. The impossible – try to find a direct, straightforward connection between a sputnik and a box on a girl's dressing table! – under the chisel of a craftsman appears as something simply, easily, quite effortlessly attainable. Applied art seems frivolous. But in fact it is a sceptical smile at the frivolity of serious art.

Anyway, there undoubtedly exists some correlation between what is depicted and what is expressed; without doubt the peculiarity of applied art lies in this correlation. But is this true only of applied art?

In no scientific article do we find anything similar to this contradictory interaction of the depicted and the expressed; nor do we find invention. And only in a work of art, even of the most mediocre, run-of-the-mill variety, does this interaction begin to expand and broaden, acquiring, in masterpieces, a scale and an unprecedented multiformity of shapes which guarantee it eternal life in the minds of generations. What is depicted gradually ages, decays, is worn away. What is expressed, on the other hand, comes to the surface not at once but in the course of a long period of time; and thus new riches are continually being revealed in the artistic inheritance of the past – riches which people could not see at the time a work was created.

Some 'general law' unites the great poet with unknown applied artists – the modeller or woodcarver. What they *express* is considerably richer and more complex than what they *say*. A work of art cannot in practice be sucked dry of content. 'Content in art', as Belinsky says

is not always that which it is immediately possible to declare and define; it is not the poet's general outlook, nor his specific view of life; not the basis or system of any beliefs or convictions, nor the creed of the philosophical school or political coterie to which he adheres; content is something more than these, something from which all beliefs, convictions and principles derive; content is the poet's vision of the world, his personal awareness of being in his worldly home.

Take the depiction as the electrodes and the content as the spark. Sparks of electricity flash between two electrodes. You may feel free to wonder at the electrodes and rhapsodize over their blinding light. Nevertheless, the electrodes exist to interact: it is more sensible to use the energy of the current running through the wire calmly and economically. (It's true that you can immediately see the wire, while it's impossible to see the electricity. Yet its existence is agreed.)

'The artist thinks in images' – a great truth. But there is no point in vulgarizing it or surreptitiously replacing it with another, more 'convenient' truth: 'He describes people, and they're all just like you and me, real ...' Let's call Tatyana, Onegin, Lensky, Skalozub, Oblomov, Davydov and Nagulnov 'heroes', 'protagonists', 'types', 'characters' (for there's a good stock of terms stored up, enough to last us for five centuries), but keep the term *artistic image* in reserve.

The 'image' enables one to systematize what the artist depicts. And we are justified in saying, for instance, that in one of his books Pushkin has given us an 'image' of the logic of history, an 'image' of the succession of generations and an 'image' of the law ruling over life and death. This 'image' really and unquestionably *is* opposed to the ideology of serfdom, which deems itself unshakeable, eternal, given once and for all time. In the plays of Ostrovsky we can see an *artistic image* of the 'benighted realm'; in Gogol's *Dead Souls* we have an 'image' of the ultimate stage of the uncivilized; in the early tales of Dostoyevsky we find an 'image' of poverty and proud destitution; Tolstoy gives us an 'image' of war and peace, human unhappiness and happiness.

But even the image cannot convey the whole content of a work of art. Even more important is the method which led the artist into the creation of this image, i.e., into knowing the place of particular things in a general order.

It is said that nature gets to know itself in art. This is true. Only it is necessary to remember that we, human beings, are also nature. Thinking nature. And in art we become aware of our inalienable 'human' peculiarity – our eternally awakening thought, our methods of creating the objective, changing and moving world.

Therefore the history of artistic thought is not the history of how different types of characters or even 'images' have displaced one another. Neither the *hero* nor the *image* is the constant and unchanging objective of art. The 'story' is the means by which the character is revealed. The character is the means by which the image is constructed. The 'image' is the *objective*, for the sake of which the artist devises the characters, *and at the same time it is the means by which a new methodology is manifested.*

It has always been so. But suppose the artist is equipped with a modern view on life, with a knowledge of scientific dialectics. Suppose he is aware that art influences reality neither by its plots (which reproduce various sorts of instructive events), nor by its characters (who carry us away 'by the force of their positive example'), but most of all by its new *methods.* And suppose he considers it his duty, both as a citizen and as an artist, to concentrate his attention precisely on the demonstration of these methods and on their manifestation by some new, up-to-date devices which were unknown to the classics. Then ...

Then the fate of the characters in a work of art can be compared conclusively – let us be rather cruel – to chess-pieces in the hands of a grandmaster. A chess-piece may be shaped out of a precious kind of wood and be in itself a work of art. But in spite of this the most 'beautiful' and the most 'exquisite' chess-king and the proudest knight have point only as a means by which the chess-player – a sportsman and of course at the same time an artist – can display his bold and far-sighted ideas.

Formerly chess-men were made of ivory. They were masterpieces of applied art. And chess-players then did not know the fundamental tactics which any amateur nowadays can master completely. A new era is approaching. You can play without a board at all, blind; in case of need you can quickly model the pieces from black bread and use a hastily marked-out piece of paper instead of a richly inlaid chess-board. But the mind of the contemporary chess-player can produce masterpieces of methodology, and not for nothing does the whole world so often hold its breath and follow the moves and development of such a mind. And to berate Mayakovsky, Picasso and the artists of the future, who beyond all doubt will flood Parnassus with intentionally 'schematic' heroes, for their 'absence of psychology' would be just as illogical as to reproach Botvinnik and Tal for the fact that the chess-men they move about the board are not in the least artistic. Schematism in the portrayal of characters is pitiful when it tries as hard as it can to pretend to be, so to say, 'non-schematism'. But today there is nothing more contemporary and artistic than the bold 'schemes' which step out of the canvases of Picasso and the verses of Mayakovsky.

The analogy with chess is a little crude, I agree. But let it be crude, if only it helps us to understand the essence of the matter: today what is important is for us to see in art the thought of the artist unfolding before us, to understand the passion of his epistemological investigations, to grasp his method – to see the morning ray being reflected in the 'images', in the composition, in the poetics of an artistic work, and coming to shine with the brightness of the sun in all its strength. 'If a man is not a natural poet,' thundered Belinsky,

> even though he has a profound, a true, even a holy thought, yet his work is bound to be shallow, deceptive, false, deformed, dead; it convinces nobody; rather, the thought it expresses, in spite of all its truthfulness, disappoints everyone. But nonetheless this is just how the mob understands art, this is just what it demands of its poets! Devise at your leisure some unexceptionable idea, and then set it in some plot like a diamond in gold! And that's all you have to do! No,

it is not ideas of this sort that are the living seeds of living works, and not in this way do they take possession of the poet! Art does not admit abstract, philosophical, and still less reasonable ideas: it admits only poetic ideas; and a poetic idea is not a syllogism, not a dogma, not a rule, but living endeavour, and *passion.*

1961
Translated by Martin Dewhirst

The views of writers of the younger generation on the nature of their art and their literary experience make an interesting addendum to the aesthetic statement of a young critic such as Turbin, and an appropriate conclusion to this section. They were canvassed by the important learned journal *Problems of Literature* in 1962, in preparation for a conference; many of the answers to the questionnaire give a remarkably frank and appealing insight into the thought-world of the new Soviet literature.

Here are the questions as they were put by the journal:

1. What experience of life did you have before you took up writing? When and where were your first works published?
2. What problems, characters and conflicts in the modern world do you consider topical? How do you study life? How do you gather material for your works?
3. What do you consider to be the writer's responsibilities in the process of forming new, communist qualities in society?
4. Which traditions in classical and modern literature do you respect? What experiments in the field of literary form do you consider the most promising?
5. Who of the writers of the older generation gave you professional help and what form did it take?
6. What are your creative plans for the near future?

We give excerpts from the answers of seven writers, most of them represented by original work elsewhere in this anthology. The numbers refer to the questions above.

From the Journal *Problems of Literature*

YOUNG WRITERS ON THEMSELVES

VASILY AKSYONOV
Russian prose writer

1. I hold a medical degree and have practised as a doctor for four years after college. So I can say that my path to literature was fairly natural, the doctor–author being a traditional figure in Russian literature.

I don't think a spell of work in some other profession is essential for a writer. What is more important is that he should have obtained some spiritual experience. However, there's no harm in his having had both.

I began to write prose when I was at college and was a member of a literary youth club in the Petrograd district of Leningrad. My first short stories were published in *Yunost* (*Youth*) in 1959. Just a year later the same magazine published my short novel *Colleagues* and in 1961 my novel *Star Ticket*.

2. I don't approach life as something to be 'studied'. The study of life is an unconscious process. People about whom you intend to write later at once put up their guard when they feel you are studying them. I try to make myself one of them. That isn't always easy because I consider it not quite playing the game to conceal the fact that you are a writer. Of course, it's very helpful to visit different parts of the country. Our country, thank God, is big.

I am still interested in the process of the formation of character of our Soviet youth. More recently I have grown interested in what goes on in characters that are already mature.

One of the most important problems of modern times is, I consider, how to overcome the inertia of the 'cult of personality' in the life of society and in people's souls.

I think that the relationship between science and life is an extremely important problem. The spiritual life of the new technical intelligentsia – isn't that interesting?

And there conflicts lie ready-made. You don't have to invent them.

3. Bearing in mind the educative role of literature, the writer must avoid like the plague any moralizing or didacticism.

Life, for all that, is probably a better teacher than literature.

The unequivocal adherence to the truth of life – that is the operative law of the writer's participation in the formation of the man of the Future.

4. The traditions of Russian classical literature, the traditions of Tolstoy and Chekhov. I am enormously interested in Soviet literature of the twenties and early thirties. Reading Babel and Andrei Platonov – that is a good school.

Hemingway, Faulkner, Böll, Salinger – that too is a first-rate school, apart from the pleasure you get from reading their books.

Experiments in form should, I think, go on in all directions. Failures and blunders are unavoidable in experiments, but in the long run progress in literature is inevitable.

I think about form when I'm not writing. When I write I don't think about it. Somehow things work out by themselves ...

*

VASIL BYKOV
Byelorussian prose writer

1. Four years on active service. Ten years in the army after the war, in the Ukraine, Byelorussia, the Far East.

2. The same problems that have always been topical – the problems of the truth of a work of art and of the sincerity of the author. For that reason I consider as really topical true-to-life characters who aren't invented or 'assembled' but are taken directly from life with all their human complexities.

3. To expose evil in all its forms and depict the goodness that is to be seen above all in the greatness of human spirit.
4. The traditions of critical realism, I think. (The second part of this question seems to me rather unimportant: form has no independent, decisive meaning. The thing is to be honest, true to life and artistic.)
5. The best help I have received from writers of the older generation has, it seems to me, been given in the form of their books. And in this connection I'd like to mention Aleksandr Fadeyev's *The Nineteen*, Mikhail Sholokhov's *And Quiet Flows the Don*, Viktor Nekrasov's *In the Trenches of Stalingrad* and also the books of some authors of my own generation—Grigory Baklanov, Yury Bondarev, Emmanuil Kazakevich, though I began to write considerably later than they did.
6. Subjects drawn from the last war, for in it are to be found many principles that are applicable to our days and will be valid in the future.

*

IVAN DRACH
Ukrainian poet

1. I like to make people face the sun. At first their eyes ache a little but then how much it improves their vision. The world becomes dearer, more familiar, more palpable. I like to make people face the sun of art. I discovered it in the sky of life some time ago but only recently have I begun to understand it.

I was born in 1936. My experience of life: school, a teacher of the Russian language and literature; then an instructor in a district Komsomol committee, military service in the sappers, the university.

My first poems worthy of the name were published in a local paper called the *Leninist Banner*.

2–3. I am worried about the pessimistic mood and scepticism of a section of the youth of my generation. The writer must help people understand the reasons for that depressing condition and assist them to overcome it. He ought to take the offensive against the inertia of those sad times of the past connected with the cult of Stalin, an inertia still to be found in many fields of our life. He should help to get rid once and for all of the fashionable influence of the *Weltschmerz*, the pessimism of West-European youth.

Very important too for me are problems of national development. The only solution here lies in the fraternal union of the Soviet socialist nations, in a true understanding of Lenin's teachings on the nationalities question. Sometimes it is annoying and shameful to find things like nihilistic moods, disrespectful of national susceptibilities, or – what is just as bad – a narrow-mindedness that reeks of nationalism. A correct understanding of the national question is necessary in art too: it must never be forgotten that a tree can grow only in its native soil, draw sustenance only from its native sap; only then can it support the wide international sky on its green shoulders.

4. I love Ukrainian literature – from Taras Shevchenko to Ivan Franko and Lesya Ukrainka – it is a very democratic literature. Vasil Stefanik, one of the most interesting and profound Ukrainian writers of the twentieth century, taught me to look hard into the human soul.

I find it difficult to imagine my inner world without Tolstoy and Dostoyevsky, García Lorca and Hemingway, the early Tychina and Blok, Rylsky, Dovzhenko and Fellini. But I think the strongest influence on my artistic perception and understanding of the world has come from the artists Vrubel, Picasso and Ciurlionis and from that giant of talent, the composer Sergei Prokofiev.

They teach me to undertake big things and not to borrow ready-made ideas. If you are an artist, then create new worlds, make your own universe with its own suns and galaxies.

5. If I am to speak of the help I have received from writers of

the older generation, then I can say that most of it has come in the form of well-wishing or passing critical remarks. One reads with envy, for example, of the severe, exacting and benevolent attitude of Flaubert to the young Maupassant.

6. At present I am working on a poem called 'In the Golden Dawn', on a film scenario *The Year of Birth 1937* and on poetic variations on the theme of the works of Taras Shevchenko and folk songs.

*

YURY KAZAKOV
Russian prose writer

1. My experience of life is probably that of most of my generation. In my childhood and youth – war, a gloomy, hungry life and then study, work and again study ... In short a not particularly rich experience.

But I am inclined to give preference to my 'inner biography'. For a writer that is particularly important. A man with a rich inner life can rise to the task of expressing his time in his writings though his life may be lacking in outward events. That, for instance, was the case of Aleksandr Blok.

My writing began to appear in print in 1952. The first work was a one-act play, *The New Lathe*, published in an anthology.

2. I have not yet chosen any special problem. It seems to me that any author who has the audacity to enrol himself in real literature is concerned for all his life with one and the same set of problems.

Happiness and its roots, suffering and the overcoming of suffering, moral responsibility to the people, love, understanding of oneself, attitude to work, the tenacity of base instincts – those are some of the problems I take an interest in. I am constantly meeting these problems in various forms in the works of all our most gifted writers of prose and poetry.

I make no special study of life and I don't collect material except in those cases when I am given a special assignment by my editors.

Generally speaking, I don't understand the term: 'the study of life'. You can understand life, you can meditate on life, but you cannot 'study' life – all you can do is to live.

I travel a great deal and after each trip I have one or two stories to tell – sometimes quite a long time after I've returned.

This doesn't depend on any plan.

3. I do not think literature has an immediate and direct effect on the life of a man and on his ethics. As an example you could take many unfair, slovenly critics who, of course, have read Tolstoy, Chekhov and Hemingway – read them but without learning a thing.

All the same, I believe in the educative power of literature. And I think a writer who spends all his life advocating the goodness, truth and beauty of man does raise the moral qualities of his contemporaries and successors, those of them, of course, who are willing to read and think over what they have read. How profound are the qualitative changes that take place in human nature under the influence of literature I do not venture to judge. It probably varies with everyone.

What is important, though, is that the writer should perfect his own moral qualities. Then he will have the right to teach others something. A low spiritual level in a writer inexorably shows in his books. And such books either bore or sadden the reader. And sometimes make him feel ashamed.

4. The tradition of being honest to oneself and to the reader.

As for experiment, the form should serve the idea. And the most fruitful are those experiments where the researcher is trying to express his idea in the fullest and most powerful way.

Generally speaking, every experimenter, if he has talent, arrives in the long run at simplicity ...

*

ANATOLY PRISTAVKIN
Russian prose writer

1. This was my experience: dozens of children's homes, years of vagrancy over the face of Russia during the war, a job in a canning factory at the age of twelve, then in an aircraft factory, a wireless operator at an aerodrome and so on until my military service started. Perhaps that is why my characters are either former inmates of children's homes or people who began working at an early age. My poems were printed in various newspapers and anthologies from 1952 onwards, but I consider that my literary career began in 1959 when *Yunost* published my first sketches.

2. Each generation has its main tasks. Every person who shuns that principal task finds himself on the fringe of life. We are first and foremost the representatives of our own generation, our task is to see the main thing and to write about it. The scale of a writer is formed by three factors – his talent, his civic or human qualities, and his correct understanding of the tasks that face the generation he belongs to. As concerns the latter, I am firmly of the opinion that one must live with one's generation, not merely visit it on a special assignment but live with it, that is, experience all its difficulties, and its joys. That is fully within the realm of possibility for young writers, and some do it. I too try to do it.

3. I see here two sides of one and the same thing. The formation of the man of the future is impossible without struggling against what hinders the process. At present that means, no doubt, struggling against the vestiges of the 'cult of personality'. The 'cult' engendered not only bad methods of leadership but brought with it indifference, bureaucracy and the degradation of the human personality. Probably the most grievous thing we had to experience in those years was the neglect of the main thing in life: everything we do should be done for man. From a match-box to the Bratsk Power Station, everything is for him, for the man of today, our own

kin, our living contemporary. In my opinion, communism is not only a society of abundance, it is something loftier, a society of great respect for the human personality. The writer is obliged to help to bring to the fore everything that serves that cause ...

5. My instructor in the seminar at the Literary Institute was the poet Lev Oshanin, to whom I owe much in my development. My other 'teachers' were the editors of the *Literaturnaya Gazeta*. But I feel a latent resentment towards the older generation of writers in general. I know from what I have read that the writer Grigorovich, having read the first stories written by the young Chekhov, sent him a friendly letter. I know that Gorky of his own free will sent his good wishes to many of the living writers of the older generation. I swear that neither I nor many of my writer friends received any such letters on their successful débuts in literature. And we, who are often working in the dark, sometimes find a few warm words indispensable. We don't want to hear them from the platform, nor at a section meeting of the Writers' Union, but the way Gorky did it, understanding everything and kind. After all, they are something like plant food for plants, they could make us work twice as hard and grow proportionally.

★

ANDREY VOZNESENSKY
Russian poet

1. I am a graduate of the Moscow Institute of Architecture. I do a lot of painting. I think the best way of acquiring experience of life is to live. And that is what I did before I took up writing. My first poems to be published appeared in 1958, in the *Literaturnaya Gazeta.*

2–3. The main problem of contemporary literature is to look deep into man's mind, into the interior of his soul.

Communism comes through the heart. And the heart belongs to the realm of poetry.

4. I don't think it profits a writer to feel any affinity with his literary predecessors. Incest leads to degeneration. Andrei Rublev, Joan Miró and the later Le Corbusier gave me more than Byron.

In poetry as in architecture technical skill has reached a high level.

You can build a house on the point of a needle. People have had enough of rhyme. Every sixteen-year-old schoolboy can rhyme brilliantly. In our poetry the future lies with associations. Metaphorism reflects the interdependence of phenomena, their mutual transformation.

However, the point is not form. Form ought to be clear, boundlessly restless and charged with profound meaning, like the sky in which only a radio locator can detect the presence of a plane.

5. Boris Pasternak. He was the only poet to whom, from my schooldays onwards, I showed my poems.

6. Poetry is an improvisation. You don't plan it.

*

YEVGENY YEVTUSHENKO
Russian poet

1. In the first place we must define what is meant by 'experience of life'. I take that phrase to mean not external events in a man's life but the refraction of those events in his psychology.

Before I started writing I had seen a good deal – the war, work on a collective farm, timber-rafting and going on geological prospecting expeditions. I thought I had acquired some experience of life. My first book *Prospectors of the Future*, published in a light-blue cover to match the contents, was full of self-confidence. However, real experience of life came later when life taught me my first lessons in suffering, doubts about myself and disillusion in many other people.

Incidentally, maturity is often conditioned by the number of mistakes one makes about others. But, of course, there is much more to it than that. Maturity is also the ability to see the good in others and to fight for that good. That is why I have remained an optimist.

But my optimism is no longer light-blue or rosy. It is made up of all the colours of the spectrum, including black.

For that reason I must say that my real experience of life did not precede my literary work but came somewhat belatedly in its wake.

My very first poems were published in the paper *Sovietsky Sport*, in 1949. They were a comparative analysis of the ethics of American and Soviet athletes. They had only a vague connection with poetry. The only thing I can say to justify them is that I was very young then and that I was most eager to get into print.

2. The word 'topical' has been so compromised by some crude critics that I prefer to substitute for it the simple Russian word 'daily' as it is employed in the phrase 'our daily bread'. For me everything is 'daily' or, if you like, vital, that can be defined briefly and universally as life. It isn't enough to limit oneself to the phrase 'to study life'. I haven't studied life with a sort of microscope; I've simply lived. Sometimes I have written poems which, incidentally, I include in the idea of 'having simply lived'.

3. I think of communism as a sort of symbolic state where the president will be Truth, served by two ministers, Gentleness and Strictness. In my view, those two ministers will be enough.

The writer, then, ought to be the prototype of a communist state of that nature. In the first place, he must be gentle in his attitude to people, he must love them and understand them. But he must be something else too: he must be implacably strict both towards his own failings and towards those of others. However, I'd like to say that an author has the right to be merciless and severe with people only if he knows how to treat them gently too.

4. I try to learn from everybody – even from minor writers.

Some writers exist, perhaps, only to write a single line which can prove useful to us. That more than justifies their existence.

I shall be happy if but one of my lines helps someone of a later generation.

If one is to speak about experiments in the field of artistic form I must say with genuine regret that I have paid insufficient attention to this. The opinion that I seem to have invented something in this field is exaggerated. But I follow with joyful envy the formal experiments that others make ...

1962

Translated by Ralph Parker

3 Nature, Countryside, Provincial Russia

Questions of man's relationship with the natural world are nothing new in Russian literature, and were revived with particular immediacy after the Revolution (encouraged, for example, by the first publication of Engels's *Dialectics of Nature*). No doubt the Russian awareness of nature is conditioned by such factors as the extreme and obtrusive climate, the vastness of the hinterland, the characteristically paradoxical combination of poor agricultural conditions and great natural riches, the 'closeness to the soil' of even the urban population. It is no surprise that consideration of such themes tends to be closely connected with interest in the way of life and physical aspect of the Russian countryside (whose undemonstrative beauty has frequently inspired a peculiarly fervent devotion, sometimes with an admixture of despair at its bleak poverty or at the uglier inroads of modern life). A feeling that the 'heart' of Russia somehow resides in the deep provinces and the ageless culture of the peasantry is a nineteenth-century legacy that has had considerable repercussions in twentieth-century thought. A striking feature of 1910s–20s literature was the active and far from unsophisticated group of 'peasant poets', whose best-known representative was Yesenin (they have had their successors in contemporary writers such as Tvardovsky, Isakovsky, Martynov, Yashin, and Soloukhin); the rhythms of popular speech entered modern literature.

Clearly there is a wide range of possible approaches to these related themes of man's proper relationship to nature and the Russian's relationship to his countryside: from the near-mystical to the down-to-earth, from the abstract-philosophical to the practical, from the 'conservationist' to the 'exploitative', from the native's intense, unsentimental involvement to the sophisticated intellectual's position as 'outside observer'. The deepest philosophical concern is probably shown by Nikolai Zabolotsky (see also pp. 65, 145): from the urban-grotesque manner of his first book he moved to the construction of a strangely stylized, Utopian and timeless perception of the countryside in his work of the 1930s, and continued this vein in some of the poetry written after his return from exile in 1946. The first of the two poems below picks up an old theme of his, that of the 'schooling' of Nature to its own and man's mutual advantage; the second was intended by the poet to open a comprehensive collection of his work (published eventually seven years after his death).

As a contrast to Zabolotsky's elevated manner we follow him with a short poem by Gleb Gorbovsky (b. 1931), often considered the most 'Russian' of the important Leningrad poets (cf. pp. 178, 185). The 'hunting scene' (given a new twist by Kazakov in *Arcturus*, q.v.) has been a common vehicle in Russian literature since Turgenev for perceptions and reflections of wider import.

Nikolai Zabolotsky

O trees, recite Hesiodic hexameters,
be amazed by Ossian, mountain ash,
nature, it is not your long sword that sounds
against the shield of Cuchulain, but the school-bell's crash.
The wind is neverending like an epic poet,
the birch forest of Morven is still crying out Irish,
but look, in the schoolhouse hares and sparrows sit:
now the ninth muse has descended to the animal.
Birches you are schoolgirls, you are chattering, be quiet,
stop that horseplay and tearing your skirts and all.
Through the storm and the mud listen how the waterfalls roar
they have joined their tongues and where the willow branches
  fall
into that mirror of rivers, and fir trees paw the air,
the small Hamlet voice of the grasshopper is groaning.
To put an end to uncertainties you must be stronger.
And again I recognize that nature is deceiving,
nature is an old madam with a house full of whores;
why, why am I in this dirt and downpour, why am I
  wandering
like a mad creature? How many times and with what force
nature said there can be no immortal illusions of the intellect
at the moment of general decay: life's a moment or worse.
I disbelieved nature and I cannot now expect
another miracle than this one I am singing about in my heart
before my soul shakes loose and my body is derelict.
Look, we have been the masters of this world from the start:

we are the sages and the pedagogues of the universe;
I hear through woods and brakes the loud harp-strings of
  Ossian's art,
from one sea to the other we can teach, we breed our brothers,
and each day playing slowly in sunlight some butterflies
settle to rest on the balding head of Socrates.

1946
Translated by Peter Levi and Robin Milner-Gulland

Nikolai Zabolotsky

I do not look for harmony in nature:
I do not discern in the inward parts of rocks,
I do not discern in the clear roof of leaves
any proportionable origins.

It is a world of sleep and unreason.
The heart bears no concordant music
in the obstinate chanting of the wind,
the soul senses neither voice nor harmony.

When in the silence of the sunsets of autumn
the wind dies in the remote distance,
when night comes down blindly to the river
all interfused with puny radiance,
and when the black water weary of its vigour
its bodily movement and its massive labours
drops into the disturbed half-sleep of exhaustion,
and is silent,
when the huge world of contradictions halts
a kind of archetype of human pain
rises to me from the abyss of waters.

Around me nature's sad and heavy breathing.
And wild freedom and good mixed with evil
are not in nature at this moment.

It is a dream of glittering turbines,
measured voices of labour and reason,
the chanting pipes, the pink glow of the dam,
electric power, human construction.

Lovesick, brainless mother: slack on her bed
with her child's whole world hidden in her
Will wake into daylight with her son.

1947
Translated by Peter Levi and Robin Milner-Gulland

Gleb Gorbovsky

ENCOUNTER

Half a minute's reflection:
Shall I fire at it or go away?
The animal's eyes for some reason
still couldn't focus me;
then it spotted the bearded
feral curve of my mouth.
It was a simpler matter to finish the shot
than to leave it permanently unfinished.
And the bullet left the rifle,
And the animal rolled its eyes,
while, near by, a bare rowan
lifted its arms to the skies.

1964
Translated by Daniel Weissbort

Solzhenitsyn, whose concern with questions of cultural heritage is as passionate as his involvement with the Russian soil, is one of the writers whose work makes a natural transition from the themes of the previous section of our anthology to those of this section. We continue with three more of his 'miniatures' (cf. p. 357).

Aleksandr Solzhenitsyn

YESENIN'S BIRTHPLACE

Four villages, one after another, stretch monotonously along one street. There are no orchards, and no near-by woods, only rickety fences and garishly painted window-frames. An obese and majestic pig scratches itself against the pump in the middle of the road. An orderly procession of geese turns in unison to send a martial challenge after the fleeting shadow of a bicycle. Busy hens scratch up the roadway and the back-yards, searching for food.

The village shop at Konstantinovo is in a hut like a rickety hen-house. There are herrings. All sorts of herrings. There are sweets, a sticky mass of those satin cushions that people everywhere stopped eating fifteen years ago. And there are black loaves the size of hefty cobblestones, loaves that need a chopper, not a knife.

Flimsy partitions divide the Yesenin house into cubby-holes and hutches – there's nothing you could call a room. In the garden there is a windowless shed, and there used to be a bath-house. Sergei crept out there in the dark to write his first verses. Beyond the stick fence there is just a strip of field.

I walk round this village which is like so many others, where everybody is preoccupied with getting a living, making money, keeping up with the neighbours . . . and I am excited. A heavenly fire once scorched this neighbourhood, and it still makes my cheeks burn. I come out on the sloping bank of the Oka, gaze into the distance and marvel: can he have been looking at that dim strip of scrubby forest in the distance when he said mysteriously: 'The pinewoods ring with the weeping of woodcocks ...' and did he think of these meadows along the bends of the Oka when he wrote about 'stooks of sun in the lap of the water ...'?

What nugget of talent did the Creator fling into this hut, into the heart of this rowdy peasant lad, who looked round amazed and found so much raw beauty – at the stove, in the pens, on the threshing-floor, in the wasteland outside the village – beauty which people had trodden under foot for a thousand years and never noticed?

1958–60
Translated by H. T. Willetts

Aleksandr Solzhenitsyn

THE ELM LOG

We were sawing firewood, picked up an elm log, and cried out in surprise – all that time since the trunk had been trimmed, and uprooted by a tractor, and sawn into pieces, and the pieces flung into barges and on to lorries, and stacked and tipped out on to the ground – and still the elm log had not given up! It had put out a new shoot, which might become an elm itself, or a leafy rustling branch.

We had already placed the log on the saw-horse – as though on the headsman's block – but we could not bring ourselves to cut into it. How could we saw it? It wanted to live too! Just look how much it wanted to live – more than we ourselves did!

1958–60
Translated by H. T. Willetts

Aleksandr Solzhenitsyn

THE KOLKHOZ RUCKSACK

When you're travelling on a country bus and somebody gives you a painful jab in the chest or the ribs with its sharp corners – don't start a row, but take a good look at it, that basket of plaited bast on its broad strap of frayed canvas. A woman takes milk and cottage cheese and tomatoes to market in it, for herself and two neighbours, and brings four dozen loaves from town to feed three families.

It is roomy, stout and cheap, this countrywoman's rucksack; its gaudy sporting brethren, all side-pockets and shining buckles, cannot compare with it. It holds so much weight that even over a jerkin its strap is too much for a practised peasant shoulder. So the women have made it the fashion to swing the plaited basket on to the small of the back and pass the strap over their heads like a horse-collar. Then the weight is evenly distributed over shoulders and breast.

Brother writers! I don't ask you to try one of these baskets on your own backs. But if you get jostled – just travel by taxi.

1958–60
Translated by H. T. Willetts

A stark, almost hallucinatory glimpse of the remote provinces is given us by Rid Grachev – a young Leningrad writer whose first book appeared in 1967 (though 'Tomatoes' was published in the excellent literary annual *Young Leningrad* in 1962).

Rid Grachev

TOMATOES

In the summer a stall had been set up next to the shop. When the cedar cones ripened the little boys from the settlement took it over with their haversacks and beakers. Frowning in agony, sucking and biting their pencils, they worked out their daily takings on scraps of paper. Sometimes they made a rouble a day.

On Mondays women took over the stall. They sold grayling – the remnants of their husbands' Sunday catch.

In September the water had warmed up, and the grayling went away into the depths of Lake Baikal. In their free time the inhabitants of the settlement dug potatoes, so there was nobody free to gather the cedar cones. The stall was deserted.

One Sunday morning a new blue Moskvich car drew up. Out of it stepped a woman in a black kerchief. The driver, an elderly, stocky man with short legs, wearing a black Russian shirt and a cap, opened the boot and pulled out a basket covered with a cloth. The woman took a pair of scales from the back seat and carried them to the stall. The man put the basket on the counter. They spoke about something and the man left.

The woman undid the cloth and began to lay out the tomatoes on the counter. She took them out and packed them into a pyramid, carefully placing one tomato next to another. Then she pulled out a piece of paper from the basket and began to arrange a second pyramid next to the first.

Amidst the brown earth round the stall, surrounded by yellow boarding and with the spotted slopes of the volcanic mounds behind, the tomatoes glowed ruby red and shone glossily under the sun, and behind them the figure of their owner loomed black and indistinct.

The woman pulled a gilded aluminium tray from under the counter and put it on the scales. On the other side she placed the weights. She weighed a kilogram of tomatoes, took off the weights, and put some more tomatoes on the other side of the scales so that both lots balanced. From the bottom of the basket she took some pieces of paper with the prices marked on, put them in front of the pyramids and started to wait. At midday the housewives began to gather at the shop. They stopped at the stall, looked down at the price tickets and went past into the shop. Then the shop closed for lunch. The street was deserted.

The woman rested against the counter and looked down the road. It was empty. She knew how to wait. She was not a young woman, but the standing wearied her. She sat herself down on her haunches, her head hidden behind the counter. Soon she heard footsteps.

She got up quickly but didn't see anyone. Then she stuck her head out of the stall and looked at the passer-by.

The sun, which had been striking down directly at the tomatoes, now shone on them from the left. The woman's face was hidden in the shadow.

To pass the time she started to move the tomatoes from one side of the scales to the other. She took two tomatoes in her hand, compared their size, placed them on the scales and took another pair.

Then she started throwing a tomato up into the air. The little scarlet ball with its shining, glossy sides flew up above the counter. The shadow hid the woman, so that it looked as though the tomato was jumping up and down by itself.

Once it fell to the ground and rolled towards a puddle. The woman found a twig and began to fish it out, while looking at the road.

When the tomato had rolled on to a dry spot she picked it up, wiped it on the hem of her skirt, went back to the stall and put it on the scales.

When the sun hung above Baikal Station and the shadows from the highway fell into the ditch, the first customer approached the stall. He was wearing a wadded jacket and a beret, and across his shoulder hung a bag.

When she saw him the woman began to transfer the tomatoes from one side of the scales to the other, putting the bigger ones on the right and the others on the left.

The customer didn't look at the prices. He handed her the money. She tipped the tomatoes out of the tray into his bag.

Straight after him came the man with short legs. He looked at the pyramids of untouched tomatoes, swore, pulled an empty vodka bottle out of his pocket and hurled it into the lake.

He helped the woman pack the tomatoes in the basket and stood the basket in the boot of the car. The woman put the scales on the back seat. The man started the engine, turned the car round and drove it out on to the road.

On the following Sunday they arrived later. The man parked the car behind the stall. He climbed out and lay down next to it on the grass.

The woman pulled the basket out of the boot herself and carried it in front of her, holding the handle with both hands. She came back for the scales and put them on the counter. Then she came back again and pulled a high stool with a small seat out of the car.

She arranged the tomatoes in two pyramids, filled both sides of the scales and began to wait.

The man lay by the car for a time and then got up and went past the woman without looking at her.

She glanced at him and straightened the price tickets leaning against the pyramids.

Soon, one after another, the women began to gather round

the shop. A few of them walked up to the stall, peering from a distance at the price, shouted angrily, gesticulated and went away.

The woman watched them go up to the door of the shop. The sun blinded her. She put her hand in front of her eyes and turned round on the stool when she wanted to see if anyone else was coming.

An hour later the man in the wadded jacket and beret passed along the road, with the bag on his shoulder. The woman quickly added another tomato to the gilded tray, and bent over the counter.

The man passed by. The woman looked after him until he disappeared round the corner.

The shop closed for lunch and then opened again. The housewives again approached the stall, looked at the prices and went away.

The woman fidgeted restlessly on her stool and then got down. She heard a noise on the road and poked her head out of the stall.

People were walking slowly along the road.

The woman looked at the people, and her lips stirred. When the people came a bit nearer, she took the extra tomato off the tray and sat down on the stool. She looked straight in front of her and saw the water running towards the shore in sloping waves.

Beyond the dark blueness of the water stood the flat-topped grey hills, and even farther away the sharp white crags with their blue edges were shining in the sun. They were already covered with snow.

The people were carrying a coffin. It was brown, with white, lacy glazed brocade inside, and behind it they were carrying the lid. At the back of the procession walked two women scattering branches of fir onto the road.

The woman looked with curiosity at the coffin and the lid. Then she looked at the road and got down from the stool.

She wanted to leave the stall, but, looking at the people walking quietly along the road, she quickly began to gather the tomatoes together and pack them into the basket. She carried the basket to the car, came back and took the scales. She locked the door and ran into the shop.

After she had disappeared behind the door the man in the wadded jacket and beret came up. He looked at the empty counter and the car, and went on his way.

The woman came out of the shop carrying a bottle of vodka and some salted herring wrapped in paper. She hid the vodka under the counter, and took the tomatoes out of the car.

She had already arranged the first pyramid when the man came. He asked her something, and she answered, shaking her head. Then she got the vodka from under the counter and gave it to the man. He took the herring from the counter, got a piece of bread from the car, and settled himself down in the sun.

When he had finished the vodka, he kicked the bottle away, went up to the counter and started to throw the tomatoes into the basket. They fell to the bottom with a dull thump.

The woman moved him away with her hand and began to collect the tomatoes herself.

After packing the load in the car, they sat on the front seat. The Moskvich turned round sharply, came out on to the road and set off between the volcanic mounds, which were covered alternately with rich green and bright yellow splashes of colour.

Then the mounds became a monotonous grey blue. Heavy, dull waves beat against the shore and the spray reached the road and fell into long rust-coloured puddles, spilling over into the ruts. Storm clouds covered the distant bank, and the lake seemed endless.

The Moskvich, splashed with yellow mud, stopped by the

stall. The woman brought out a bucket piled to the top with tomatoes, and laid out a high pyramid on the counter.

The car drove out on to the road and was hidden behind the bend. The woman gazed after it and began to wait.

When the housewives began to come to the shop the woman hid at the back of the stall. But no one came up to her. Then she went out to them herself. She stopped one of the housewives carrying a shopping bag and asked her something, but the latter shook her head and went away.

Now along the road came a small boy in a torn cotton jersey and long blue trousers. Seeing the scarlet tomatoes on the counter, he stopped in front of the stall and looked at them. He smoothed his close-cropped head and eyed the tomatoes.

'Do you want a tomato?' asked the woman.

'Yes,' he said.

He got up on tip-toe and pointed at the top of the pyramid. The woman slapped his hand and he went away.

The Moskvich came out from behind the bend. Seeing it, the woman began gathering the tomatoes into the bucket.

The car stopped on the road. It was washed and gleamed freshly blue against the background of the brown water. The windows sparkled while the tyres looked dark and damp. In the clean, nickel-plated hub-caps, without a single scratch on them, shone the reflections of a paunchy stall, a bucket and a woman with a tiny head and a huge black body. The rear-lights glowed with a full, tomato-like lustre.

It was the latest model.

The man leaned out of the door and beckoned to the woman. She hurriedly grabbed the bucket and, picking up her skirts, quickly went towards the car.

The man climbed out of the car and walked up to the woman. She said something to him.

He hit her across the face.

The woman stepped back, trying not to tilt the bucket. Then he struck her again. The woman slipped and fell. She was holding the bucket in one hand and did not let it go when she fell.

The tomatoes rolled along the ruts. Their ruby tops stuck up out of the reddish water. The woman knelt in the mud and began to gather the tomatoes. She wiped them on the hem of her skirt, laying bare a pink, unsightly leg, and carefully lowered them into the bucket.

The man stood behind and looked at her. Then he pulled a bottle out of his pocket, swung his arm round and hurled the bottle at the stall.

It crashed against the side of the stall and smashed.

The man got into the car and started the engine. The woman sat on the back seat with the bucket.

The car moved off, rolling from side to side and bouncing gently on its new springs.

1962

Translated by D. M. Dewhirst

The greatest 'nature poet' of modern Russia is doubtless Boris Pasternak (see also p. 121); but, in the highly sophisticated textures of his earlier poetry, nature is approached quite differently from, say, the 'folkloristic' manner of the peasant poets – its role is the (usually sudden) illumination of the poet himself, 'momentarily-eternally' as he puts it, and natural objects are shamelessly anthropomorphized (or Pasternakomorphized). From the 1940s his more outward-looking approach continues to give nature an important place, though not primacy, in his poetic scheme of things. How intellectual as well as simple man can sense and respond to the 'wind' of natural (which includes historical) forces becomes a pressing concern – in his novel as well as in his poetry. It is worked out with characteristic humour and humanity in a cycle of four poems in memory of Blok, a writer with whom Pasternak felt instinctive kinship despite their very different literary methods, and whose presence (despite his short life: 1880–1921) seems to haunt twentieth-century Russian culture.

Boris Pasternak

THE WIND

Four fragments about Blok

I

Only the influential yes-men know
  Whom critics are to propagate
    With praise, or criticize
      And liquidate.

Without their Ph.D.s to light the world
  And tell us Pushkin was a writer,
    How should we ever know
      He was, poor blighter?

But Blok, thank God, is a different sort of being
  From all those condescending ones
    Who step from Sinai
      To look for sons.

No school or system pickled him alive
  In well-planned glory. What he wrote
    Keeps him, neither cooked up
      Nor stuffed down throat.

II

He blows like the wind
That roared in the country
When Philip the outrider
Galloped six horses

And grandfather Blok
Was a crystal-souled Jacobin;
The gusty grandson
Is more than his match.

For better for worse
Blok's poems remember
That wind, whistling
Through ribs to soul,

That blows where it wills,
In trees and houses,
The rain, Book Three,
The Twelve, death, all.

III

River and meadow
Spread widely, widely.
Harvest hustles
With reaping and threshing.
No time for the reapers
To gaze at the river.
Harvest is catching;
Blok, the squire's son,
Picks up a scythe,
Lunges, lucky
To miss a hedgehog,
Carves two snakes,

But hasn't finished his homework;
'Lazybones,' they grumble.
Childhood, leadweight of lessons
And singing from the fields.

Clouds in the east, at evening;
North and south at war.
A wind, savage, unseasonal
Hurls itself on the scythes,
Bleeds on the blades of rushes
That crowd the bending river.

Childhood, leadweight of lessons
And singing from the fields.
River and meadow spread widely,
Widely.

IV

Abrupt horizons menace
The unhealed twilight, bruised
And bleeding like the scar-crossed
  Legs of the reaper.

The sky has many gashes,
Gale-warnings of disaster.
The marshes smell of rust,
  Water and iron.

On roads, in woods and gullies,
In big and little hamlets,
These cloud-inscribing zigzags
  Promise a downpour.

But purple-rusting rims
About a capital city
Mean state events, the cyclone
  Poised for attacking.

Blok saw these patterned heavens
And knew their prophecy.

He waited; the ugly weather
  Gathered its forces,

Blew up, concussed the earth
And signed his life and poems
In flaming strokes, with a frightened
  Thirst for the outcome.

1956
Translated by Michael Harari

From the late 1960s Russian readers and Western observers have become slowly aware of the emergence of a distinctive 'school' of Russian writing, which remains to this day the most promising contemporary trend in Soviet literature: the so-called 'village' (or 'country') prose-writers (in Russian, *derevenshchiki*). Rather diverse names, including some we have met earlier in the anthology (Voinovich, Kazakov, Iskander, Soloukhin), are often grouped under this heading; what they have in common is a desire to perceive contemporary Soviet provincial life, its traditions, tensions and evolution, from 'inside', rather than through the spectacles of the urban intelligentsia. Semi-fictional genres (the *Village Diary* of Ye. Dorosh), the 'sketch' and the short story (whose best practitioners include V. Belov, V. Ovechkin and F. Abramov) predominate in their work.

Not long before his recent untimely death, Vasily Shukshin (1929–74), perhaps the most characteristic of the *derevenshchiki*, complained in a newspaper interview of the town-bred reader's 'country-cottage attitude' towards the Russian village and its critical problems. Shukshin himself had most successful 'city' careers as a film-director and as an actor, but continually put his native awareness of peasant life to good use in his many brief stories. They are full of elemental vigour, often rather unpolished, with a sense of the mixed humour, irony and pathos behind the clash of new values and technical prowess with the archetypal and inward-looking way of peasant life. The two we print here show respectively the darker and the more light-hearted sides of his talent.

Vasily Shukshin

IN PROFILE AND FULL FACE

An old man was sitting on the bench by his front gate. He felt as weary and dull as the warm evening which was drawing on. Long ago he too had known his morning sunshine, when he had stepped out boldly and felt the earth light beneath his feet. Now, however, it was evening, and peaceful, with a touch of mist over the village.

A thin gangling youth with a lined face sat down on the bench beside him. Young men like that look weedy, but actually they have the stamina of a horse. And they sweat well in a steam-bath, too.

The lad sighed deeply and lit a cigarette.

'Not working?' the old man asked.

'Well, I'm not exactly merry-making, grandad,' Ivan said, after a pause. 'It's enough to make you weep. Have you got a rouble fifty on you?'

'Huh, what a hope!'

'Ugh, my head's splitting.'

'How's work going, then?'

'Bloody awful. "Get yourself a pitchfork," he says, "and report to the pig-sty." '

'Who, the director?'

'Yes, the director. And, mark you, I've got three certificates and I did pretty well nine years of school as well. So I told him: "Sweat it out yourself, if you're so keen." '

'Hm. How long did they confiscate your licence for?'

'A year. And I only drank a mug of beer. Well, and a glass of red wine. But he was on to me like a shot. Been watching his chance for months, he had. So I told him where he got off, and then he really turned nasty.'

'Ah, you know, lad, you're mighty ... er ... bumptious. You should watch your step. What'll you do with them now? They're the bosses.'

'Well, and so what?'

'You'll just have to stay where you are, that's what. You may have three certificates, but that won't help. You should learn when to hold your tongue.'

In the garden plots they were burning loose foliage in preparation for ploughing. Every year it was exactly the same, yet one would never tire of breathing in the acrid, mouldering smell of smoke and damp earth.

'Aye, you should learn when to hold your tongue, son,' repeated the old man, gazing at the bonfires in the gardens. 'That's our lot in life.'

'But I don't really swear at them or anything,' Ivan grumbled. 'At least, only if one of them really gets his teeth into me ... And anyway the thing is I didn't even break the law,' he shouted out exasperatedly. 'How can you confiscate somebody's driving licence for a year just for a mug of beer and a glass of wine? The bastard.'

'Take a look over the fence. Is my old woman in the garden?'

'Why?'

'I've got a bottle of my home brew under the stove. I could bring it out to cure your hangover.'

Ivan got up quickly and looked into the garden.

'She's there,' he said. 'In the far corner. She's not watching.'

The old man went into the house and returned with a bottle of his spirit and a bunch of spring onions. And a glass.

'Why didn't you say straight away you had some of this?' asked Ivan impatiently. 'Sitting there keeping quiet about it.' He poured a glass and threw it back in one gulp. 'I prefer the real home-made brew to the factory stuff: it has a good strong smell, like petrol. You don't pussy around in front of it. A-a-ah! There, have one yourself. In one gulp, mind.'

The old man drunk unhurriedly, nibbling at an onion.

'Like petrol, isn't it?'

'What d'you mean, like petrol? It's ordinary, home-made vodka.'

'Well, there we are!' Ivan slapped his chest. 'Now life seems worth living again. Thanks, grandad. Want a fag?' He held out a packet of Pamir cigarettes.

The old man took one, fumbling with his stiff fingers, rolled it over and over again, stared at it, and then took a light from Ivan.

'Does Petya write?' Ivan asked him.

'Uh-huh. But I'll be dead soon, anyway, Ivan.'

Ivan looked up at him in surprise: 'Come off it!'

'There's no getting round it.' The old man spoke calmly.

'Have you got a pain then somewhere?'

'No. I just feel it. When you're my age you'll feel it too.'

Ivan was in a good mood from the vodka, and didn't feel like talking about death.

'Come off it!' he said. 'You've got plenty of life in you yet. Would you like me to fetch my accordion?'

'Aye, you do that.'

Ivan crossed the road, went into the house ... and did not return for a long time. Eventually he appeared with his accordion, but frowning again.

'Mother,' he said. 'Course, you can't help feeling sorry for her ...'

'You're still bent on leaving, then?'

'Well, what else can I do?' Ivan had evidently just said the same thing to his mother. 'I can't work in that ... Oh, to hell with it, why discuss it? I've been round the Northern Sea Route, let me tell you. I'm a motor mechanic and a grade-five metalworker. Okay then, I won't drive for a year, but do they really expect me to ... Oh, what's the point, to hell with it, he squeezed the accordion, struck up a tune and then abandoned it. He became downcast. 'I get all the rotten luck, grandad, I really do. I got married in Eastern Siberia, remember? We had a little daughter. But then my wife sold me the buck and cleared off home to her mum in Leningrad. What d'you make of that?' He would often tell the story of his marriage.

'Why to Leningrad?'

'Oh, she was only working off her college years in Eastern Siberia. I don't care about the wife, to hell with her, but I do miss my daughter. I dream of her sometimes.'

'Are you going to see her now when you leave?'

'My wife? She's been married again for more than a year ... She's young and attractive, the bitch.'

'Where are you off to, then?'

'To see an old mate. In the mines. Maybe not for good. Maybe for a year or so.'

'Young people don't seem able to go away just for a year nowadays. They all seem to leave for good now, without a second thought.'

'Well, what would I do here?' Ivan flared up again. 'Go and work in the ... oh, to hell with it!' He pulled out the accordion and started to play, singing with a forced, almost vindictive gaiety:

So I was living with this woman,
Tarum-tarum-tum-tum,
And this woman, see, she left me,
She left me just like that!
Got frightened, did you, darling,
When the fun came to an end?

The old man still sat peacefully listening.

'I make 'em up,' Ivan said. 'As I go along. I can sing the whole night through.'

So we won't take up our poses –
In profile and full face;
In a little golden frame ...

'You ask for trouble, you do, Vanya,' the old man broke in. 'You could quite well go and put in a year here, looking after the pigs. You don't think of your mother. She's been alone all her life.'

Ivan broke off and sat silent a while.

'That isn't the point, grandad. What galls me is that they could perfectly well have found me a job. D'you think they couldn't do with another metalworker? I ask you! The point is, the director's got a grudge against me as well. I took his daughter home a couple of times from the club, and he started to get the wind up. And well he might: she's fair game for anybody. And I know how to handle a woman ... I could have given him quite a surprise. Pity I didn't.'

'You mean, got her in the family way?'

'Uh-huh. A nice little surprise for Mothering Sunday.'

'Aye, you could have done that in style.'

'I feel really low, grandad. I don't know why. I just don't feel like doing anything, like a ... what d'you call it? ... a bystander. I was a bystander once: one fellow punched another in the glasses, and ruined his eyesight. And there I was sitting in the court and I had no idea what I was doing there. All for an absurd punch-up. All right, so I saw it happen – so what? I was in a terrible state throughout the trial.' Ivan looked over at the bonfires in the garden plots, sighed and fell silent. 'It's just like that now. I sit here and think "What am I doing here?". The trial was a long one, but at least eventually it came to an end and I got away. But where can I go from here? There's nowhere to go to.'

'There's only one way out of here – to the other world.'

Ivan poured out another glass and drank it.

'There's no happiness in life,' he said and spat. 'Shall I pour you some?'

'No, that's enough.'

'Well, was your life a happy one?'

The old man sat in silence for a time.

'At your age I didn't think like that,' he began quietly. 'I used to do enough work for three people. Why, if you were to take just the grain I grew, you could probably feed the whole village for a year. I had no time to think the way you do.'

'But I don't know what I'm working for. Do you understand? I was taken on, I do my bit. But if you ask me why, I don't know. Just to stuff myself? Well, okay then, my belly's full – now what?' Ivan's question was serious: he paused to see what the old man would say. 'Now what, eh? I feel like a damp rag.'

'Things cloy when you've eaten too much,' the old man explained.

'What do you know about it? You had no horizons in your day, so you were satisfied. You were cavemen. I could live the way you used to, but I need something more.'

'Pour me one,' the old man asked. He drank and then spat too. 'Centipedes,' he suddenly burst out. 'You scamper hither and thither, and where does it get you? Look at all the cars they make nowadays – ugh! Where d'you think cancer comes from? From your bloody petrol, from the fumes. Soon you'll forget how to produce children ...'

'Huh, that's not likely.'

'And you sense there's something wrong with your lives, but you still insist on your "hori-i-izons"! Well, what are you bellyaching about, then?'

'What's biting you? Annoyed that I called you a caveman? Well, what are you, then?'

'You're layabouts. Think yourselves clever! Look how a young fellow behaves nowadays: they offer him a rouble twenty five a trip – okay, so he could easily earn four roubles a day, but not on your life: he does two trips and unharnesses his horses. A great strapping lad, bursting with health. Now I only used to get a quarter of a labour-day per trip, and I used to do five a day, sometimes with three or four carts behind me. And even when I'd earned my labour-day, I'd have to wait a year to see how much I'd get paid for it. Often it was damn all. And you can complain you don't know what you're working for! You can't be bothered to earn 1,500 roubles a month, where I used to break my back right through the summer for a few miserable kopecks.'

'But I don't need that much money,' said Ivan, as though to provoke him. 'Don't you see that? It's something else I need.'

'You don't need the money, yet you haven't a rouble fifty to your name for a drink. So you go scrounging instead ... Don't need it, indeed. While your mother shrivels up working. It's criminal. Layabouts. The sun's still way up in the sky, and they're already coming back from the fields. In lorries, singing! There's workmen for you! All they can do is wolf-whistle at the club and prepare little surprises for Daddy ...'

'No, life'll never be ... I suppose in theory you're right, but after all we're not horses ...'

'You think it's beneath you to do a spot of work in the pig-sty! But it's not beneath you to eat meat, I dare say?'

'You'll never understand, grandad,' sighed Ivan.

'How d'you expect me to?'

'As I say, I've eaten as much as I want already. So what now? I don't know. But I do know this doesn't suit me. I can't work just to fill my stomach.

Just to fill my stomach, oh,
Tum-tarum-tum-tum ...

– he sang.

The old man gave a laugh.

'You rascal. Why did your wife leave you? Did you drink, eh?'

'The thing is, grandad, I'm not a grasshopper. I'm serious about things. I was a first-grade specialist in the navy, you know. Why she left? I don't know. Probably because I wasn't a grasshopper.'

'What weren't you?'

'Doesn't matter.' Ivan put his accordion down on the bench, lit a cigarette and sat silent for a while. Suddenly he said without any flippancy and with a certain veiled alarm, even anguish, in his voice: 'It's true I don't know what I'm living for.'

'You should get married.'

'It's crazy. I'm not a fool, am I? But how do I find peace of mind? I don't even know where to look. How stupid can one get?'

'Get married. That'll stop you fretting. You'll have other things on your mind.'

'No, that's not right either. I've got to be consumed by love. Fat chance of that here! I don't get it. Am I the only fool that feels this way, or does everybody, only they all keep quiet about it? You know, at night I lie awake thinking and thinking, and I feel so ghastly I could scream. What's it all for?'

'Ugh!' the old man shook his head. 'People are going to the dogs.'

Meanwhile the day gently declined, melting away in the damp warmth. It was getting darker and darker. The flames in the gardens flared brighter. And the smell of smoke grew sharper. Far into the evening people would burn foliage and chat to one another. Their voices would carry clearly and the noise and bustle of the village would die away. Then it would get completely dark. The flames in the gardens would go out. And somewhere, very near, a man's deep voice would say:

'Oh, well, let's call it a day.'

★

The next day dawned as noisy, bright and full-throated as the previous one had faded peacefully, gently and sadly. The cocks crowed all over the village. People bestirred themselves and bustled about, losing no time.

Ivan got up early. He sat on his bed and stared at the floor. He felt sick and tense. He started to get dressed.

His mother was fanning up the stove, and he smelt smoke again, only now it was different: woody and dry, a morning smell. When mother opened the door and went into the street, the air from outside smelt fresh from puddles covered by bright, glassy ice, from clods of earth dappled with touches of hoar-frost, from yesterday's bonfires, whose ash was now grey, moist and heavy, and from fallen leaves which had dampened in the spring but still rustled loudly whenever anyone walked through them.

'What if I went to the director and asked him?' mother began.

Ivan was shaving.

'You're joking. Why don't you go on bended knees: he'll be really tickled.'

'Well, what's to be done, then?' Mother was trying not to whine, and to make her points as telling as possible, realizing that this was probably their last chance to talk. 'People do go and ask for things. My tongue won't drop off.'

'I've been. And asked.'

'I know you, son. You don't ask. You put your nose in the air and bark your orders.'

'Stop it, mum.'

Mother could stand it no longer. She sat down on the step, began to cry quietly and wailed: 'Wherever do you think you'll finish up? In some god-forsaken hole ... Was I condemned from birth to suffer all my days? Why do you think only of yourself, son?'

Ivan had known there would be tears. That was why he had felt so lousy. And tense. And why he had frowned in anticipation.

'Anyone would think you were seeing me off to war. What's so dreadful? Ah, damn it all! Always tears, whatever I do. I can't get away from them.'

'I could easily go and ask – he isn't made of stone, he would find you something. Or why don't you see the inspector? Why leave straight away like this? When they confiscated

Kolya Zavyalov's licence, why, the lad went and had a word with them ... A quiet word is all that's needed.'

'But the police already have my licence. It's too late.'

'Well, you could go to the police station, then.'

'Oh-ho!' exclaimed Ivan. 'Just catch me going there!'

'Oh, lord. Oh, lord ... All my life it's been like this. Why have I been singled out for this misery? Am I damned ...?'

It was getting too much for him. Ivan went out into the yard, washed at the hand-basin, and stood for a moment at the gate in his vest. He looked at the village. He knew everything in it. He had waited longingly in those alleyways on moonlit nights ... And now he didn't feel in himself the firmness he would have liked before a long journey. Not that he was afraid to go, but he would have preferred to have a proper grip on himself, and to feel a bit more cheer in parting.

His dog, Dick, appeared from nowhere – a good-looking dog, but a mongrel – and jumped up to lick him.

'Down!' Ivan brushed him off and went inside.

His mother was laying the table.

'Why don't you try it just for a bit in the pig-sty?'

They are persistent, mothers are. And helpless.

'Not a hope,' said Ivan firmly. 'I'd have the whole village laughing at me. I know why he wants to shove me into the pig-sty. Well, it won't work.'

'Oh, lord. Oh, lord ...'

... They had breakfast.

Mother packed everything in a suitcase, and then sat on the floor in front of the open lid and started to cry again. This time without saying anything.

'I'll work for a year or so and then come back. What's the matter with you?'

'Let me go and try, son?' She looked up at her son, and her eyes were full of grief, entreaty, hope and despair. 'I'll get round him. He's a good sort.'

'Oh, mother ... This is hard for me too.'

'Or perhaps you could slip one of the policemen something. You think they'd refuse? Course they wouldn't! D'you think Kolya Zavyalov didn't slip them something? Course he did. And they returned his licence to him just like that.'

'It'd be more to the point if *they* bribed *me*.'

The next stage was to say good-bye to the stove. Whenever Ivan left on a long journey, his mother made him kiss the stove three times and say: 'Mother stove, as you have given me food and drink, bless me for my long journey.' And each time she would remind him of the words, though he had long known them by heart.

Ivan pecked the stove's warm brow three times and repeated: 'Mother stove, as you have given me food and drink, bless me for my long journey.'

... And they set off down the street, mother, son and dog.

Ivan didn't want his mother to see him off, didn't want people to stare out of their windows and say: 'Vanya's off somewhere then, is he?'

On the way they met the old man with whom Ivan had talked the previous evening. Ivan stopped. It occurred to him that mother, after chatting a while, would not walk on, but turn round and go back with their neighbour.

'So you're off.'

'Yes, I'm off.'

They both lit cigarettes.

'Been fishing?'

'I've put the nets out just in case. But it's early yet.'

'Yes, that's true.'

Mother stood to one side, clutching her hands in her apron, not listening to the conversation, but gazing thoughtfully, or perhaps unthinkingly, in the direction in which her son was leaving.

'Don't start drinking there,' grandad advised. 'You know what the town is like: everyone's a stranger there. Feel your way first ...'

'What d'you think I am, an alcoholic?'

They stood still a moment.

'Well, God be with you!' said the old man.

'Mind how you go.'

The old man went his way. Ivan glanced at his mother ... Staring in front of her as before, she strode out in the direction they both had to go. Ivan walked beside her.

They went a little way.

'Mum ... you go home now.'

Mother stopped obediently. Ivan put an arm round her. Her head quivered against his chest. That was always the worst moment. He must push her away, turn round and go.

'Right then, mum ... You go. I'll write you a letter straight away. As soon as I arrive. Nothing can happen to me! People are always going on journeys. So off you go.'

Mother made the sign of the cross over him. And then just stood there. But Ivan walked on. His stupid dog started to chase after him. It always went to work with its master.

'Go away!' said Ivan angrily.

Dick wagged his tail and carried on running ahead.

'Dick! Dick!' Ivan called.

Dick ran up to him. Ivan kicked him hard. Dick bared his teeth and ran off to one side. And stared at his master in astonishment. Ivan turned. Dick gave a wag of his tail and made as if to follow him, but stayed where he was, still staring at his master in astonishment.

A little farther off stood his mother.

'No, one must live alone in this world. Then it will be easy,' thought Ivan, clenching his teeth. And he strode out along the road – towards the bus.

His mother was still standing there, watching him go.

1967/70

Translated by Geoffrey Hosking

Vasily Shukshin

DEPTH OF CHARACTER

A party of young people from town (from the House of Fashion) arrived in the village of Krasny Yar. They had come to give a fashion show.

It was early summer. The red bus rolled along the village street, stopped at the club and a crowd of dazzling girls and young men carrying musical instruments got out.

The club manager, Ilya Degtyaryov, a very lazy and crafty fellow, was on the spot to meet them. He met them and took them off to the houses where they would be put up for the night.

An announcement was posted up on the notice-board outside the club, or H. C. (short for House of Culture) as Degtyaryov insisted on calling it.

ANNOUNCEMENT!
Today at the H. C. there will be a
demonstration for young people of fashions for the
spring and summer seasons.
Demonstration begins at 9 p.m.
Afterwards there will be a film.
No charge for admission to the demonstration.

A lot of people attended, most of them girls.

Degtyaryov came out with one of his usual speeches.

'In this day and age of astonishingly admirable achievements', he said, 'we must all be well dressed, comrades! And yet it is no secret that we sometimes let such matters slide. So today the employees of the town House of Fashion will demonstrate to us a series of achievements in the sphere of the light industry.'

Degtyaryov ended his speech as follows:

'There may have been a time when certain scoffers could say sceptically, "Try and make Russia cultured!" but today we can declare with complete assurance, "Yes, comrades, we stand for higher standards of culture in the village!" '

The young men with their musical instruments came on to the stage, sat down in a semi-circle and played some light, gay music. A girl wearing a beautiful silvery white dress made her entry, walked gracefully across the stage, smiled at the audience and walked back again.

'This is a formal evening gown,' a plain middle-aged woman, whom no one had noticed up to now, began her commentary. 'Though fairly simple in style, it is, as you see, strikingly effective.'

The girl in the evening gown kept walking to and fro and smiling. The musicians went on playing, particularly the drummer, who jiggled with his sticks and tapped his foot. The accordionist also tapped his foot. And so did the guitarist.

No sooner had the girl in the silvery dress left the stage than another girl in a different dress appeared. She was very young and slender with a small red mouth. She too walked across the stage with very short steps and whirled round. She whirled round so gracefully that the hall buzzed with approval.

'Here we have a dress for everyday wear. It is very comfortable and inexpensive. It can also be worn in the evening.'

The Vinokurov brothers were sitting in the front row and had a fine view.

Ivan, the elder of the two, sat with his elbow resting on the back of the seat and at first surveyed the proceedings with some contempt. But the band played more and more gaily, and other girls in other dresses came on the stage and smiled, and Ivan sat up straight.

His younger brother, Sergei, remained quite still all the time, watching the girls.

A plump little blonde in a simple navy-blue dress made her appearance and walked back and forth.

'This dress is just the thing for the beach. It is so easy to take off.'

The plump girl stopped just in front of the brothers and started unbuttoning her dress. Ivan nudged Sergei with his knee; Sergei didn't stir.

The girl took off her dress and walked across the stage again in nothing but a bathing-suit.

There was dead silence in the hall.

The girl smiled and put on her dress, then left the stage.

Ilya Degtyaryov (he was sitting in the front row, by the gangway) turned round and surveyed the audience with a severe look on his face, then turned back to the stage and, having given the matter some thought, began to clap. He was supported, but in a half-hearted manner; many thought it was not the thing to applaud.

Then some young men in smart suits came out and also walked to and fro, smiling.

Then there was a film.

When the brothers left the club, Ivan started discussing the models.

'If you ask me, they're just a waste of time,' he declared. Ivan lived in town and, whenever he was on holiday in the village, he liked to look down on everything and pass judgement. Generally speaking he was always making himself out a great brain these days. 'It's all on the surface with them. There's no depth of character.'

'Come off it,' Sergei protested. He didn't like it when his brother tried to show off his mind. 'You'll be dreaming of them soon yourself.'

'I will?'

'Yes, you.'

'For a start, they're not my taste – they're too skinny,' Ivan said. 'But above all, there's no depth of character.'

'In hell's name, what do I need their depth of character for?' Sergei demanded.

'Well, that's great, that is!' his elder brother stared at him in surprise. 'Sergei, you're ... what's come over you?'

'What do you think?'

'Character is everything,' Ivan said with conviction. 'A woman without depth of character – why, that's – I don't know – that's a nightmare!'

'Stuff it,' Sergei muttered.

There was a surprise for the brothers when they got home. Two of the girl models were staying with them. They heard the news from their father, Kuzma Vinokurov. Kuzma was sitting on the porch, smoking.

'They've billeted a couple of the lasses on us,' he said. 'Just till tomorrow.'

The brothers exchanged glances.

'The ones that came to the club? From town?'

'Aye.'

'Well, fancy that! ...' Ivan was slightly baffled. 'Where are they now?'

'In the best room.'

Sergei sat down on the porch step and lit a cigarette.

'Shall we go and see 'em, Sergei?' Ivan suggested.

Sergei said nothing.

'Well?'

'What for?'

'Just to see. Come on?'

'Knock on the door first – they'll be changing their clothes, I reckon,' their father warned. 'Otherwise you'll go bursting in.'

Sergei stubbed out his cigarette and rose.

'What are we going to say?'

'Good evening and all that. Chat 'em up a bit.'

Sergei went into the house, took a new shirt out of the big chest in the passage and put it on.

'Mind how you go,' he warned his brother. 'Don't be too forward.'

Ivan frowned condescendingly.

'Keep calm, Sergei. I've handled bigger things than this.'

Sergei nodded at the door of the best room.

'Well ...'

Ivan knocked.

'Come in!'

The brothers entered.

'Good evening!' Ivan said loudly, and halted in the doorway.

Sergei found himself in the foolish position of not being able to go forward or back. Ivan had blocked the way into the room, and it was equally impossible to withdraw. He, too, uttered a loud 'good evening' and jabbed his fist into Ivan's back. Ivan didn't budge.

The girls responded to their greeting and looked at them inquiringly.

'We live here,' Ivan found it necessary to explain.

'Do you? Is anything wrong? Are we taking your room?'

'Not a bit!' Ivan exclaimed, and advanced into the room. 'Live here as long as you like.'

Sergei followed him in. His flesh was crawling with embarrassment and shame.

One girl, the one who had strolled about the stage in the bathing-suit, was combing her hair in front of a mirror, the other was sitting at the table, drumming on the tablecloth with her long, slender fingers.

'Well, how do you find it here?' Ivan asked. 'Not so bad?'

'In what way?' The girl who was combing her hair turned to him and smiled.

'Made yourselves comfortable?'

'It's all right, thank you.'

Ivan also smiled and sat down on a bench. Sergei remained standing for a minute, then joined him.

Not knowing what else to say, Ivan sat there smiling. Sergei also forced a smile. For want of something to do, he took a penknife out of his pocket, opened it and started feeling the blade with his thumb, as if to test its sharpness.

The girl with the long slender fingers broke into a loud laugh.

'Is that what you're here for – to cut our throats?'

Ivan sniggered and looked at his brother.

Sergei blushed and wiped the knife blade on his trousers.

'I can if you like,' he grunted, and blushed even redder.

'A little while ago, just before I left town, someone got stabbed,' Ivan said. 'It was one of the lads from our pit. He was just walking down the street and he came up to him and stuck it in – right here. The other one doubles up and he says, "What are you bending down for? Stand up straight!" But he was in such pain ...'

'I don't follow. Who said that to whom?' the girl who had performed at the 'demonstration' in the bathing-suit asked; she had finished combing her hair and was sitting at the table, eyeing the brothers merrily.

Ivan realized that he had said the wrong thing in the wrong way.

'The one who poked him with the knife,' he explained grudgingly.

Sergei slipped the knife away into his pocket and looked wistfully at his brother.

'Him and his tales,' he thought.

'Do you work in the mines?' the tall slim girl asked.

'Yes.'

'Right underground?'

Ivan smiled.

'Where else?'

'It must be hard work?'

'No! Only for the first month or two. Then you get used to it. The night shift's hard, of course. And it's hard for anyone who smokes; you're not allowed to smoke.'

'Mustn't you smoke?'

'It's because of the gases. It gave me a bit of trouble, then I dropped it.'

'What did you drop? Smoking?'

'Yeah.'

The conversation just wouldn't go. The plump girl openly showed her boredom, yawning and covering her mouth with a tiny hand. She looked at the clock.

'They seem to be a long time coming,' she said to her friend.

The other also looked at the clock.

'They'll be here in a minute.'

Sergei was looking at the plump little one; she gave him a glance too. Sergei looked away and frowned.

'Do you work down a mine too?' the girl asked.

Sergei shook his head.

'He's a driver,' Ivan said, and looked at his brother as elder brothers always look at younger brothers, as though apologizing slightly for their foolishness but with affection. 'That's his "grey mare" standing by the fence. I used to be a driver myself, then gave it up.'

'Why?'

'It doesn't pay.'

'Doesn't it?'

'What's the matter? Are you expecting someone?' Sergei asked.

'Some of our boys were going to come round,' the tall slim one answered.

'A-ah.' Ivan nodded understandingly. 'Good work.'

'By the way, I know a conjuring trick,' Sergei said suddenly and looked straight at the small plump girl.

The girls exchanged glances.

'Oh? What is it?'

'You take an ordinary handkerchief ...' Sergei searched his pockets in vain for a handkerchief, then asked his brother. His brother also searched and couldn't find one either.

'Haven't got one.'

The small plump girl sniggered into her hand.

Sergei looked at her, gave her one of his shy, friendly smiles and said simply, 'I'll go and fetch one'.

He went out into the passage and returned with a handkerchief, which he spread out on his broad palm.

'See?'

'And now what?' Ivan asked.

'Nothing there, is there?'

The girls also showed an interest.

'No, nothing. What now?'

'Keep calm everybody!' Sergei had suddenly become much bolder. 'I take a match and put it here. See?' He placed the match on the handkerchief. 'Did you see that?'

'Well?'

'I fold the handkerchief ...' Sergei folded the handkerchief with deliberate care, putting each corner into the middle, and allowed everyone in turn to feel the match through the handkerchief. 'Feel the match there?'

'Yes, it's there,' the small girl said (Sergei had given her first turn).

'Yes, it is,' said the tall slim girl.

'Yes, it's there,' said Ivan, and looked at his brother in surprise; he had not expected such initiative from him.

'Now break it!' Sergei commanded, and let the small girl break the match. She broke it in the handkerchief. Sergei looked at her joyfully.

'Broken it?'

'Yes.'

'Let me check that,' Ivan demanded.

'Certainly.'

Ivan checked.

'Is it broken?'

'It is.'

Sergei unfolded the handkerchief, and there was the match – all in one piece. Everyone was surprised. Sergei laughed.

'Show us again! Do show us again!' the small plump girl begged.

'Again? All right.'

Sergei went out into the passage for a few minutes and returned.

'What were you doing out there?' Ivan asked suspiciously.

'Having a smoke.'

'Let's break some more matches!' the small girl demanded.

Again they wrapped up the match and all three of them saw to it that it was broken, and again, when Sergei unfolded the handkerchief, the match was whole. The small plump girl squealed with delight and clapped her hands.

'Oooh! How's it done! Please, tell us!'

Just then there was a knock at the door.

'That's them!' the tall slim girl exclaimed joyfully. 'Yes, come in!'

Two young fellows entered the room. They had a guitar with them. The trick was forgotten, and so were the Vinokurov brothers. One of the newcomers said he had just heard a song in the street and promptly performed it 'country style'.

The townees laughed. Ivan laughed too – putting on airs again.

Sergei rose to his feet and said, 'I must have a look at the truck – it's been playing up a bit lately.'

He went out into the yard, sat down on the chopping block and lighted a cigarette.

From the windows of the best room came sounds of laughter and the strumming of the guitar – they were having fun. Sergei liked these handsome carefree people. He felt a sudden intense longing to be gay and handsome too. But he did not know how.

His father crossed the yard. He had been down to the cellar for some freshly salted cucumbers.

'What's the matter?' he asked his son.

'Nothing.'

'Where's Ivan?'

'In there.' Sergei nodded towards the window of the best room.

'Want a drink?'

'No, thanks.'

His father went back to the house, where his son's godfather was waiting for him.

Sergei finished his cigarette and stood up. He didn't feel like going to bed. The gaiety in the best room was disturbing. He pictured the small plump girl laughing, putting her hand over her mouth so that you could only see her shining eyes. She was a treat! He picked up the chopper and started splitting some thick logs. He split about three of them, then threw down the chopper and went up to the hayloft to sleep. Just as he was, in his new shirt. He could think of nothing but that sweet small girl.

Ivan climbed into the loft and sat down beside him.

'Well?' Sergei asked.

'Waste of time really,' Ivan replied. 'I told you it's all on the surface with them.'

Sergei turned away to the bare wooden wall.

'Why did you leave?'

'Never mind.'

They fell silent. Ivan sat for a while, whistling thoughtfully to himself, and went back to the house, to his father and godfather.

Peals of laughter were still coming from the windows of the best room.

In the morning Sergei rose at the crack of dawn. He walked aimlessly about the yard and peered in at the girls' window.

The small plump one was sleeping with her white plump arms lying across the pillow. Her mouth was slightly open and a bit of fluff was stuck to her lower lip; when she breathed out, the bit of fluff stood up and quivered in a funny way.

'Just like a kid,' Sergei thought tenderly. He stood watching the sleeping girl for some time, then he took a notebook from the cab of his lorry, tore out a clean page and wrote:

'It's dead easy really. All you have to do is hide a match beforehand in the hem of the handkerchief, then slip it in and see it's the one that gets broken. Let them break it till they're blue in the face – the other match is still whole! Get it? Try it on somebody. Sergei.'

He folded the sheet and put it on the window-sill with a stone on top of it, so that the wind wouldn't blow it away.

Then he started his engine and drove off.

The village streets were still deserted; the sun was just rising over the house-tops.

Perhaps I ought to buy myself a hat? Sergei wondered. He looked at himself in the driving mirror and grinned.

1964
Translated by Robert Daglish

We must return to Solzhenitsyn for a writer who penetrates to the very roots of peasant Russia, and finds there resonances that give sudden meaning to our search for the spiritual sources of modern Russian literature. His 'long short story' *Matryona's Home* seems not to be well known abroad; but some would say that it (together perhaps with *Ivan Denisovich*) represents his finest work so far. It 'selects itself' to close our anthology as naturally as Platonov's 'Seventh Man' did to start it.

Aleksandr Solzhenitsyn

MATRYONA'S HOME

A hundred and fifteen miles from Moscow trains were still slowing down to a crawl a good six months after it happened. Passengers stood glued to the windows or went out to stand by the doors. Was the line under repair, or what? Would the train be late?

It was all right. Past the crossing the train picked up speed again and the passengers went back to their seats.

Only the engine-drivers knew what it was all about.

The engine-drivers and I.

In the summer of 1953 I was coming back from the hot and dusty desert, just following my nose – so long as it led me back to European Russia. Nobody waited or wanted me at any particular place, because I was a little matter of ten years overdue. I just wanted to get to the central belt, away from the great heats, close to the leafy muttering of forests. I wanted to efface myself, to lose myself in deepest Russia ... if it was still to be found.

A year earlier I should have been lucky to get a job carrying a hod this side of the Urals. They wouldn't have taken me as an electrician on a decent construction job. And I had an itch to teach. Those who knew told me that it was a waste of money buying a ticket, that I should have a journey for nothing.

But things were beginning to move. When I went up the stairs of the N— Regional Education Department and asked for the Personnel Section, I was surprised to find Personnel sitting behind a glass partition, like in a chemist's shop, instead of the usual black leather-padded door. I went timidly up to the window, bowed, and asked, 'Please, do you need any mathematicians somewhere where the trains don't run? I should like to settle there for good.'

They passed every dot and comma in my documents through a fine comb, went from one room to another, made telephone calls. It was something out of the ordinary for them too – people always wanted the towns, the bigger the better. And lo and behold, they found just the place for me – Vysokoye Polye [High Field]. The very sound of it gladdened my heart.

Vysokoye Polye did not belie its name. It stood on rising ground, with gentle hollows and other little hills around it. It was enclosed by an unbroken ring of forest. There was a pool behind a weir. Just the place where I wouldn't mind living and dying. I spent a long time sitting on a stump in a coppice and wishing with all my heart that I didn't need breakfast and dinner every day but could just stay here and listen to the branches brushing against the roof in the night, with not a wireless anywhere to be heard and the whole world silent.

Alas, nobody baked bread in Vysokoye Polye. There was nothing edible on sale. The whole village lugged its victuals in sacks from the big town.

I went back to Personnel Section and raised my voice in prayer at the little window. At first they wouldn't even talk to me. But then they started going from one room to another, made a telephone call, scratched with their pens and stamped on my orders the word 'Torfoprodukt' [Peat product].

Torfoprodukt? Turgenev never knew that you can put words like that together in Russian.

On the station building at Torfoprodukt, an antiquated temporary hut of grey wood, hung a stern notice, BOARD TRAINS ONLY FROM THE PASSENGERS' HALL. A further message had been scratched on the boards with a nail, *And Without Tickets.* And by the booking-office, with the same melancholy wit, somebody had carved for all time the words, *No Tickets.* It was only later that I fully appreciated the meaning of these addenda. Getting to Torfoprodukt was easy. But not getting away.

Here too, deep and trackless forests had once stood, and were still standing after the Revolution. Then they were chopped down by the peat-cutters and the neighbouring kolkhoz. Its chairman, Shashkov, had razed quite a few hectares of timber and sold it at a good profit down in Odessa region.

The workers' settlement sprawled untidily among the peat bogs – monotonous shacks from the thirties, and little houses with carved façades and glass verandas, put up in the fifties. But inside these houses I could see no partitions reaching up to the ceilings, so there was no hope of renting a room with four real walls.

Over the settlement hung smoke from the factory chimney. Little locomotives ran this way and that along narrow-gauge railway lines, giving out more thick smoke and piercing whistles, pulling loads of dirty brown peat in slabs and briquettes. I could safely assume that in the evening a loudspeaker would be crying its heart out over the door of the club and there would be drunks roaming the streets and, sooner or later, sticking knives in each other.

This was what my dream about a quiet corner of Russia had brought me to ... when I could have stayed where I was and lived in an adobe hut looking out on the desert, with a fresh breeze at night and only the starry dome of the sky overhead.

I couldn't sleep on the station bench, and as soon as it started getting light I went for another stroll round the settlement. This time I saw a tiny market-place. Only one woman stood there at that early hour, selling milk, and I took a bottle and started drinking it on the spot.

I was struck by the way she talked. Instead of a normal speaking voice she used an ingratiating sing-song, and her words were the ones I was longing to hear when I left Asia for this place.

'Drink, and God bless you. You must be a stranger round here?'

'And where are you from?' I asked, feeling more cheerful.

I learnt that the peat workings weren't the only thing, that over the railway lines there was a hill, and over the hill a village, that this village was Talnovo, and it had been there ages ago, when the 'gipsy woman' lived in the big house and the wild woods stood all round. And farther on there was a whole countryside full of villages – Chaslitsy, Ovintsy, Spudni, Shevertni, Shestimirovo, deeper and deeper into the woods, farther and farther from the railway, up towards the lakes.

The names were like a soothing breeze to me. They held a promise of backwoods Russia. I asked my new acquaintance to take me to Talnovo after the market was over, and find a house for me to lodge in.

It appeared that I was a lodger worth having: in addition to my rent, the school offered a lorry-load of peat for the winter to whoever took me. The woman's ingratiating smile gave way to a thoughtful frown. She had no room herself, because she and her husband were 'keeping' her aged mother, so she took me first to one lot of relatives then to another. But there wasn't a separate room to be had and both places were crowded and noisy.

We had come to a dammed-up stream that was short of water and had a little bridge over it. No other place in all the village took my fancy as this did: there were two or three willows, a lop-sided house, ducks swimming on the pond, geese shaking themselves as they stepped out of the water.

'Well, perhaps we might just call on Matryona,' said my guide, who was getting tired of me by now. 'Only it isn't so neat and cosy-like in her house, neglects things she does. She's unwell.'

Matryona's house stood quite near by. Its row of four windows looked out on the cold backs, the two slopes of the roof were covered with shingles, and a little attic window was decorated in the old Russian style. But the shingles were rotting, the beam-ends of the house and the once mighty gates had turned grey with age, and there were gaps in the little shelter over the gate.

The small door let into the gate was fastened, but instead of knocking my companion just put her hand under and turned the catch, a simple device to prevent animals from straying. The yard was not covered, but there was a lot under the roof of the house. As you went through the outer door a short flight of steps rose to a roomy landing, which was open to the roof high overhead. To the left, other steps led up to the top room, which was a separate structure with no stove, and yet another flight down to the basement. To the right lay the house proper, with its attic and its cellar.

It had been built a long time ago, built sturdily, to house a big family, and now one lonely woman of nearly sixty lived in it.

When I went into the cottage she was lying on the Russian stove under a heap of those indeterminate dingy rags which are so precious to a working man or woman.

The spacious room, and especially the best part near the windows, was full of rubber plants in pots and tubs standing on stools and benches. They peopled the householder's loneliness like a speechless but living crowd. They had been allowed to run wild, and they took up all the scanty light on the north side. In what was left of the light, and half-hidden by the stove-pipe, the mistress of the house looked yellow and weak. You could see from her clouded eyes that illness had drained all the strength out of her.

While we talked she lay on the stove face downwards, without a pillow, her head towards the door, and I stood looking up at her. She showed no pleasure at getting a lodger, just complained about the wicked disease she had. She was just getting over an attack; it didn't come upon her every month, but when it did, 'It hangs on two or three days so as I shan't manage to get up and wait on you. I've room and to spare, you can live here if you like.'

Then she went over the list of other housewives with whom I should be quieter and cosier, and wanted me to make the round of them. But I had already seen that I was destined to settle in this dimly lit house with the tarnished mirror in which you couldn't see yourself, and the two garish posters (one advertising books, the other about the harvest), bought for a rouble each to brighten up the walls.

Matryona Vasilyevna made me go off round the village again, and when I called on her the second time she kept trying to put me off, 'We're not clever, we can't cook, I don't know how we shall suit ...' But this time she was on her feet when I got there, and I thought I saw a glimmer of pleasure in her eyes to see me back. We reached agreement about the rent and the load of peat which the school would deliver.

Later on I found out that, year in year out, it was a long time since Matryona Vasilyevna had earned a single rouble. She didn't get a pension. Her relatives gave her very little help. In the kolkhoz she had worked not for money but for credits: the marks recording her labour days in her well-thumbed work-book.

So I moved in with Matryona Vasilyevna. We didn't divide the room. Her bed was in the corner between the door and the stove, and I unfolded my camp-bed by one window and pushed Matryona's beloved rubber plants out of the light to make room for a little table by another. The village had electric light, laid on back in the twenties, from Shatura. The newspapers were writing about 'Ilyich's little lamps', but the peasants talked wide-eyed about 'Tsar Light'.

Some of the better-off people in the village might not have thought Matryona's house much of a home, but it kept us snug enough that autumn and winter. The roof still held the rain out, and the freezing winds could not blow the warmth of the stove away all at once, though it was cold by morning, especially when the wind blew on the shabby side.

In addition to Matryona and myself, a cat, some mice, and some cockroaches lived in the house.

The cat was no longer young, and gammy-legged as well. Matryona had taken her in out of pity, and she had stayed. She walked on all four feet but with a heavy limp: one of her feet was sore and she favoured it. When she jumped from the stove she didn't land with the soft sound a cat usually makes, but with a heavy thud as three of her feet struck the floor at once – such a heavy thud that until I got used to it, it gave me a start. This was because she stuck three feet out together to save the fourth.

It wasn't because the cat couldn't deal with them that there were mice in the cottage: she would pounce into the corner like lightning, and come back with a mouse between her teeth. But the mice were usually out of reach because somebody, back in the good old days, had stuck embossed wallpaper of a greenish colour on Matryona's walls, and not just one layer of it but five. The layers held together all right, but in many places the whole lot had come away from the wall, giving the room a sort of inner skin. Between the timber of the walls and the skin of wallpaper the mice had made themselves runs where they impudently scampered about, running at times right up to the ceiling. The cat followed their scamperings with angry eyes, but couldn't get at them.

Sometimes the cat ate cockroaches as well, but they made her sick. The only thing the cockroaches respected was the partition which screened the mouth of the Russian stove and the kitchen from the best part of the room.

They did not creep into the best room. But the kitchen at night swarmed with them, and if I went in late in the evening for a drink of water and switched on the light the whole floor, the big bench, and even the wall would be one rustling brown mass. From time to time I brought home some borax from the school laboratory and we mixed it with dough to poison them. There would be fewer cockroaches for a while, but Matryona was afraid that we might poison the cat as well. We stopped puting down poison and the cockroaches multiplied anew.

At night, when Matryona was already asleep and I was working at my table, the occasional rapid scamper of mice behind the wallpaper would be drowned in the sustained and ceaseless rustling of cockroaches behind the screen, like the sound of the sea in the distance. But I got used to it because there was nothing evil in it, nothing dishonest. Rustling was life to them.

I even got used to the crude beauty on the poster, for ever reaching out from the wall to offer me Belinsky, Panferov, and a pile of other books – but never saying a word. I got used to everything in Matryona's cottage.

Matryona got up at four or five o'clock in the morning. Her wall-clock was twenty-seven years old, and had been bought in the village shop. It was always fast, but Matryona didn't worry about that – just so long as it didn't lose and make her late in the morning. She switched on the light behind the kitchen screen and moving quietly, considerately, doing her best not to make a noise, she lit the stove, went to milk the goat (all the livestock she had was this one dirty-white goat with twisted horns), fetched water and boiled it in three iron pots: one for me, one for herself, and one for the goat. She fetched potatoes from the cellar, picking out the littlest for the goat, little ones for herself and egg-sized ones for me. There were no big ones, because her garden was sandy, had not been manured since the war and was always planted with potatoes, potatoes, and potatoes again, so that it wouldn't grow big ones.

I scarcely heard her about her morning tasks. I slept late, woke up in the wintry daylight, stretched a bit and stuck my head out from under my blanket and my sheep-skin. These, together with the prisoner's jerkin round my legs and a sack stuffed with straw underneath me, kept me warm in bed even on nights when the cold wind rattled our wobbly windows from the north. When I heard the discreet noises on the other side of the screen, I spoke to her, slowly and deliberately.

'Good morning, Matryona Vasilyevna!'

And every time the same good-natured words came to me from behind the screen. They began with a warm, throaty gurgle, the sort of sound grandmothers make in fairy-tales.

'M-m-m ... same to you too!'

And after a little while, 'Your breakfast's ready for you now.'

She didn't announce what was for breakfast, but it was easy to guess: taters in their jackets or tatty soup (as everybody in the village called it), or barley gruel (no other grain could be bought in Torfoprodukt that year, and even the barley you had to fight for, because it was the cheapest and people bought it up by the sack to fatten their pigs on it). It wasn't always salted as it should be, it was often slightly burnt, it furred the palate and the gums, and it gave me heartburn.

But Matryona wasn't to blame: there was no butter in Torfoprodukt either, margarine was desperately short, and only mixed cooking fat was plentiful, and when I got to know it I saw that the Russian stove was not convenient for cooking: the cook cannot see the pots and they are not heated evenly all round. I suppose the stove came down to our ancestors from the Stone Age because you can stoke it up once before daylight, and food and water, mash and swill, will keep warm in it all day long. And it keeps you warm while you sleep.

I ate everything that was cooked for me without demur, patiently putting aside anything uncalled-for that I came across: a hair, a bit of peat, a cockroach's leg. I hadn't the heart to find fault with Matryona. After all, she had warned me herself.

'We aren't clever, we can't cook – I don't know how we shall suit ...'

'Thank you,' I said quite sincerely.

'What for? For what is your own?' she answered, disarming me with a radiant smile. And, with a guileless look of her faded-blue eyes, she would ask, 'And what shall I cook you for just now?'

For just now meant for supper. I ate twice a day, like at the Front. What could I order for just now? It would have to be one of the same old things, taters or tater soup.

I resigned myself to it, because I had learnt by now not to look for the meaning of life in food. More important to me was the smile on her roundish face, which I tried in vain to catch when at last I had earned enough to buy a camera. As soon as she saw the cold eye of the lens upon her Matryona assumed a strained or else an exaggeratedly severe expression.

Just once I did manage to get a snap of her looking through the window into the street and smiling at something.

Matryona had a lot of worries that winter. Her neighbours put it into her head to try and get a pension. She was all alone in the world, and when she began to be seriously ill she had been dismissed from the kolkhoz as well. Injustices had piled up, one on top of another. She was ill, but not regarded as a disabled person. She had worked for a quarter of a century in the kolkhoz, but it was a kolkhoz and not a factory, so she was not entitled to a pension for herself. She could only try and get one for her husband, for the loss of her bread-winner. But she had had no husband for twelve years now, not since the beginning of the war, and it wasn't easy to obtain all the particulars from different places about his length of service and how much he had earned. What a bother it was getting those forms through! Getting somebody to certify that he'd earned, say, 300 roubles a month; that she lived alone and nobody helped her; what year she was born in. Then all this had to be taken to the Pensions Office. And taken somewhere else to get all the mistakes corrected. And taken back again. Then you had to find out whether they would give you a pension.

To make it all more difficult the Pensions Office was twelve miles east of Talnovo, the Rural Council Offices six miles to the west, the Factory District Council an hour's walk to the north. They made her run around from office to office for two months on end, to get an *i* dotted or a *t* crossed. Every trip took a day. She goes down to the Rural District Council – and the secretary isn't there today. Secretaries of rural councils often aren't here today. So come again tomorrow. Tomorrow the secretary is in, but he hasn't got his rubber stamp. So come again the next day. And the day after that back she goes yet again, because all her papers are pinned together and some cock-eyed clerk has signed the wrong one.

'They shove me around, Ignatich,' she used to complain to me after these fruitless excursions. 'Worn out with it I am.'

But she soon brightened up. I found that she had a sure means of putting herself in a good humour. She worked. She would grab a shovel and go off to lift potatoes. Or she would tuck a sack under her arm and go after peat. Or take a wicker basket and look for berries deep in the woods. When she'd been bending her back to bushes instead of office desks for a while, and her shoulders were aching from a heavy load, Matryona would come back cheerful, at peace with the world and smiling her nice smile.

'I'm on to a good thing now, Ignatich. I know where to go for it (peat she meant), a lovely place it is.'

'But surely my peat is enough, Matryona Vasilyevna? There's a whole lorry-load of it.'

'Pooh! Your peat! As much again, and then as much again, that might be enough. When the winter gets really stiff and the wind's battling at the windows, it blows the heat out of the house faster than you can make the stove up. Last year we got heaps and heaps of it. I'd have had three loads in by now. But they're out to catch us. They've summoned one woman from our village already.'

That's how it was. The frightening breath of winter was already in the air. There were forests all round, and no fuel to be had anywhere. Excavators roared away in the bogs, but there was no peat on sale to the villagers. It was delivered, free, to the bosses and the people round the bosses, and teachers, doctors, and workers got a load each. The people of Talnovo were not supposed to get any peat, and they weren't supposed to ask about it. The chairman of the kolkhoz walked about the village looking people in the eye while he gave his orders or stood chatting, and talked about anything you liked except fuel. He was stocked-up. Who said anything about winter coming?

So just as in the old days they used to steal the squire's wood, now they pinched peat from the trust. The women went in parties of five or ten, so that they would be less frightened. They went in the daytime. The peat cut during the summer had been stacked up all over the place to dry. That's the good thing about peat, it can't be carted off as soon as it's cut. It lies around drying till autumn or, if the roads are bad, till the snow starts falling. This was when the women used to come and take it. They could get six peats in a sack if it was damp, or ten if it was dry. A sackful weighed about half a hundredweight and it sometimes had to be carried two miles. This was enough to make the stove up once. There were 200 days in the winter. The Russian stove had to be lit in the mornings, and the 'Dutch' stove in the evenings.

'Why beat about the bush?' said Matryona angrily to someone invisible. 'Since there've been no more horses, what you can't heave around yourself you haven't got. My back never heals up. Winter you're pulling sledges, summer it's bundles on your back, it's God's truth I'm telling you.'

The women went more than once in a day. On good days Matryona brought six sacks home. She piled my peat up where it could be seen, and hid her own under the passageway, boarding up the hole every night.

'If they don't just happen to think of it, the devils will never find it in their born days,' said Matryona smiling and wiping the sweat from her brow.

What could the peat trust do? Its establishment didn't run to a watchman for every bog. I suppose they had to show a rich haul in their returns, and then write off so much for crumbling, so much washed away by the rain ... Sometimes they would take it into their heads to put out patrols and try to catch the women as they came into the village. The women would drop their sacks and scatter. Or somebody would inform and there would be a house-to-house search. They would draw up a report on the stolen peat, and threaten a court action. The women would stop fetching it for a while, but the approach of winter drove them out with sledges in the middle of the night.

When I had seen a little more of Matryona, I noticed that, apart from cooking and looking after the house, she had quite a lot of other jobs to do every day. She kept all her jobs, and the proper times for them, in her head and always knew when she woke up in the morning how her day would be occupied. Apart from fetching peat, and stumps which the tractors unearthed in the bogs, apart from the cranberries which she put to soak in big jars for the winter ('Give your teeth an edge,

Ignatich,' she used to say when she offered me some), apart from digging potatoes and all the coming and going to do with her pension, she had to get hay from somewhere for her one and only dirty-white goat.

'Why don't you keep a cow, Matryona?'

Matryona stood there in her grubby apron, by the opening in the kitchen screen, facing my table, and explained to me.

'Oh, Ignatich, there's enough milk from the goat for me. And if I started keeping a cow she'd eat me out of house and home in no time. You can't cut the grass by the railway track, because it belongs to the railway, and you can't cut any in the woods, because it belongs to the foresters, and they won't let me have any at the kolkhoz because I'm not a member any more, they reckon. And those who are members have to work there every day till the white flies swarm, and make their own hay when there's snow on the ground – what's the good of grass like that? In the old days they used to be sweating to get the hay in at midsummer, between the end of June and the end of July, while the grass was sweet and juicy ...'

So it meant a lot of work for Matryona to gather enough hay for one skinny little goat. She took her sickle and a sack and went off early in the morning to places where she knew there was grass growing – round the edges of fields, on the roadside, on hummocks in the bog. When she had stuffed her sack with heavy fresh grass she dragged it home and spread it out in her yard to dry. From a sackful of grass she got one forkload of dry hay.

The farm had a new chairman, sent down from the town not long ago, and the first thing he did was to cut down the garden-plots for those who were not fit to work. He left Matryona a third of an acre of sand – when there was over a thousand square yards just lying idle on the other side of the fence. Yet when they were short of working hands, when the women dug in their heels and wouldn't budge, the chairman's wife would come to see Matryona. She was from the town as well, a determined woman whose short grey overcoat and intimidating glare gave her a somewhat military appearance. She walked into the house without so much as a good-morning and looked sternly at Matryona. Matryona was uneasy.

'Well now, Comrade Vasilyevna,' said the chairman's wife, drawing out her words. 'You will have to help the kolkhoz! You will have to go and help cart muck out tomorrow!'

A little smile of forgiveness wrinkled Matryona's face – as though she understood the embarrassment which the chairman's wife must feel, not being able to pay her for her work.

'Well – er,' she droned. 'I'm not well, of course, and I'm not attached to you any more ...' then she hurried to correct herself, 'What time should I come then?'

'And bring your own fork!' the chairman's wife instructed her. Her stiff skirt crackled as she walked away.

'Think of that!' grumbled Matryona as the door closed. 'Bring your own fork! They've got neither forks nor shovels on the kolkhoz. And I don't have a man who'll put a handle on for me!'

She went on thinking about it out loud all evening.

'What's the good of talking, Ignatich. I must help, of course. Only the way they work it's all a waste of time – don't know whether they're coming or going. The women stand propped up on their shovels and waiting for the factory hooter to blow twelve o'clock. Or else they get on to adding up who's earned what and who's turned up for work and who hasn't. Now what I call work, there isn't a sound out of anybody, only ... oh dear, dear – dinner-time's soon rolled round – what, getting dark already ...'

In the morning she went off with her fork.

But it wasn't just the kolkhoz – any distant relative, or just a neighbour, could come to Matryona of an evening and say, 'Come and give me a hand tomorrow, Matryona. We'll finish lifting the potatoes.'

Matryona couldn't say no. She gave up what she should be doing next and went to help her neighbour, and when she came back she would say without a trace of envy, 'Ah, you should see the size of her potatoes, Ignatich! It was a joy to dig them up. I didn't want to leave the allotment, God's truth I didn't.'

Needless to say, not a garden could be ploughed without Matryona's help. The women of Talnovo had got it neatly worked out that it was a longer and harder job for one woman to dig her garden with a spade than for six of them to put themselves in harness and plough six gardens. So they sent for Matryona to help them.

'Well – did you pay her?' I asked sometimes.

'She won't take money. You have to try and hide it on her when she's not looking.'

Matryona had yet another troublesome chore when her turn came to feed the herdsmen. One of them was a hefty deaf mute, the other a boy who was never without a cigarette in his drooling mouth. Matryona's turn only came round every six weeks, but it put her to great expense. She went to the shop to buy tinned fish, and was lavish with sugar and butter, things she never ate herself. It seems that the housewives showed off in this way, trying to outdo each other in feeding the herdsmen.

'You've got to be careful with tailors and herdsmen,' Matryona explained. 'They'll spread your name all round the village if something doesn't suit them.'

And every now and then attacks of serious illness broke in on this life that was already crammed with troubles. Matryona would be off her feet for a day or two, lying flat out on the stove. She didn't complain, and didn't groan, but she hardly stirred either. On these days Masha, Matryona's closest friend from her earliest years, would come to look after the goat and light the stove. Matryona herself ate nothing, drank nothing, asked for nothing. To call in the doctor from the clinic at the settlement would have seemed strange in Talnovo, and would have given the neighbours something to talk about – what does she think she is, a lady? They did call her in once, and she arrived in a real temper and told Matryona to come down to the clinic when she was on her feet again. Matryona went, although she didn't really want to; they took specimens and sent them off to the district hospital – and that's the last anybody heard about it. Matryona was partly to blame herself.

But there was work waiting to be done, and Matryona soon started getting up again, moving slowly at first and then as briskly as ever.

'You never saw me in the old days, Ignatich. I'd lift any sack you liked, I didn't think a hundredweight was too heavy. My father-in-law used to say, "Matryona, you'll break your back". And my brother-in-law didn't have to come and help me lift on the cart. Our horse was a war-horse, a big strong one ...'

'What do you mean, a war-horse?'

'They took ours for the war and gave us this one instead – he'd been wounded. But he turned out a bit spirited. Once he bolted with the sledge right into the lake, the men-folk hopped out of the way, but I grabbed the bridle, as true as I'm here, and stopped him ... Full of oats that horse was. They liked to feed their horses well in our village. If a horse feels his oats he doesn't know what heavy means.'

But Matryona was a long way from being fearless. She was afraid of fire, afraid of 'the lightning', and most of all she was for some reason afraid of trains.

'When I had to go to Cherusti, the train came up from Nechayevka way with its great big eyes popping out and the rails humming away – put me in a proper fever. My knees started knocking. God's truth I'm telling you!' Matryona raised her shoulders as though she surprised herself.

'Maybe it's because they won't give people tickets, Matryona Vasilyevna?'

'At the window? They try to shove first-class tickets on to you. And the train was starting to move. We dashed about all over the place: "Give us tickets for pity's sake."

'The men-folk had climbed on top of the carriages. Then we found a door that wasn't locked and shoved straight in without tickets ... and all the carriages were empty, they were all empty, you could stretch out on the seat if you wanted to. Why they wouldn't give us tickets, the hard-hearted parasites, I don't know ...'

Still, before winter came Matryona's affairs were in a better state than ever before. They started paying her at last a pension of eighty roubles. Besides this she got just over 100 from the school and me.

Some of her neighbours began to be envious.

'Hm! Matryona can live for ever now. If she had any more money she wouldn't know what to do with it at her age.'

Matryona had herself some new felt boots made. She bought a new jerkin. And she had an overcoat made out of the worn-out railwayman's greatcoat given to her by the engine-driver from Cherusti who had married Kira, her foster-daughter. The hump-backed village tailor put a padded lining under the cloth and it made a marvellous coat, such as Matryona had never worn before in all her sixty years.

In the middle of winter Matryona sewed 200 roubles into the lining of this coat for her funeral. This made her quite cheerful.

'Now my mind's a bit easier, Ignatich.'

December went by, January went by – and in those two months Matryona's illness held off. She started going over to Masha's house more often in the evening, to sit chewing sunflower seeds with her. She didn't invite guests herself in the evening out of consideration for my work. Once, on the feast of the Epiphany, I came back from school and found a party going on and was introduced to Matryona's three sisters who called her 'nan-nan' or 'nanny' because she was the oldest. Until then not much had been heard of the sisters in our cottage – perhaps they were afraid that Matryona might ask them for help.

But one ominous event cast a shadow on the holiday for Matryona. She went to the church three miles away for the blessing of the water, and put her pot down among the others. When the blessing was over, the women went rushing and jostling to get their pots back again. There were a lot of women in front of Matryona and when she got there her pot was missing, and no other vessel had been left behind. The pot had vanished as though the Devil had run off with it.

Matryona went around the worshippers asking them, 'Has any of you girls accidentally mistook somebody's else's holy water? In a pot?'

Nobody owned up. There had been some boys there, and boys got up to mischief sometimes. Matryona came home sad.

No one could say that Matryona was a devout believer. If anything, she was a heathen, and her strongest beliefs were superstitious: you mustn't go into the garden on the fast of St John or there would be no harvest next year. A blizzard meant that somebody had hanged himself. If you pinched your foot in the door, you could expect a guest. All the time I lived with her I didn't once see her say her prayers or even cross herself. But, whatever job she was doing, she began with a 'God bless us', and she never failed to say 'God bless you', when I set out for school. Perhaps she did say her prayers, but on the quiet, either because she was shy or because she didn't want to embarrass me. There were ikons on the walls. Ordinary days they were left in darkness, but for the vigil of a great feast, or on the morning of a holiday, Matryona would light the little lamp.

She had fewer sins on her conscience than her gammy-legged cat. The cat did kill mice ...

Now that her life was running more smoothly, Matryona

started listening more carefully to my radio. (I had, of course, installed a speaker, or as Matryona called it, a peeker.)

When they announced on the radio that some new machine had been invented, I heard Matryona grumbling out in the kitchen, 'New ones all the time, nothing but new ones. People don't want to work with the old ones any more, where are we going to store them all?'

There was a programme about the seeding of clouds from aeroplanes. Matryona, listening up on the stove, shook her head, 'Oh, dear, dear, dear, they'll do away with one of the two – summer or winter.'

Once Chaliapin was singing Russian folk-songs. Matryona stood listening for a long time before she gave her emphatic verdict, 'Queer singing, not our sort of singing.'

'You can't mean that, Matryona Vasilyevna ... just listen to him.'

She listened a bit longer, and pursed her lips, 'No, it's wrong. It isn't our sort of tune, and he's tricky with his voice.'

She made up for this another time. They were broadcasting some of Glinka's songs. After half a dozen of these drawing-room ballads, Matryona suddenly came from behind the screen clutching her apron, with a flush on her face and a film of tears over her dim eyes.

'That's our sort of singing,' she said in a whisper.

So Matryona and I got used to each other and took each other for granted. She never pestered me with questions about myself. I don't know whether she was lacking in normal female curiosity or just tactful, but she never once asked if I had been married. All the Talnovo women kept at her to find out about me. Her answer was, 'You want to know – you ask him. All I know is he's from distant parts.'

And when I got round to telling her that I had spent a lot of time in prison she said nothing but just nodded, as though she had already suspected it.

And I thought of Matryona only as the helpless old woman she was now, and didn't try to rake up her past, didn't even suspect that there was anything to be found there.

I knew that Matryona had got married before the Revolution and come to live in the house I now shared with her, that she had gone 'to the stove' immediately. (She had no mother-in-law and no older sister-in-law, so it was her job to put the pots in the oven on the very first morning of her married life.) I knew that she had had six children and that they had all died very young, so that there were never two of them alive at once. Then there was a sort of foster-daughter, Kira. Matryona's husband had not come back from the last war. She received no notification of his death. Men from the village who had served in the same company said that he might have been taken prisoner, or he might have been killed and his body not found. In the eight years that had gone by since the war Matryona had decided that he was not alive. It was a good thing that she thought so. If he was still alive, he was probably in Brazil or Australia, and married again. The village of Talnovo, and the Russian language, would be fading from his memory.

One day, when I got back from school, I found a guest in the house. A tall, dark man, with his hat on his lap, was sitting on a chair which Matryona had moved up to the Dutch stove in the middle of the room. His face was completely surrounded by bushy black hair with hardly a trace of grey in it. His thick black moustaches ran into his full black beard, so that his mouth could hardly be seen. Black side-whiskers merged with the black locks which hung down from his crown, leaving only the tips of his ears visible; and broad black eyebrows met in a wide double span. But the front of his head as far as the crown was a spacious bald dome. His whole appearance made an impression of wisdom and dignity. He sat squarely on his chair, with his hands folded on his stick, and his stick resting vertically on the floor, in an attitude of patient expectation, and he obviously hadn't much to say to Matryona, who was busy behind the screen.

When I came in, he eased his majestic head round towards me and suddenly addressed me, 'Master, I can't see you very well. My son goes to your school. Grigoryev, Antoshka ...'

There was no need for him to say any more ... However strongly inclined I felt to help this worthy old man, I knew and dismissed in advance all the pointless things he was going to say. Antoshka Grigoryev was a plump, red-faced lad in 8-D who looked like a cat that's swallowed the cream. He seemed to think that he came to school for a rest and sat at his desk with a lazy smile on his face. Needless to say, he never did his homework. But the worst of it was that he had been put up into the next class from year to year because our district, and indeed the whole region and the neighbouring region, were famous for the high percentage of passes they obtained, and the school had to make an effort to keep its record up. So Antoshka had got it clear in his mind that, however much the teachers threatened him, they would put him up in the end, and there was no need for him to learn anything. He just laughed at us. There he sat in the eighth class, and he hadn't even mastered his decimals and didn't know one triangle from another. In the first two terms of the school year I had kept him firmly below the pass line and the same treatment awaited him in the third.

But now this half-blind old man, who should have been Antoshka's grandfather rather than his father, had come to humble himself before me – how could I tell him that the school had been deceiving him for years, and that I couldn't go on deceiving him, because I didn't want to ruin the whole class, to become a liar and a fake, to start despising my work and my profession.

For the time being I patiently explained that his son had been very slack, that he told lies at school and at home, that his mark-book must be checked frequently, and that we must both take him severely in hand.

'Severe as you like, master,' he assured me, 'I beat him every week now. And I've got a heavy hand.'

While we were talking I remembered Matryona had once interceded for Antoshka Grigoryev, but I hadn't asked what relation of hers he was and I had refused to do what she wanted. Matryona was standing in the kitchen doorway like a mute suppliant on this occasion too. When Faddei Mironovich left, saying that he would call on me to see how things were going, I asked her, 'I can't make out what relation this Antoshka is to you, Matryona Vasilyevna'.

'My brother-in-law's son,' said Matryona shortly, and went out to milk the goat.

When I'd worked it out, I realized that this determined old man with the black hair was the brother of the missing husband.

The long evening went by, and Matryona didn't bring up the subject again. But late at night, when I had stopped thinking about the old man and was working in silence broken only by the rustling of the cockroaches and the heavy tick of the wall-clock, Matryona suddenly spoke from her dark corner: 'You know, Ignatich, I nearly married him once.'

I had forgotten that Matryona was in the room. I hadn't heard a sound from her – and suddenly her voice came out of the darkness, as agitated as if the old man were still trying to win her.

I could see that Matryona had been thinking about nothing else all evening.

She got up from her wretched rag bed and walked slowly towards me, as though she were following her own words. I sat back in my chair and caught my first glimpse of a quite different Matryona.

There was no overhead light in our big room with its forest

of rubber plants. The table lamp cast a ring of light round my exercise books, and when I tore my eyes from it the rest of the room seemed to be half-dark and faintly tinged with pink. I thought I could see the same pinkish glow in her usually sallow cheeks.

'He was the first one who came courting me, before Yefim did ... he was his brother ... the older one ... I was nineteen and Faddei was twenty-three ... They lived in this very same house. Their house it was. Their father built it.'

I looked round the room automatically. Instead of the old grey house rotting under the faded green skin of wallpaper where the mice had their playground, I suddenly saw new timbers, freshly trimmed, and not yet discoloured, and caught the cheerful smell of pine-tar.

'Well, and what happened then?'

'That summer we went to sit in the coppice together,' she whispered. 'There used to be a coppice where the stableyard is now. They chopped it down ... I was just going to marry him, Ignatich. Then the German war started. They took Faddei in the army.'

She let fall these few words – and suddenly the blue and white and yellow July of the year 1914 burst into flower before my eyes: the sky still peaceful, the floating clouds, the people sweating to get the ripe corn in. I imagined them side by side, the black-haired Hercules with a scythe over his shoulder, and the red-faced girl clasping a sheaf. And there was singing out under the open sky, such songs as nobody can sing nowadays, with all the machines in the fields.

'He went to the war – and vanished. For three years I kept to myself and waited. Never a sign of life did he give ...'

Matryona's round face looked out at me from an elderly threadbare head-scarf. As she stood there in the gentle reflected light from my lamp her face seemed to lose its slovenly workaday covering of wrinkles, and she was a scared young girl again with a frightening decision to make.

Yes ... I could see it ... The trees shed their leaves, the snow fell and melted. They ploughed and sowed and reaped again. Again the trees shed their leaves, and snow fell. There was a revolution. Then another revolution. And the whole world was turned upside down.

'Their mother died and Yefim came to court me. You wanted to come to our house, he says, so come. He was a year younger than me, Yefim was. It's a saying with us – sensible girls get married after Michaelmas, and silly ones at midsummer. They were short-handed. I got married ... The wedding was on St Peter's day, and then about St Nicolas's day in the winter he came back ... Faddei, I mean, from being a prisoner in Hungary.'

Matryona covered her eyes.

I said nothing.

She turned towards the door as though somebody were standing there. 'He stood there at the door. What a scream I let out! I wanted to throw myself at his feet! ... but I couldn't. If it wasn't my own brother, he says, I'd take my axe to the both of you.'

I shuddered. Matryona's despair, or her terror, conjured up a vivid picture of him standing in the dark doorway and raising his axe to her.

But she quietened down and went on with her story in a sing-song voice, leaning on a chair-back, 'Oh dear, dear me, the poor dear man! There were so many girls in the village – but he wouldn't marry. I'll look for one with the same name as you, a second Matryona, he said. And that's what he did – fetched himself a Matryona from Lipovka. They built themselves a house of their own and they're still living in it. You pass their place every day on your way to school.'

So that was it. I realized that I had seen the other Matryona quite often. I didn't like her. She was always coming to my Matryona to complain about her husband – he beat her, he was stingy, he was working her to death. She would weep and weep, and her voice always had a tearful note in it. As it turned out, my Matryona had nothing to regret, with Faddei beating his Matryona every day of his life and being so tight-fisted.

'Mine never beat me once,' said Matryona of Yefim. 'He'd pitch into another man in the street, but me he never hit once ... Well, there was one time ... I quarrelled with my sister-in-law and he cracked me on the forehead with a spoon. I jumped up from the table and shouted at them, "Hope it sticks in your gullets, you idle lot of beggars, hope you choke!" I said. And off I went into the woods. He never touched me any more.'

Faddei didn't seem to have any cause for regret either. The other Matryona had borne him six children (my Antoshka was one of them, the littlest, the runt) and they had all lived, whereas the children of Matryona and Yefim had died, every one of them, before they reached the age of three months, without any illness.

'One daughter, Yelena, was born and was alive when they washed her, and then she died right after ... My wedding was on St Peter's day, and it was St Peter's day I buried my sixth, Aleksandr.'

The whole village decided that there was a curse on Matryona.

Matryona still nodded emphatic belief when she talked about it. 'There was a *course* on me. They took me to a woman as used to be a nun to get cured, she set me off coughing and waited for the *course* to jump out of me like a frog. Only nothing jumped out ...'

And the years had run by like running water ... In 1941 they didn't take Faddei into the army because of his poor sight, but they took Yefim. And what had happened to the elder brother in the First World War happened to the younger in the Second ... he vanished without trace. Only he never came back at all. The once noisy cottage was deserted, it became old and rotten, and Matryona, all alone in the world, grew old in it.

So she begged from the other Matryona, the cruelly beaten Matryona, a child of her womb (or was it a spot of Faddei's blood?), the youngest daughter, Kira.

For ten years she brought the girl up in her own house, in place of the children who had not lived. Then, not long before I arrived, she had married her off to a young engine-driver from Cherusti. The only help she got from anywhere came in dribs and drabs from Cherusti: a bit of sugar from time to time, or some of the fat when they killed a pig.

Sick and suffering, and feeling that death was not far off, Matryona had made known her will: the top room, which was a separate frame joined by tie-beams to the rest of the house, should go to Kira when she died. She said nothing about the house itself. Her three sisters had their eyes on it too.

That evening Matryona opened her heart to me. And, as often happens, no sooner were the hidden springs of her life revealed to me than I saw them in motion.

Kira arrived from Cherusti. Old Faddei was very worried. To get and keep a plot of land in Cherusti the young couple had to put up some sort of building. Matryona's top-room would do very well. There was nothing else they could put up, because there was no timber to be had anywhere. It wasn't Kira herself so much, and it wasn't her husband, but old Faddei who was consumed with eagerness for them to get their hands on the plot at Cherusti.

He became a frequent visitor, laying down the law to Matryona and insisting that she should hand over the top room right away, before she died. On these occasions I saw a different Faddei. He was no longer an old man propped up by a stick, whom a push or a harsh word would bowl over.

Although he was slightly bent by back-ache, he was still a fine figure; he had kept the vigorous black hair of a young man in his sixties; he was hot and urgent.

Matryona had not slept for two nights. It wasn't easy for her to make up her mind. She didn't grudge them the top room, which was standing there idle, any more than she ever grudged her labour or her belongings. And the top room was willed to Kira in any case. But the thought of breaking up the roof she had lived under for forty years was torture to her. Even I, a mere lodger, found it painful to think of them stripping away boards and wrenching out beams. For Matryona it was the end of everything.

But the people who were so insistent knew that she would let them break up her house before she died.

So Faddei and his sons and sons-in-law came along one February morning, the blows of five axes were heard and boards creaked and cracked as they were wrenched out. Faddei's eyes twinkled busily. Although his back wasn't quite straight, yet he scrambled nimbly up under the rafters and bustled about down below, shouting at his assistants. He and his father had built this house when he was a lad, a long time ago. The top room had been put up for him, the oldest son, to move in with his bride. And now he was furiously taking it apart, board by board, to carry it out of somebody else's yard.

After numbering the beam-ends and the ceiling boards they dismantled the top room and the store-room underneath it. The living-room, and what was left of the landing, they boarded up with a thin wall of deal. They did nothing about the cracks in the wall. It was plain to see that they were wreckers, not builders, and that they did not expect Matryona to be living there very long.

While the men were busy wrecking, the women were getting the drink ready for moving day – vodka would cost a lot too much. Kira brought forty pounds of sugar from Moscow region, and Matryona carried the sugar and some bottles to the distiller under cover of night.

The timbers were carried out and stacked in front of the gates, and the engine-driver son-in-law went off to Cherusti for the tractor.

But the very same day a blizzard, or 'a blower' as Matryona called it, began. It howled and whirled for two days and nights and buried the road under enormous drifts. Then, no sooner had they made the road passable and a couple of lorries gone by, than it got suddenly warmer. Within a day everything was thawing out, damp mist hung in the air and rivulets gurgled as they burrowed into the snow, and you could get stuck up to the top of your knee-boots.

Two weeks passed before the tractor could get at the dismantled top room. All this time Matryona went around like someone lost. What particularly upset her was that her three sisters came and with one voice called her a fool for giving the top room away, said they didn't want to see her any more, and went off. At about the same time the lame cat strayed and was seen no more. It was just one thing after another. This was another blow to Matryona.

At last the frost got a grip on the slushy road. A sunny day came along and everybody felt more cheerful. Matryona had had a lucky dream the night before. In the morning she heard that I wanted to take a photograph of somebody at an old-fashioned hand-loom. (There were looms still standing in two cottages in the village; they wove coarse rugs on them.) She smiled shyly and said, 'You just wait a day or two, Ignatich, I'll just send the top room there off and I'll put my loom up, I've still got it, you know, and then you can snap me. Honest to God!'

She was obviously attracted by the idea of posing in an old-fashioned setting. The red, frosty sun tinged the window of the curtailed passageway with a faint pink, and this reflected light warmed Matryona's face. People who are at ease with their consciences always have nice faces.

Coming back from school before dusk I saw some movement near our house. A big new tractor-drawn sledge was already fully loaded, and there was no room for a lot of the timbers, so old Faddei's family and the helpers they had called in had nearly finished knocking together another home-made sledge. They were all working like madmen, in the frenzy that comes upon people when there is a smell of good money in the air or when they are looking forward to some treat. They were shouting at one another and arguing.

They could not agree whether the sledges should be hauled separately or both together. One of Faddei's sons (the lame one) and the engine-driver son-in-law reasoned that the sledges couldn't both be taken at once because the tractor wouldn't be able to pull them. The man in charge of the tractor, a hefty fat-faced fellow who was very sure of himself, said hoarsely that he knew best, he was the driver, and he would take both at once. His motives were obvious: according to the agreement the engine-driver was paying him for the removal of the upper room not for the number of trips he had to make. He could never have made two trips in a night – twenty-five kilometres each way, and one return journey. And by morning he had to get the tractor back in the garage from which he had sneaked it out for this job on the side.

Old Faddei was impatient to get the top room moved that day, and at a nod from him his lads gave in. To the stout sledge in front they hitched the one which they had knocked together in such a hurry.

Matryona was running about amongst the men, fussing and helping them to heave the beams on to the sledge. Suddenly I noticed that she was wearing my jerkin and had dirtied the sleeves on the frozen mud round the beams. I was annoyed, and told her so. That jerkin held memories for me: it had kept me warm in the bad years.

This was the first time that I was ever angry with Matryona Vasilyevna.

Matryona was taken aback. 'Oh dear, dear me,' she said. 'My poor head. I picked it up in a rush, you see, and never thought about it being yours. I'm sorry, Ignatich.'

And she took it off and hung it up to dry.

The loading was finished, and all the men who had been working, about ten of them, clattered past my table and dived under the curtain into the kitchen. I could hear the muffled rattle of glasses and, from time to time, the clink of a bottle, the voices got louder and louder, the boasting more reckless. The biggest braggart was the tractor-driver. The stench of hooch floated in to me. But they didn't go on drinking long. It was getting dark and they had to hurry. They began to leave. The tractor-driver came out first, looking pleased with himself and fierce. The engine-driver son-in-law, Faddei's lame son and one of his nephews were going to Cherusti. The others went off home. Faddei was flourishing his stick, trying to overtake somebody and put him right about something. The lame son paused at my table to light up and suddenly started telling me how he loved Aunt Matryona, and that he had got married not long ago, and his wife had just had a son. Then they shouted for him and he went out. The tractor set up a roar outside.

After all the others had gone Matryona dashed out from behind the screen. She looked after them, anxiously shaking her head. She had put on her jerkin and her head-scarf. As she was going through the door she said to me, 'Why ever couldn't they hire two? If one tractor had cracked up, the other would have pulled them. What'll happen now, God only knows!'

She ran out after the others.

After the booze-up and the arguments and all the coming and going it was quieter than ever in the deserted cottage, and very chilly because the door had been opened so many times. I got into my jerkin and sat down to mark exercise books. The noise of the tractor died away in the distance.

An hour went by. And another. And a third. Matryona still hadn't come back, but I wasn't surprised. When she had seen the sledge off she must have gone round to her friend Masha.

Another hour went by. And yet another. Darkness and with it a deep silence had descended on the village. I couldn't understand at the time why it was so quiet. Later I found out that it was because all evening not a single train had gone along the line five hundred yards from the house. No sound was coming from my radio and I noticed that the mice were wilder than ever. Their scampering and scratching and squeaking behind the wallpaper was getting noisier and more defiant all the time.

I woke up. It was one o'clock in the morning and Matryona still hadn't come home.

Suddenly I heard several people talking loudly. They were still a long way off, but something told me that they were coming to our house. And sure enough I heard soon afterwards a heavy knock at the gate. A commanding voice, strange to me, yelled out an order to open up. I went out into the pitch darkness with a torch. The whole village was asleep, there was no light in the windows and the snow had started melting in the last week so that it gave no reflected light. I turned the catch and let them in. Four men in greatcoats went on towards the house. It's a very unpleasant thing to be visited at night by noisy people in greatcoats.

When we got into the light though, I saw that two of them were wearing railway uniforms. The older of the two, a fat man with the same sort of face as the tractor-driver, asked, 'Where's the woman of the house?'

'I don't know.'

'This is the place the tractor with a sledge came from?'

'This is it.'

'Had they been drinking before they left?'

All four of them were looking around them, screwing up their eyes in the dim light from the table-lamp. I realized that they had either made an arrest or wanted to make one.

'What's happened then?'

'Answer the question!'

'But ...'

'Were they drunk when they went?'

'Were they drinking here?'

Had there been a murder? Or hadn't they been able to move the top room? The men in greatcoats had me off balance. But one thing was certain: Matryona could do time for making hooch.

I stepped back to stand between them and the kitchen door. 'I honestly didn't notice. I didn't see anything.' (I really hadn't seen anything – only heard.) I made what was supposed to be a helpless gesture, drawing attention to the state of the cottage: a table-lamp shining peacefully on books and exercises, a crowd of frightened rubber plants, the austere couch of a recluse, not a sign of debauchery.

They had already seen for themselves, to their annoyance, that there had been no drinking in that room. They turned to leave, telling each other this wasn't where the drinking had been then, but it would be a good thing to put in that it was. I saw them out and tried to discover what had happened. It was only at the gate that one of them growled. 'They've all been cut to bits. Can't find all the pieces.'

'That's a detail. The nine o'clock express nearly went off the rails. That would have been something.' And they walked briskly away.

I went back to the hut in a daze. Who were 'they'? What did 'all of them' mean? And where was Matryona?

I moved the curtain aside and went into the kitchen. The

stink of hooch rose and hit me. It was a deserted battlefield: a huddle of stools and benches, empty bottles lying around, one bottle half-full, glasses, the remains of pickled herring, onion and sliced fat pork.

Everything was deathly still. Just cockroaches creeping unperturbed about the field of battle.

They had said something about the nine o'clock express. Why? Perhaps I should have shown them all this? I began to wonder whether I had done right. But what a damnable way to behave – keeping their explanations for official persons only.

Suddenly the small gate creaked. I hurried out on to the landing. 'Matryona Vasilyevna?'

The yard door opened, and Matryona's friend Masha came in, swaying and wringing her hands. 'Matryona ... our Matryona, Ignatich ...'

I sat her down and through her tears she told me the story.

The approach to the crossing was a steep rise. There was no barrier. The tractor and the first sledge went over, but the tow-rope broke and the second sledge, the home-made one, got stuck on the crossing and started falling apart – the wood Faddei had given them to make the second sledge was no good. They towed the first sledge out of the way and went back for the second. They were fixing the tow-rope – the tractor-driver and Faddei's lame son, and Matryona, heaven knows what brought her there, was with them, between the tractor and the sledge. What help did she think she could be to the men? She was for ever meddling in men's work. Hadn't a bolting horse nearly tipped her into the lake once, through a hole in the ice?

Why did she have to go to the damned crossing? She had handed over the top room, and owed nothing to anybody ... The engine-driver kept a look-out in case the train from Cherusti rushed up on them. Its headlamps would be visible a long way off. But two engines coupled together came from the other direction, from our station, backing without lights. Why they were without lights nobody knows. When an engine is backing, coal-dust blows into the driver's eyes from the tender and he can't see very well. The two engines flew into them and crushed three people between the tractor and the sledge to pulp. The tractor was wrecked, the sledge was matchwood, the rails were buckled, and both engines turned over.

'But how was it they didn't hear the engines coming?'

'The tractor engine was making such a din.'

'What about the bodies?'

'They won't let anybody in. They've roped them off.'

'What was that somebody was telling me about the express?'

The nine o'clock express goes through our station at a good speed and on to the crossing. But the two drivers weren't hurt when their engines crashed, they jumped out and ran back along the line waving their hands and they managed to stop the train ... The nephew was hurt by a beam as well. He's hiding at Klavka's now so that they won't know he was at the crossing. If they find out, they'll drag him in as a witness ... 'Don't know lies up, and do know gets tied up. Kira's husband didn't get a scratch. He tried to hang himself, they had to cut him down. It's all because of me, he says, my aunty's killed and my brother. Now he's gone and given himself up. But the mad-house is where he'll be going, not prison. Oh, Matryona, my dearest Matryona ...'

Matryona was gone. Someone close to me had been killed. And on her last day I had scolded her for wearing my jerkin.

The lovingly-drawn red and yellow woman in the book advertisement smiled happily on.

Old Masha sat there weeping a little longer. Then she got up to go. And suddenly she asked me, 'Ignatich, you remember, Matryona had a grey shawl. She meant it to go to my Tanya when she died, didn't she?'

She looked at me hopefully in the half-darkness ... surely I hadn't forgotten?

No, I remembered. 'She said so, yes.'

'Well, listen, maybe you could let me take it with me now. The family will be swarming in tomorrow and I'll never get it then.' And she gave me another hopeful, imploring look. She had been Matryona's friend for half a century, the only one in the village who truly loved her.

No doubt she was right.

'Of course ... take it.'

She opened the chest, took out the shawl, tucked it under her coat and went out.

The mice had gone mad. They were running furiously up and down the walls, and you could almost see the green wall-paper rippling and rolling over their backs.

In the morning I had to go to school. The time was three o'clock. The only thing to do was to lock up and go to bed.

Lock up, because Matryona would not be coming.

I lay down, leaving the light on. The mice were squeaking, almost moaning, racing and running. My mind was weary and wandering, and I couldn't rid myself of an uneasy feeling that an invisible Matryona was flitting about and saying good-bye to her home.

And suddenly I imagined Faddei standing there, young and black-haired, in the dark patch by the door, with his axe up-lifted. 'If it wasn't my own brother, I'd chop the both of you to bits.'

The threat had lain around for forty years, like an old broad-sword in a corner, and in the end it had struck its blow.

When it was light the women went to the crossing and brought back all that was left of Matryona on a hand-sledge with a dirty sack over it. They threw off the sack to wash her. There was just a mess ... no feet, only half a body, no left hand. One woman said, 'The Lord has left her her right hand. She'll be able to say her prayers where she's going ...'

Then the whole crowd of rubber plants was carried out of the cottage ... these plants that Matryona had loved so much that once when smoke woke her up in the night she didn't rush to save her house but to tip the plants on to the floor in case they were suffocated. The women swept the floor clean. They hung a wide towel of old home-spun over Matryona's dim mirror. They took down the jolly posters. They moved my table out of the way. Under the icons, near the windows, they stood a rough unadorned coffin on a row of stools.

In the coffin lay Matryona. Her body, mangled and lifeless, was covered with a clean sheet. Her head was swathed in a white kerchief. Her face was almost undamaged, peaceful, more alive than dead.

The villagers came to pay their last respects. The women even brought their small children to take a look at the dead. And if anyone raised a lament, all the women, even those who had looked in out of idle curiosity, always joined in, wailing where they stood by the door or the wall, as though they were providing a choral accompaniment. The men stood stiff and silent with their caps off.

The formal lamentation had to be performed by the women of Matryona's family. I observed that the lament followed a coldly calculated age-old ritual. The more distant relatives went up to the coffin for a short while and made low wailing noises over it. Those who considered themselves closer kin to the dead woman began their lament in the doorway and when they got as far as the coffin, bowed down and roared out their grief right in the face of the departed. Every lamenter made up her own melody. And expressed her own thoughts and feelings.

I realized that a lament for the dead is not just a lament, but a kind of politics. Matryona's three sisters swooped, took possession of the cottage, the goat, and the stove, locked up the chest, ripped the 200 roubles for the funeral out of the coat lining, and drummed it into everybody who came that only they were near relatives. Their lament over the coffin went like this, '*Oh, nanny, nanny! Oh nan-nan!* All we had in the world was you! You could have lived in peace and quiet, you could. And we should always have been kind and loving to you. Now your top room's been the death of you. Finished you off it has, the cursed thing! Oh why did you have to take it down? Why didn't you listen to us?'

Thus the sisters' lament were indictments of Matryona's husband's family: they shouldn't have made her take the top room down. (There was an underlying meaning too: you've taken the top room all right but we won't let you have the house itself!)

Matryona's husband's family, her sisters-in-law, Yefim and Faddei's sisters, and various nieces lamented like this, '*Oh poor auntie, poor auntie!* Why didn't you take better care of yourself! Now they're angry with us for sure. Our own dear Matryona you were, and it's your own fault! The top room is nothing to do with it. Oh why did you go where death was waiting for you? Nobody asked you to go there. And what a way to die! Oh why didn't you listen to us?' (Their answer to the others showed through these laments: we are not to blame for her death, and the house we'll talk about later.)

But the 'second' Matryona, a coarse, broad-faced woman, the substitute Matryona whom Faddei had married so long ago for the sake of her name, got out of step with family policy, wailing and sobbing over the coffin in her simplicity, '*Oh my poor dear sister!* You won't be angry with me, will you now? Oh-oh-oh! How we used to talk and talk, you and me! Forgive a poor miserable woman! You've gone to be with your dear mother, and you'll come for me some day for sure! Oh-oh-oh-oh!...'

At every 'oh-oh-oh' it was as though she were giving up

the ghost. She writhed and gasped, with her breasts against the side of the coffin. When her lament went beyond the ritual prescription the women, as though acknowledging its success, all started saying, 'Come away now, come away.'

Matryona came away, but back she went again, sobbing with even greater abandon. Then an ancient woman came out of a corner, put her hand on Matryona's shoulder and said: 'There are two riddles in this world: how I was born I don't remember, how I shall die I don't know.'

And Matryona fell silent at once, and all the others were silent, so that there was an unbroken hush.

But the old woman herself, who was much older than all the other old women there and didn't seem to belong to Matryona at all, after a while started wailing, 'Oh, my poor sick Matryona! Oh my poor Vasilyevna! Oh what a weary thing it is to be seeing you into your grave!'

There was one who didn't follow the ritual, but wept straightforwardly, in the fashion of our age, which has had plenty of practice at it. This was Matryona's unfortunate foster-daughter, Kira, from Cherusti, for whom the top room had been taken down and moved. Her ringlets were pitifully out of curl. Her eyes looked red and bloodshot. She didn't notice that her headscarf was slipping off out in the frosty air and that her arm hadn't found the sleeve of her coat. She walked in a stupor from her foster-mother's coffin in one house to her brother's in another. They were afraid she would lose her mind, because her husband had to go for trial as well.

It looked as if her husband was doubly at fault: not only had he been moving the top room, but as an engine-driver he knew the regulations about unprotected crossings, and should have gone down to the station to warn them about the tractor. There were a thousand people on the Urals express that night, peacefully sleeping in the upper and lower berths of their dimly lit carriages, and all those lives were nearly cut short. All because of a few greedy people, wanting to get their hands on a plot of land, or not wanting to make a second trip with a tractor.

All because of the top room, which had been under a curse ever since Faddei's hands had started itching to take it down.

The tractor-driver was already beyond human justice. And the railway authorities were also at fault, both because a busy crossing was unguarded and because the coupled engines were travelling without lights. That was why they had tried at first to blame it all on the drink, and then to keep the case out of court.

The rails and the track were so twisted and torn that for three days, while the coffins were still in the house, no trains ran – they were diverted on to another line. All Friday, Saturday and Sunday, from the end of the investigation until the funeral, the work of repairing the line went on day and night. The repair gang was frozen, and they made fires to warm themselves and to light their work at night, using the boards and beams from the second sledge which were there for the taking, scattered around the crossing.

The first sledge just stood there, undamaged and still loaded, a little way beyond the crossing.

One sledge, tantalizingly ready to be towed away, and the other perhaps still to be plucked from the flames – that was what harrowed the soul of black-bearded Faddei all day Friday and all day Saturday. His daughter was going out of her mind, his son-in-law had a criminal charge hanging over him, in his own house lay the son he had killed, and along the street the woman he had killed and whom he had once loved. But Faddei stood by the coffins clutching his beard only for a short time, and went away again. His tall brow was clouded by painful thoughts, but what he was thinking about was how to save the timbers of the top room from the flames and from Matryona's scheming sisters.

Going over the people of Talnovo in my mind I realized that Faddei was not the only one like that.

Property, the people's property, or my property, is strangely called our 'goods'. If you lose your goods, people think you disgrace yourself and make yourself look foolish.

Faddei dashed about, never stopping to sit down, from the settlement to the station, from one official to another, stood there with his bent back, leaning heavily on his stick, and begged them all to take pity on an old man and give him permission to recover the top room.

Somebody gave permission. And Faddei gathered together his surviving sons, sons-in-law and nephews, got horses from the kolkhoz and from the other side of the wrecked crossing, by a roundabout way that led through three villages, brought the remnants of the top room home to his yard. He finished the job in the early hours of Sunday morning.

On Sunday afternoon they were buried. The two coffins met in the middle of the village, and the relatives argued about which of them should go first. Then they put them side by side on an open sledge, the aunt and the nephew, and carried the dead over the damp snow, with a gloomy February sky above, to the churchyard two villages away. There was an unkind wind, so the priest and the deacon waited inside the church and didn't come out to Talnovo to meet them.

A crowd of people walked slowly behind the coffins, singing in chorus. Outside the village they fell back.

When Sunday came the women were still fussing around the house. An old woman mumbled psalms by the coffin, Matryona's sisters flitted about, popping things into the oven, and the air round the mouth of the stove trembled with the heat of red-hot peats, those which Matryona had carried in a sack from a distant bog. They were making unappetizing pies with poor flour.

When the funeral was over and it was already getting on towards evening, they gathered for the wake. Tables were put together to make a long one, which hid the place where the coffin had stood in the morning. To start with they all stood round the table, and an old man, the husband of a sister-in-law, said the Lord's Prayer. Then they poured everybody a little honey and warm water, just enough to cover the bottom of the bowl. We spooned it up without bread or anything, in memory of the dead. Then we ate something and drank vodka, and the conversation became more animated. Before the jelly they all stood up and sang 'Eternal remembrance' (they explained to me that it had to be sung before the jelly). There was more drinking. By now they were talking louder than ever, and not about Matryona at all. The sister-in-law's husband started boasting, 'Did you notice, brother Christians, that they took the funeral service slowly today? That's because Father Mikhail noticed me. He knows I know the service. Other times it's saints defend us, homeward wend us, and that's all.'

At last the supper was over. They all rose again. They sang 'Worthy is she'. Then again, with a triple repetition of 'Eternal remembrance'. But the voices were hoarse and out of tune, their faces drunken, and nobody put any feeling into this 'eternal memory'.

Then the main guests went away, and only the near relatives were left. They pulled out their cigarettes and lit up, there were jokes and laughter. There was some mention of Matryona's husband and his disappearance. The sister-in-law's husband, striking himself on the chest, assured me and the cobbler who was married to one of Matryona's sisters, 'He was dead, Yefim was dead! What could stop him coming back if he wasn't? If I knew they were going to hang me when I got to the old country, I'd come back just the same!'

The cobbler nodded in agreement. He was a deserter and had never left the old country. All through the war he was hiding in his mother's cellar.

The stern and silent old woman who was more ancient than

all the ancients was staying the night and sat high up on the stove. She looked down in mute disapproval on the indecently animated youngsters of fifty and sixty.

But the unhappy foster-daughter, who had grown up within these walls, went away behind the kitchen screen to cry.

Faddei didn't come to Matryona's wake – perhaps because he was holding a wake for his son. But twice in the next few days he walked angrily into the house for discussions with Matryona's sisters and the deserting cobbler.

The argument was about the house. Should it go to one of the sisters or to the foster-daughter? They were on the verge of taking it to court, but they made peace because they realized that the court would hand over the house to neither side, but to the Rural District Council. A bargain was struck. One sister took the goat, the cobbler and his wife got the house, and to make up Faddei's share, since he had 'nursed every bit of timber here in his arms', in addition to the top room which had already been carried away, they let him have the shed which had housed the goat, and the whole of the inner fence between the yard and the garden.

Once again the insatiable old man got the better of sickness and pain and became young and active. Once again he gathered together his surviving sons and sons-in-law, and they dismantled the shed and the fence, and he hauled the timbers himself, sledge by sledge, and only towards the end did he have Antoshka of 8-D, who didn't slack this time, to help him.

They boarded Matryona's house up till the spring, and I moved in with one of her sisters-in-law, not far away. This sister-in-law on several occasions came out with some recollection of Matryona, and made me see the dead woman in a new light. 'Yefim didn't love her. He used to say, "I like to dress in an educated way, but she dresses any old way, like they do in the country." Well then, he thinks, if she doesn't want anything, he might as well drink whatever's to spare. One time I went with him to the town to work, and he got himself a madam there and never wanted to come back to Matryona.'

Everything she said about Matryona was disapproving. She was slovenly, she made no effort to get a few things about her. She wasn't the saving kind. She didn't even keep a pig, because she didn't like fattening them up for some reason. And the silly woman helped other people without payment. (What brought Matryona to mind this time was that the garden needed ploughing and she couldn't find enough helpers to pull the plough.)

Matryona's sister-in-law admitted that she was warm-hearted and straightforward, but pitied and despised her for it.

It was only then, after these disapproving comments from her sister-in-law, that a true likeness of Matryona formed itself before my eyes, and I understood her as I never had when I lived side by side with her.

Of course! Every house in the village kept a pig. But she didn't. What can be easier than fattening a greedy piglet that cares for nothing in the world but food! You warm his swill three times a day, you live for him – then you cut his throat and you have some fat.

But she had none ...

She made no effort to get things round her ... She didn't struggle and strain to buy things and then care for them more than life itself.

She didn't go all out after fine clothes. Clothes, that beautify what is ugly and evil.

She was misunderstood and abandoned even by her husband. She had lost six children, but not her sociable ways. She was a stranger to her sisters and sisters-in-law, a ridiculous creature who stupidly worked for others without pay. She didn't accumulate property against the day she died. A dirty-white goat, a gammy-legged cat, some rubber plants ...

We had all lived side by side with her and never understood that she was that righteous one without whom, as the proverb says, no village can stand.

Nor any city.

Nor our whole land.

1959–60

Translated by H. T. Willetts